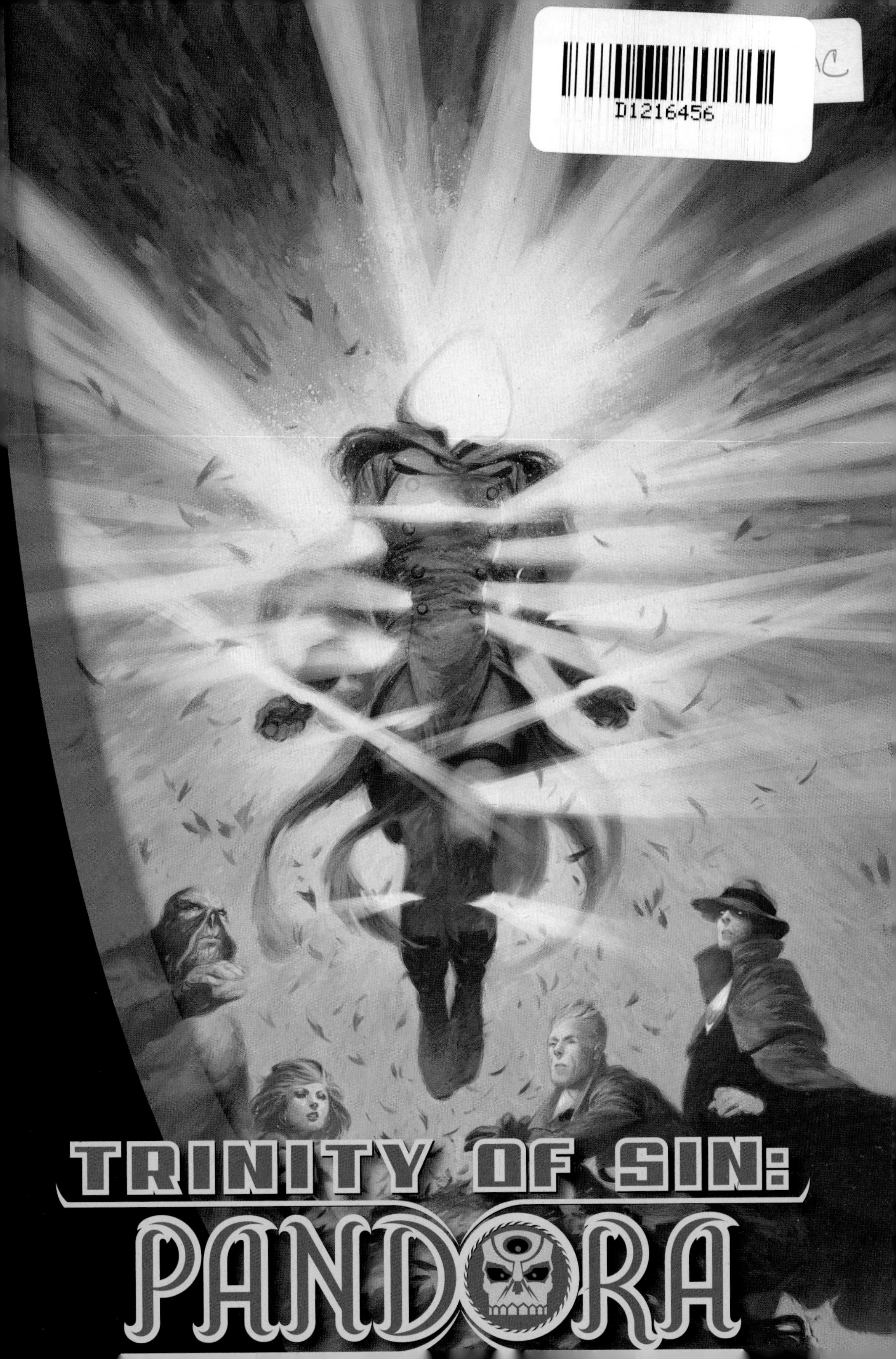
TRINITY OF SIN:
PANDORA

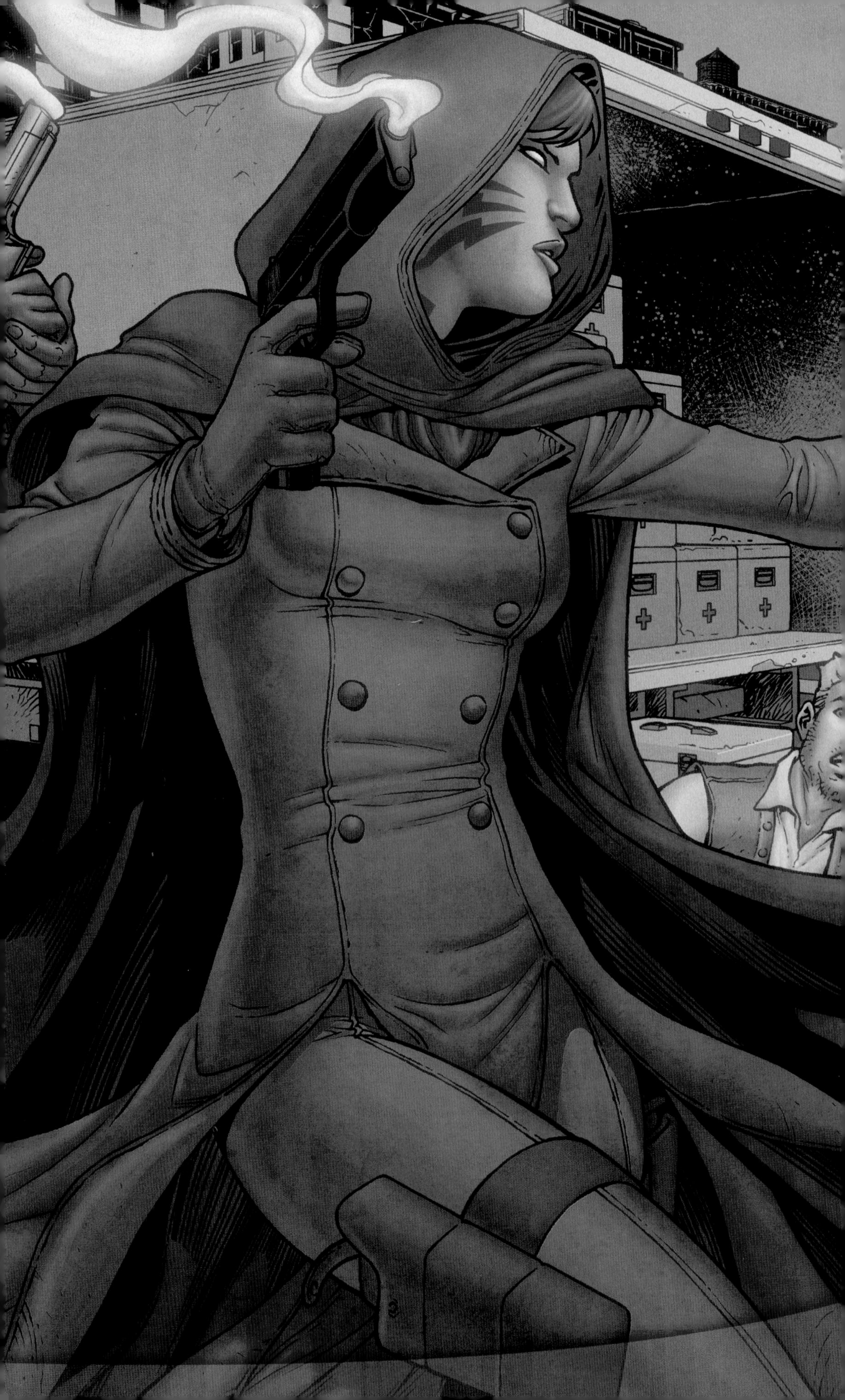

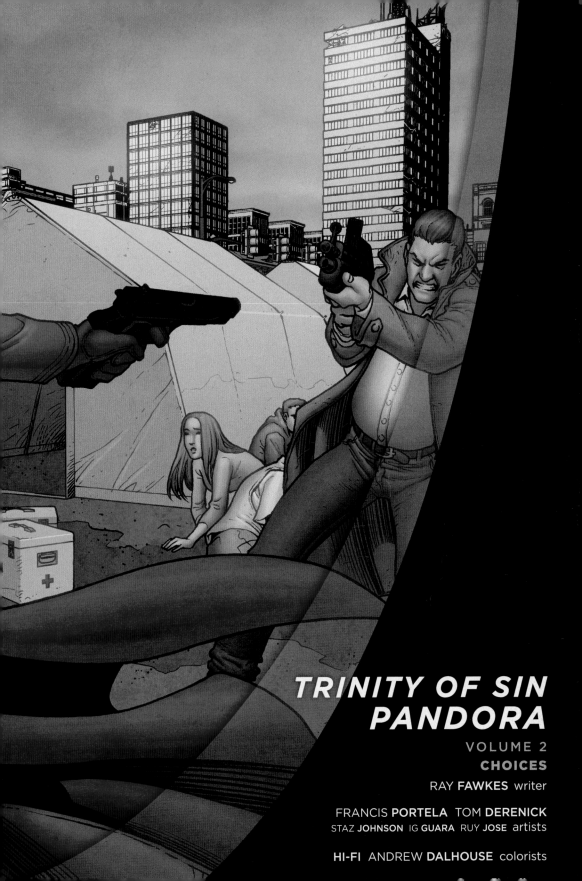

TRINITY OF SIN
PANDORA

VOLUME 2
CHOICES

RAY **FAWKES** writer

FRANCIS **PORTELA**   TOM **DERENICK**
STAZ **JOHNSON**   IG **GUARA**   RUY **JOSE** artists

HI-FI   ANDREW **DALHOUSE** colorists

BRIAN CUNNINGHAM WIL MOSS CHRIS CONROY Editors - Original Series
HARVEY RICHARDS Associate Editor - Original Series PETER HAMBOUSSI Editor
ROBBIN BROSTERMAN Design Director - Books ROBBIE BIEDERMAN Publication Design

BOB HARRAS Senior VP - Editor-in-Chief, DC Comics

DIANE NELSON President DAN DIDIO and JIM LEE Co-Publishers GEOFF JOHNS Chief Creative Officer
AMIT DESAI Senior VP - Marketing and Franchise Management
AMY GENKINS Senior VP - Business and Legal Affairs NAIRI GARDINER Senior VP - Finance
JEFF BOISON VP - Publishing Planning MARK CHIARELLO VP - Art Direction and Design
JOHN CUNNINGHAM VP - Marketing TERRI CUNNINGHAM VP - Editorial Administration
LARRY GANEM VP - Talent Relations and Services ALISON GILL Senior VP - Manufacturing and Operations
HANK KANALZ Senior VP - Vertigo and Integrated Publishing JAY KOGAN VP - Business and Legal Affairs, Publishing
JACK MAHAN VP - Business Affairs, Talent NICK NAPOLITANO VP - Manufacturing Administration SUE POHJA VP - Book Sales
FRED RUIZ VP - Manufacturing Operations COURTNEY SIMMONS Senior VP - Publicity BOB WAYNE Senior VP - Sales

TRINITY OF SIN: PANDORA VOLUME 2: CHOICES

DC Comics, 1700 Broadway, New York, NY 10019
A Warner Bros. Entertainment Company.
Printed by Transcontinental Interglobe, Beauceville, QC, Canada. 10/17/14. First Printing.
ISBN: 978-1-4012-5013-3

Library of Congress Cataloging-in-Publication Data

Fawkes, Ray, author.
Trinity of Sin: Pandora. Volume 2 / Ray Fawkes, Francis Portela.
pages cm. — (The New 52!)
ISBN 978-1-4012-5013-3 (paperback)
1. Graphic novels. I. Portela, Francis, illustrator. II. Title.
PN6728.T77F43 2014
741.5'973—dc23
2014015072

SUSTAINABLE FORESTRY INITIATIVE Certified Chain of Custody Promoting Sustainable Forestry www.sfiprogram.org

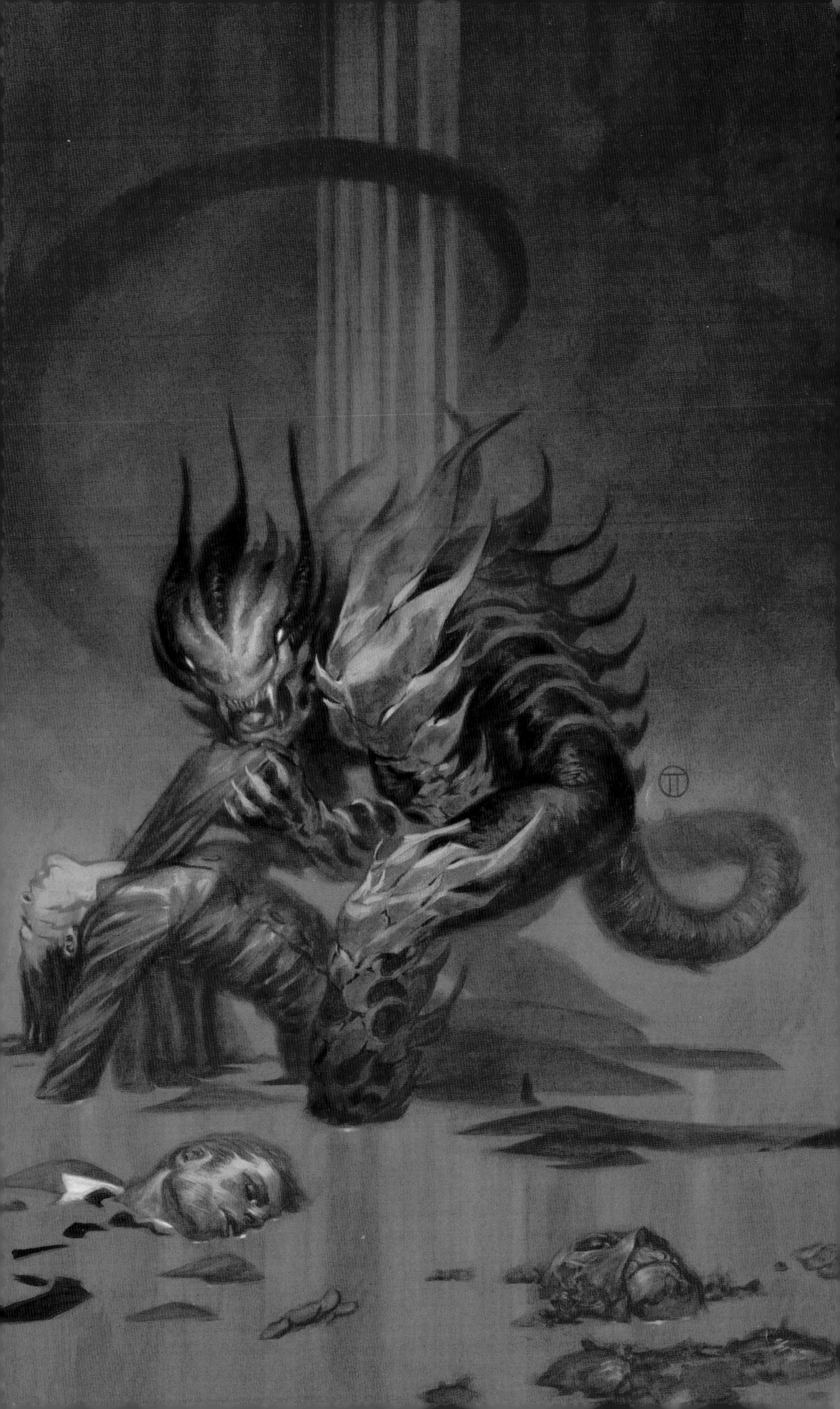

PRECIOUS LITTLE

RAY FAWKES
writer

FRANCIS PORTELA (PAGES 7-13, 18-26)
STAZ JOHNSON (PAGES 14-17)
artists

HI-FI
colorist

TRAVIS LANHAM
letterer

cover art by
JULIAN TOTINO TEDESCO

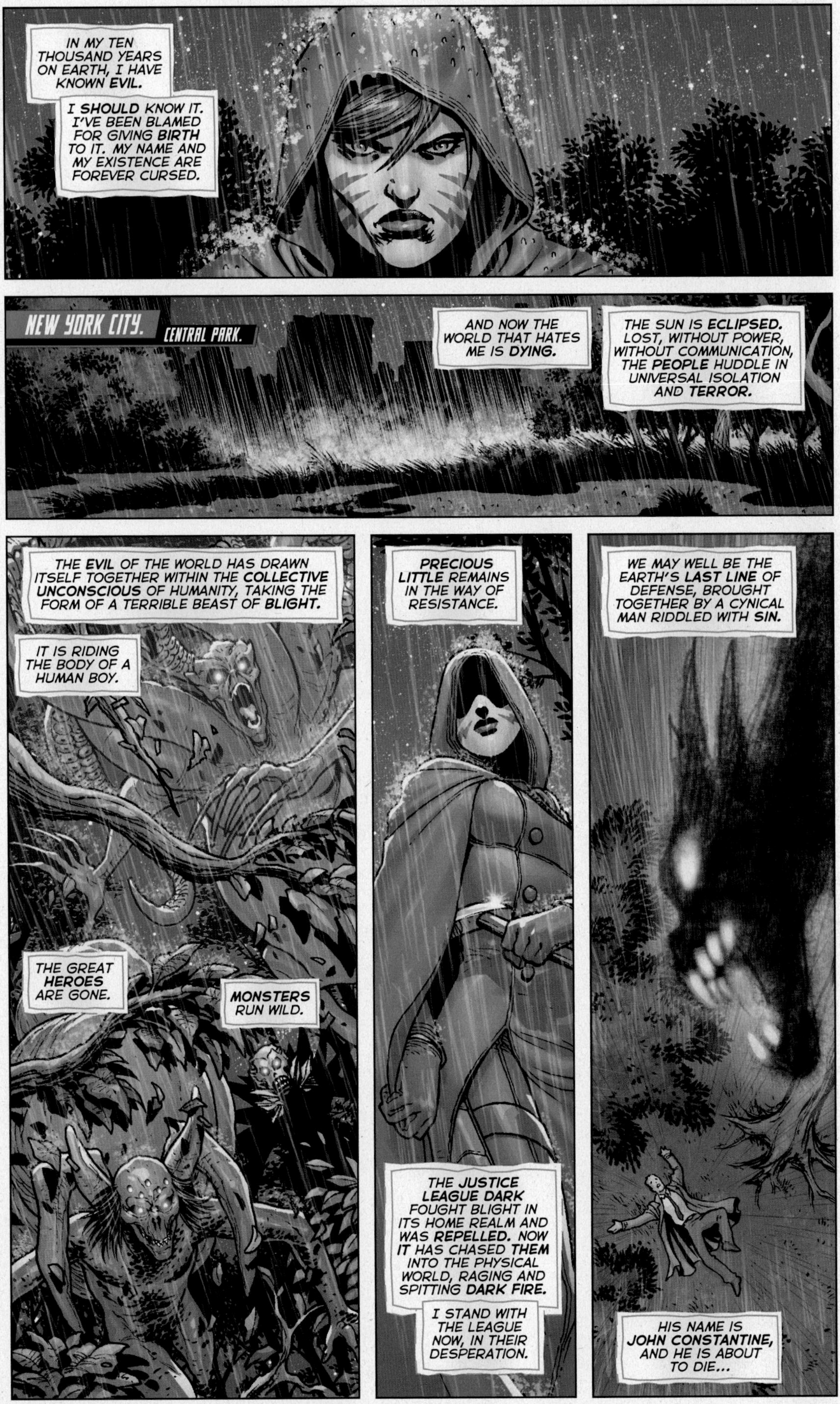
IN MY TEN THOUSAND YEARS ON EARTH, I HAVE KNOWN EVIL.
I SHOULD KNOW IT. I'VE BEEN BLAMED FOR GIVING BIRTH TO IT. MY NAME AND MY EXISTENCE ARE FOREVER CURSED.
NEW YORK CITY.
CENTRAL PARK.
AND NOW THE WORLD THAT HATES ME IS DYING.
THE SUN IS ECLIPSED. LOST, WITHOUT POWER, WITHOUT COMMUNICATION, THE PEOPLE HUDDLE IN UNIVERSAL ISOLATION AND TERROR.
THE EVIL OF THE WORLD HAS DRAWN ITSELF TOGETHER WITHIN THE COLLECTIVE UNCONSCIOUS OF HUMANITY, TAKING THE FORM OF A TERRIBLE BEAST OF BLIGHT.
IT IS RIDING THE BODY OF A HUMAN BOY.
THE GREAT HEROES ARE GONE.
MONSTERS RUN WILD.
PRECIOUS LITTLE REMAINS IN THE WAY OF RESISTANCE.
THE JUSTICE LEAGUE DARK FOUGHT BLIGHT IN ITS HOME REALM AND WAS REPELLED. NOW IT HAS CHASED THEM INTO THE PHYSICAL WORLD, RAGING AND SPITTING DARK FIRE.
I STAND WITH THE LEAGUE NOW, IN THEIR DESPERATION.
WE MAY WELL BE THE EARTH'S LAST LINE OF DEFENSE, BROUGHT TOGETHER BY A CYNICAL MAN RIDDLED WITH SIN.
HIS NAME IS JOHN CONSTANTINE, AND HE IS ABOUT TO DIE...

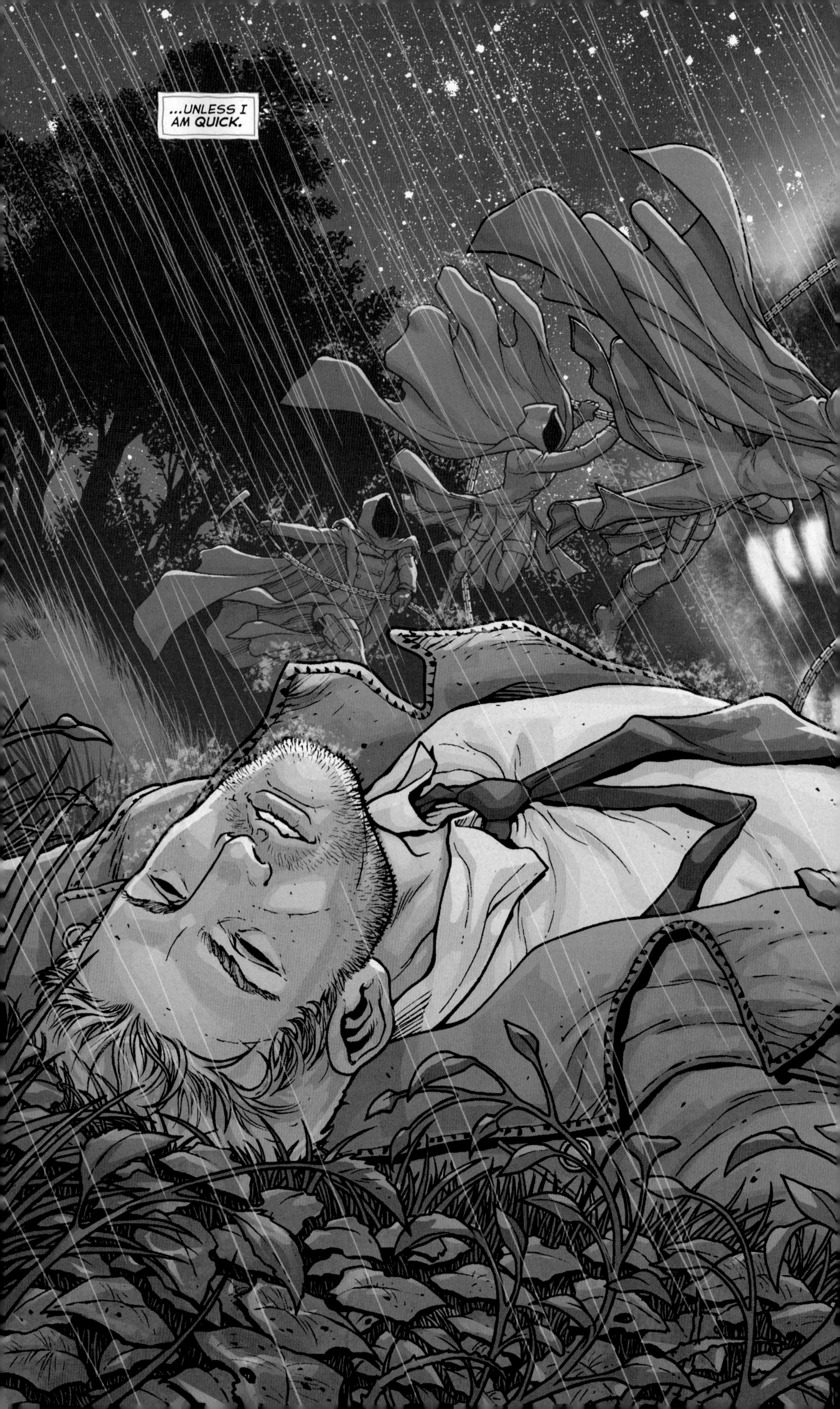
...UNLESS I AM QUICK.

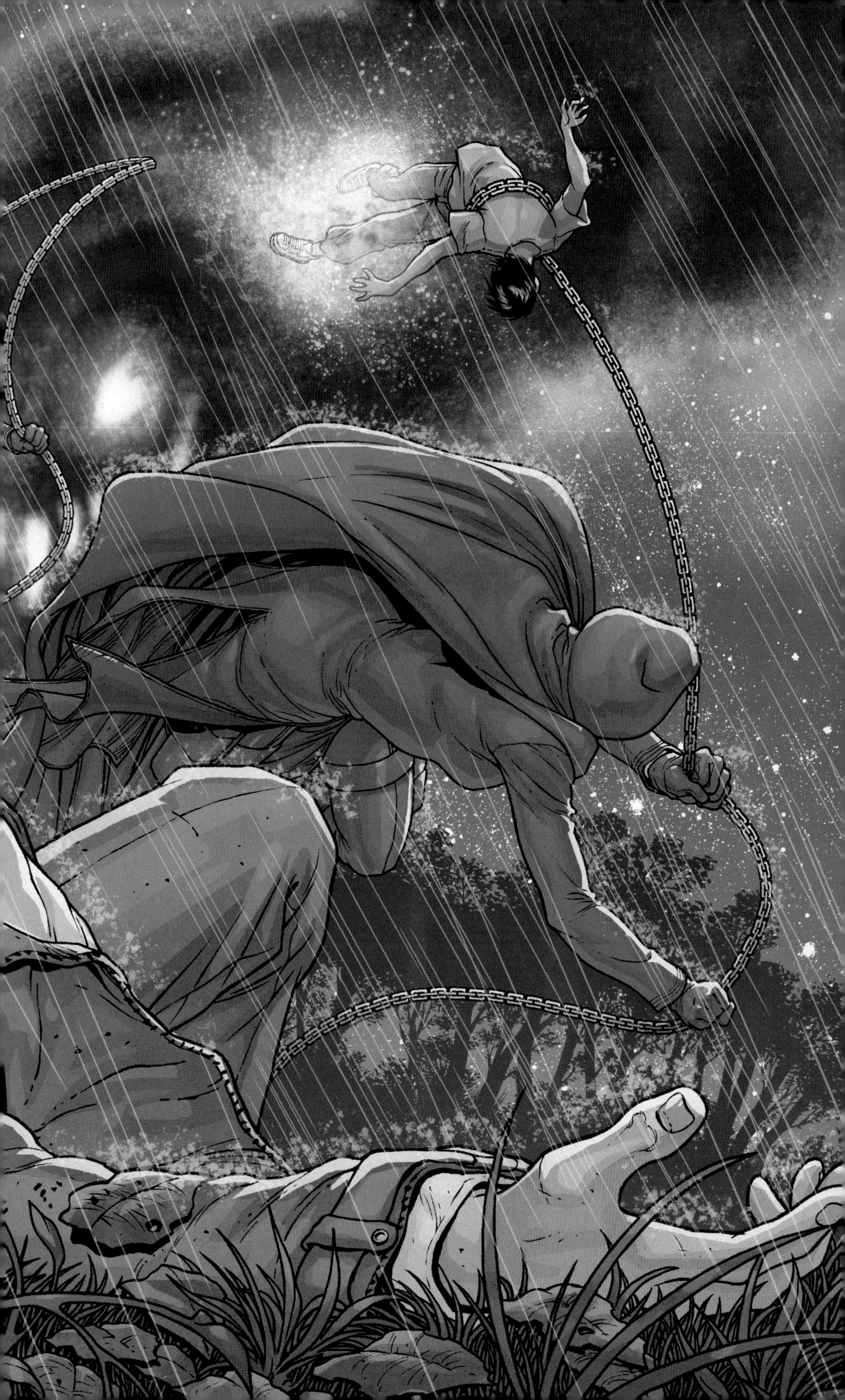

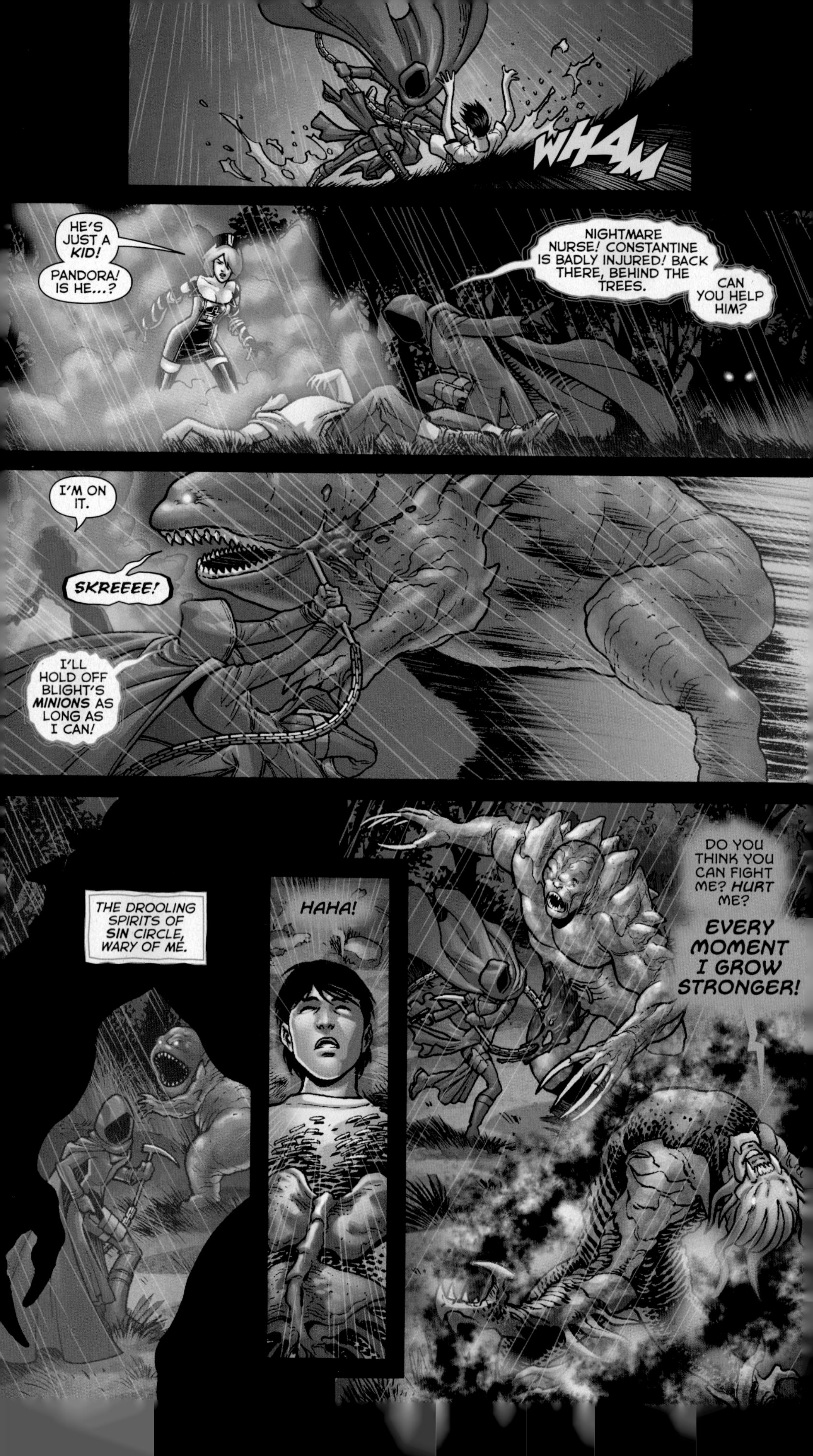
WHAM
HE'S JUST A KID!
PANDORA! IS HE...?
NIGHTMARE NURSE! CONSTANTINE IS BADLY INJURED! BACK THERE, BEHIND THE TREES.
CAN YOU HELP HIM?
I'M ON IT.
SKREEEE!
I'LL HOLD OFF BLIGHT'S MINIONS AS LONG AS I CAN!
THE DROOLING SPIRITS OF SIN CIRCLE, WARY OF ME.
HAHA!
DO YOU THINK YOU CAN FIGHT ME? HURT ME?
EVERY MOMENT I GROW STRONGER!

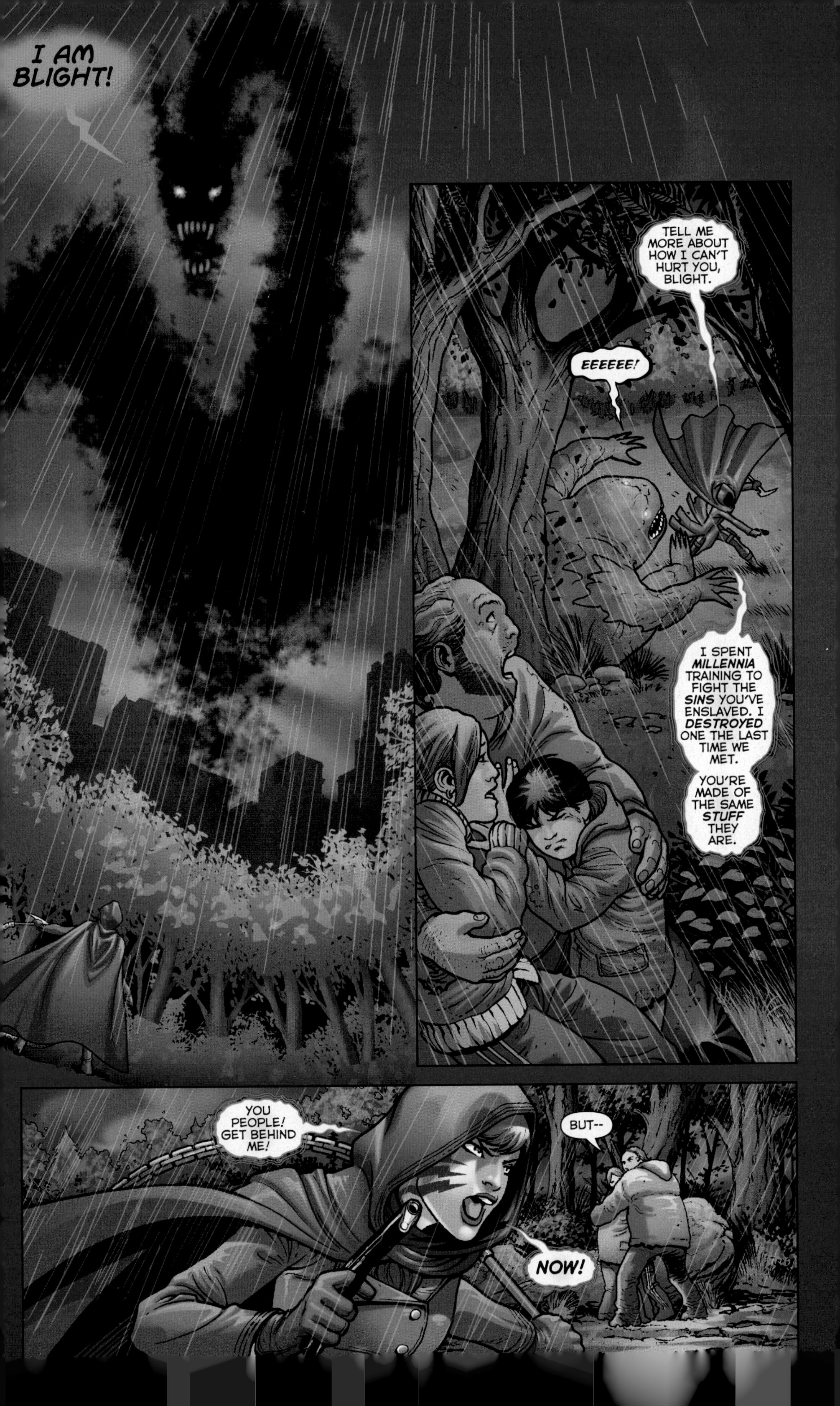
I AM BLIGHT!
TELL ME MORE ABOUT HOW I CAN'T HURT YOU, BLIGHT.
EEEEEE!
I SPENT MILLENNIA TRAINING TO FIGHT THE SINS YOU'VE ENSLAVED. I DESTROYED ONE THE LAST TIME WE MET.
YOU'RE MADE OF THE SAME STUFF THEY ARE.
YOU PEOPLE! GET BEHIND ME!
BUT--
NOW!

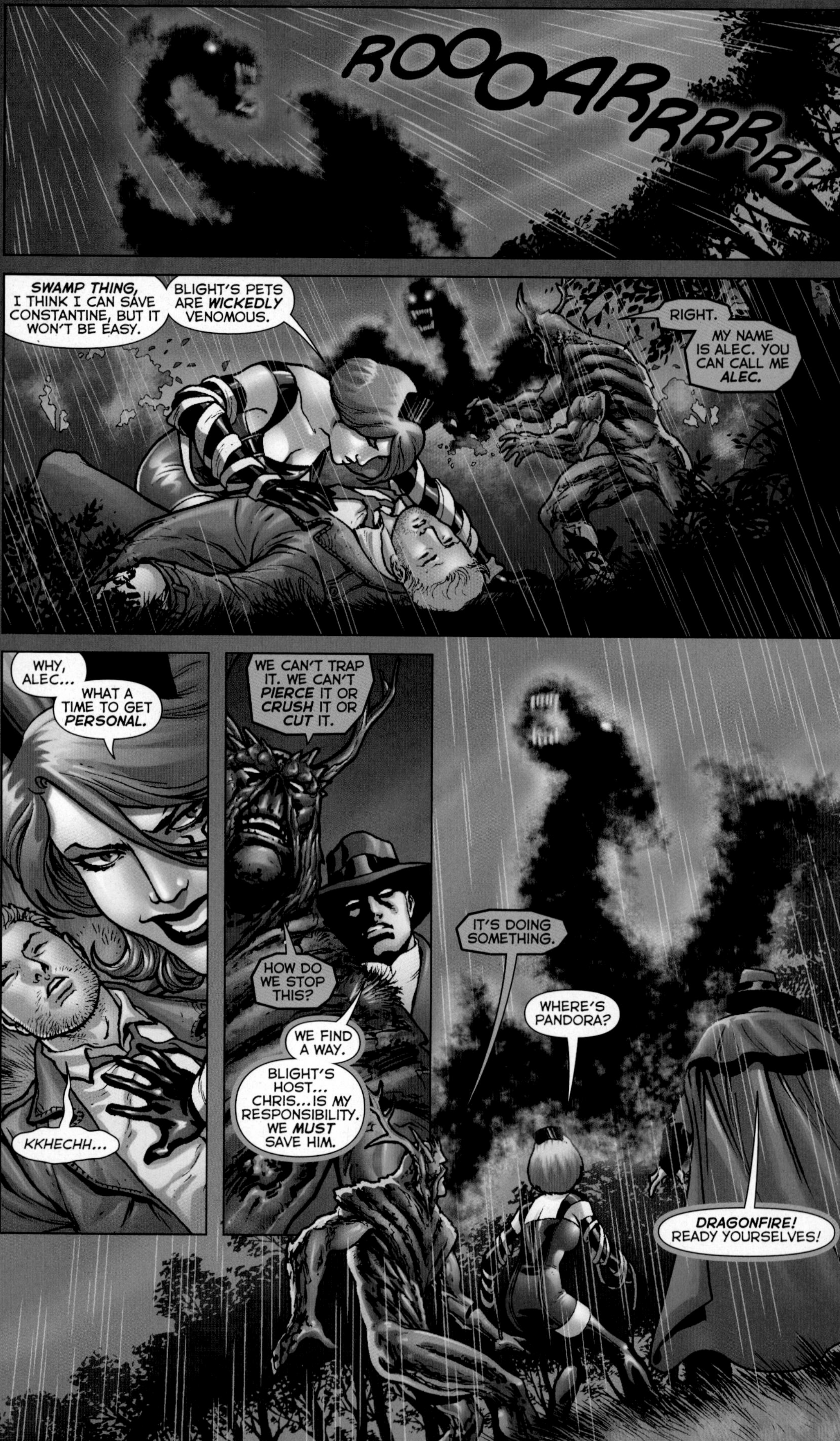
ROOOARRRRR!
SWAMP THING, I THINK I CAN SAVE CONSTANTINE, BUT IT WON'T BE EASY.
BLIGHT'S PETS ARE WICKEDLY VENOMOUS.
RIGHT.
MY NAME IS ALEC. YOU CAN CALL ME ALEC.
WHY, ALEC...
WHAT A TIME TO GET PERSONAL.
KKHECHH...
WE CAN'T TRAP IT. WE CAN'T PIERCE IT OR CRUSH IT OR CUT IT.
HOW DO WE STOP THIS?
WE FIND A WAY.
BLIGHT'S HOST... CHRIS...IS MY RESPONSIBILITY. WE MUST SAVE HIM.
IT'S DOING SOMETHING.
WHERE'S PANDORA?
DRAGONFIRE! READY YOURSELVES!

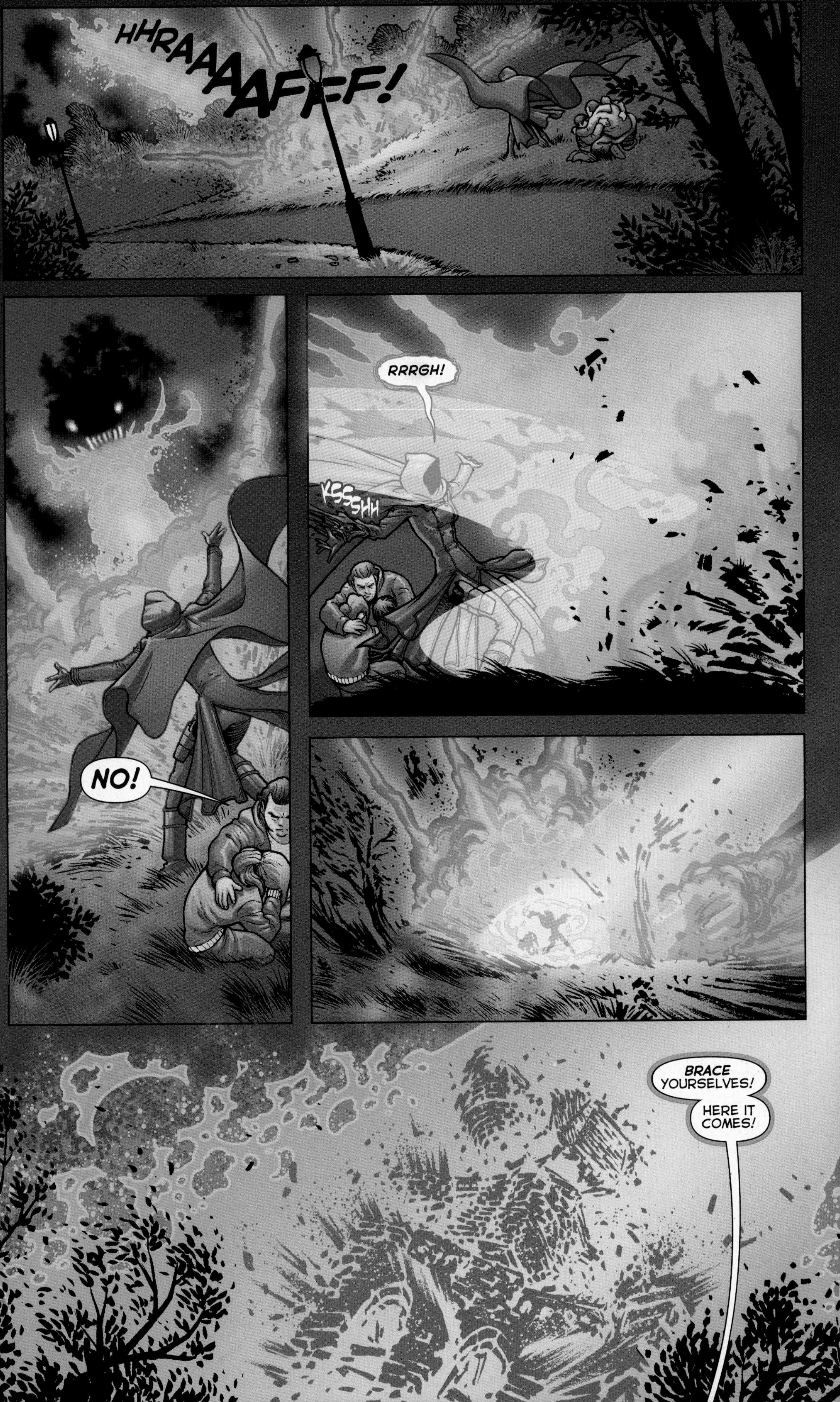
HHRAAAAAFFFF!
NO!
RRRGH!
KSSSHH
BRACE YOURSELVES!
HERE IT COMES!

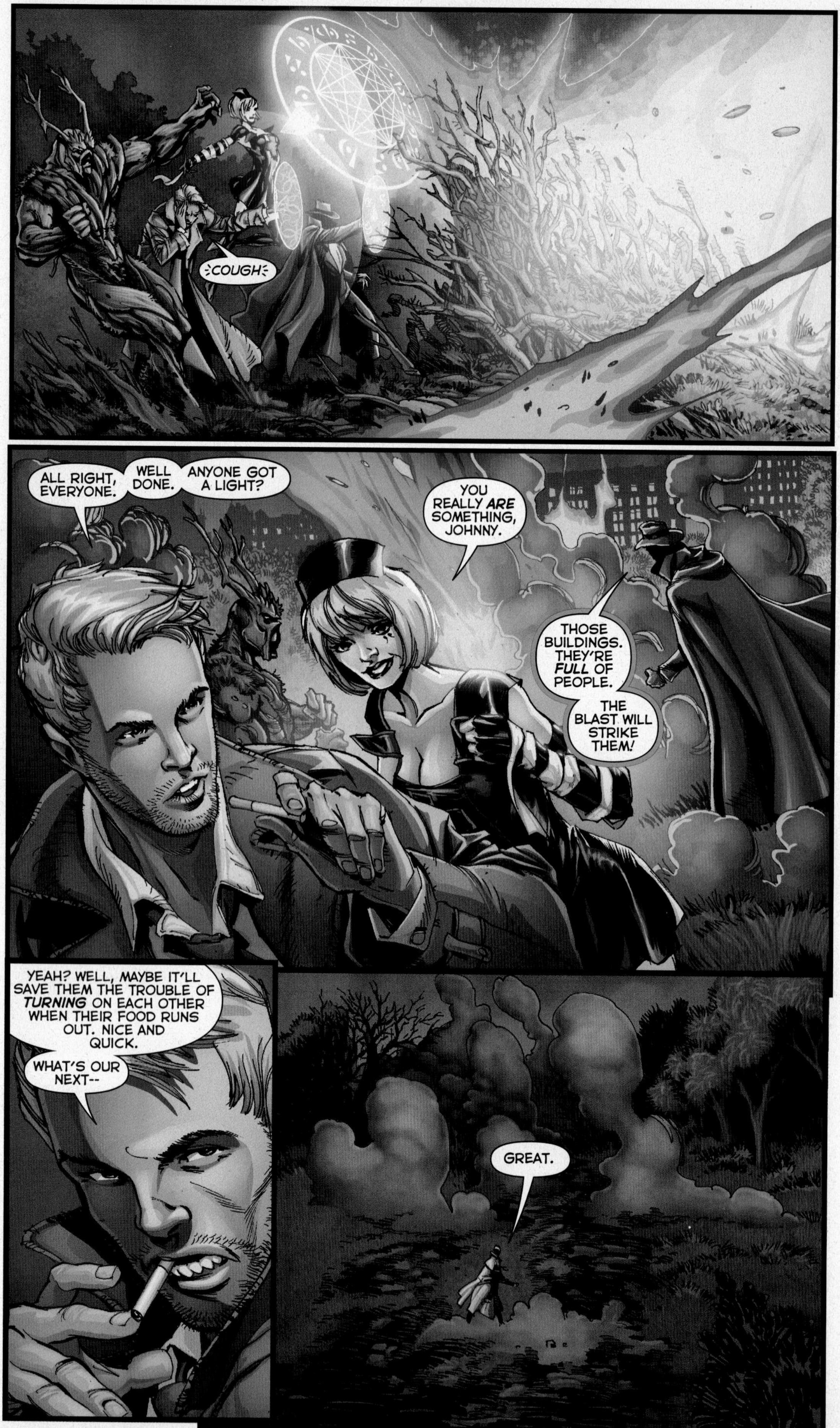

COUGH
ALL RIGHT, EVERYONE.
WELL DONE.
ANYONE GOT A LIGHT?
YOU REALLY ARE SOMETHING, JOHNNY.
THOSE BUILDINGS. THEY'RE FULL OF PEOPLE.
THE BLAST WILL STRIKE THEM!
YEAH? WELL, MAYBE IT'LL SAVE THEM THE TROUBLE OF TURNING ON EACH OTHER WHEN THEIR FOOD RUNS OUT. NICE AND QUICK.
WHAT'S OUR NEXT--
GREAT.

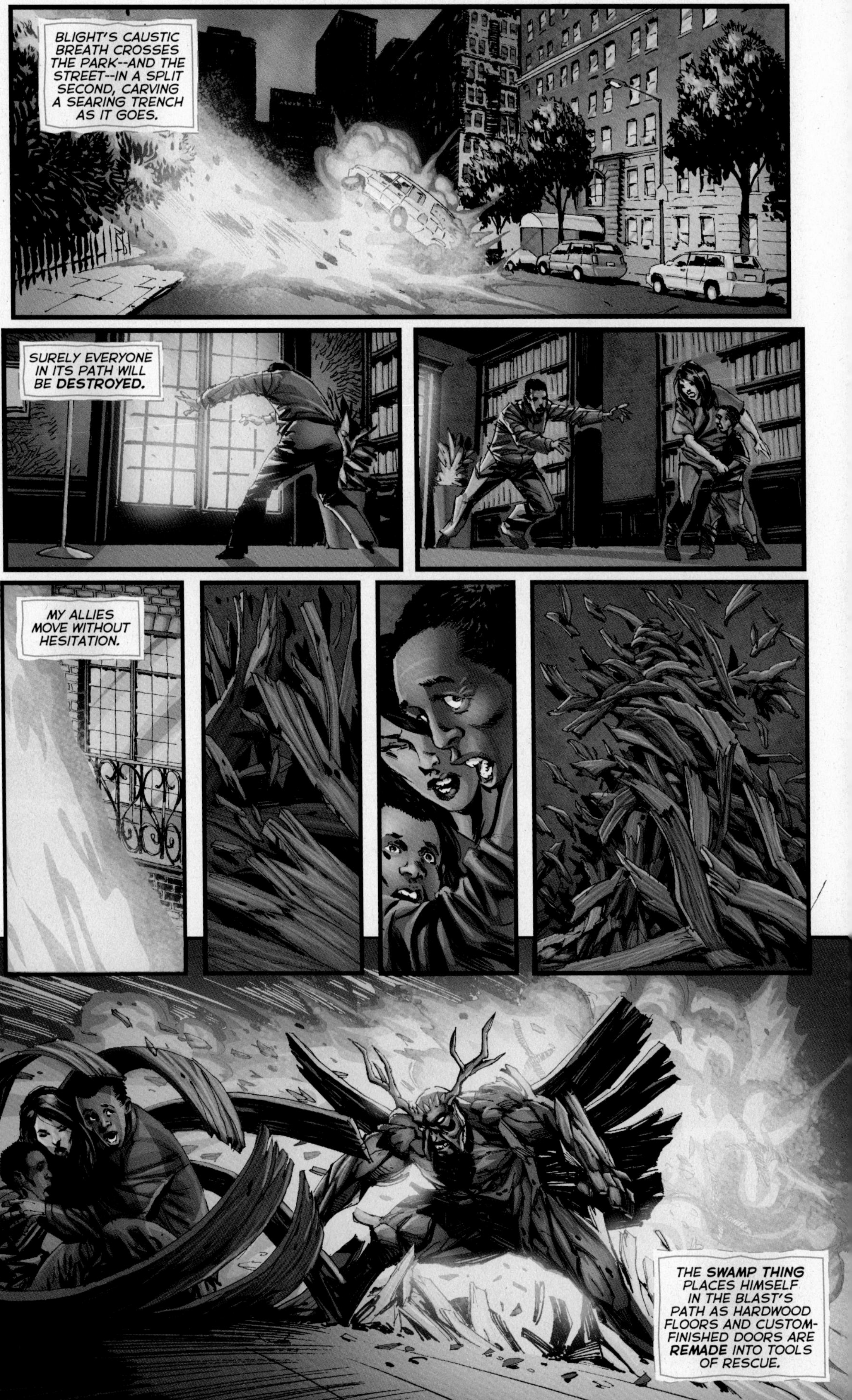
BLIGHT'S CAUSTIC BREATH CROSSES THE PARK--AND THE STREET--IN A SPLIT SECOND, CARVING A SEARING TRENCH AS IT GOES.
SURELY EVERYONE IN ITS PATH WILL BE **DESTROYED.**
MY ALLIES MOVE WITHOUT HESITATION.
THE **SWAMP THING** PLACES HIMSELF IN THE BLAST'S PATH AS HARDWOOD FLOORS AND CUSTOM-FINISHED DOORS ARE **REMADE** INTO TOOLS OF RESCUE.

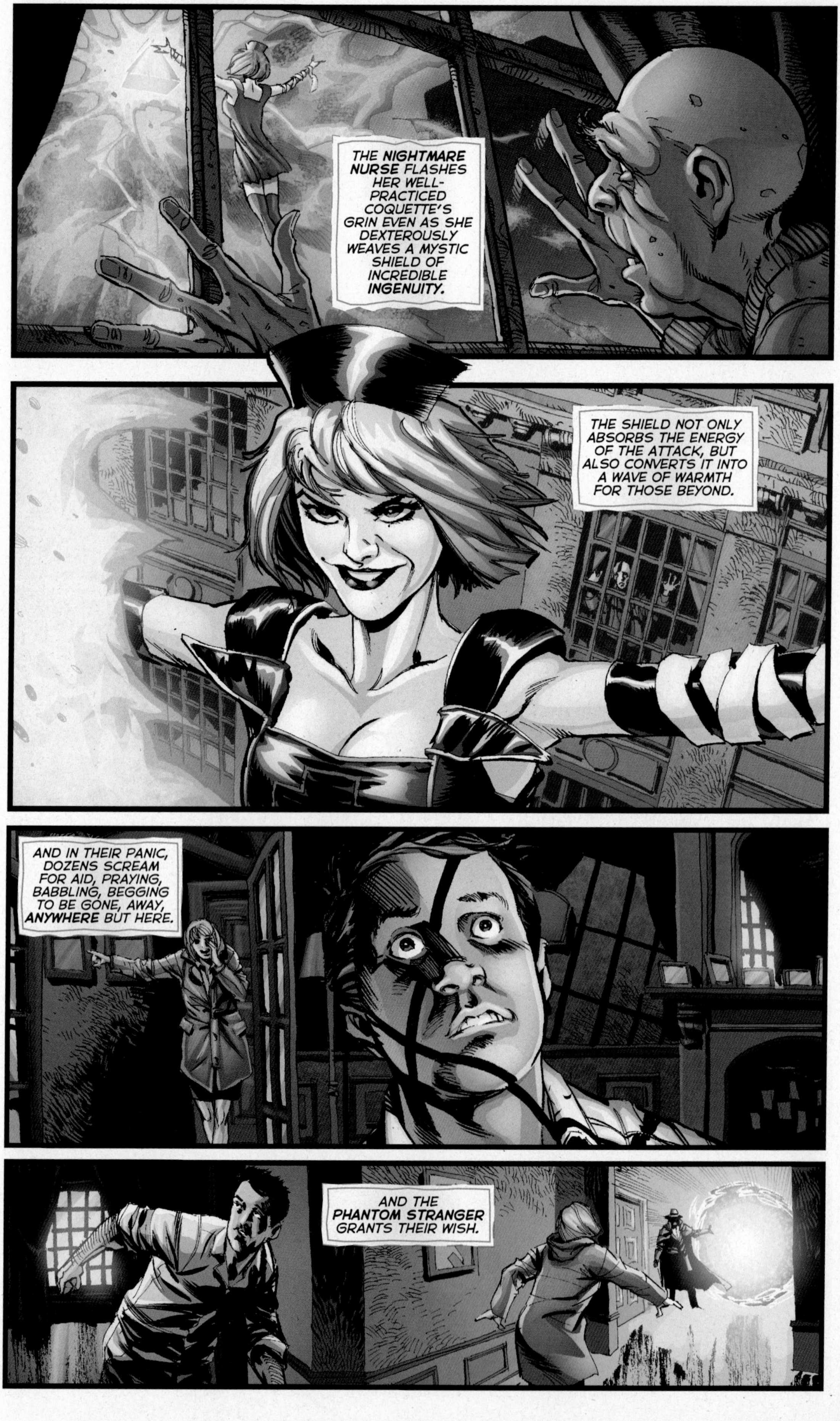

THE NIGHTMARE NURSE FLASHES HER WELL-PRACTICED COQUETTE'S GRIN EVEN AS SHE DEXTEROUSLY WEAVES A MYSTIC SHIELD OF INCREDIBLE INGENUITY.
THE SHIELD NOT ONLY ABSORBS THE ENERGY OF THE ATTACK, BUT ALSO CONVERTS IT INTO A WAVE OF WARMTH FOR THOSE BEYOND.
AND IN THEIR PANIC, DOZENS SCREAM FOR AID, PRAYING, BABBLING, BEGGING TO BE GONE, AWAY, ANYWHERE BUT HERE.
AND THE PHANTOM STRANGER GRANTS THEIR WISH.

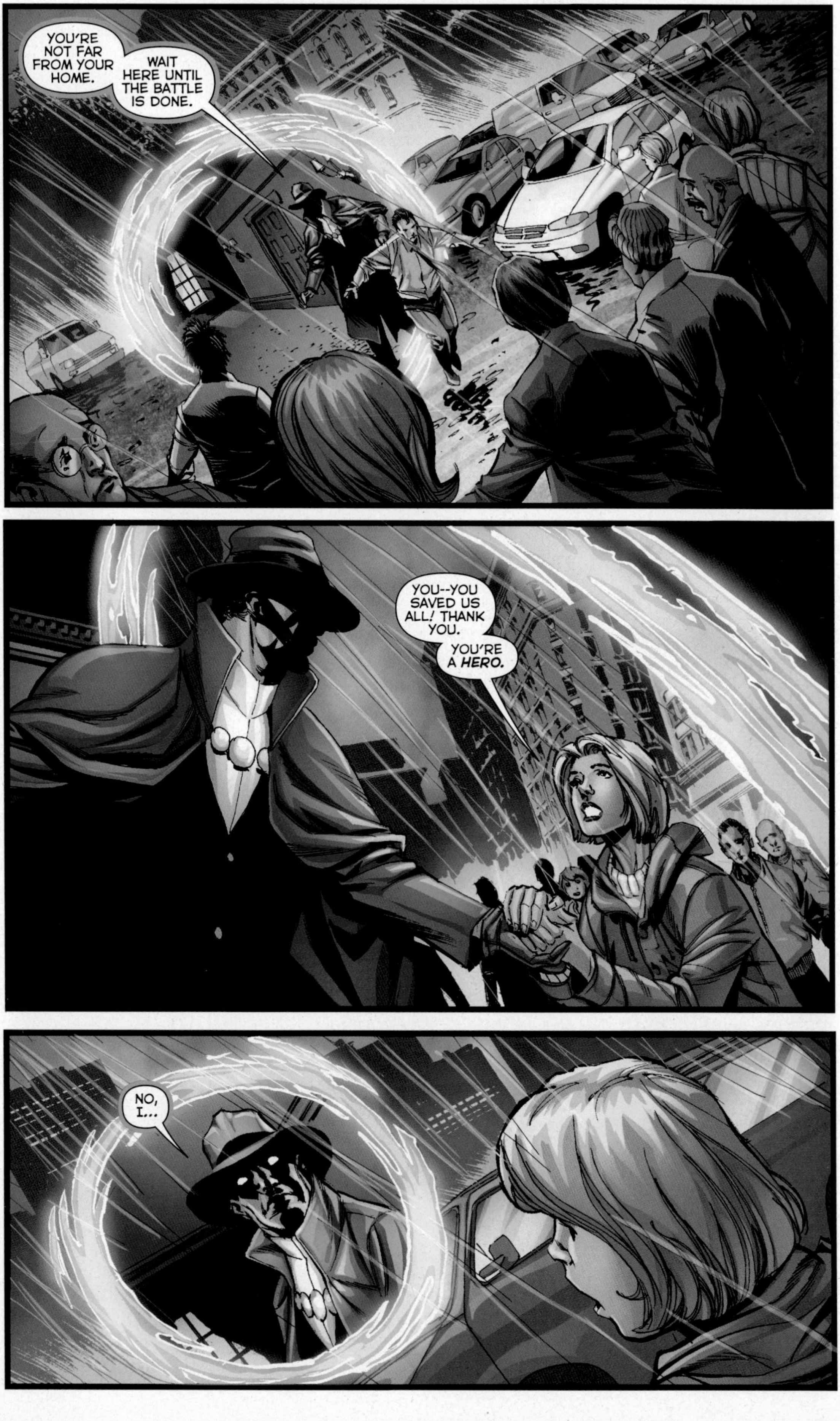
YOU'RE NOT FAR FROM YOUR HOME.
WAIT HERE UNTIL THE BATTLE IS DONE.
YOU--YOU SAVED US ALL! THANK YOU.
YOU'RE A *HERO.*
NO, I...

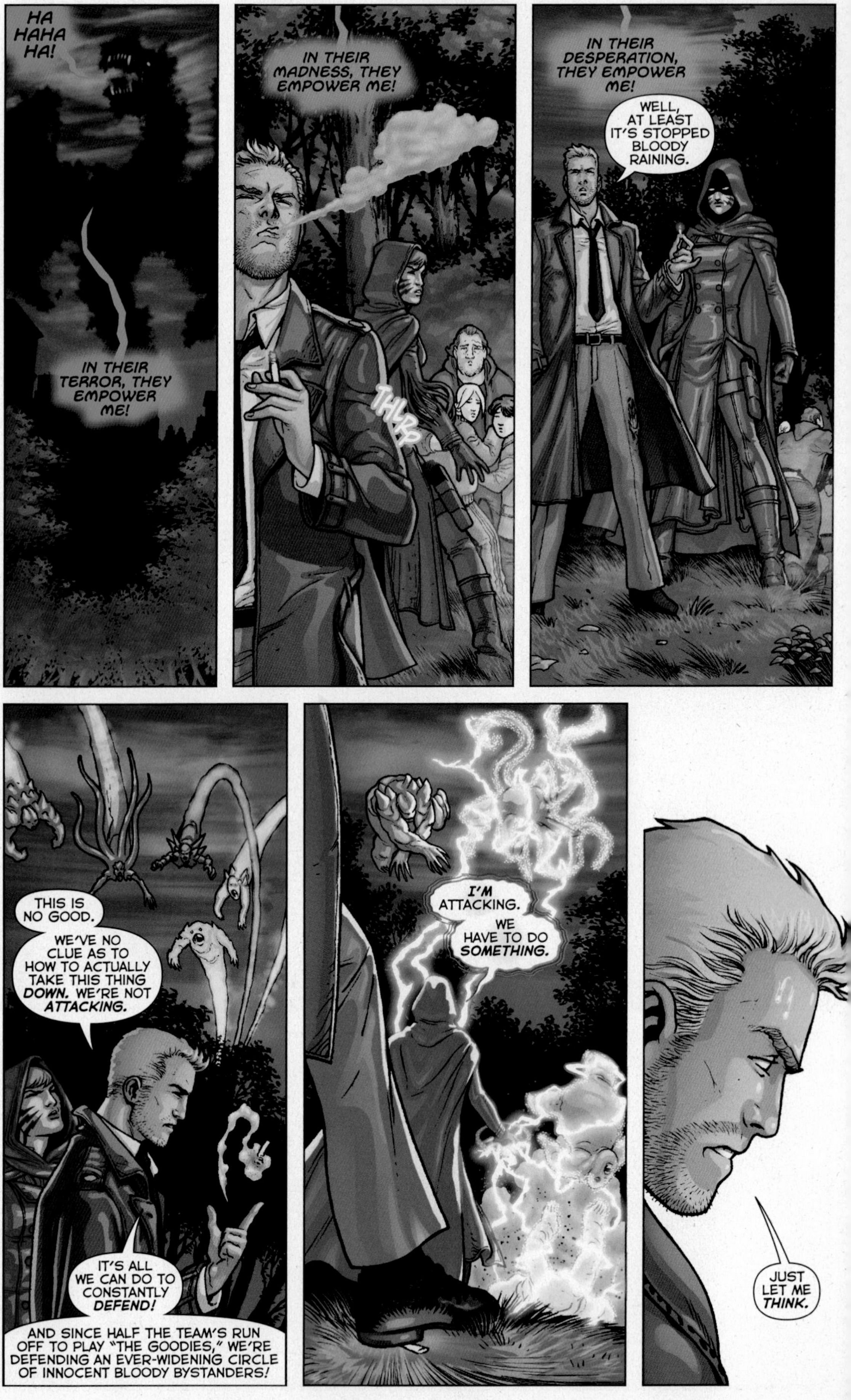
HA HAHA HA!
IN THEIR TERROR, THEY EMPOWER ME!
IN THEIR MADNESS, THEY EMPOWER ME!
THLRP
IN THEIR DESPERATION, THEY EMPOWER ME!
WELL, AT LEAST IT'S STOPPED BLOODY RAINING.
THIS IS NO GOOD.
WE'VE NO CLUE AS TO HOW TO ACTUALLY TAKE THIS THING DOWN. WE'RE NOT ATTACKING.
IT'S ALL WE CAN DO TO CONSTANTLY DEFEND!
AND SINCE HALF THE TEAM'S RUN OFF TO PLAY "THE GOODIES," WE'RE DEFENDING AN EVER-WIDENING CIRCLE OF INNOCENT BLOODY BYSTANDERS!
I'M ATTACKING.
WE HAVE TO DO SOMETHING.
JUST LET ME THINK.

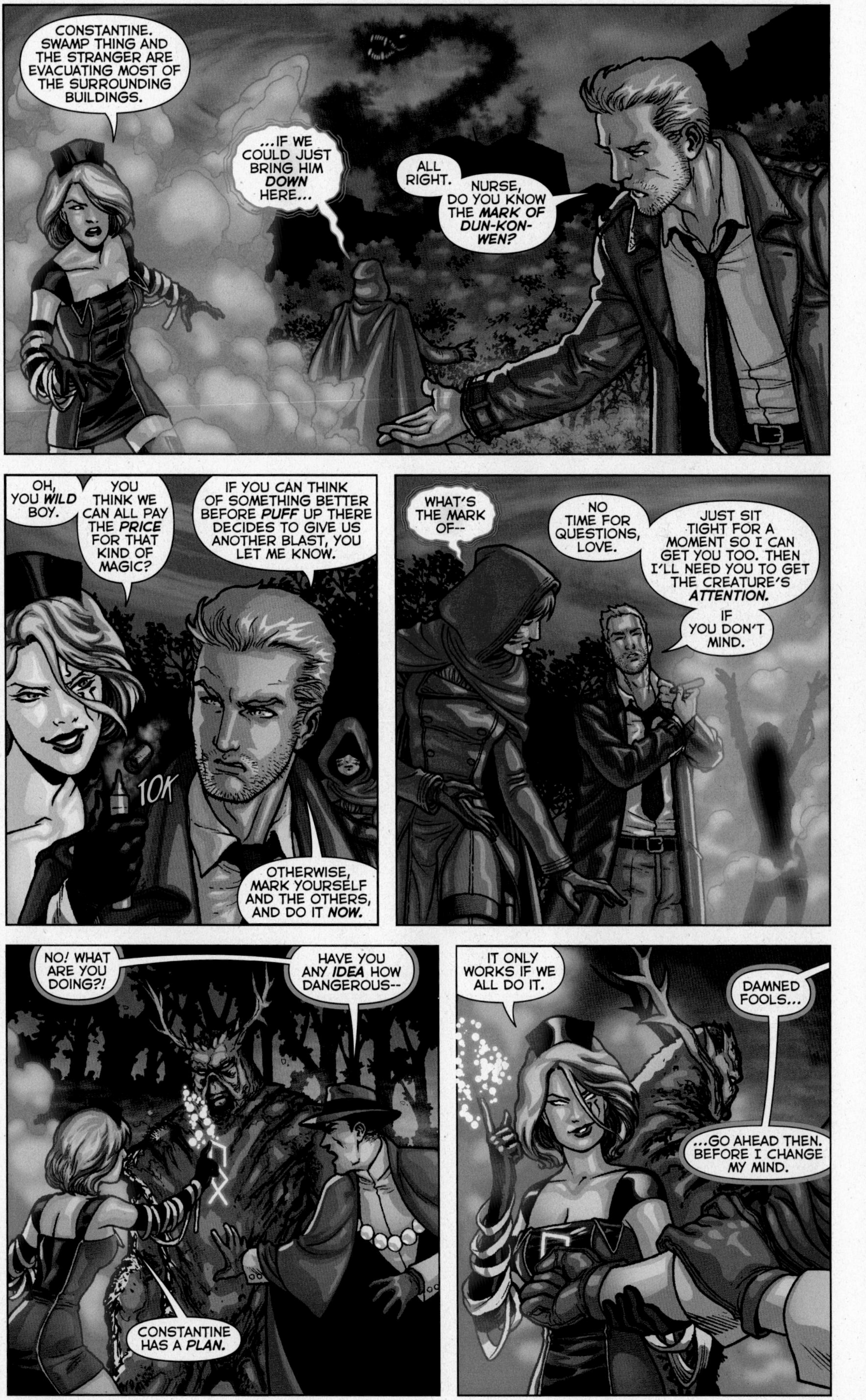
CONSTANTINE. SWAMP THING AND THE STRANGER ARE EVACUATING MOST OF THE SURROUNDING BUILDINGS.
...IF WE COULD JUST BRING HIM DOWN HERE...
ALL RIGHT.
NURSE, DO YOU KNOW THE MARK OF DUN-KON-WEN?
OH, YOU WILD BOY.
YOU THINK WE CAN ALL PAY THE PRICE FOR THAT KIND OF MAGIC?
IF YOU CAN THINK OF SOMETHING BETTER BEFORE PUFF UP THERE DECIDES TO GIVE US ANOTHER BLAST, YOU LET ME KNOW.
TOK
OTHERWISE, MARK YOURSELF AND THE OTHERS, AND DO IT NOW.
WHAT'S THE MARK OF--
NO TIME FOR QUESTIONS, LOVE.
JUST SIT TIGHT FOR A MOMENT SO I CAN GET YOU TOO. THEN I'LL NEED YOU TO GET THE CREATURE'S ATTENTION.
IF YOU DON'T MIND.
NO! WHAT ARE YOU DOING?!
HAVE YOU ANY IDEA HOW DANGEROUS--
CONSTANTINE HAS A PLAN.
IT ONLY WORKS IF WE ALL DO IT.
DAMNED FOOLS...
...GO AHEAD THEN. BEFORE I CHANGE MY MIND.

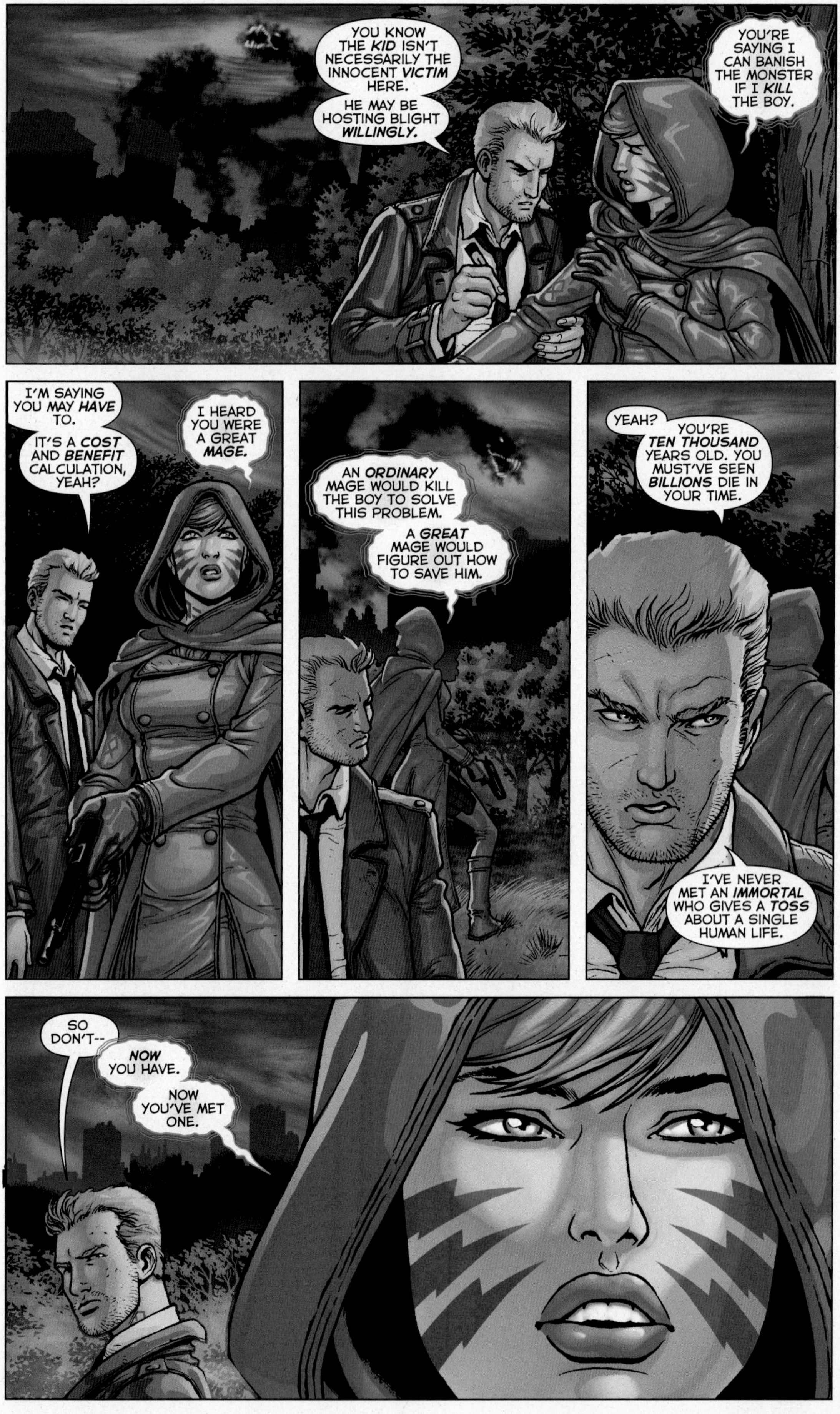
YOU KNOW THE KID ISN'T NECESSARILY THE INNOCENT VICTIM HERE.
HE MAY BE HOSTING BLIGHT WILLINGLY.
YOU'RE SAYING I CAN BANISH THE MONSTER IF I KILL THE BOY.
I'M SAYING YOU MAY HAVE TO.
IT'S A COST AND BENEFIT CALCULATION, YEAH?
I HEARD YOU WERE A GREAT MAGE.
AN ORDINARY MAGE WOULD KILL THE BOY TO SOLVE THIS PROBLEM.
A GREAT MAGE WOULD FIGURE OUT HOW TO SAVE HIM.
YEAH?
YOU'RE TEN THOUSAND YEARS OLD. YOU MUST'VE SEEN BILLIONS DIE IN YOUR TIME.
I'VE NEVER MET AN IMMORTAL WHO GIVES A TOSS ABOUT A SINGLE HUMAN LIFE.
SO DON'T--
NOW YOU HAVE.
NOW YOU'VE MET ONE.

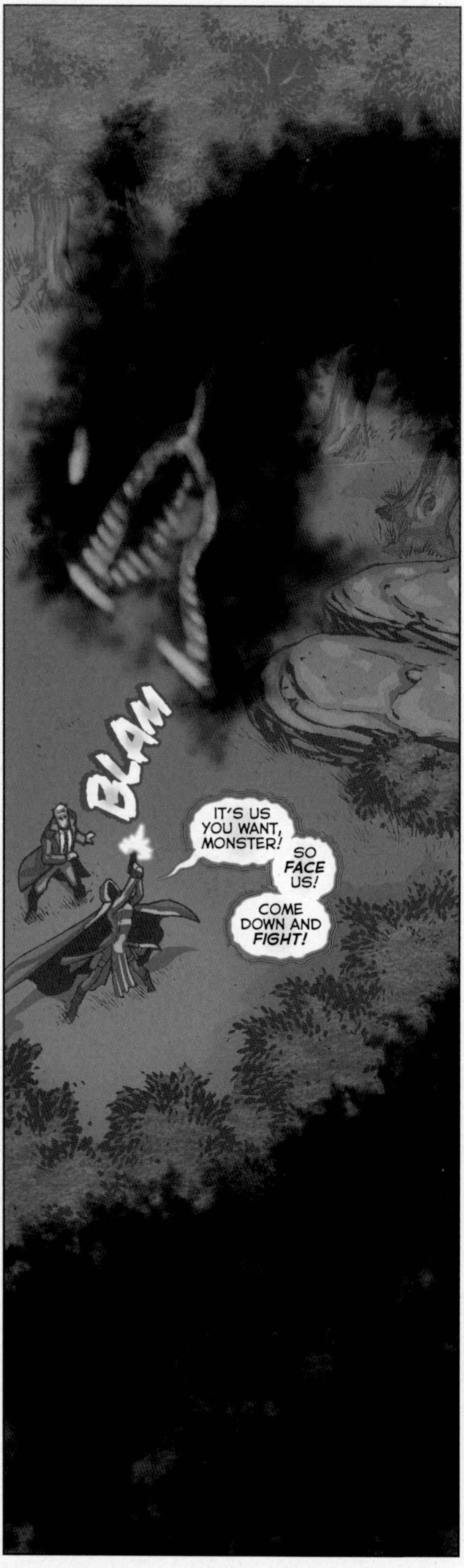
BLAM
IT'S US YOU WANT, MONSTER!
SO FACE US!
COME DOWN AND FIGHT!

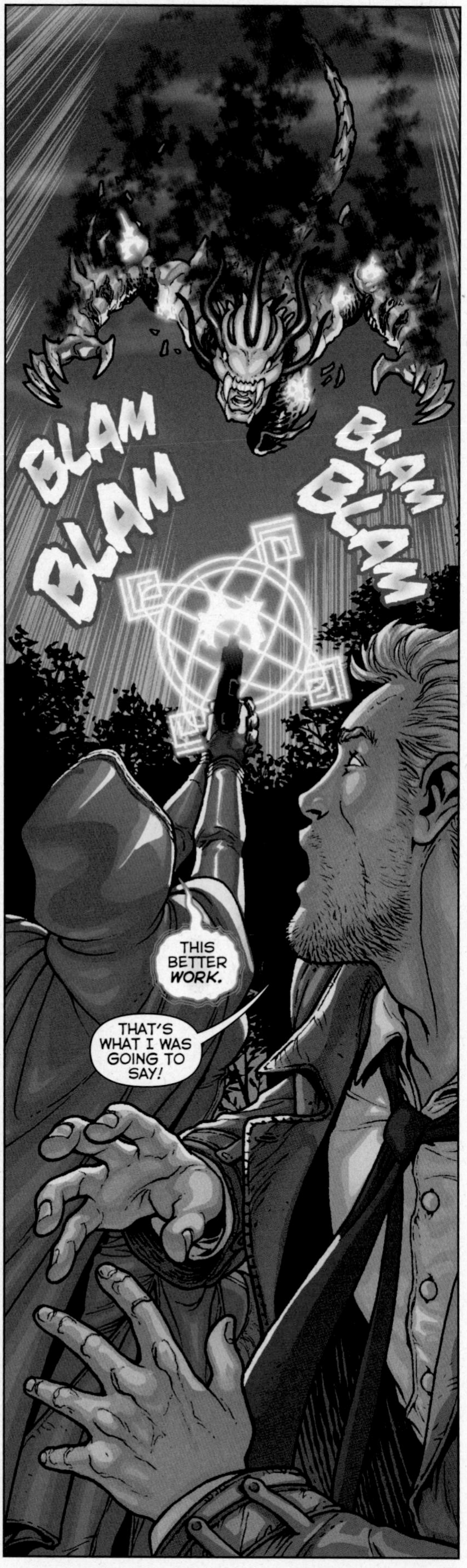
BLAM BLAM
BLAM BLAM
THIS BETTER WORK.
THAT'S WHAT I WAS GOING TO SAY!

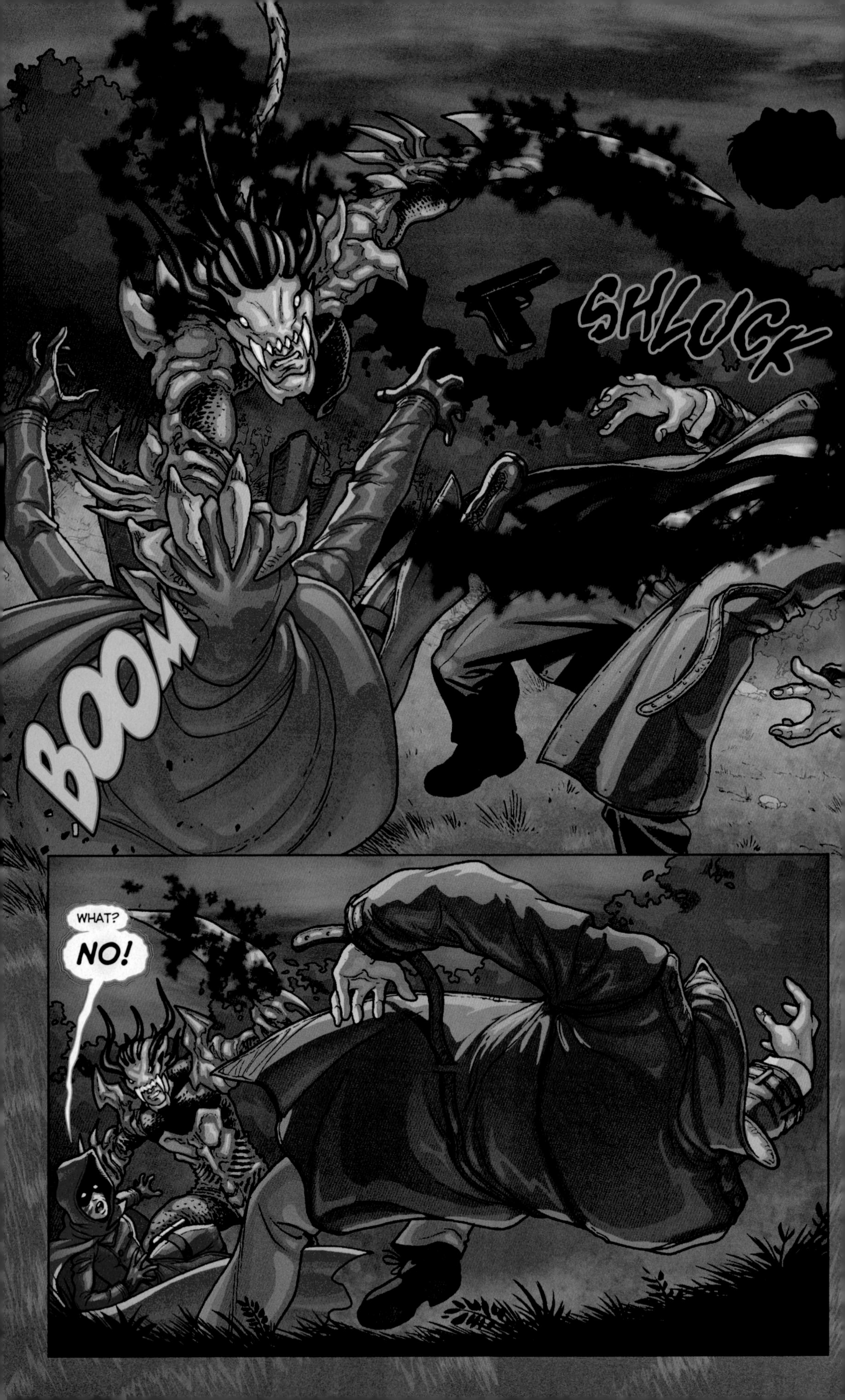
SHLUCK
BOOM
WHAT?
NO!

DEAD. THAT WAS EASY.

DAMN YOU!

:GGHKK:

NNAAA!

YOU WANTED ME? HERE I AM.

FIGHTING.

YOU SEE HOW *EASY* THIS IS?

NAGGH...

THING!

NO. YOU *DON'T* GET TO WIN. EVEN IF I'M ALL THAT'S *LEFT.*

THESE WERE *GOOD* PEOPLE!

HAHA!

"GOOD PEOPLE." THERE'S NO SUCH

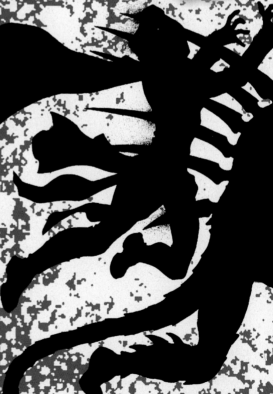

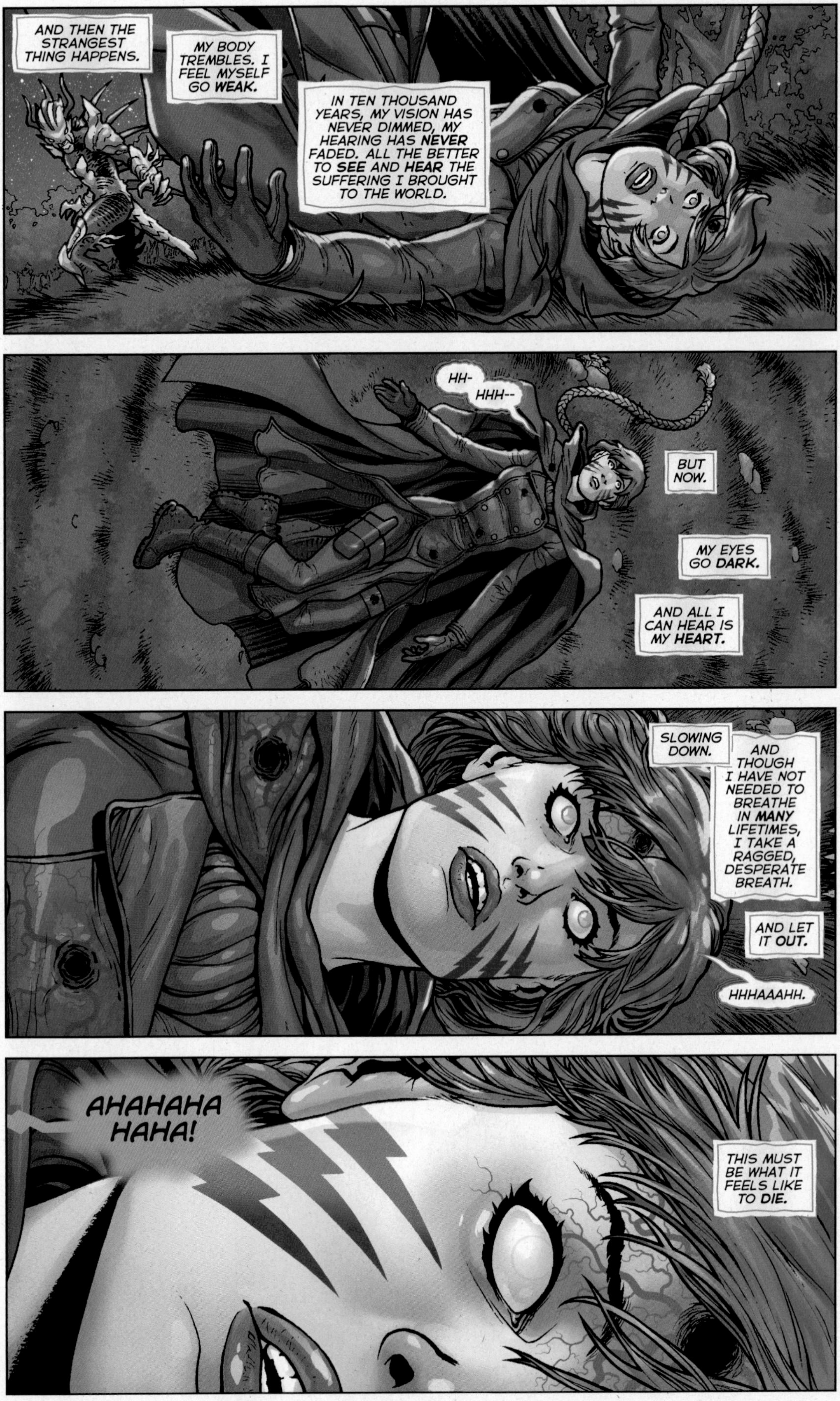
AND THEN THE STRANGEST THING HAPPENS.
MY BODY TREMBLES. I FEEL MYSELF GO WEAK.
IN TEN THOUSAND YEARS, MY VISION HAS NEVER DIMMED, MY HEARING HAS NEVER FADED. ALL THE BETTER TO SEE AND HEAR THE SUFFERING I BROUGHT TO THE WORLD.
HH-
HHH--
BUT NOW.
MY EYES GO DARK.
AND ALL I CAN HEAR IS MY HEART.
SLOWING DOWN.
AND THOUGH I HAVE NOT NEEDED TO BREATHE IN MANY LIFETIMES, I TAKE A RAGGED, DESPERATE BREATH.
AND LET IT OUT.
HHHAAAHH.
AHAHAHA HAHA!
THIS MUST BE WHAT IT FEELS LIKE TO DIE.

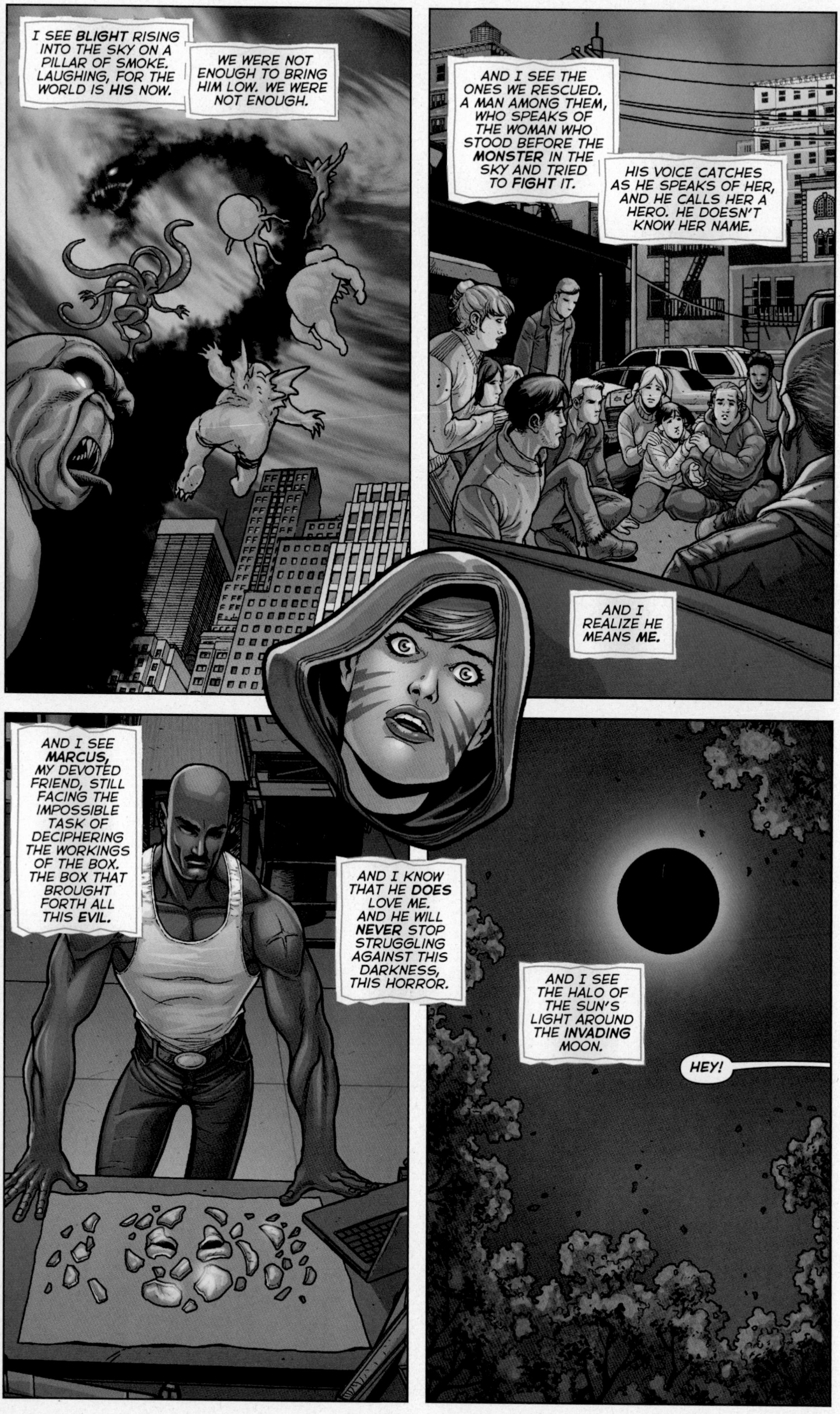
I SEE BLIGHT RISING INTO THE SKY ON A PILLAR OF SMOKE. LAUGHING, FOR THE WORLD IS HIS NOW.
WE WERE NOT ENOUGH TO BRING HIM LOW. WE WERE NOT ENOUGH.
AND I SEE THE ONES WE RESCUED. A MAN AMONG THEM, WHO SPEAKS OF THE WOMAN WHO STOOD BEFORE THE MONSTER IN THE SKY AND TRIED TO FIGHT IT.
HIS VOICE CATCHES AS HE SPEAKS OF HER, AND HE CALLS HER A HERO. HE DOESN'T KNOW HER NAME.
AND I REALIZE HE MEANS ME.
AND I SEE MARCUS, MY DEVOTED FRIEND, STILL FACING THE IMPOSSIBLE TASK OF DECIPHERING THE WORKINGS OF THE BOX. THE BOX THAT BROUGHT FORTH ALL THIS EVIL.
AND I KNOW THAT HE DOES LOVE ME. AND HE WILL NEVER STOP STRUGGLING AGAINST THIS DARKNESS, THIS HORROR.
AND I SEE THE HALO OF THE SUN'S LIGHT AROUND THE INVADING MOON.
HEY!

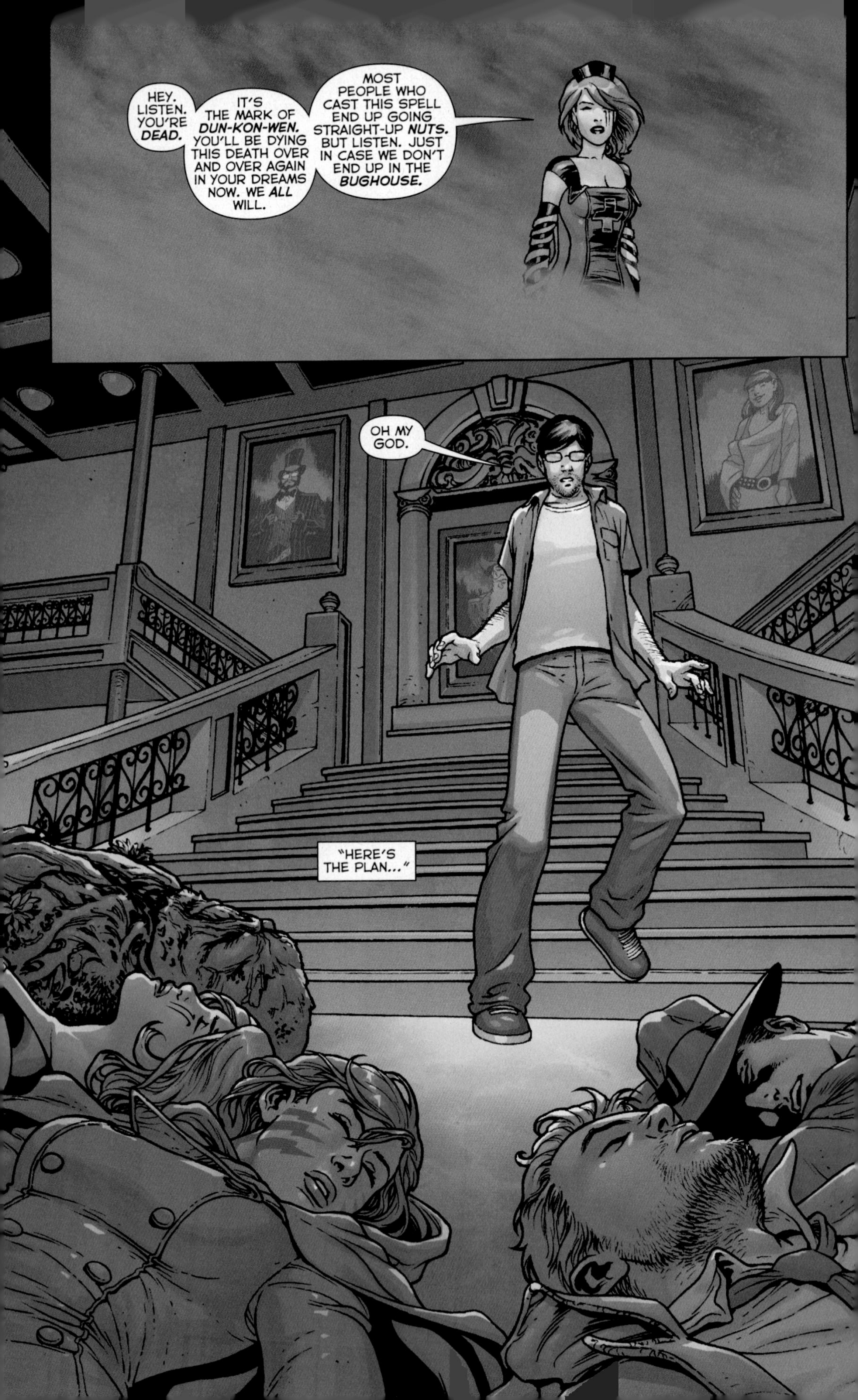

HEY. LISTEN. YOU'RE DEAD.
IT'S THE MARK OF DUN-KON-WEN. YOU'LL BE DYING THIS DEATH OVER AND OVER AGAIN IN YOUR DREAMS NOW. WE ALL WILL.
MOST PEOPLE WHO CAST THIS SPELL END UP GOING STRAIGHT-UP NUTS. BUT LISTEN. JUST IN CASE WE DON'T END UP IN THE BUGHOUSE.
OH MY GOD.
"HERE'S THE PLAN..."

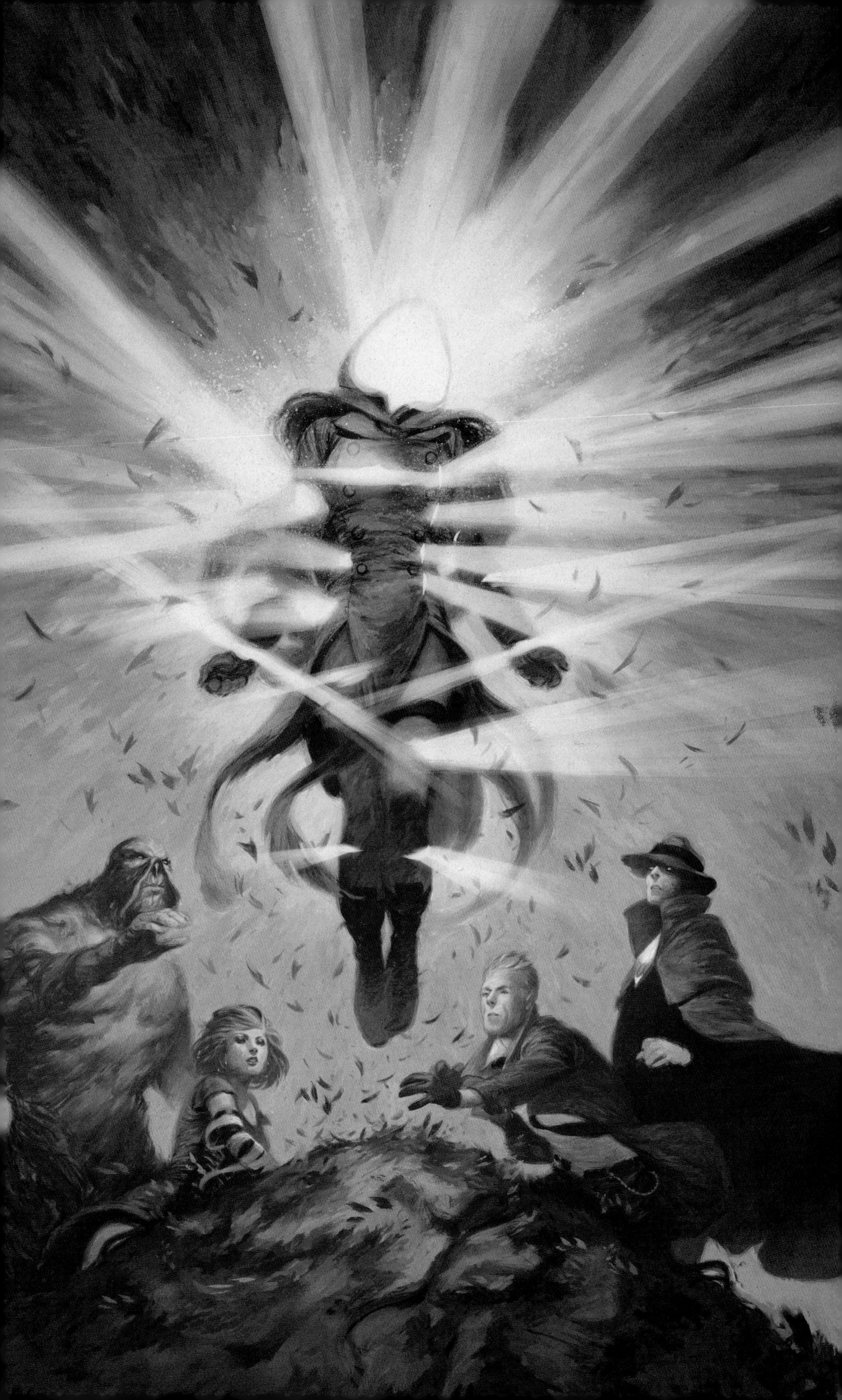

THE RESPONSE

RAY FAWKES
writer

FRANCIS PORTELA
STAZ JOHNSON
artists

HI-FI
colorist

TAYLOR ESPOSITO
letterer

cover art by
JULIAN TOTINO TEDESCO

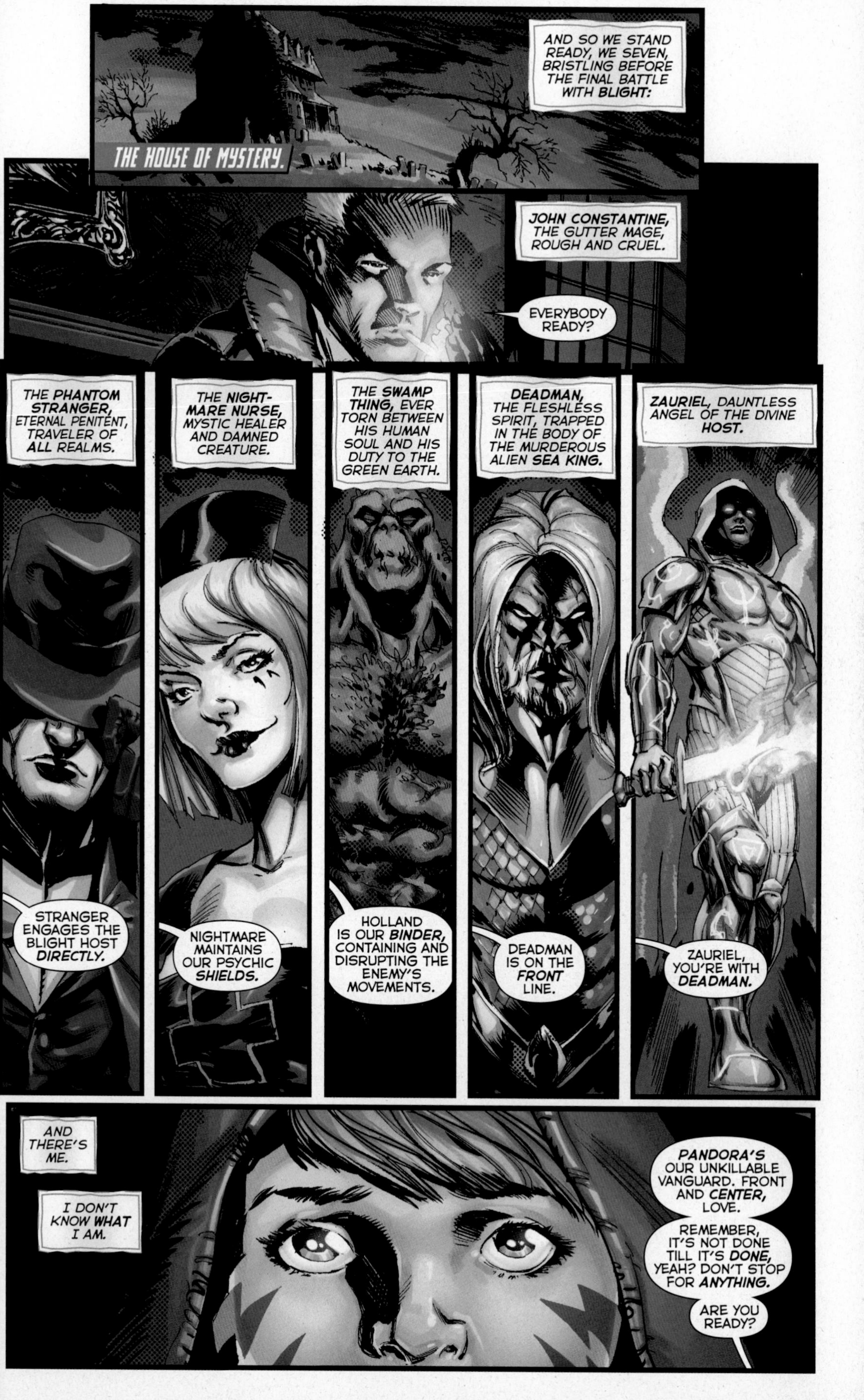
AND SO WE STAND READY, WE SEVEN, BRISTLING BEFORE THE FINAL BATTLE WITH BLIGHT:
THE HOUSE OF MYSTERY.
JOHN CONSTANTINE, THE GUTTER MAGE, ROUGH AND CRUEL.
EVERYBODY READY?
THE PHANTOM STRANGER, ETERNAL PENITENT, TRAVELER OF ALL REALMS.
STRANGER ENGAGES THE BLIGHT HOST DIRECTLY.
THE NIGHT-MARE NURSE, MYSTIC HEALER AND DAMNED CREATURE.
NIGHTMARE MAINTAINS OUR PSYCHIC SHIELDS.
THE SWAMP THING, EVER TORN BETWEEN HIS HUMAN SOUL AND HIS DUTY TO THE GREEN EARTH.
HOLLAND IS OUR BINDER, CONTAINING AND DISRUPTING THE ENEMY'S MOVEMENTS.
DEADMAN, THE FLESHLESS SPIRIT, TRAPPED IN THE BODY OF THE MURDEROUS ALIEN SEA KING.
DEADMAN IS ON THE FRONT LINE.
ZAURIEL, DAUNTLESS ANGEL OF THE DIVINE HOST.
ZAURIEL, YOU'RE WITH DEADMAN.
AND THERE'S ME.
I DON'T KNOW WHAT I AM.
PANDORA'S OUR UNKILLABLE VANGUARD. FRONT AND CENTER, LOVE.
REMEMBER, IT'S NOT DONE TILL IT'S DONE, YEAH? DON'T STOP FOR ANYTHING.
ARE YOU READY?

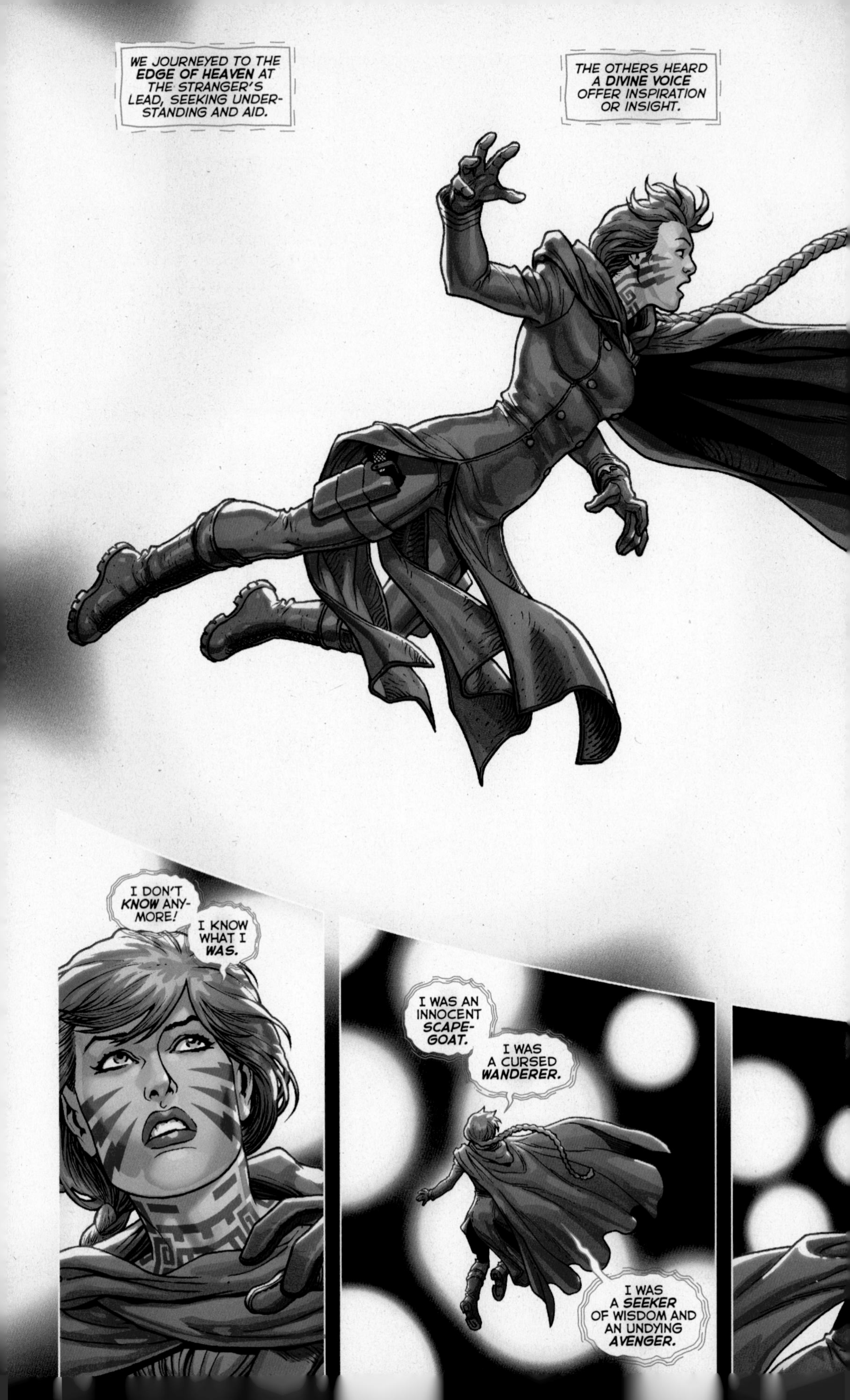
WE JOURNEYED TO THE EDGE OF HEAVEN AT THE STRANGER'S LEAD, SEEKING UNDER-STANDING AND AID.
THE OTHERS HEARD A DIVINE VOICE OFFER INSPIRATION OR INSIGHT.
I DON'T KNOW ANY-MORE!
I KNOW WHAT I WAS.
I WAS AN INNOCENT SCAPE-GOAT.
I WAS A CURSED WANDERER.
I WAS A SEEKER OF WISDOM AND AN UNDYING AVENGER.

I HEARD ONLY AN ENIGMATIC CHALLENGE.

WHAT ARE YOU?

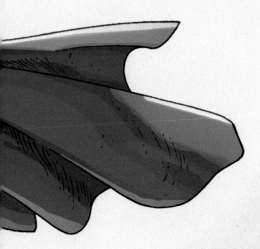

BUT I'M LONG *PAST* DESPAIR.

I'M SO *OLD* THAT MY CURSE IS BLUNTED AND TEDIOUS. I HAVE *FOUND* WISDOM, BUT DO NOT *POSSESS* IT.

THE OBJECTS OF MY VENGEANCE ARE *SADDER* AND *SMALLER* THAN I ONCE BELIEVED.

WHAT *AM I?*

WHAT AM I *NOW?*

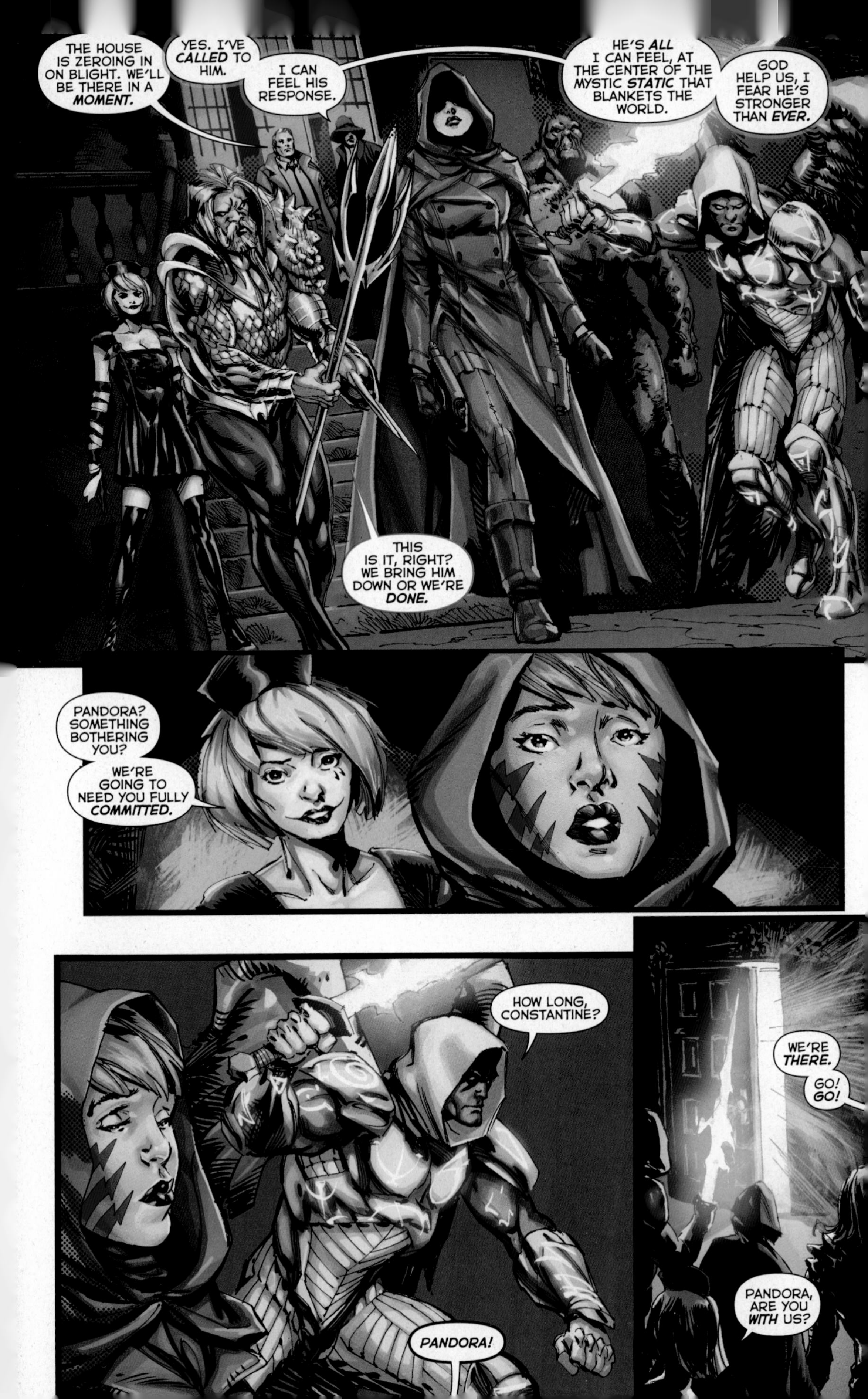
THE HOUSE IS ZEROING IN ON BLIGHT. WE'LL BE THERE IN A MOMENT.
YES. I'VE CALLED TO HIM.
I CAN FEEL HIS RESPONSE.
HE'S ALL I CAN FEEL, AT THE CENTER OF THE MYSTIC STATIC THAT BLANKETS THE WORLD.
GOD HELP US, I FEAR HE'S STRONGER THAN EVER.
THIS IS IT, RIGHT? WE BRING HIM DOWN OR WE'RE DONE.
PANDORA? SOMETHING BOTHERING YOU?
WE'RE GOING TO NEED YOU FULLY COMMITTED.
HOW LONG, CONSTANTINE?
PANDORA!
WE'RE THERE.
GO! GO!
PANDORA, ARE YOU WITH US?

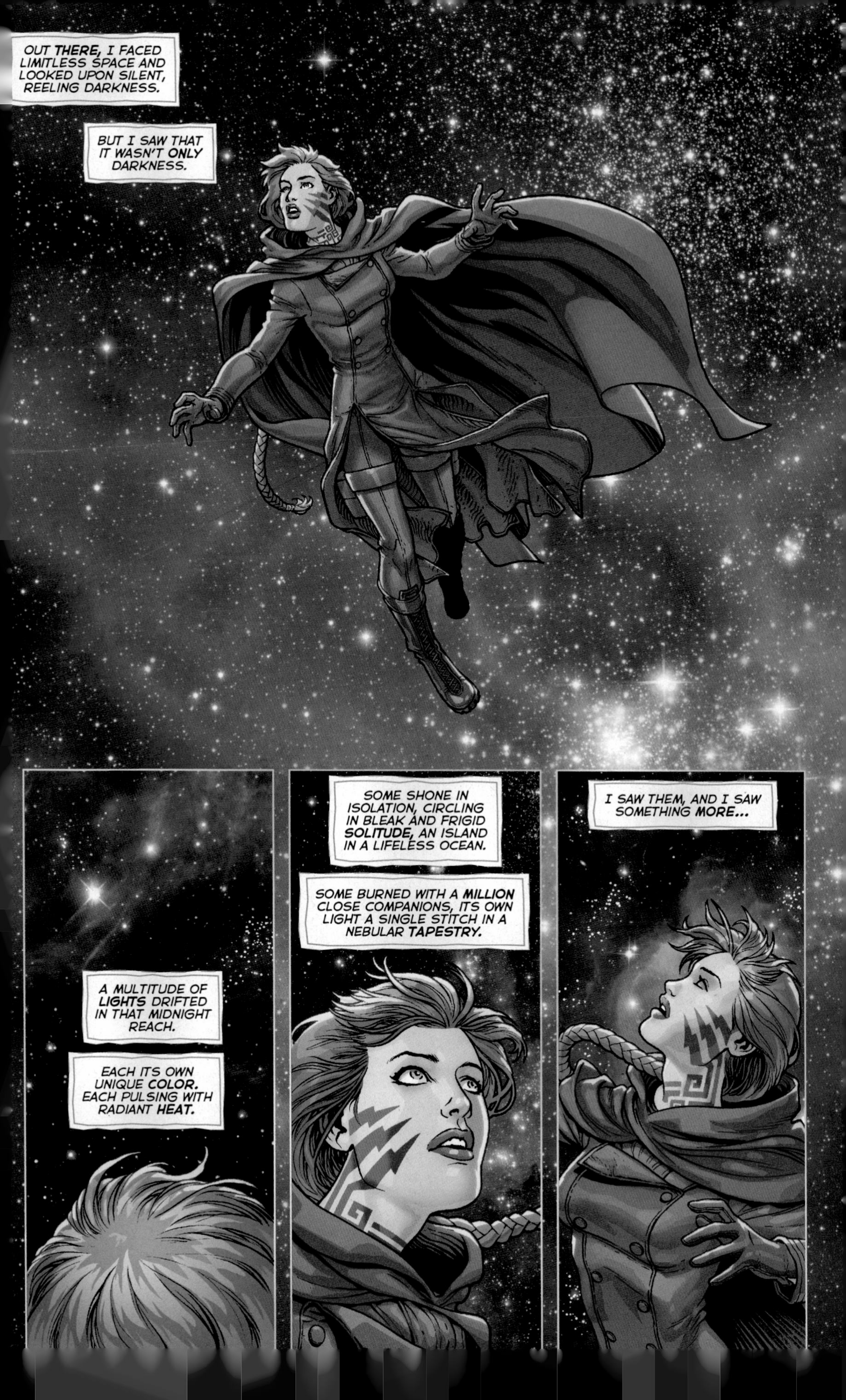
OUT THERE, I FACED LIMITLESS SPACE AND LOOKED UPON SILENT, REELING DARKNESS.
BUT I SAW THAT IT WASN'T ONLY DARKNESS.
A MULTITUDE OF LIGHTS DRIFTED IN THAT MIDNIGHT REACH.
EACH ITS OWN UNIQUE COLOR. EACH PULSING WITH RADIANT HEAT.
SOME SHONE IN ISOLATION, CIRCLING IN BLEAK AND FRIGID SOLITUDE, AN ISLAND IN A LIFELESS OCEAN.
SOME BURNED WITH A MILLION CLOSE COMPANIONS, ITS OWN LIGHT A SINGLE STITCH IN A NEBULAR TAPESTRY.
I SAW THEM, AND I SAW SOMETHING MORE...

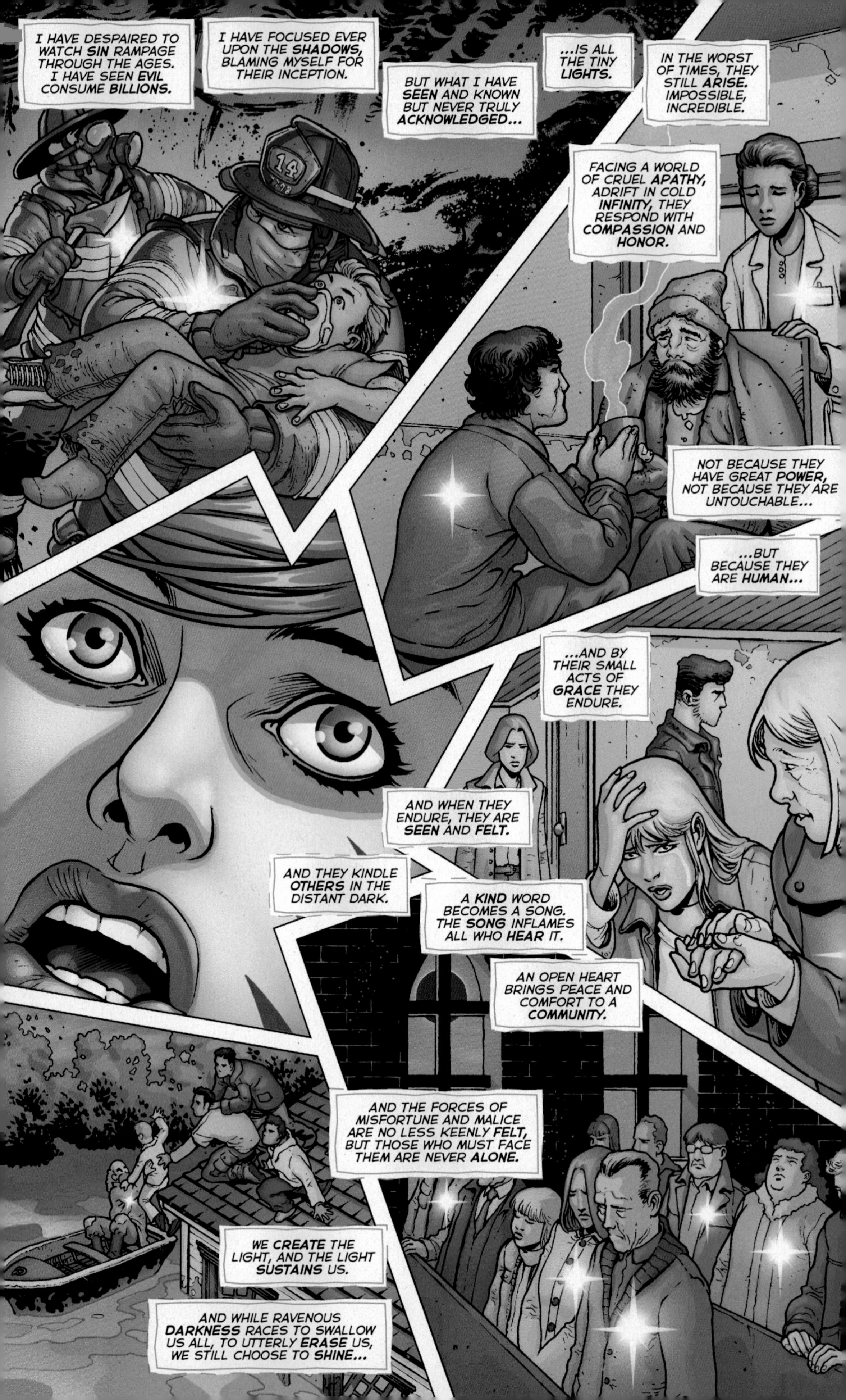
I HAVE DESPAIRED TO WATCH SIN RAMPAGE THROUGH THE AGES. I HAVE SEEN EVIL CONSUME BILLIONS.
I HAVE FOCUSED EVER UPON THE SHADOWS, BLAMING MYSELF FOR THEIR INCEPTION.
BUT WHAT I HAVE SEEN AND KNOWN BUT NEVER TRULY ACKNOWLEDGED...
...IS ALL THE TINY LIGHTS.
IN THE WORST OF TIMES, THEY STILL ARISE. IMPOSSIBLE, INCREDIBLE.
FACING A WORLD OF CRUEL APATHY, ADRIFT IN COLD INFINITY, THEY RESPOND WITH COMPASSION AND HONOR.
NOT BECAUSE THEY HAVE GREAT POWER, NOT BECAUSE THEY ARE UNTOUCHABLE...
...BUT BECAUSE THEY ARE HUMAN...
...AND BY THEIR SMALL ACTS OF GRACE THEY ENDURE.
AND WHEN THEY ENDURE, THEY ARE SEEN AND FELT.
AND THEY KINDLE OTHERS IN THE DISTANT DARK.
A KIND WORD BECOMES A SONG. THE SONG INFLAMES ALL WHO HEAR IT.
AN OPEN HEART BRINGS PEACE AND COMFORT TO A COMMUNITY.
AND THE FORCES OF MISFORTUNE AND MALICE ARE NO LESS KEENLY FELT, BUT THOSE WHO MUST FACE THEM ARE NEVER ALONE.
WE CREATE THE LIGHT, AND THE LIGHT SUSTAINS US.
AND WHILE RAVENOUS DARKNESS RACES TO SWALLOW US ALL, TO UTTERLY ERASE US, WE STILL CHOOSE TO SHINE...

...AND THIS IS THE RESULT.
AND I AM ONE OF THEM. WITH MY LIVING FAITH IN HUMANITY, EVEN AFTER ALL THESE MANY YEARS.
THE JUSTICE LEAGUE DARK HAS PLUMBED THE COLLECTIVE UNCONSCIOUS OF HUMANITY AND PETITIONED AT THE GATES OF DIVINITY SEEKING THE POWER TO DEFEAT OUR ENEMIES.
BUT WE ALREADY HAVE THAT POWER.
WE'VE ALWAYS HAD IT.
AND I THINK I'M BEING OFFERED THE CHANCE TO HOST IT, JUST AS BLIGHT HOSTS THE DARKNESS.
THE CRIME SYNDICATE HASN'T COMPLETELY WON. EVEN IF THEIR BLOODY HANDPRINT IS PRESSED INTO THE WORLD. BLIGHT HASN'T WON...

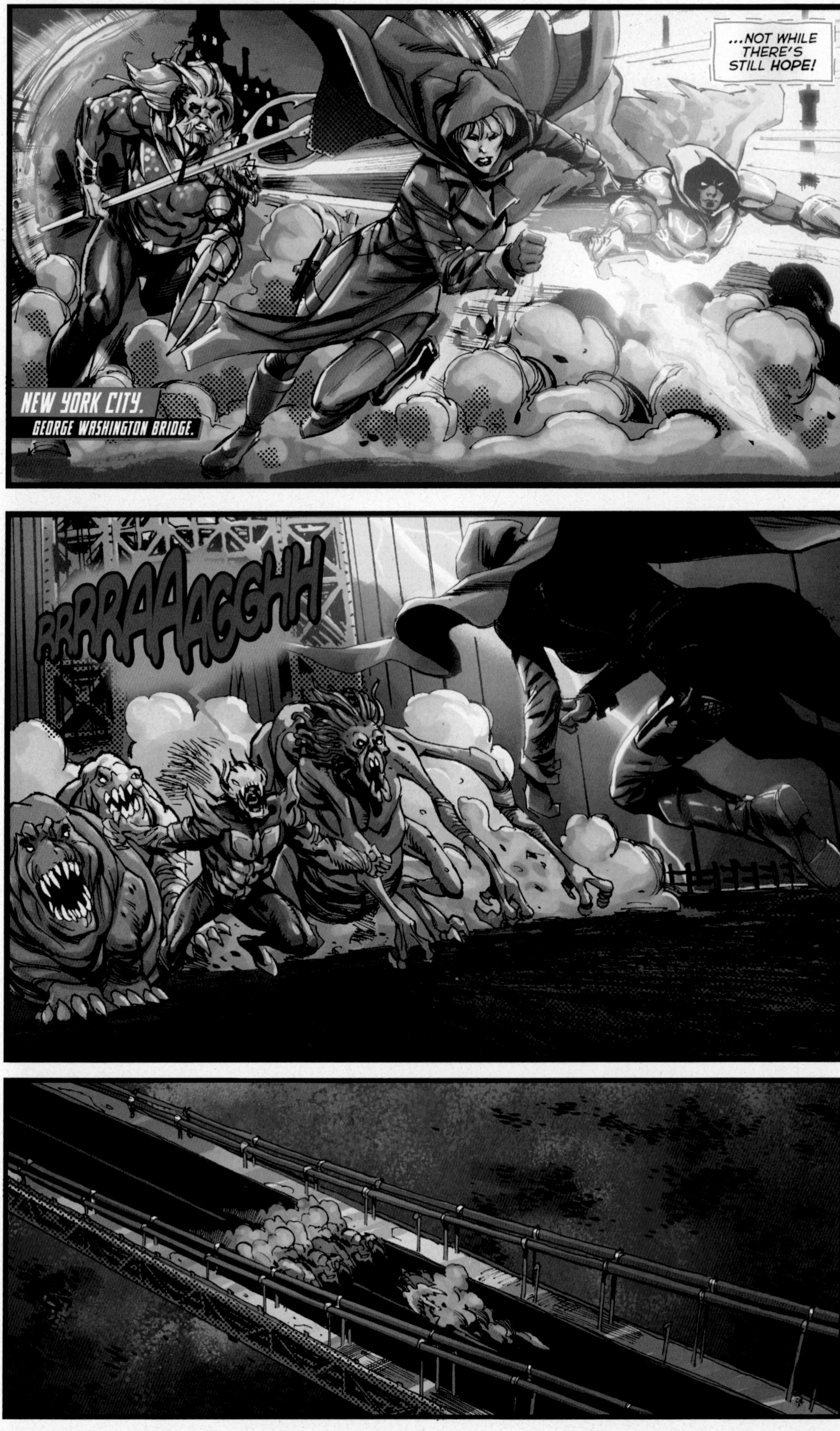
...NOT WHILE THERE'S STILL HOPE!
NEW YORK CITY.
GEORGE WASHINGTON BRIDGE.
RRRRAAAAGGHH

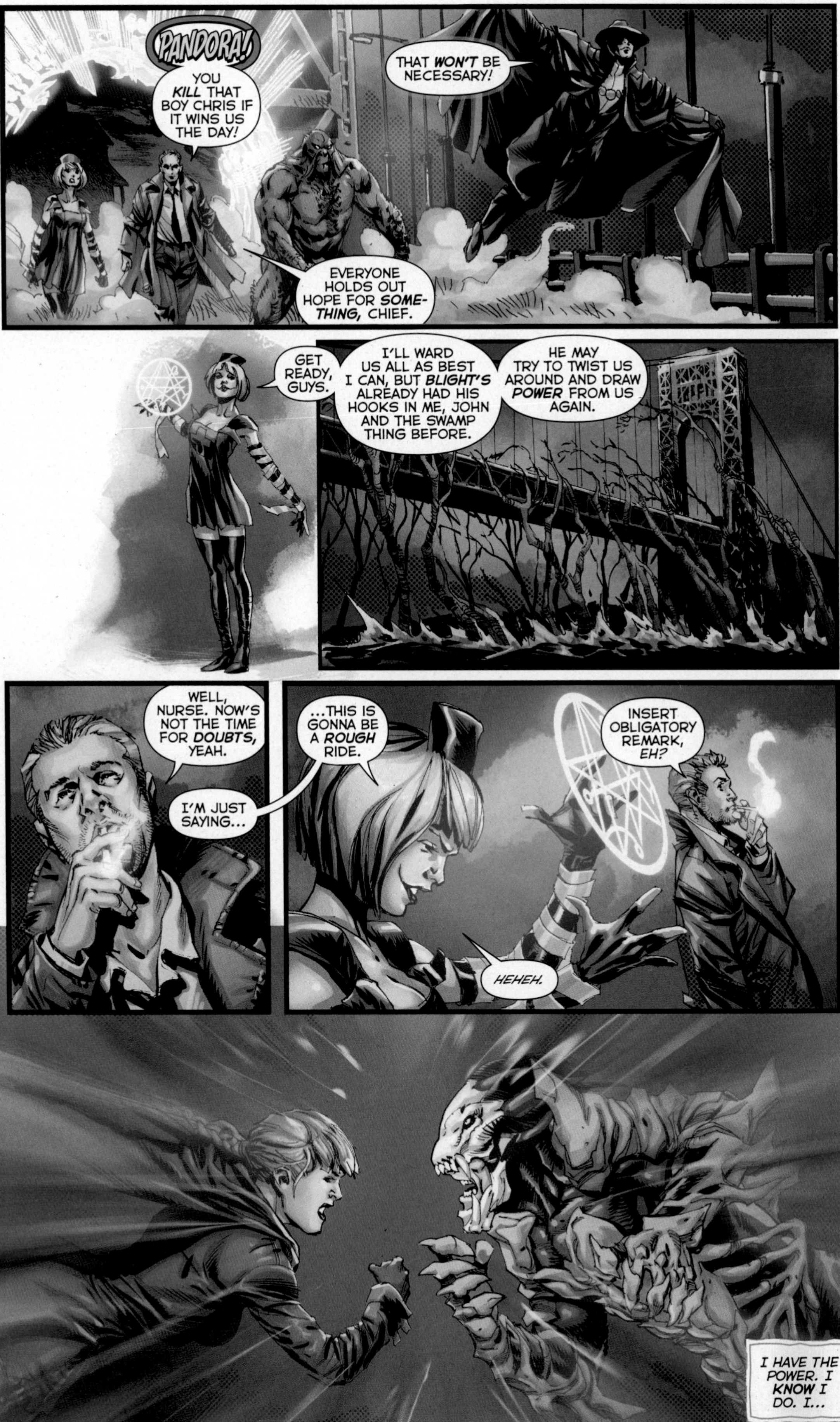
PANDORA!
YOU KILL THAT BOY CHRIS IF IT WINS US THE DAY!
THAT WON'T BE NECESSARY!
EVERYONE HOLDS OUT HOPE FOR SOME-THING, CHIEF.
GET READY, GUYS.
I'LL WARD US ALL AS BEST I CAN, BUT BLIGHT'S ALREADY HAD HIS HOOKS IN ME, JOHN AND THE SWAMP THING BEFORE.
HE MAY TRY TO TWIST US AROUND AND DRAW POWER FROM US AGAIN.
WELL, NURSE. NOW'S NOT THE TIME FOR DOUBTS, YEAH.
I'M JUST SAYING...
...THIS IS GONNA BE A ROUGH RIDE.
INSERT OBLIGATORY REMARK, EH?
HEHEH.
I HAVE THE POWER. I KNOW I DO. I...

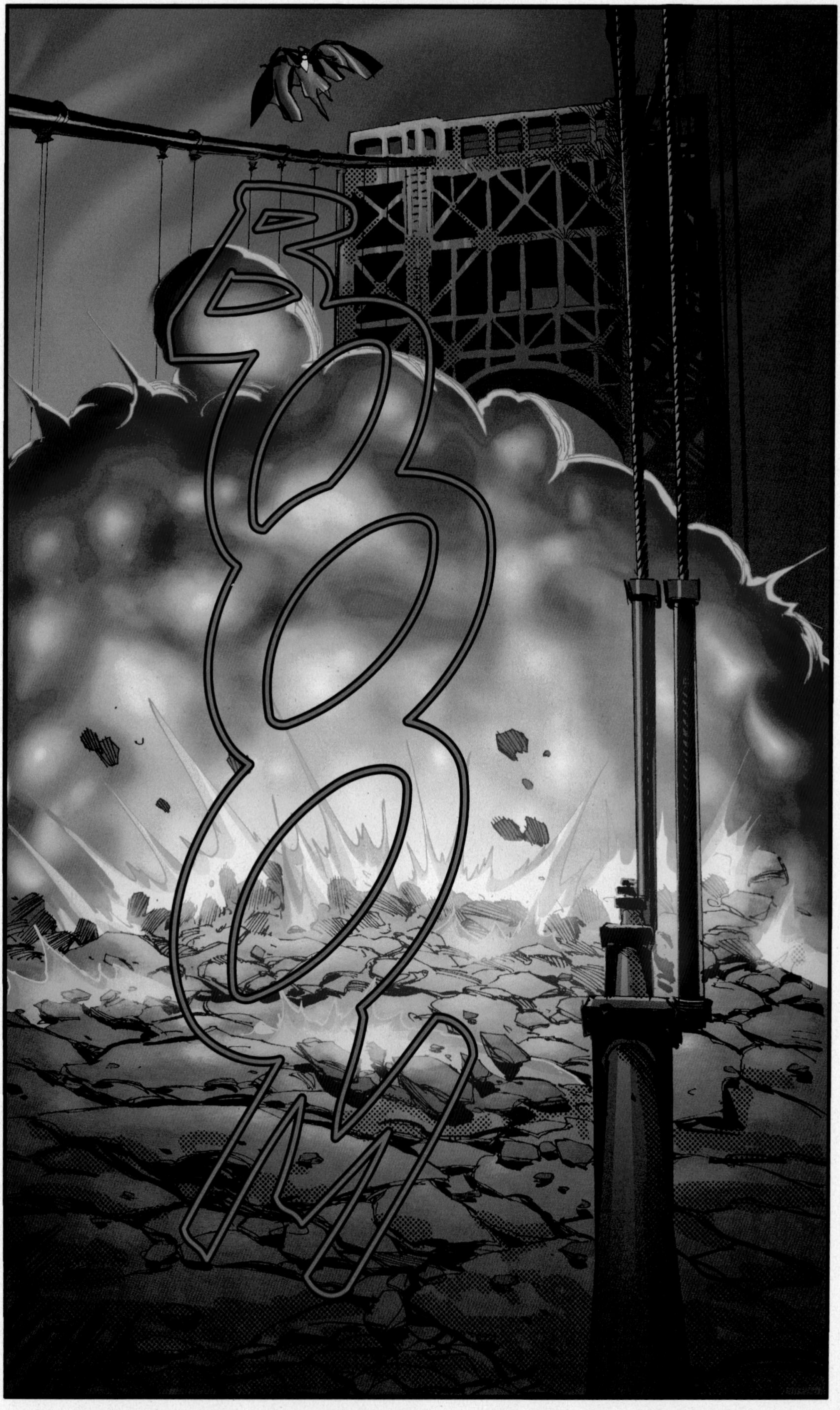
BOOM

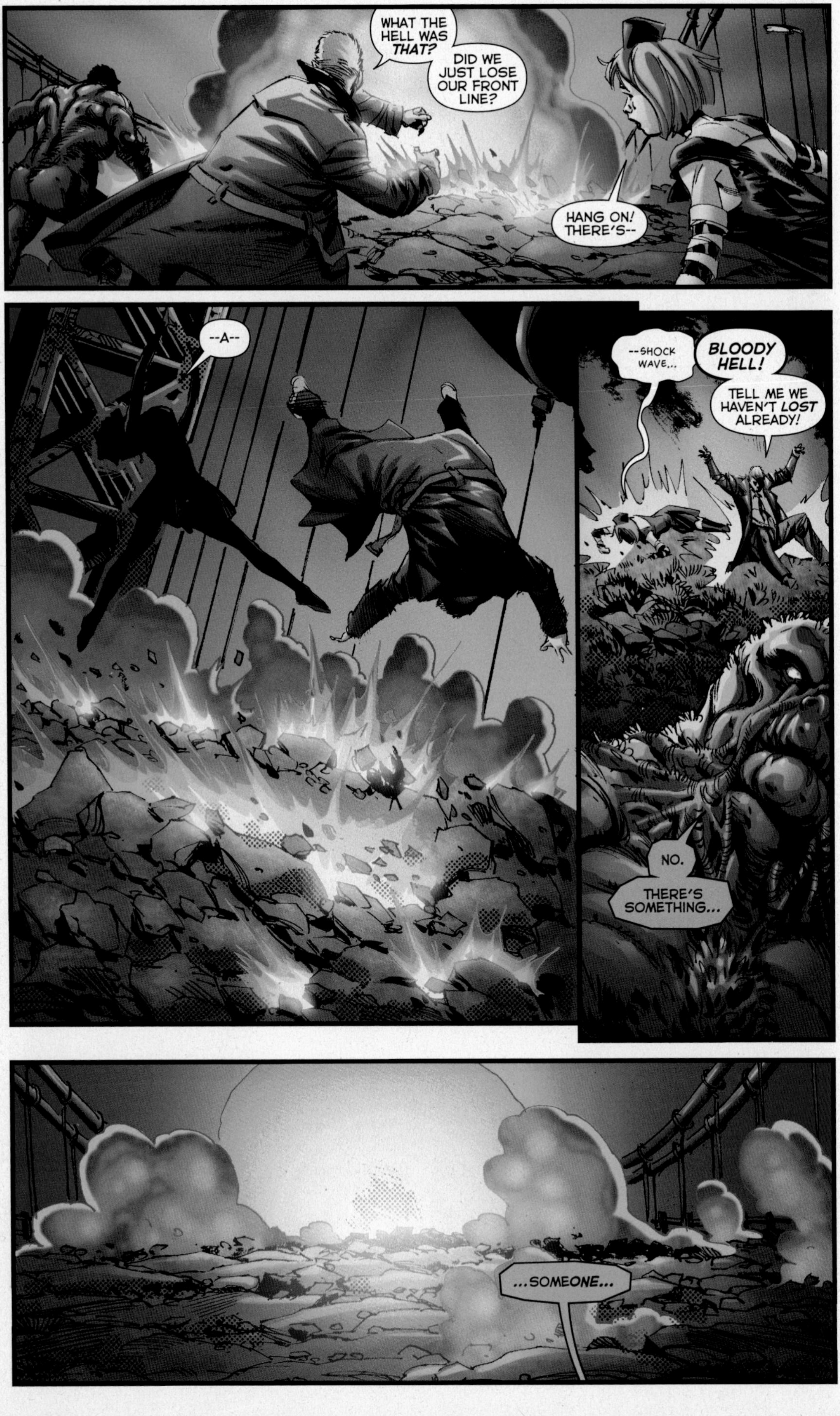
WHAT THE HELL WAS *THAT?*
DID WE JUST LOSE OUR FRONT LINE?
HANG ON! THERE'S--
--A--
--SHOCK WAVE...
BLOODY HELL!
TELL ME WE HAVEN'T *LOST* ALREADY!
NO.
THERE'S SOMETHING...
...SOME*ONE*...

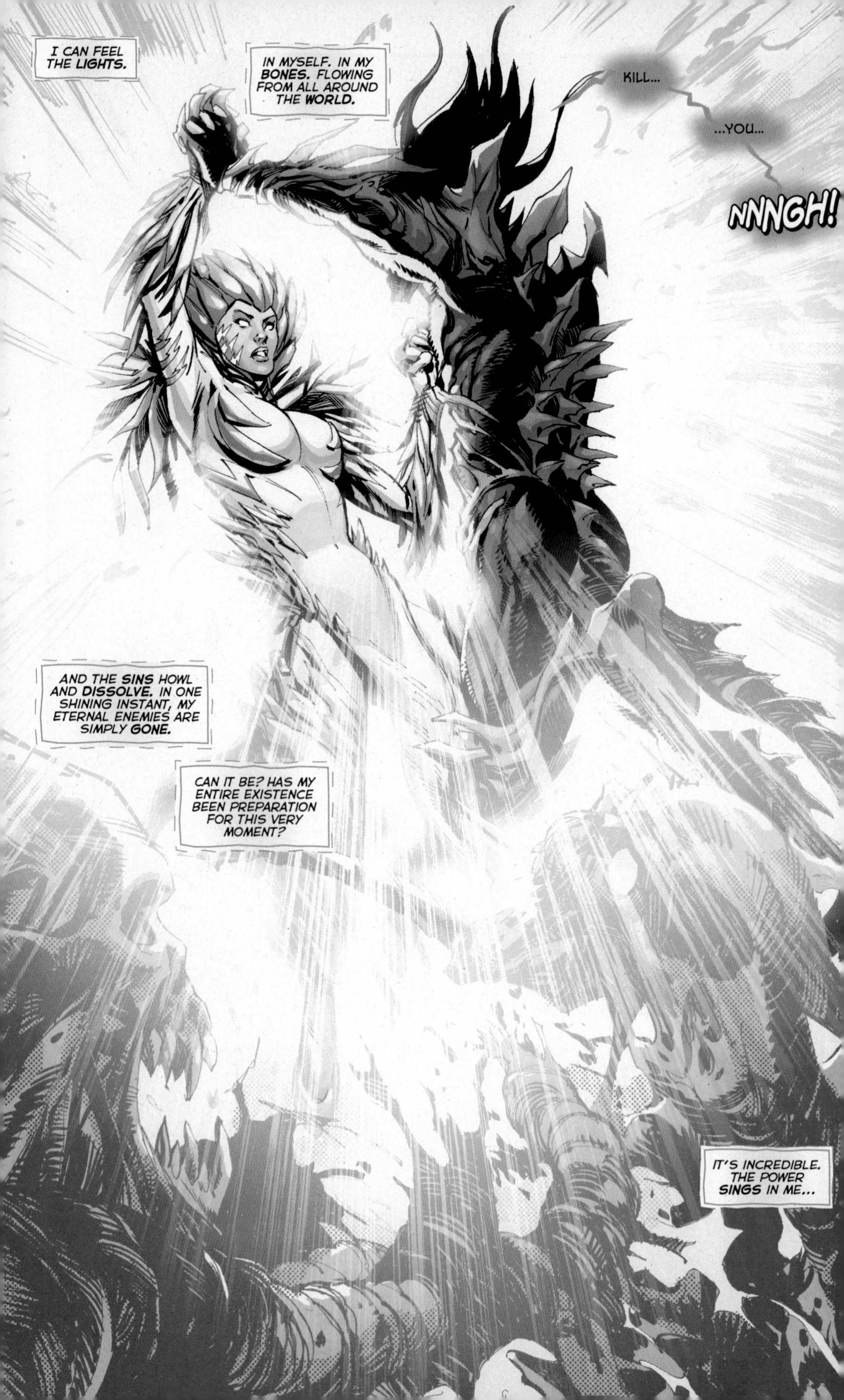
I CAN FEEL THE LIGHTS.
IN MYSELF. IN MY BONES. FLOWING FROM ALL AROUND THE WORLD.
KILL...
...YOU...
NNNGH!
AND THE SINS HOWL AND DISSOLVE. IN ONE SHINING INSTANT, MY ETERNAL ENEMIES ARE SIMPLY GONE.
CAN IT BE? HAS MY ENTIRE EXISTENCE BEEN PREPARATION FOR THIS VERY MOMENT?
IT'S INCREDIBLE. THE POWER SINGS IN ME...

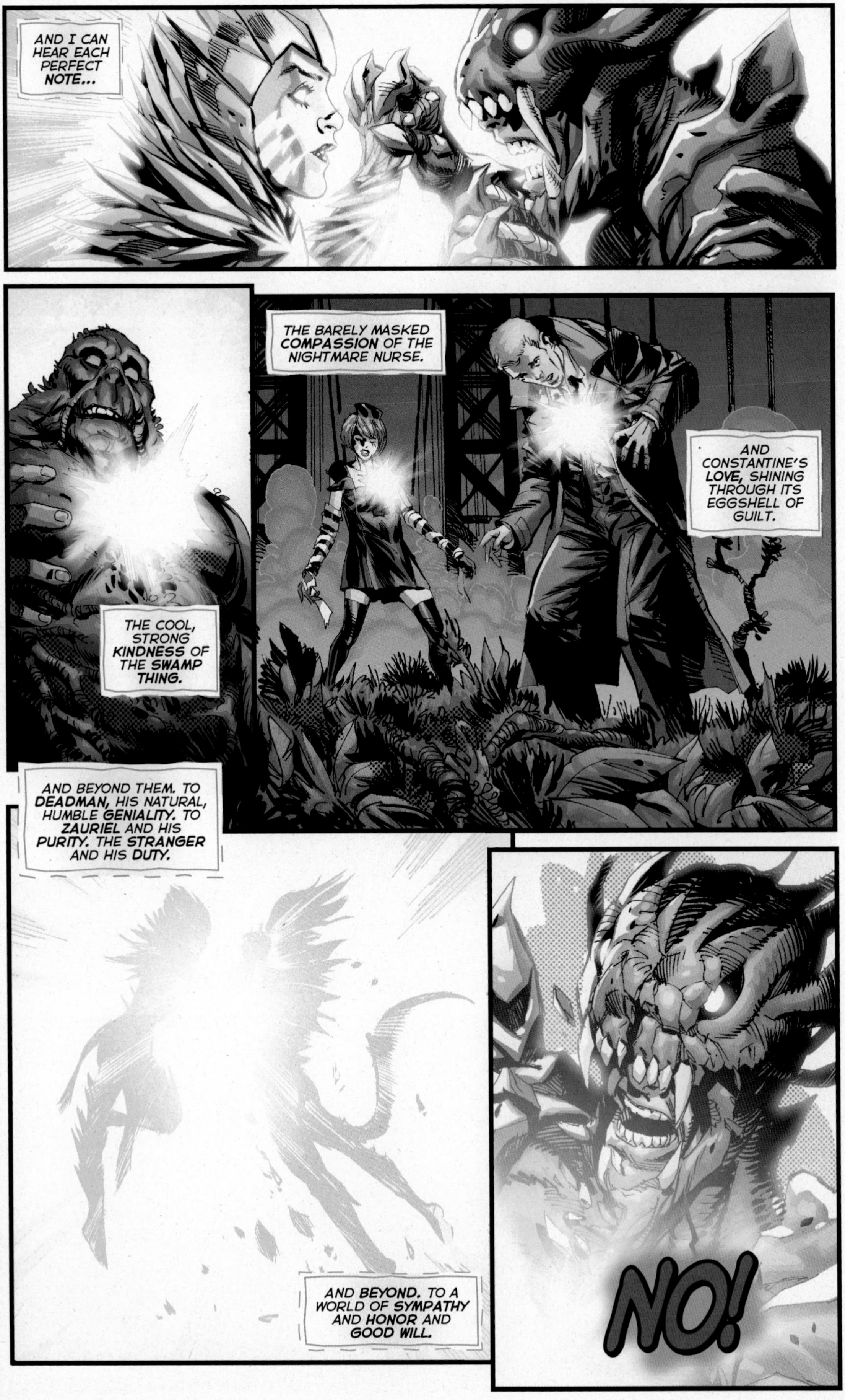
AND I CAN HEAR EACH PERFECT NOTE...
THE BARELY MASKED COMPASSION OF THE NIGHTMARE NURSE.
AND CONSTANTINE'S LOVE, SHINING THROUGH ITS EGGSHELL OF GUILT.
THE COOL, STRONG KINDNESS OF THE SWAMP THING.
AND BEYOND THEM. TO DEADMAN, HIS NATURAL, HUMBLE GENIALITY. TO ZAURIEL AND HIS PURITY. THE STRANGER AND HIS DUTY.
AND BEYOND. TO A WORLD OF SYMPATHY AND HONOR AND GOOD WILL.
NO!

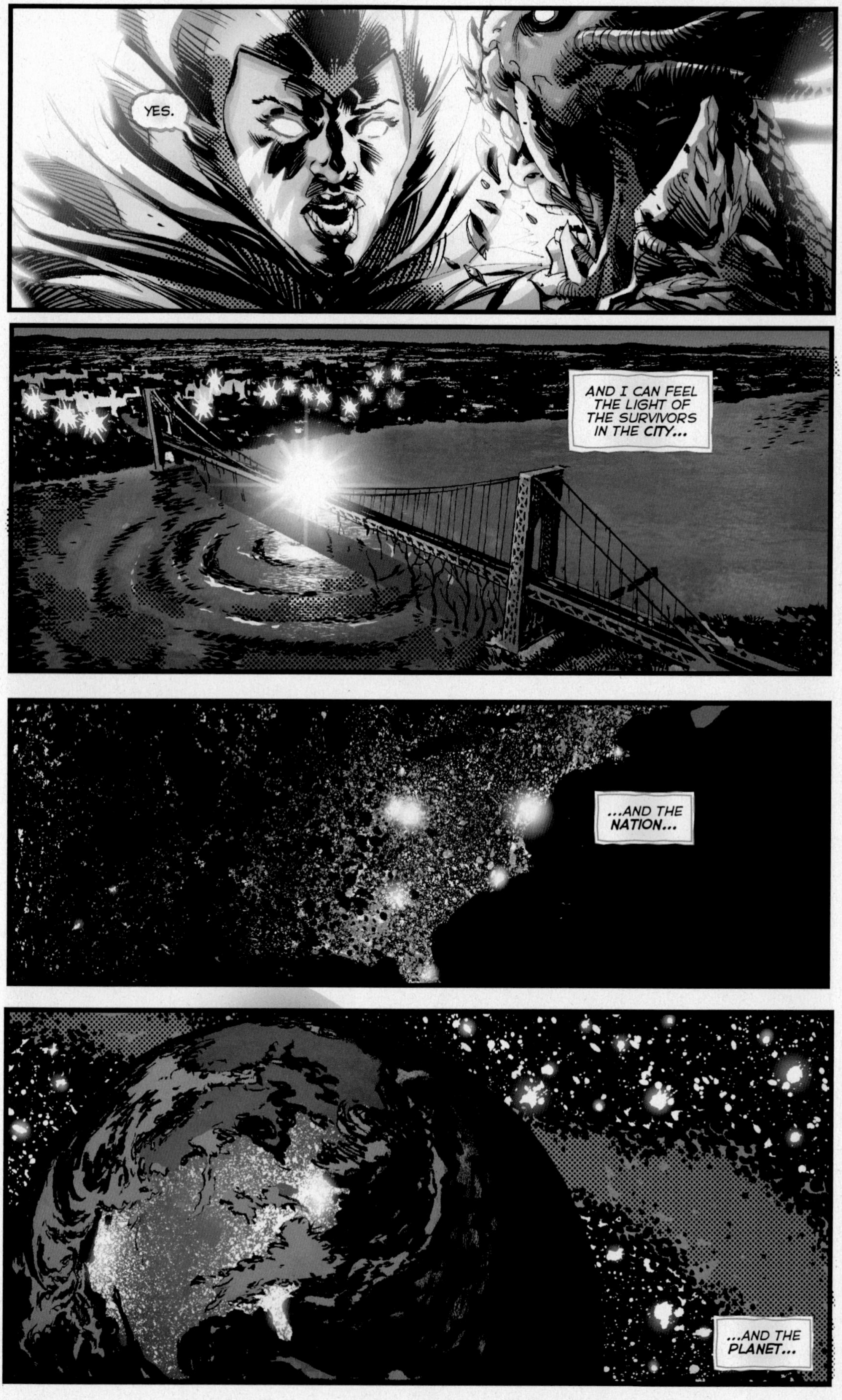
YES.
AND I CAN FEEL THE LIGHT OF THE SURVIVORS IN THE CITY...
...AND THE NATION...
...AND THE PLANET...

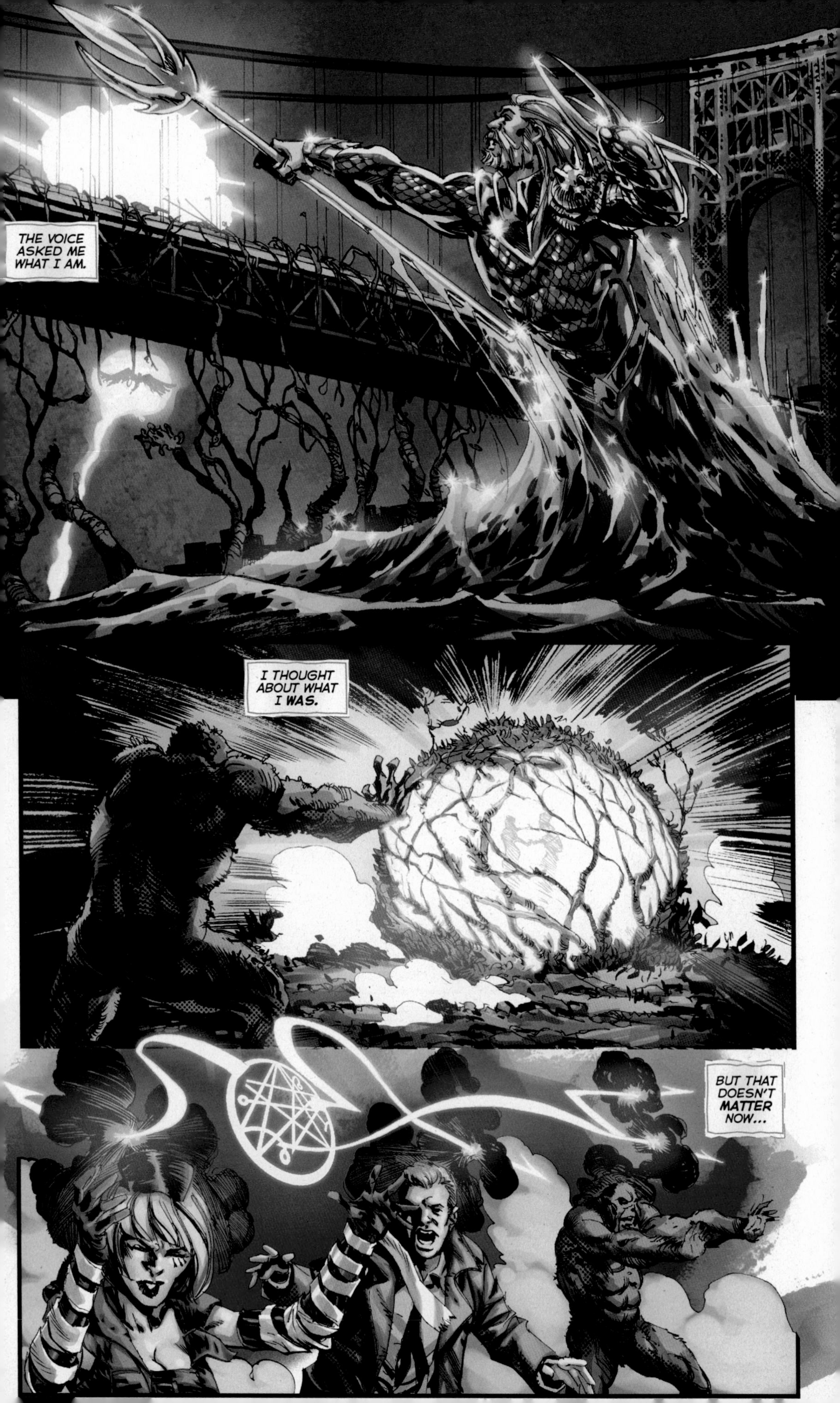
THE VOICE ASKED ME WHAT I AM.
I THOUGHT ABOUT WHAT I WAS.
BUT THAT DOESN'T MATTER NOW...

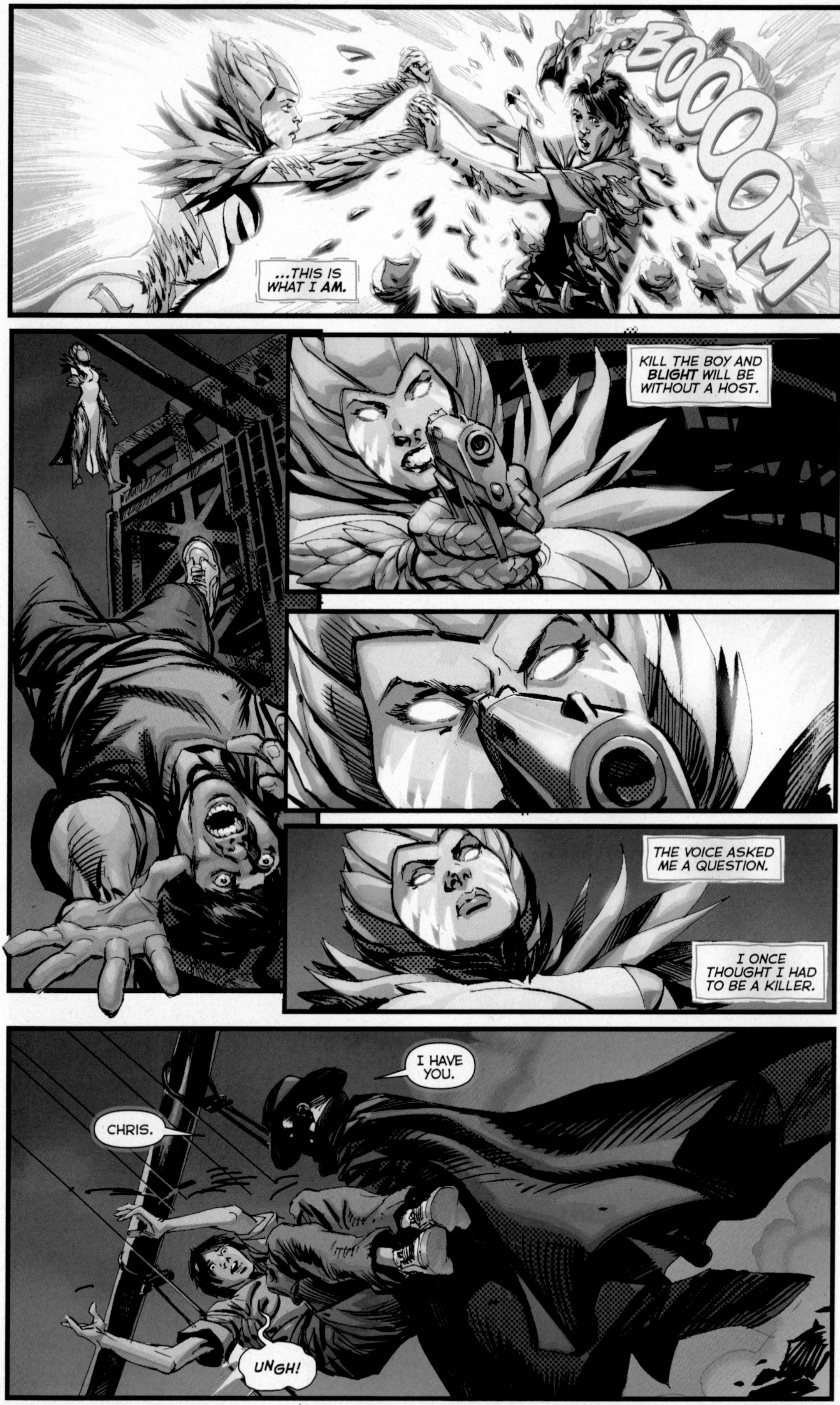
BOOOOM
...THIS IS WHAT I AM.
KILL THE BOY AND BLIGHT WILL BE WITHOUT A HOST.
THE VOICE ASKED ME A QUESTION.
I ONCE THOUGHT I HAD TO BE A KILLER.
I HAVE YOU.
CHRIS.
UNGH!

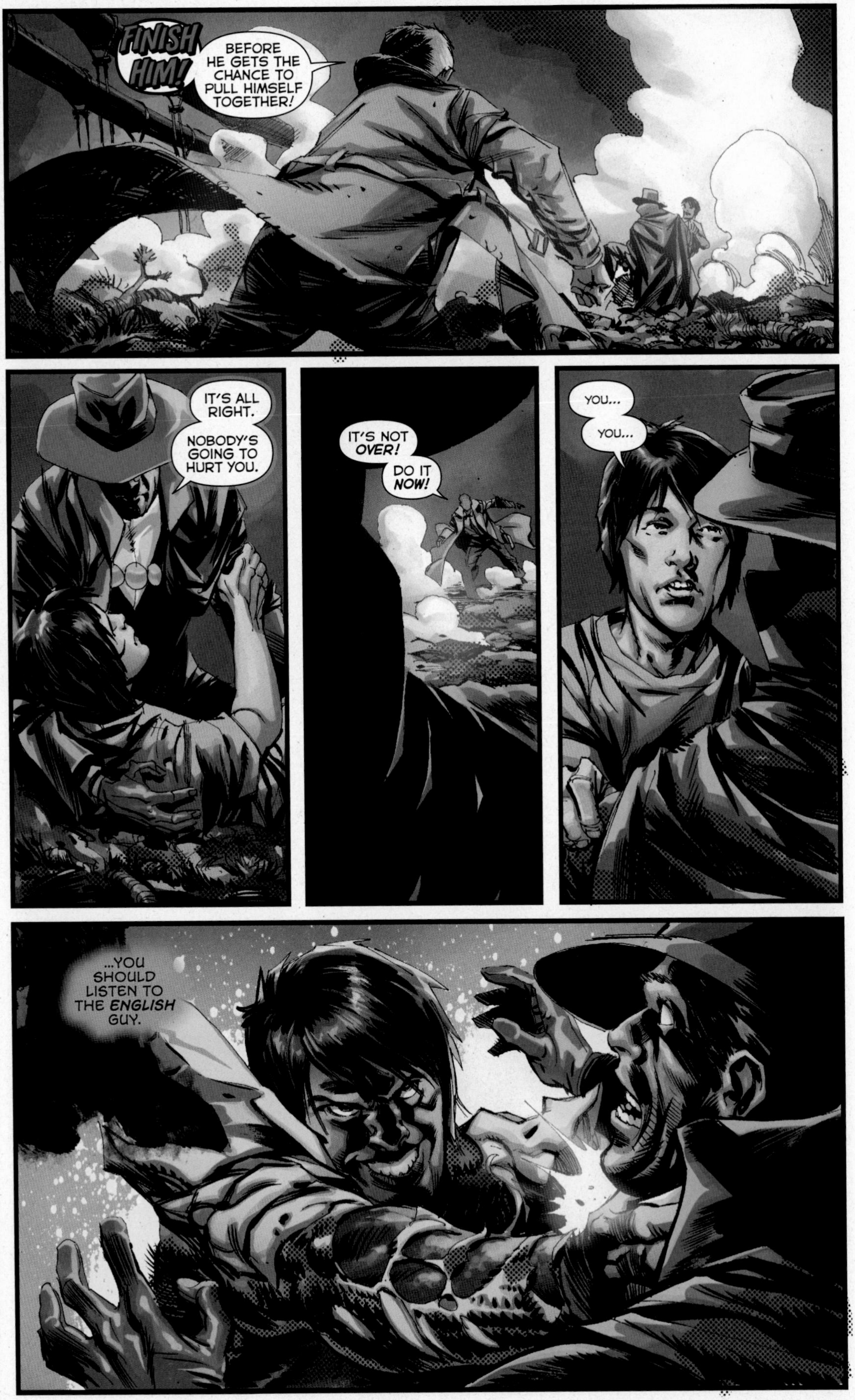
FINISH HIM!
BEFORE HE GETS THE CHANCE TO PULL HIMSELF TOGETHER!
IT'S ALL RIGHT.
NOBODY'S GOING TO HURT YOU.
IT'S NOT OVER!
DO IT NOW!
YOU...
YOU...
...YOU SHOULD LISTEN TO THE ENGLISH GUY.

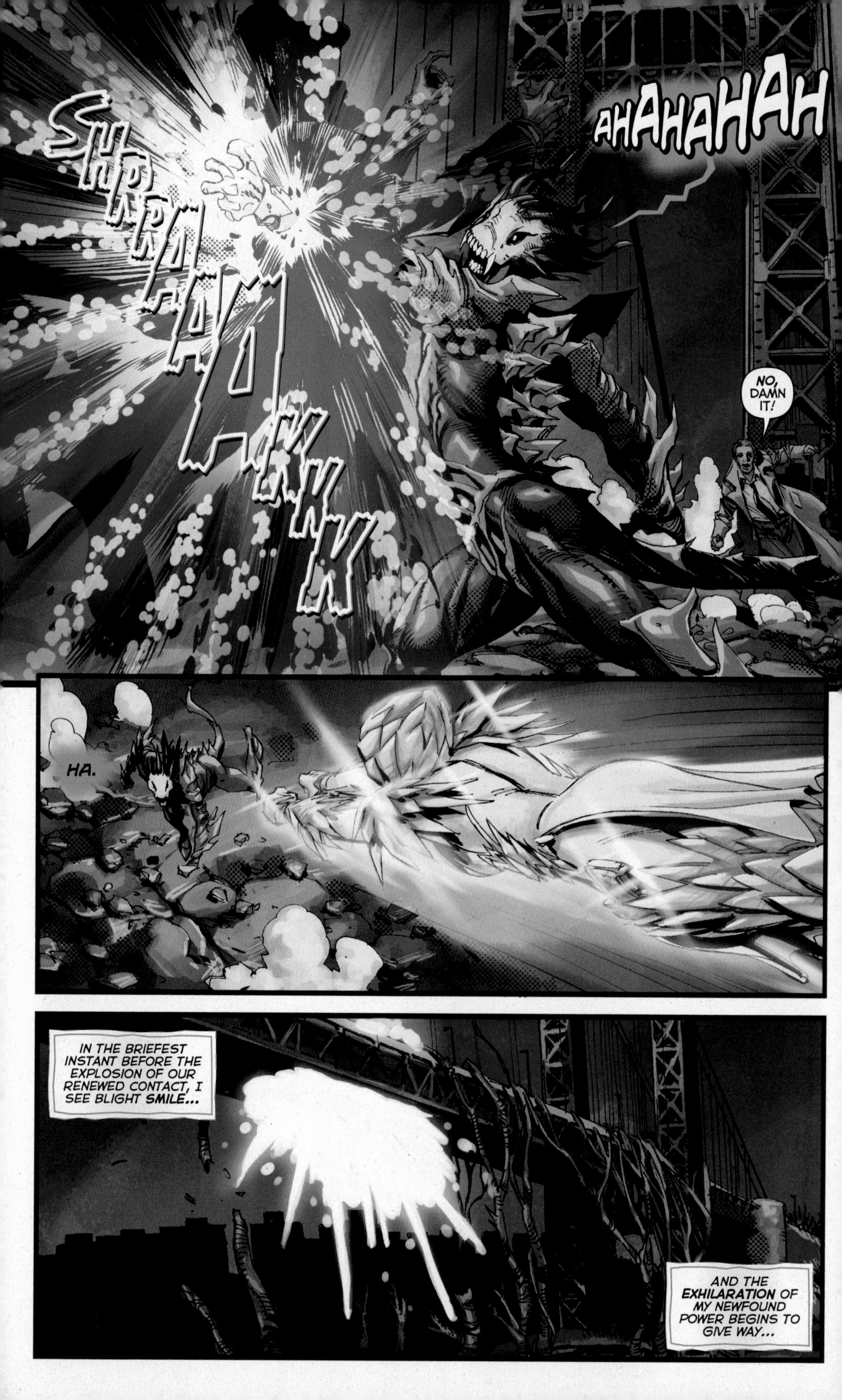
SHRRAAAAKKKK
AHAHAHAH
NO, DAMN IT!
HA.
IN THE BRIEFEST INSTANT BEFORE THE EXPLOSION OF OUR RENEWED CONTACT, I SEE BLIGHT **SMILE**...
AND THE **EXHILARATION** OF MY NEWFOUND POWER BEGINS TO GIVE WAY...

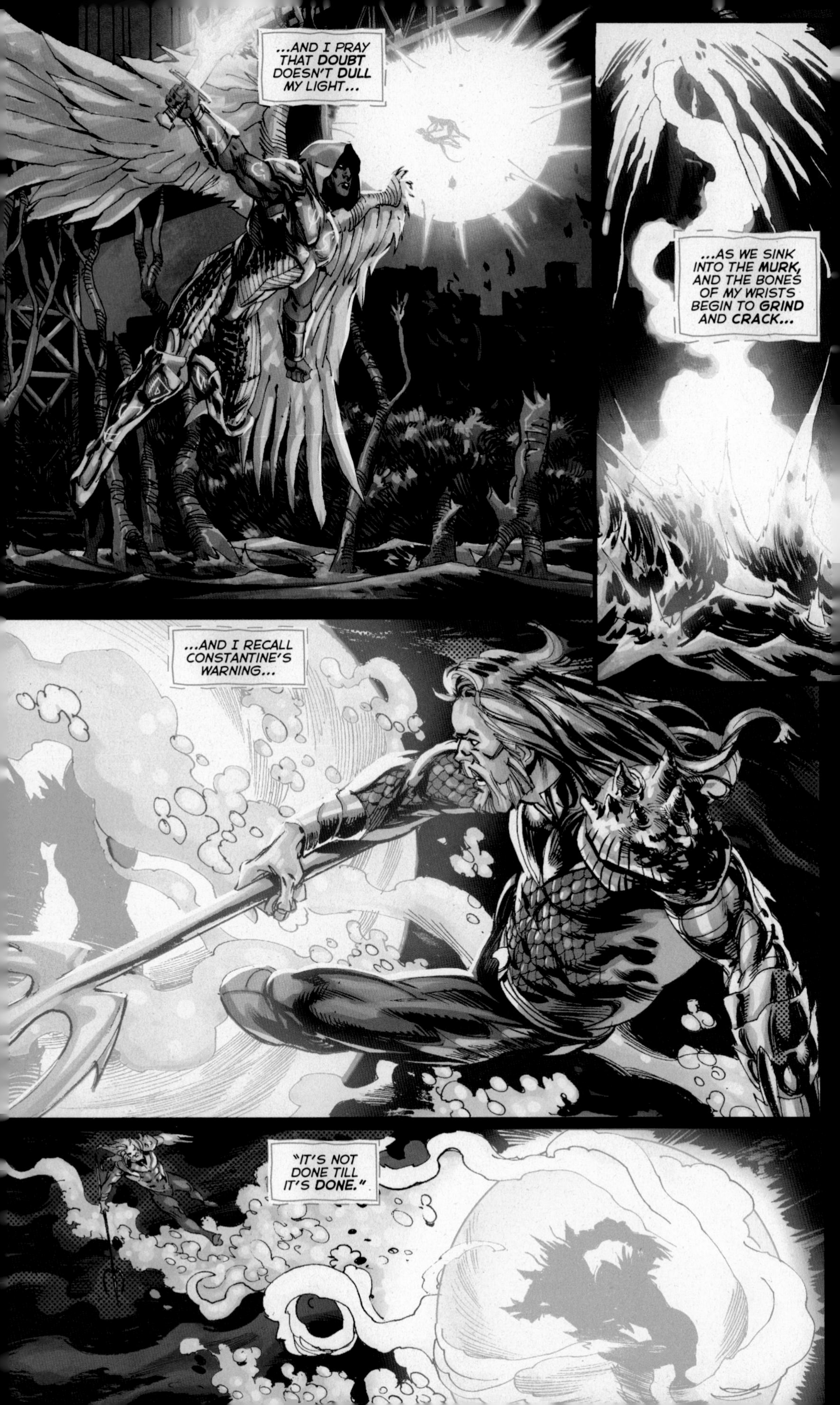
...AND I PRAY THAT DOUBT DOESN'T DULL MY LIGHT...
...AS WE SINK INTO THE MURK, AND THE BONES OF MY WRISTS BEGIN TO GRIND AND CRACK...
...AND I RECALL CONSTANTINE'S WARNING...
"IT'S NOT DONE TILL IT'S DONE."

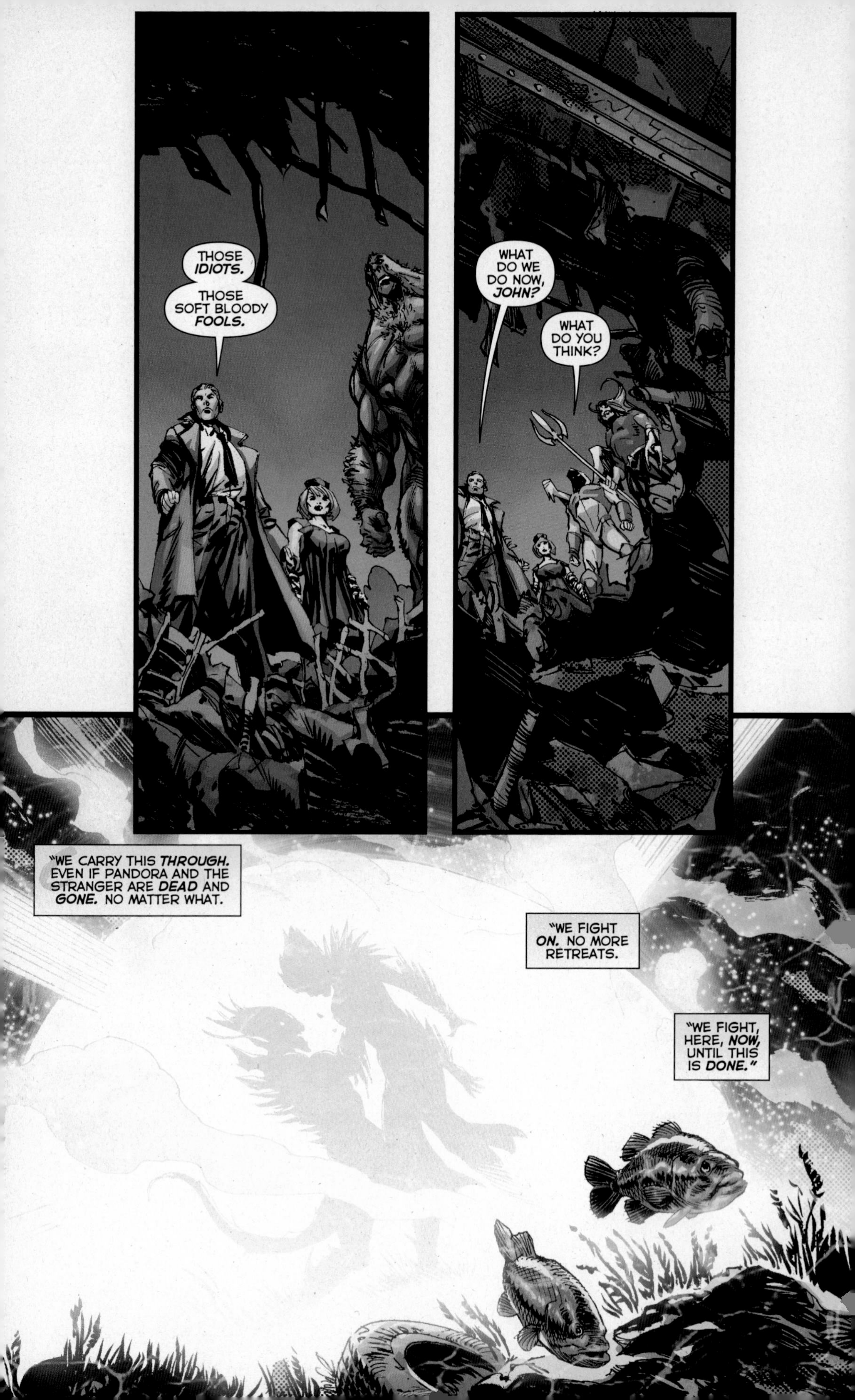
THOSE IDIOTS.
THOSE SOFT BLOODY FOOLS.
WHAT DO WE DO NOW, JOHN?
WHAT DO YOU THINK?
"WE CARRY THIS THROUGH. EVEN IF PANDORA AND THE STRANGER ARE DEAD AND GONE. NO MATTER WHAT.
"WE FIGHT ON. NO MORE RETREATS.
"WE FIGHT, HERE, NOW, UNTIL THIS IS DONE."

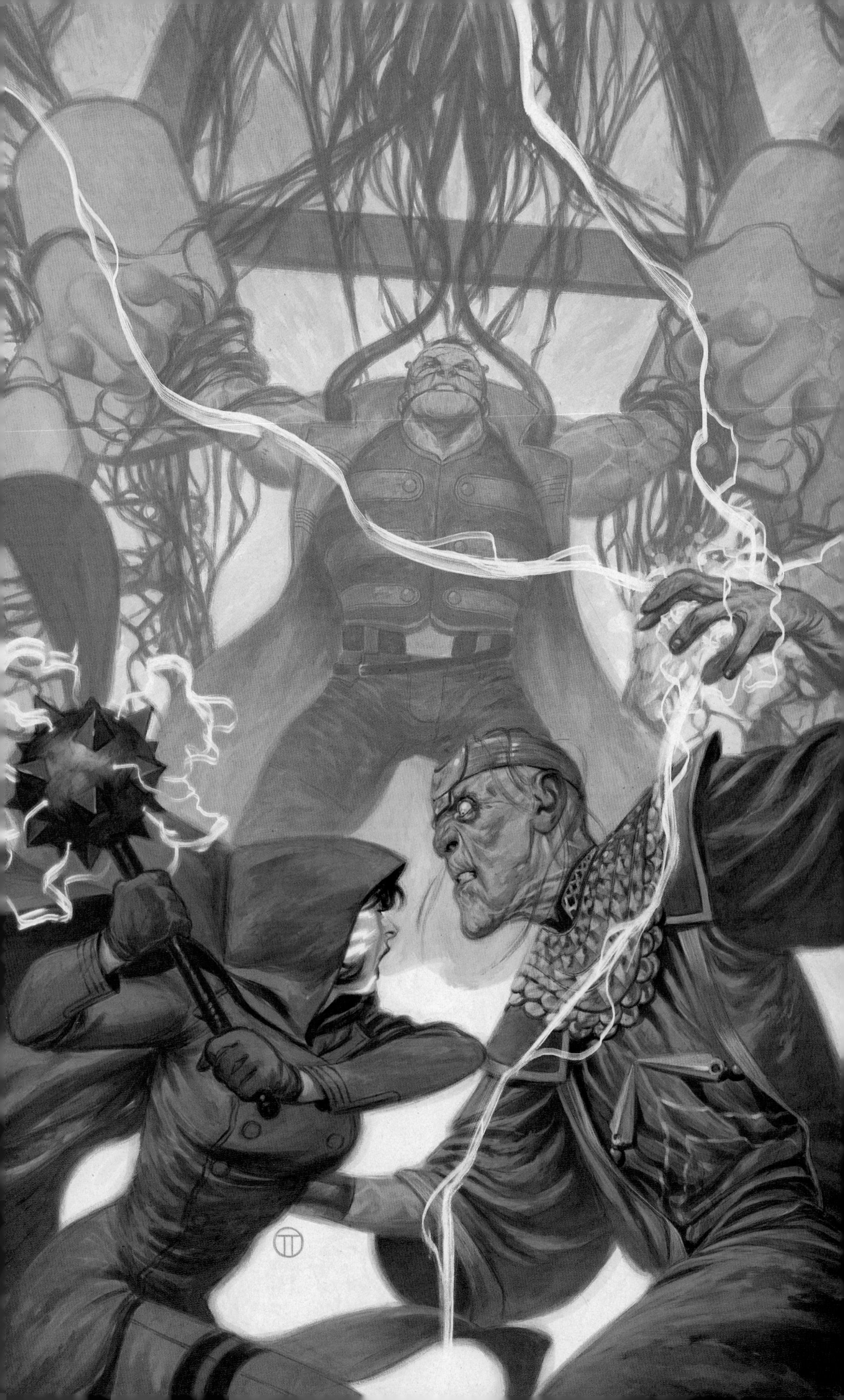

EYES OPEN

RAY FAWKES
writer

FRANCIS PORTELA
artist

HI-FI
colorist

DEZI SIENTY
TAYLOR ESPOSITO
letterers

cover art by
JULIAN TOTINO TEDESCO

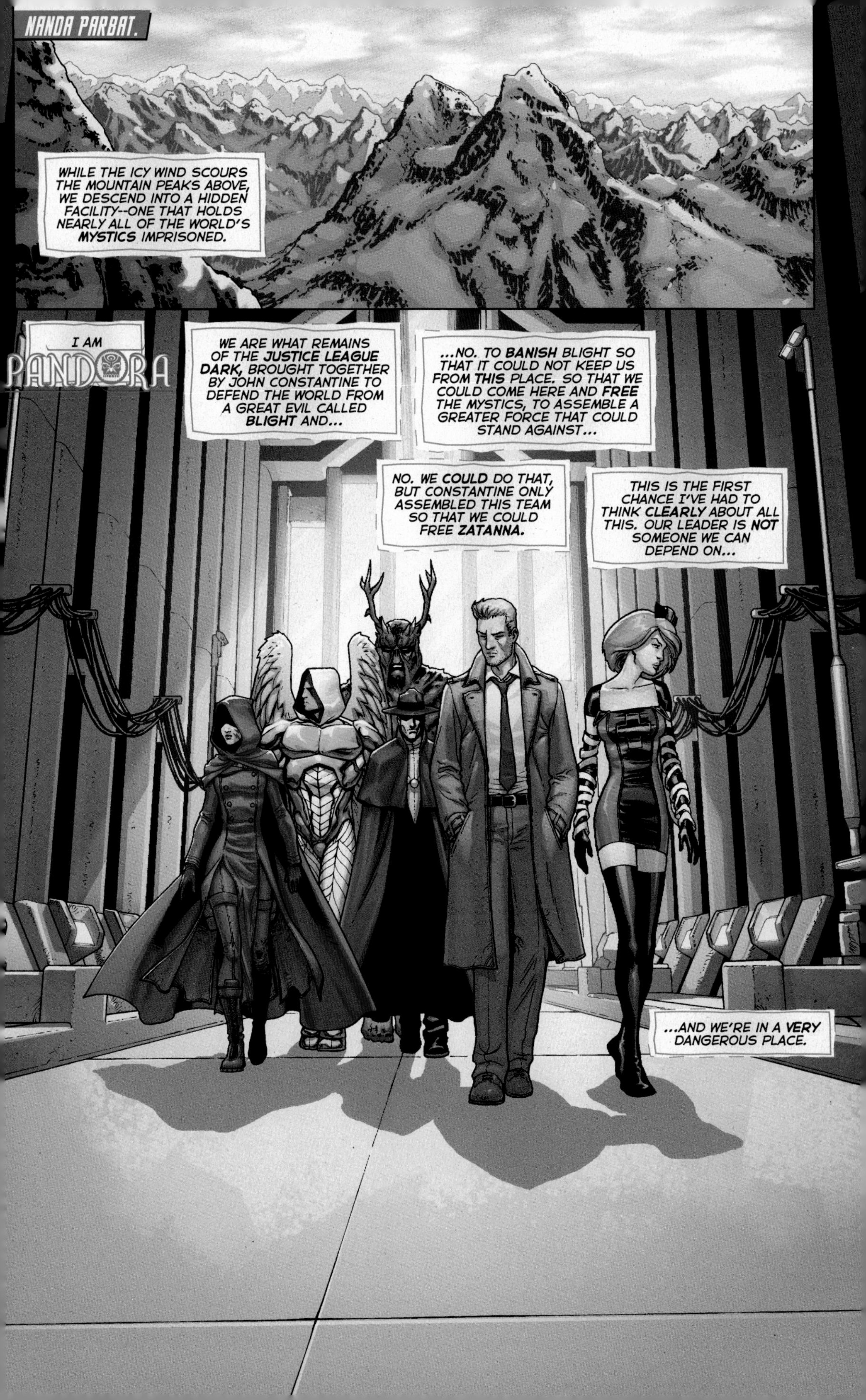
NANDA PARBAT.
WHILE THE ICY WIND SCOURS THE MOUNTAIN PEAKS ABOVE, WE DESCEND INTO A HIDDEN FACILITY--ONE THAT HOLDS NEARLY ALL OF THE WORLD'S MYSTICS IMPRISONED.
I AM PANDORA
WE ARE WHAT REMAINS OF THE JUSTICE LEAGUE DARK, BROUGHT TOGETHER BY JOHN CONSTANTINE TO DEFEND THE WORLD FROM A GREAT EVIL CALLED BLIGHT AND...
...NO. TO BANISH BLIGHT SO THAT IT COULD NOT KEEP US FROM THIS PLACE. SO THAT WE COULD COME HERE AND FREE THE MYSTICS, TO ASSEMBLE A GREATER FORCE THAT COULD STAND AGAINST...
NO. WE COULD DO THAT, BUT CONSTANTINE ONLY ASSEMBLED THIS TEAM SO THAT WE COULD FREE ZATANNA.
THIS IS THE FIRST CHANCE I'VE HAD TO THINK CLEARLY ABOUT ALL THIS. OUR LEADER IS NOT SOMEONE WE CAN DEPEND ON...
...AND WE'RE IN A VERY DANGEROUS PLACE.

THOUGH I THINK *DEADMAN* IS IN MORE DANGER THAN *WE* ARE...

CONSTANTINE LOCKED HIM INSIDE THE BODY OF THE *SEA KING*--ONE OF THE SYNDICATE'S MEMBERS-- AND HE IS THE ONE WHO BROUGHT US *INSIDE.*

THIS WAY, YOUR MAJESTY.

NOT BAD, *FAUST.*

LOOKS LIKE YOU AND *NICK NECRO* ARE DOING A BANG-UP JOB.

OH, WE ARE *HONORED* BY YOUR PRAISE.

IF YOU'LL ALLOW ME TO DEMONSTRATE...

NO. I'M ALREADY SICK OF YOUR TOADYING.

I WANT *NECRO* TO SHOW ME HOW IT WORKS.

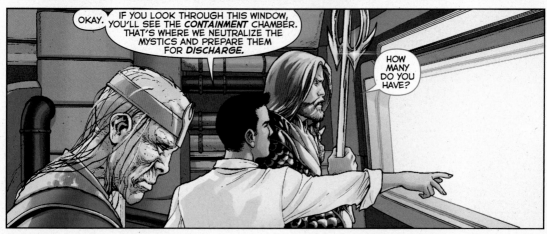

OKAY. IF YOU LOOK THROUGH THIS WINDOW, YOU'LL SEE THE *CONTAINMENT* CHAMBER. THAT'S WHERE WE NEUTRALIZE THE MYSTICS AND PREPARE THEM FOR *DISCHARGE.*

HOW MANY DO YOU HAVE?

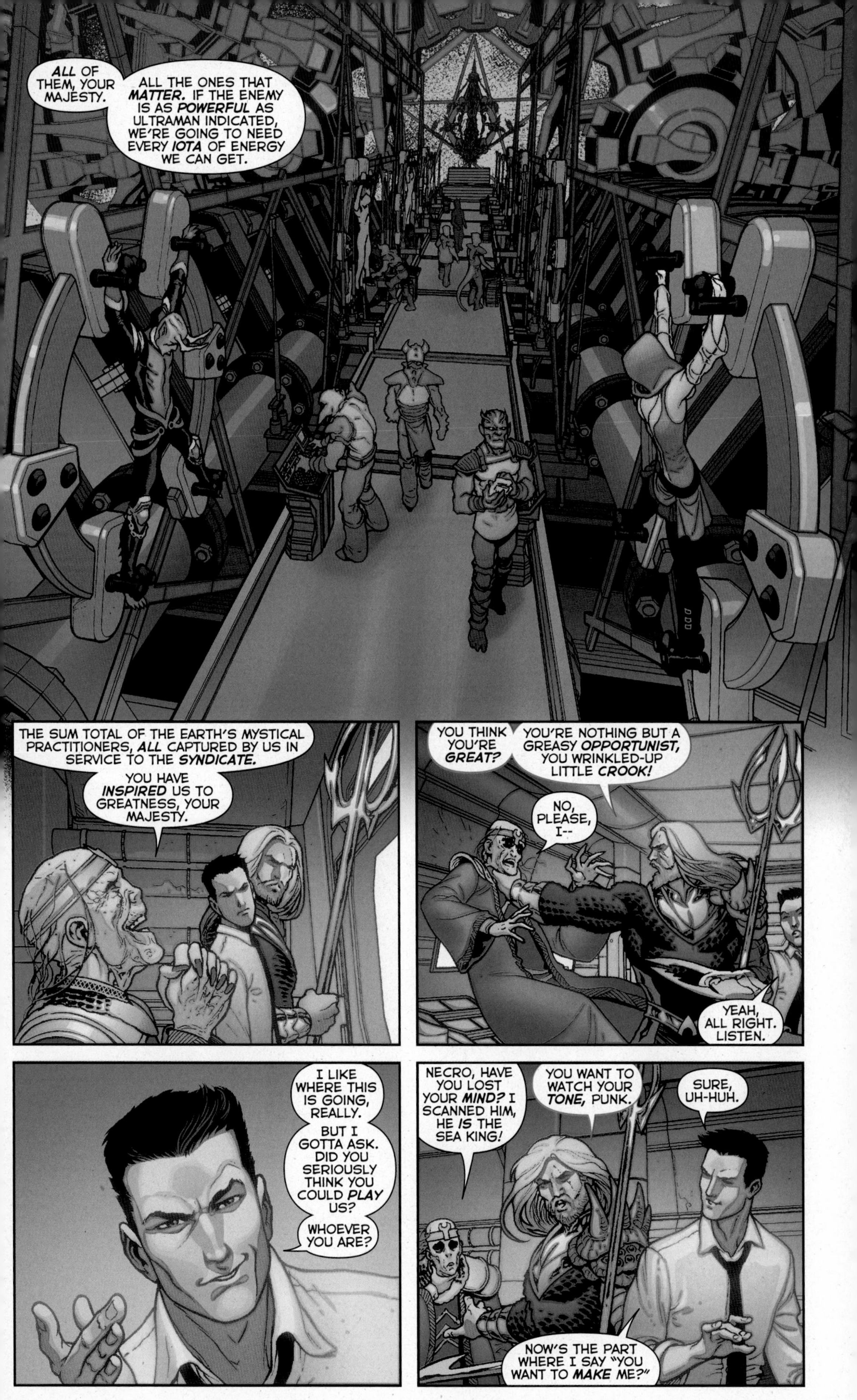
ALL OF THEM, YOUR MAJESTY.
ALL THE ONES THAT MATTER. IF THE ENEMY IS AS POWERFUL AS ULTRAMAN INDICATED, WE'RE GOING TO NEED EVERY IOTA OF ENERGY WE CAN GET.
THE SUM TOTAL OF THE EARTH'S MYSTICAL PRACTITIONERS, ALL CAPTURED BY US IN SERVICE TO THE SYNDICATE.
YOU HAVE INSPIRED US TO GREATNESS, YOUR MAJESTY.
YOU THINK YOU'RE GREAT?
YOU'RE NOTHING BUT A GREASY OPPORTUNIST, YOU WRINKLED-UP LITTLE CROOK!
NO, PLEASE, I--
YEAH, ALL RIGHT. LISTEN.
I LIKE WHERE THIS IS GOING, REALLY.
BUT I GOTTA ASK. DID YOU SERIOUSLY THINK YOU COULD PLAY US?
WHOEVER YOU ARE?
NECRO, HAVE YOU LOST YOUR MIND? I SCANNED HIM, HE IS THE SEA KING!
YOU WANT TO WATCH YOUR TONE, PUNK.
SURE, UH-HUH.
NOW'S THE PART WHERE I SAY "YOU WANT TO MAKE ME?"

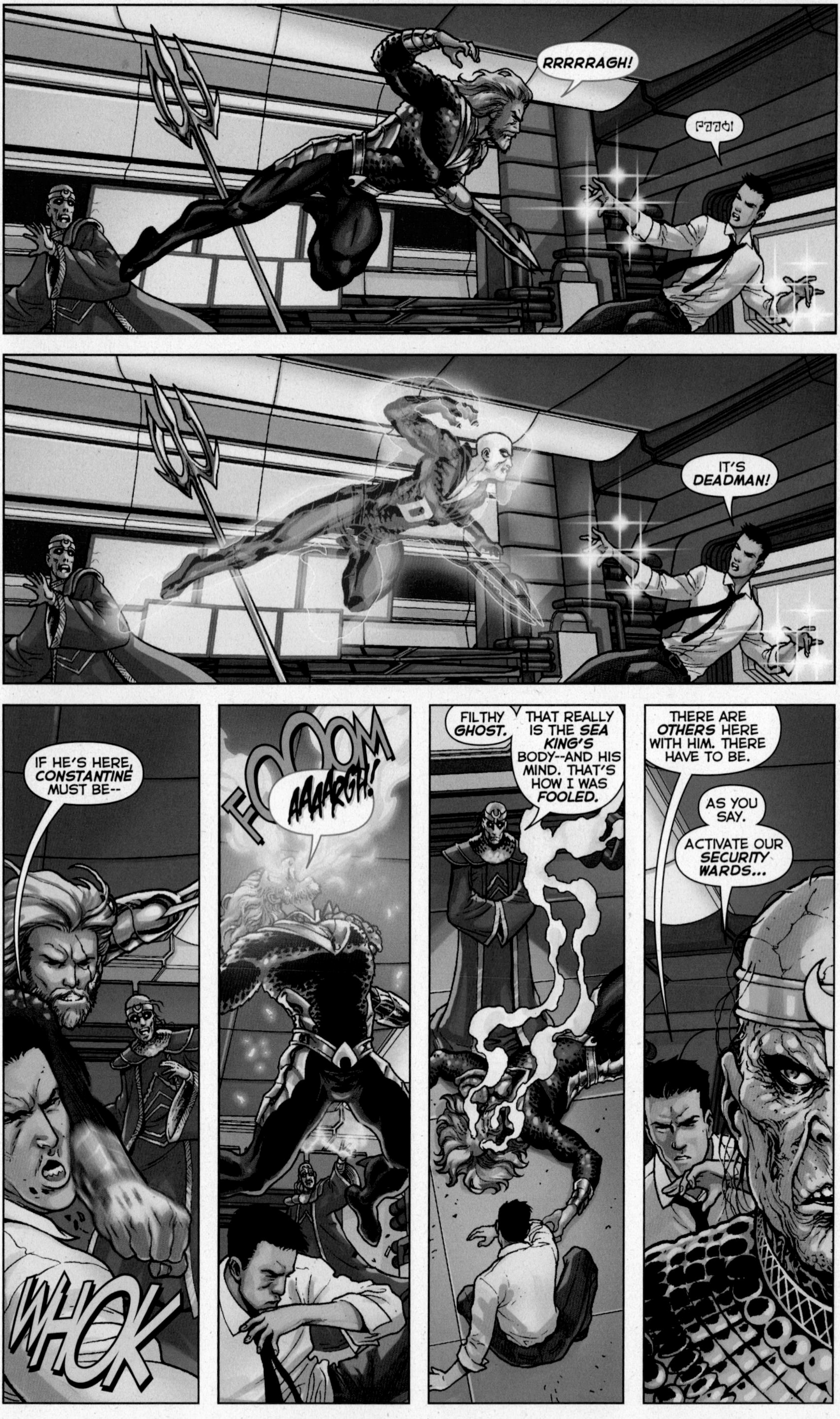
RRRRRAGH!
IT'S DEADMAN!
IF HE'S HERE, CONSTANTINE MUST BE--
WHOK
FOOOM
AAAARGH!
FILTHY GHOST.
THAT REALLY IS THE SEA KING'S BODY--AND HIS MIND. THAT'S HOW I WAS FOOLED.
THERE ARE OTHERS HERE WITH HIM. THERE HAVE TO BE.
AS YOU SAY.
ACTIVATE OUR SECURITY WARDS...

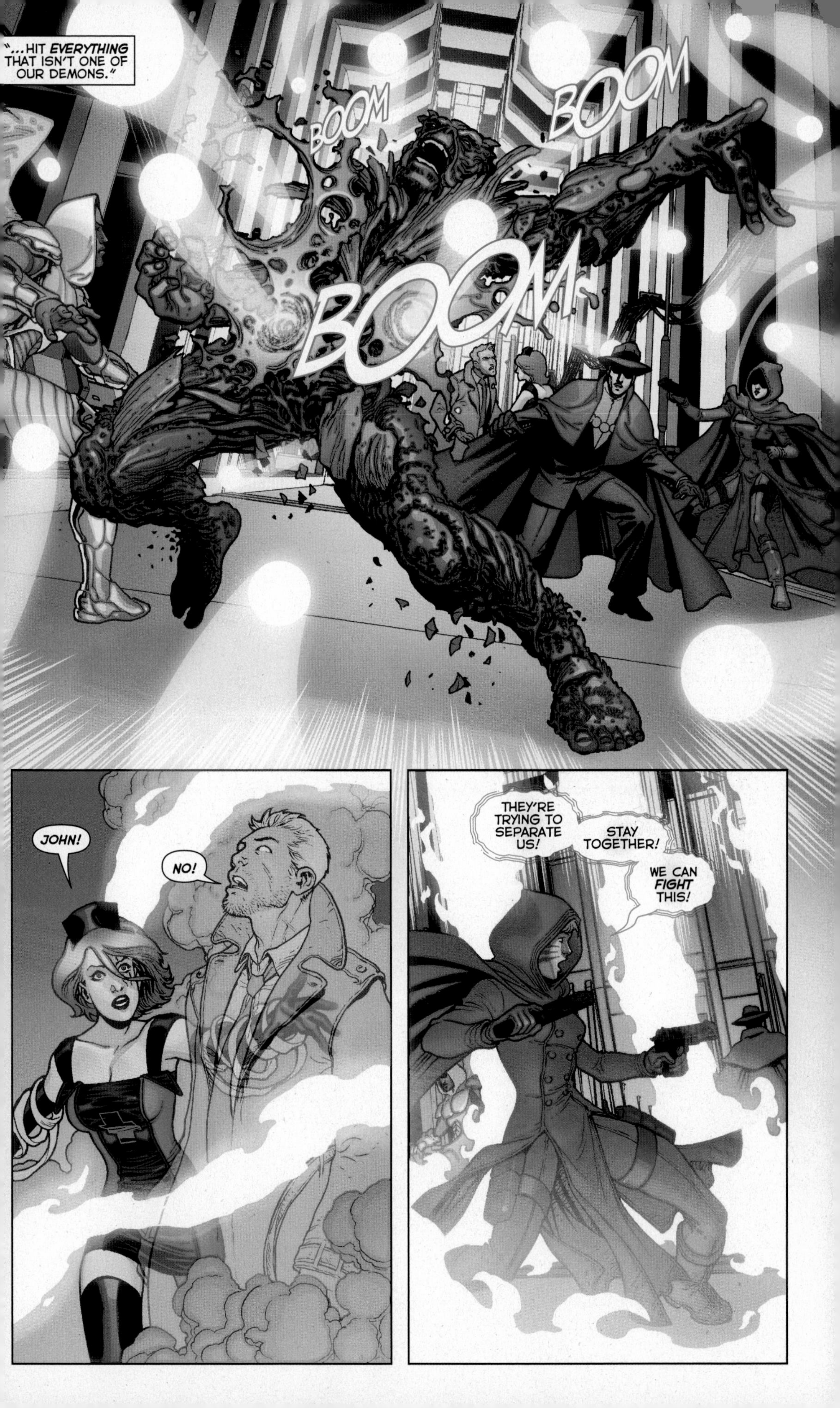
"...HIT EVERYTHING THAT ISN'T ONE OF OUR DEMONS."
BOOM
BOOM
BOOM!
JOHN!
NO!
THEY'RE TRYING TO SEPARATE US!
STAY TOGETHER!
WE CAN FIGHT THIS!

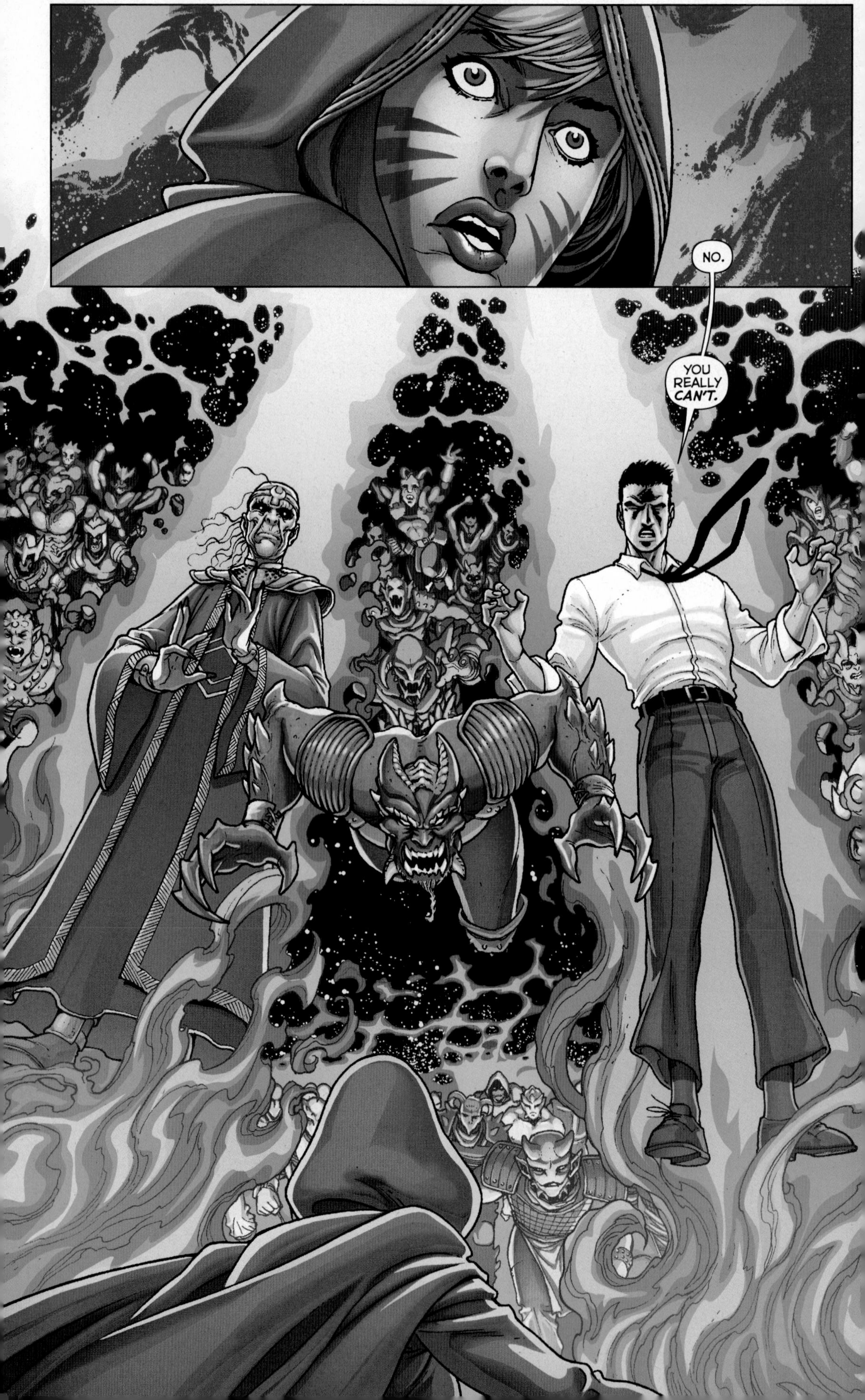
NO.
YOU REALLY CAN'T.

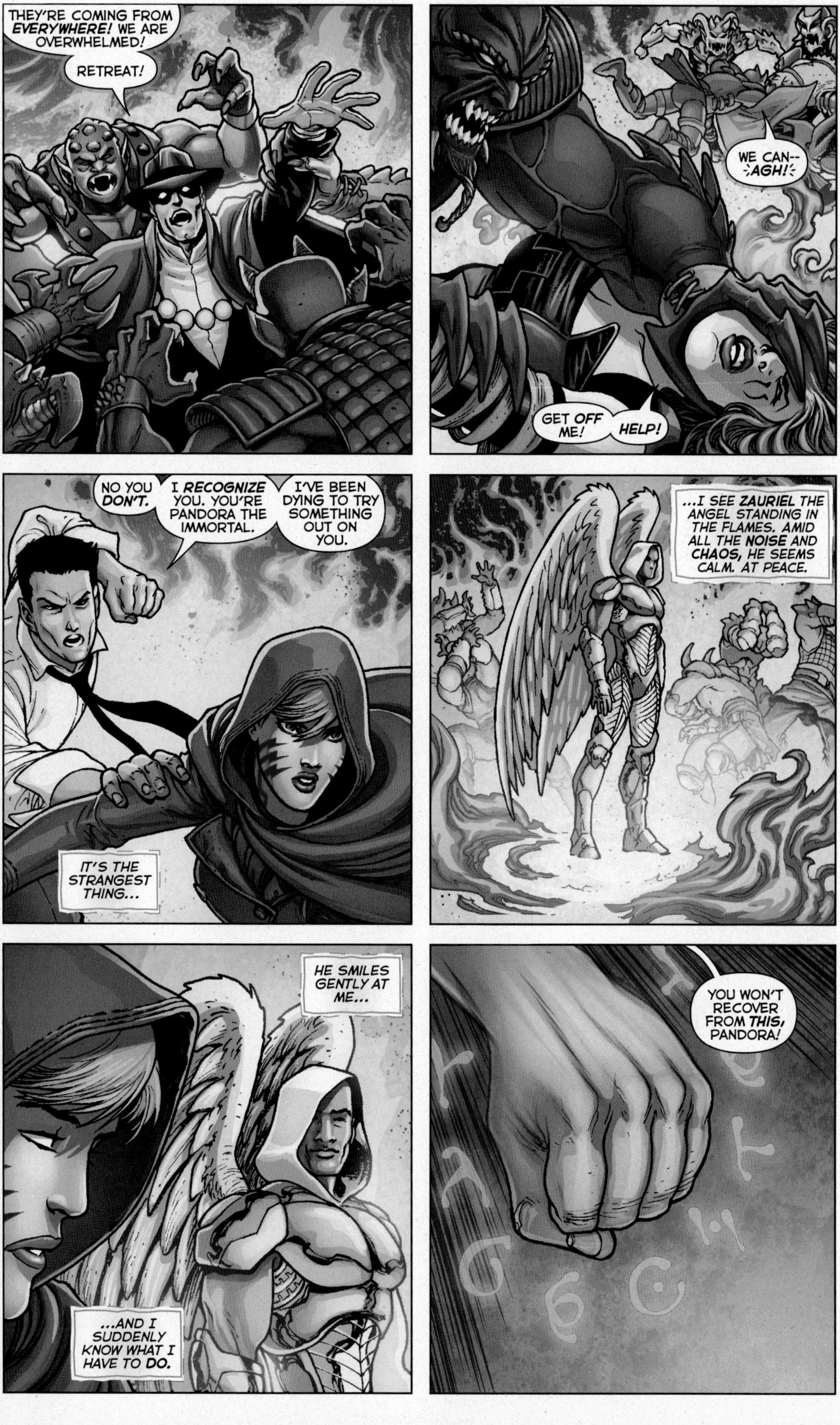
THEY'RE COMING FROM EVERYWHERE! WE ARE OVERWHELMED!
RETREAT!
WE CAN-- AGH!
GET OFF ME!
HELP!
NO YOU DON'T.
I RECOGNIZE YOU. YOU'RE PANDORA THE IMMORTAL.
I'VE BEEN DYING TO TRY SOMETHING OUT ON YOU.
IT'S THE STRANGEST THING...
...I SEE ZAURIEL THE ANGEL STANDING IN THE FLAMES. AMID ALL THE NOISE AND CHAOS, HE SEEMS CALM. AT PEACE.
HE SMILES GENTLY AT ME...
...AND I SUDDENLY KNOW WHAT I HAVE TO DO.
YOU WON'T RECOVER FROM THIS, PANDORA!

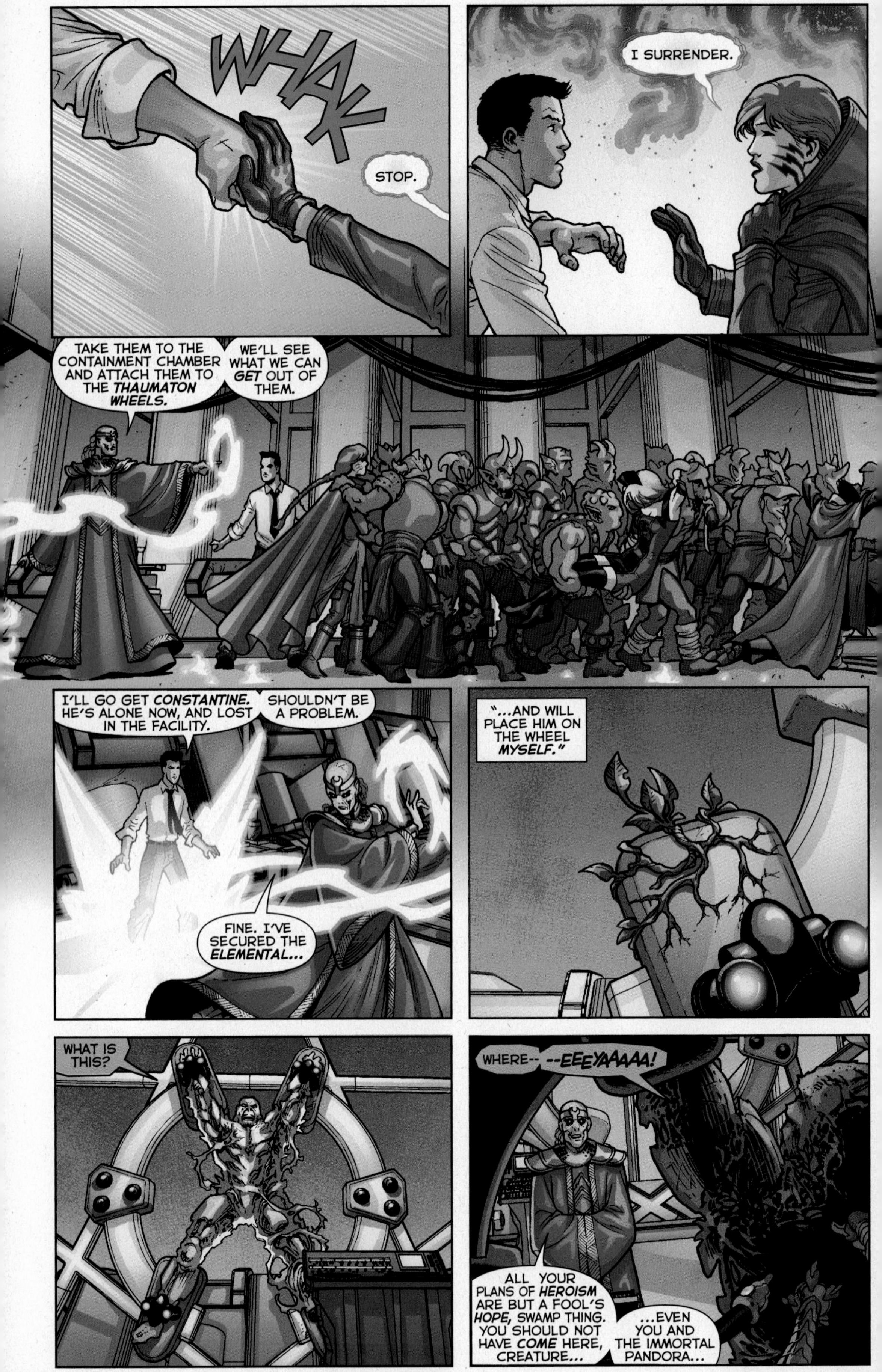
WHAK
STOP.
I SURRENDER.
TAKE THEM TO THE CONTAINMENT CHAMBER AND ATTACH THEM TO THE THAUMATON WHEELS.
WE'LL SEE WHAT WE CAN GET OUT OF THEM.
I'LL GO GET CONSTANTINE. HE'S ALONE NOW, AND LOST IN THE FACILITY.
SHOULDN'T BE A PROBLEM.
FINE. I'VE SECURED THE ELEMENTAL...
"...AND WILL PLACE HIM ON THE WHEEL MYSELF."
WHAT IS THIS?
WHERE--
--EEEYAAAAA!
ALL YOUR PLANS OF HEROISM ARE BUT A FOOL'S HOPE, SWAMP THING. YOU SHOULD NOT HAVE COME HERE, CREATURE...
...EVEN YOU AND THE IMMORTAL PANDORA...

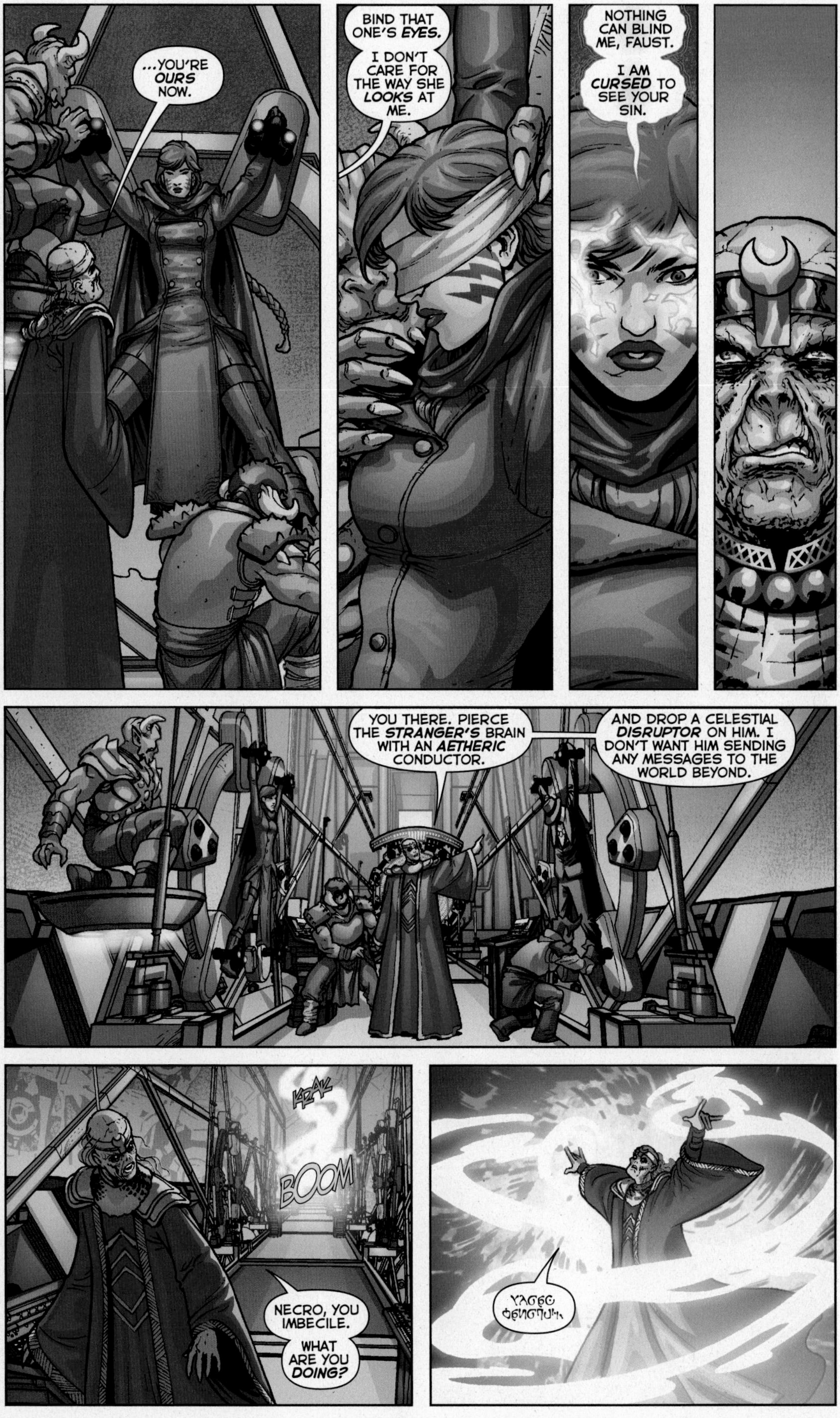
...YOU'RE OURS NOW.
BIND THAT ONE'S EYES.
I DON'T CARE FOR THE WAY SHE LOOKS AT ME.
NOTHING CAN BLIND ME, FAUST.
I AM CURSED TO SEE YOUR SIN.
YOU THERE. PIERCE THE STRANGER'S BRAIN WITH AN AETHERIC CONDUCTOR.
AND DROP A CELESTIAL DISRUPTOR ON HIM. I DON'T WANT HIM SENDING ANY MESSAGES TO THE WORLD BEYOND.
KRAK
BOOM
NECRO, YOU IMBECILE.
WHAT ARE YOU DOING?

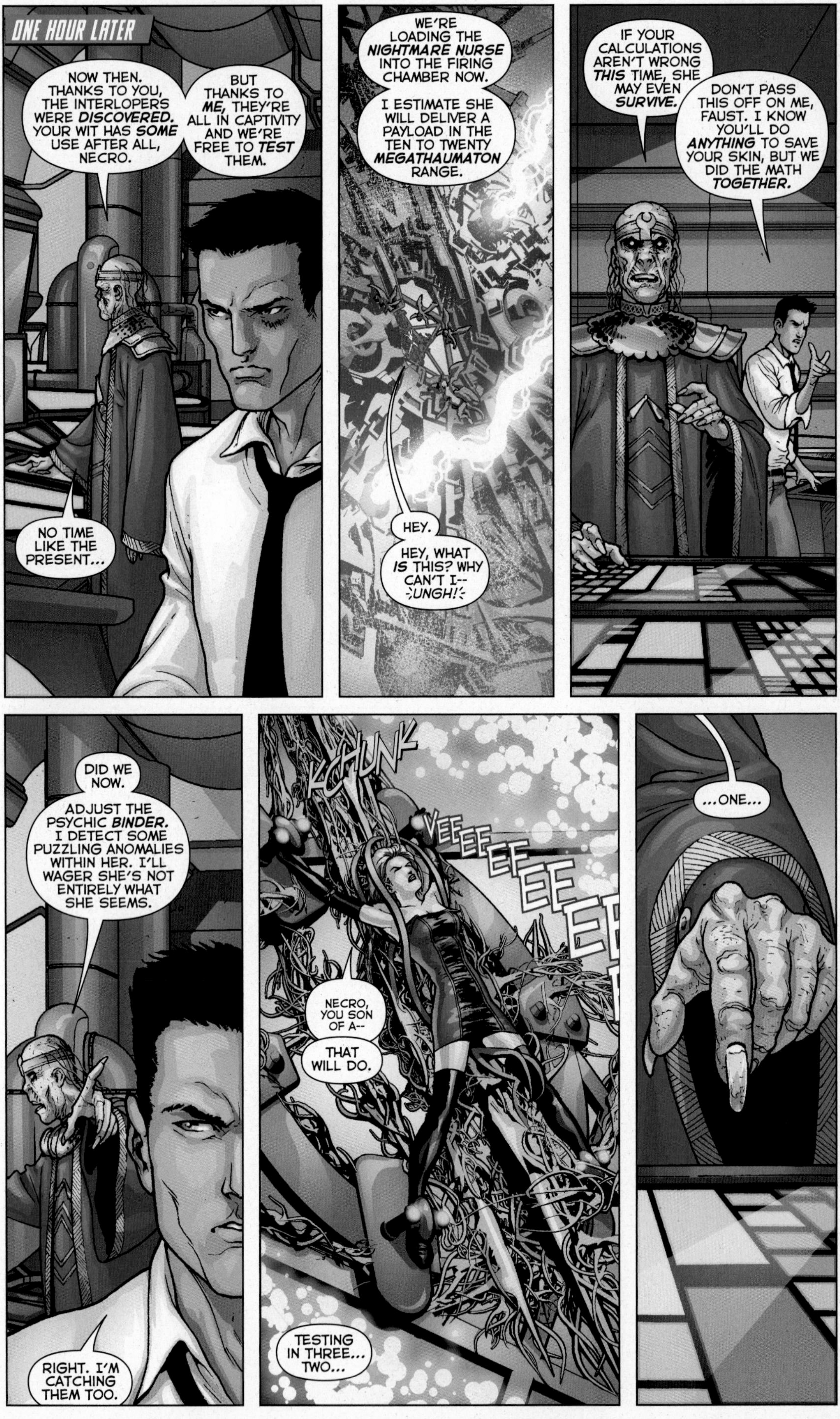
ONE HOUR LATER
NOW THEN. THANKS TO YOU, THE INTERLOPERS WERE DISCOVERED. YOUR WIT HAS SOME USE AFTER ALL, NECRO.
BUT THANKS TO ME, THEY'RE ALL IN CAPTIVITY AND WE'RE FREE TO TEST THEM.
NO TIME LIKE THE PRESENT...
WE'RE LOADING THE NIGHTMARE NURSE INTO THE FIRING CHAMBER NOW.
I ESTIMATE SHE WILL DELIVER A PAYLOAD IN THE TEN TO TWENTY MEGATHAUMATON RANGE.
HEY.
HEY, WHAT IS THIS? WHY CAN'T I-- UNGH!
IF YOUR CALCULATIONS AREN'T WRONG THIS TIME, SHE MAY EVEN SURVIVE.
DON'T PASS THIS OFF ON ME, FAUST. I KNOW YOU'LL DO ANYTHING TO SAVE YOUR SKIN, BUT WE DID THE MATH TOGETHER.
DID WE NOW.
ADJUST THE PSYCHIC BINDER. I DETECT SOME PUZZLING ANOMALIES WITHIN HER. I'LL WAGER SHE'S NOT ENTIRELY WHAT SHE SEEMS.
RIGHT. I'M CATCHING THEM TOO.
K-CHUNK
VEEEEEEEEEE
NECRO, YOU SON OF A--
THAT WILL DO.
TESTING IN THREE... TWO...
...ONE...

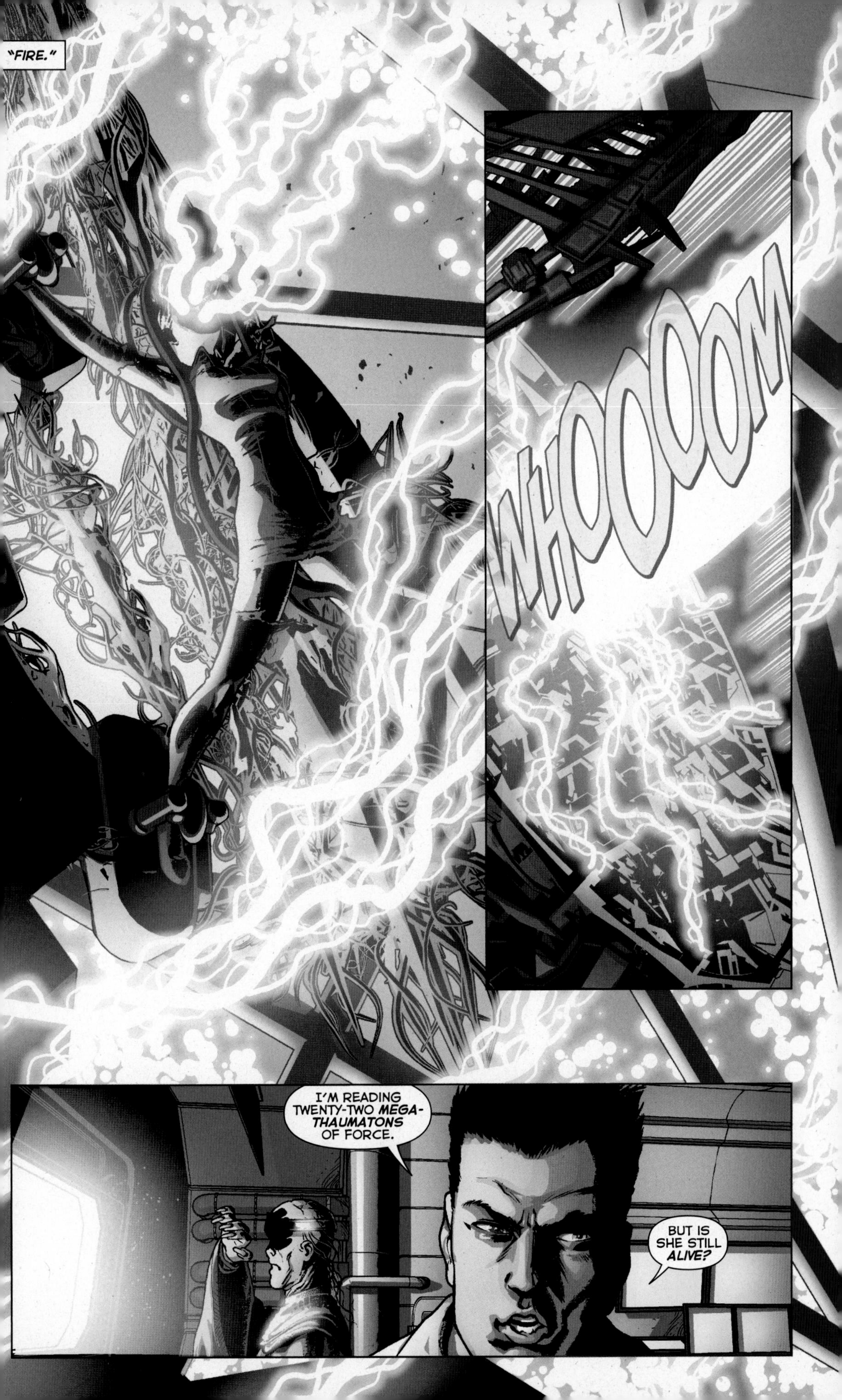
"FIRE."
WHOOOOOM
I'M READING TWENTY-TWO MEGA-THAUMATONS OF FORCE.
BUT IS SHE STILL ALIVE?

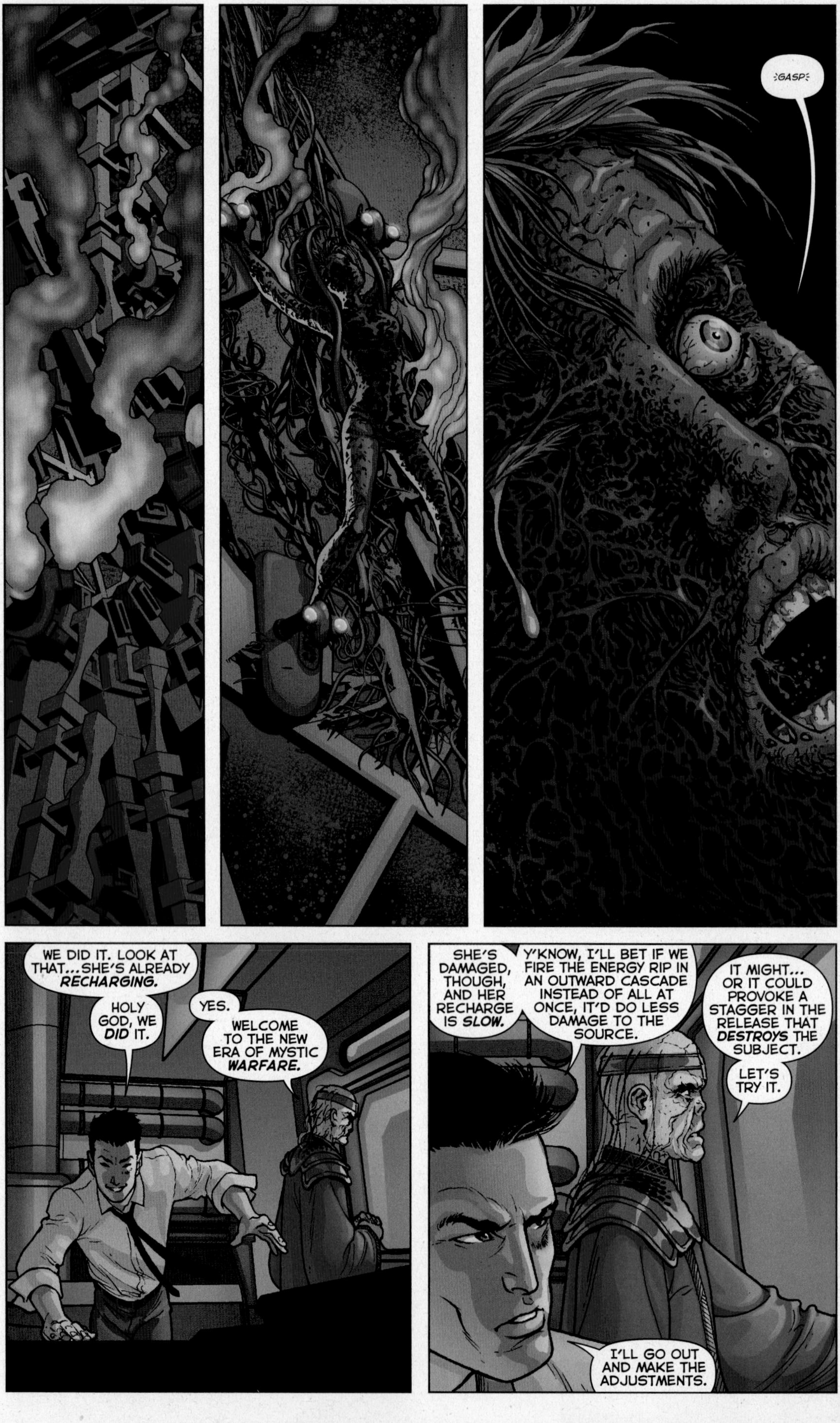

GASP
WE DID IT. LOOK AT THAT...SHE'S ALREADY RECHARGING.
HOLY GOD, WE DID IT.
YES.
WELCOME TO THE NEW ERA OF MYSTIC WARFARE.
SHE'S DAMAGED, THOUGH, AND HER RECHARGE IS SLOW.
Y'KNOW, I'LL BET IF WE FIRE THE ENERGY RIP IN AN OUTWARD CASCADE INSTEAD OF ALL AT ONCE, IT'D DO LESS DAMAGE TO THE SOURCE.
IT MIGHT... OR IT COULD PROVOKE A STAGGER IN THE RELEASE THAT DESTROYS THE SUBJECT.
LET'S TRY IT.
I'LL GO OUT AND MAKE THE ADJUSTMENTS.

WHAT... WHAT ARE YOU *DOING* TO US?

WE'RE *PEOPLE*, NECRO. NOT *LAB RATS*.

IT'S NO USE, HOLLAND.

OUR FRIEND HERE NEVER *DID* HAVE MUCH SYMPATHY FOR HIS FELLOW MAN. I'VE SEEN HIM SHRED MINDS FOR A LAUGH OVER A PINT.

EH, NICK? GOOD TIMES.

THAT'S *RIGHT*, JOHN.

SO I NEED ONE OF YOU FOR A POTENTIALLY FATAL TEST. IT'S VERY PAINFUL.

I WAS THINKING MAYBE *ZATANNA* COULD BE FUN. WE COULD WAKE HER UP, MAYBE MAKE YOU *WATCH...*

YOU'RE *SCARED*.

YOU'RE TRYING TO TERRORIZE US, BUT IT'S SO OBVIOUS.

YOU'RE LIKE A PLAY-GROUND *BULLY*.

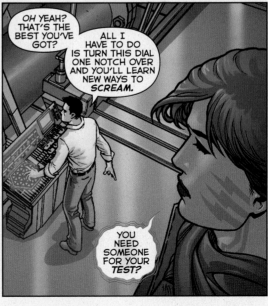

OH YEAH? THAT'S THE BEST YOU'VE GOT?

ALL I HAVE TO DO IS TURN THIS DIAL ONE NOTCH OVER AND YOU'LL LEARN NEW WAYS TO *SCREAM*.

YOU NEED SOMEONE FOR YOUR *TEST*?

PICK ME.

YEAH, YOU'D LIKE THAT? MAYBE YOU'RE *INTO* GETTING HURT.

ALL ON A *PENITENT* TRIP? DON'T WORRY, WE'LL GET TO YOU.

YOU WERE A *GOOD* PERSON, ONCE.

SUCH A SMART CHILD, SO SENSITIVE.

ALL YOU WANTED WAS TO BE GOOD AT SOMETHING, AND TO BE *LIKED.* REMEMBER WHEN THE KIDS IN YOUR NEIGHBORHOOD WERE THROWING STONES AT THAT JUNKYARD DOG AND YOU FELT *SORRY* FOR IT...

BUT YOU PICKED UP A ROCK...

NICE TRICK.

YOU WANT TO VOLUNTEER? BE MY *GUEST.* WE'RE GONNA TRY SOMETHING *NEW* AND IT'S GOING TO HURT LIKE *HELL.*

TRUST ME, I'VE *BEEN* TO HELL.

YOU'RE NOT THE ONLY SO-CALLED *IMMORTAL* IN HERE, YOU KNOW. YOU THINK YOU'VE EXPERIENCED EVERY KIND OF PAIN THERE IS? YOU DON'T KNOW *ANYTHING.*

FROM NOW ON, YOU CAN CONSIDER *ME* YOUR NEW *TEACHER.*

LOAD THIS FREAK INTO THE MACHINE.

CHOP CHOP.

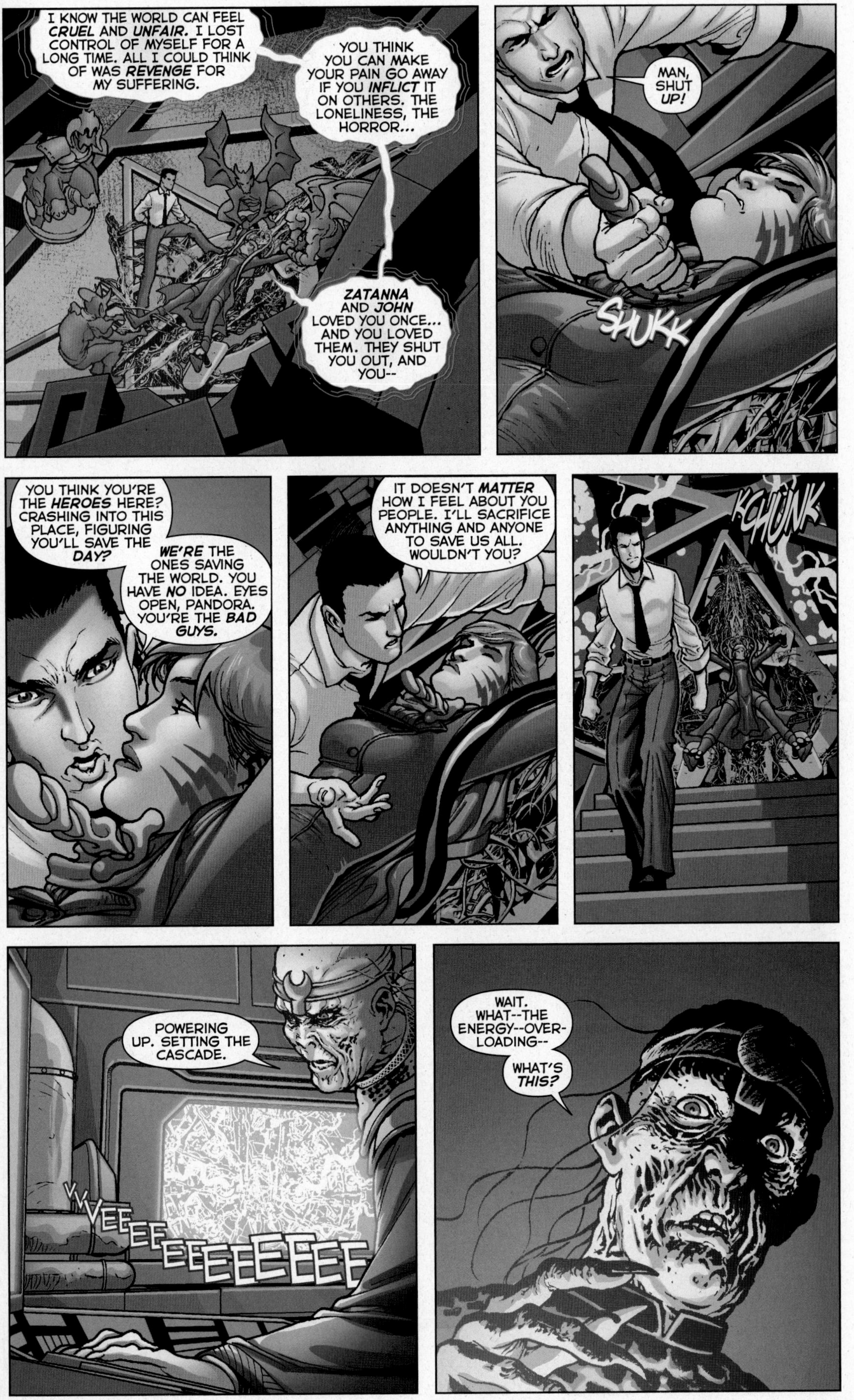
I KNOW THE WORLD CAN FEEL CRUEL AND UNFAIR. I LOST CONTROL OF MYSELF FOR A LONG TIME. ALL I COULD THINK OF WAS REVENGE FOR MY SUFFERING.
YOU THINK YOU CAN MAKE YOUR PAIN GO AWAY IF YOU INFLICT IT ON OTHERS. THE LONELINESS, THE HORROR...
ZATANNA AND JOHN LOVED YOU ONCE... AND YOU LOVED THEM. THEY SHUT YOU OUT, AND YOU--
MAN, SHUT UP!
SHUKK
YOU THINK YOU'RE THE HEROES HERE? CRASHING INTO THIS PLACE, FIGURING YOU'LL SAVE THE DAY?
WE'RE THE ONES SAVING THE WORLD. YOU HAVE NO IDEA. EYES OPEN, PANDORA. YOU'RE THE BAD GUYS.
IT DOESN'T MATTER HOW I FEEL ABOUT YOU PEOPLE. I'LL SACRIFICE ANYTHING AND ANYONE TO SAVE US ALL. WOULDN'T YOU?
KCHUNK
POWERING UP. SETTING THE CASCADE.
VVEEEEEEEEEEEEE
WAIT. WHAT--THE ENERGY--OVER-LOADING--
WHAT'S THIS?

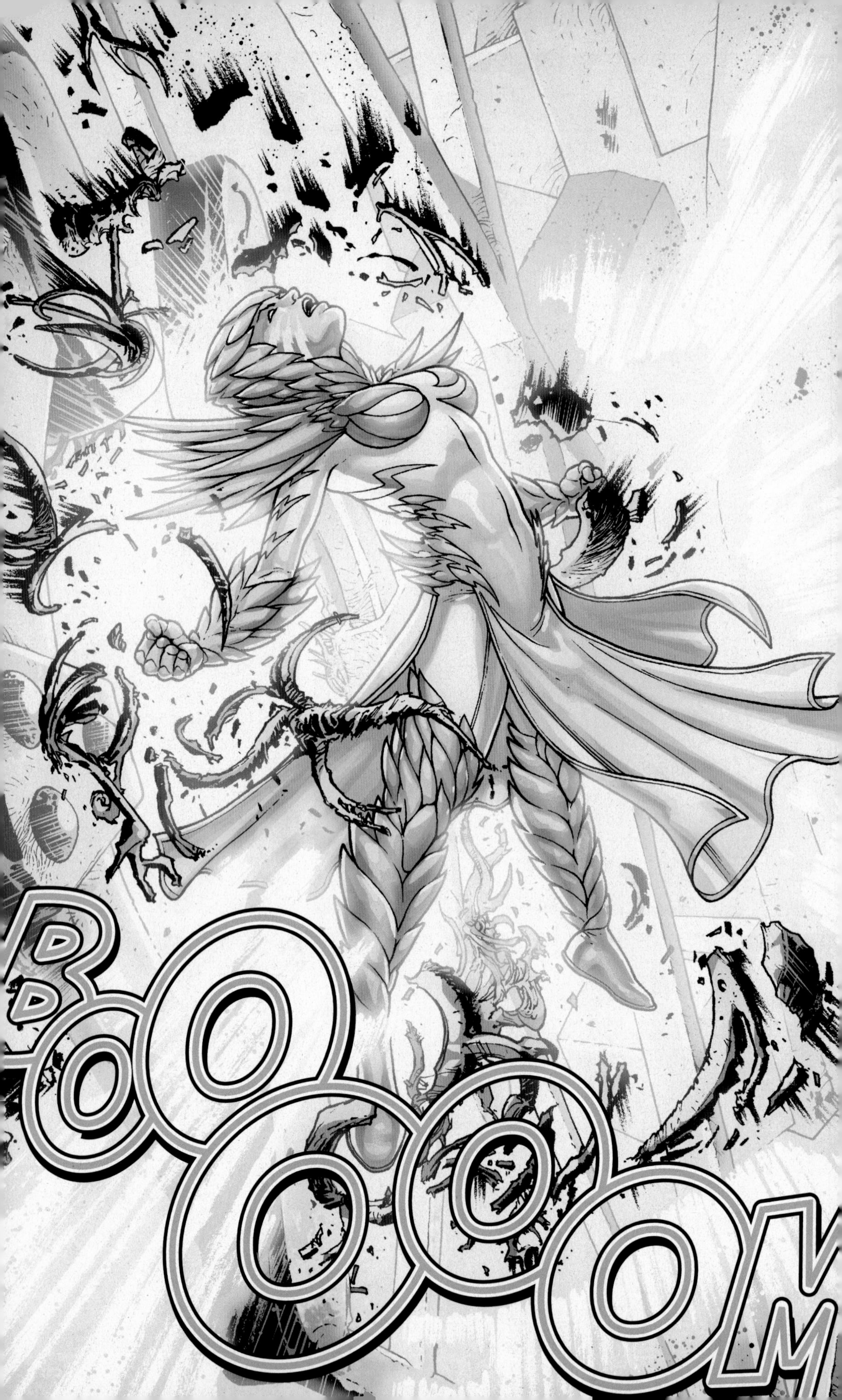
BOOOOOOM

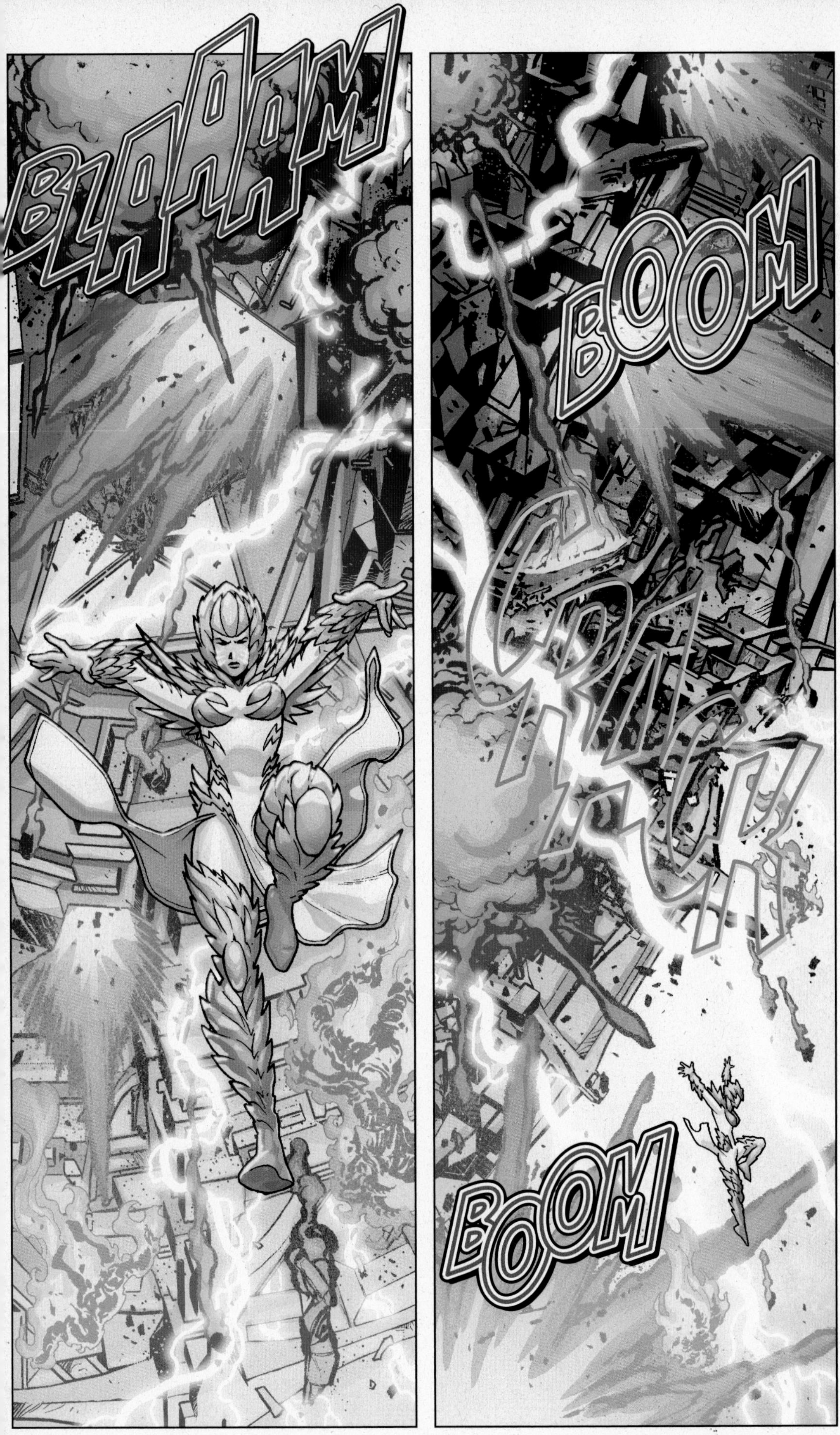
BLAAAAM
BOOM
BOOM

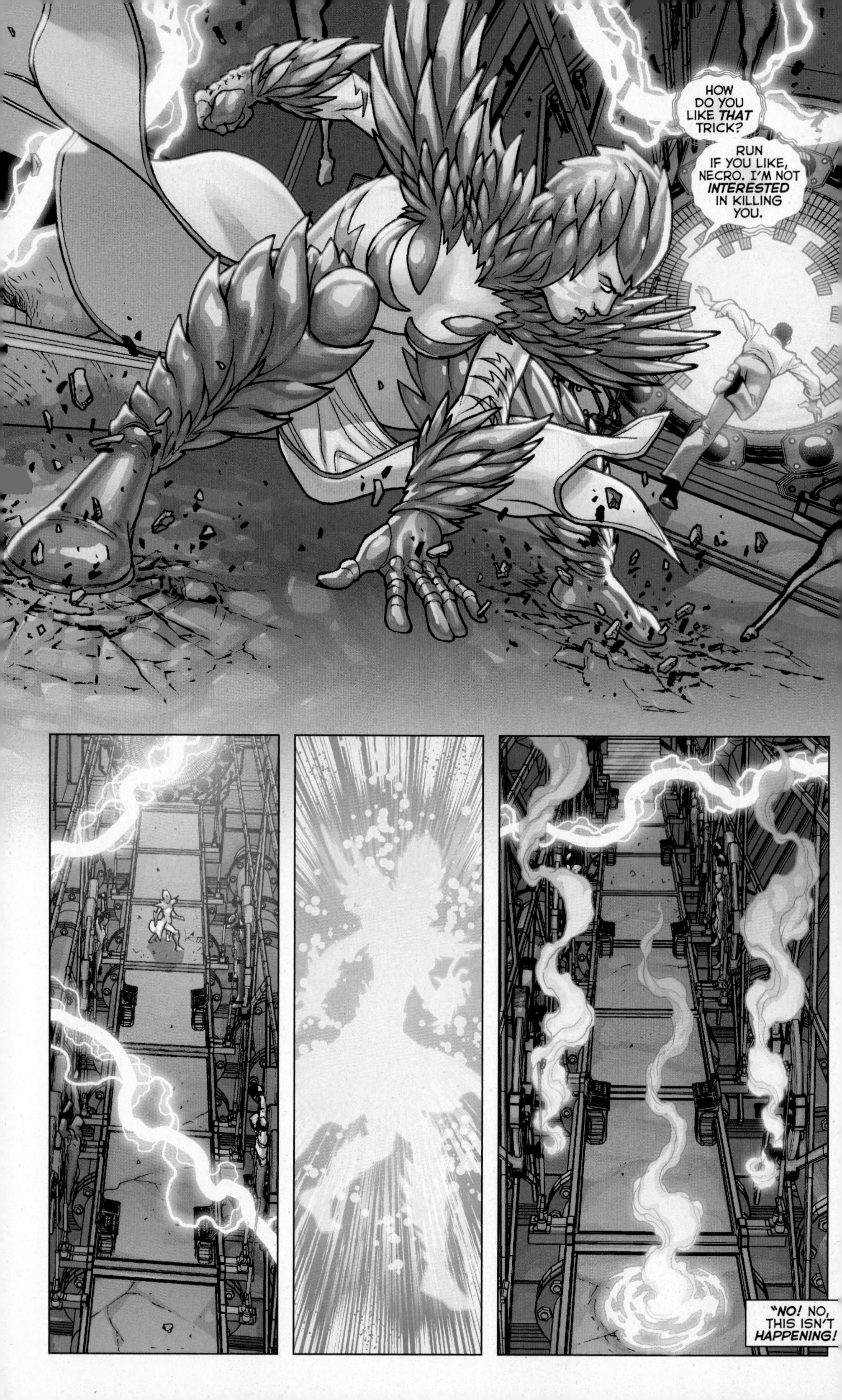
HOW DO YOU LIKE THAT TRICK?
RUN IF YOU LIKE, NECRO. I'M NOT INTERESTED IN KILLING YOU.
"NO! NO, THIS ISN'T HAPPENING!

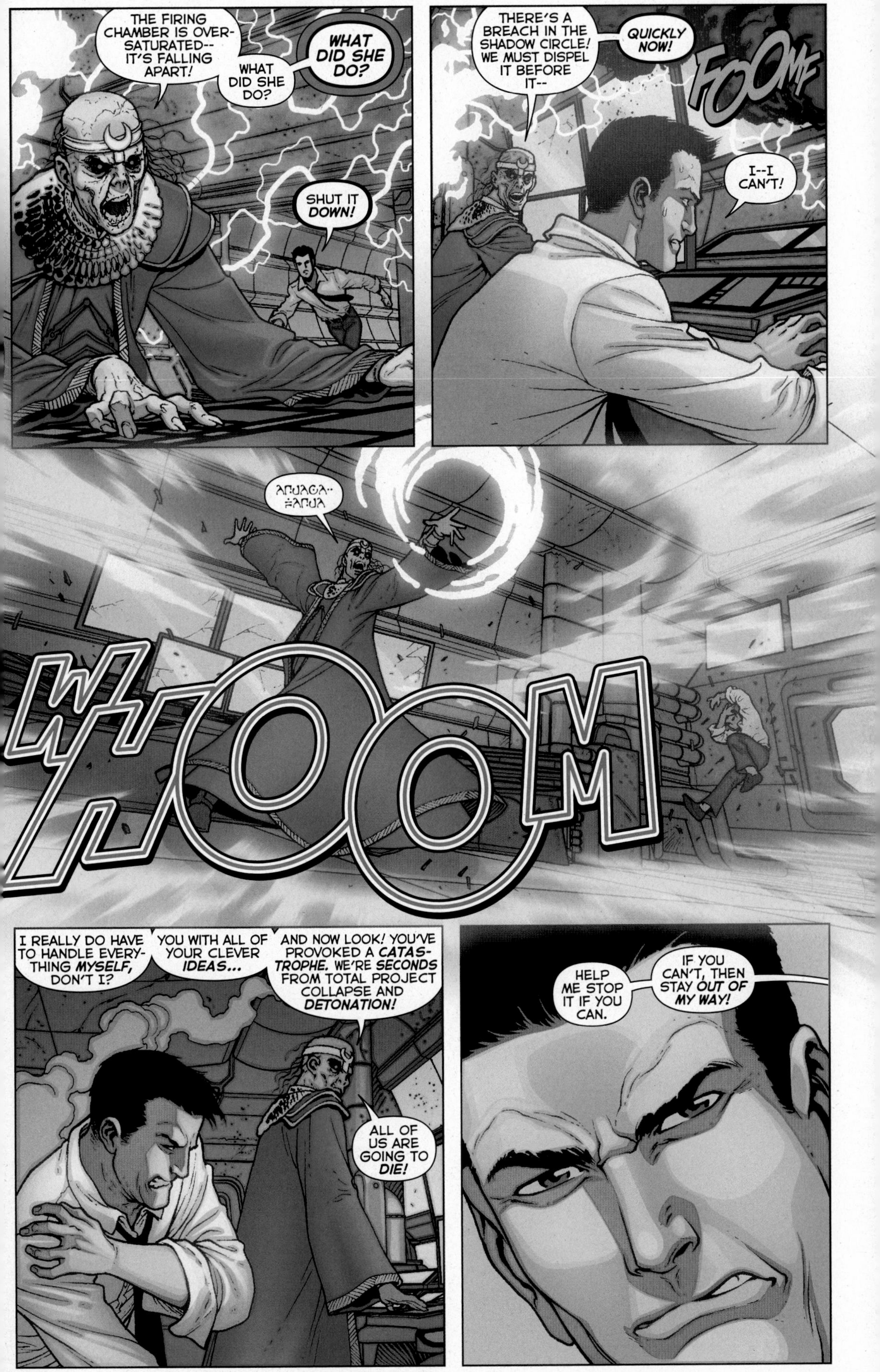
THE FIRING CHAMBER IS OVER-SATURATED-- IT'S FALLING APART!
WHAT DID SHE DO?
WHAT DID SHE DO?
SHUT IT DOWN!
THERE'S A BREACH IN THE SHADOW CIRCLE! WE MUST DISPEL IT BEFORE IT--
QUICKLY NOW!
FOOMF
I--I CAN'T!
WHOOM
I REALLY DO HAVE TO HANDLE EVERY-THING MYSELF, DON'T I?
YOU WITH ALL OF YOUR CLEVER IDEAS...
AND NOW LOOK! YOU'VE PROVOKED A CATAS-TROPHE. WE'RE SECONDS FROM TOTAL PROJECT COLLAPSE AND DETONATION!
ALL OF US ARE GOING TO DIE!
HELP ME STOP IT IF YOU CAN.
IF YOU CAN'T, THEN STAY OUT OF MY WAY!

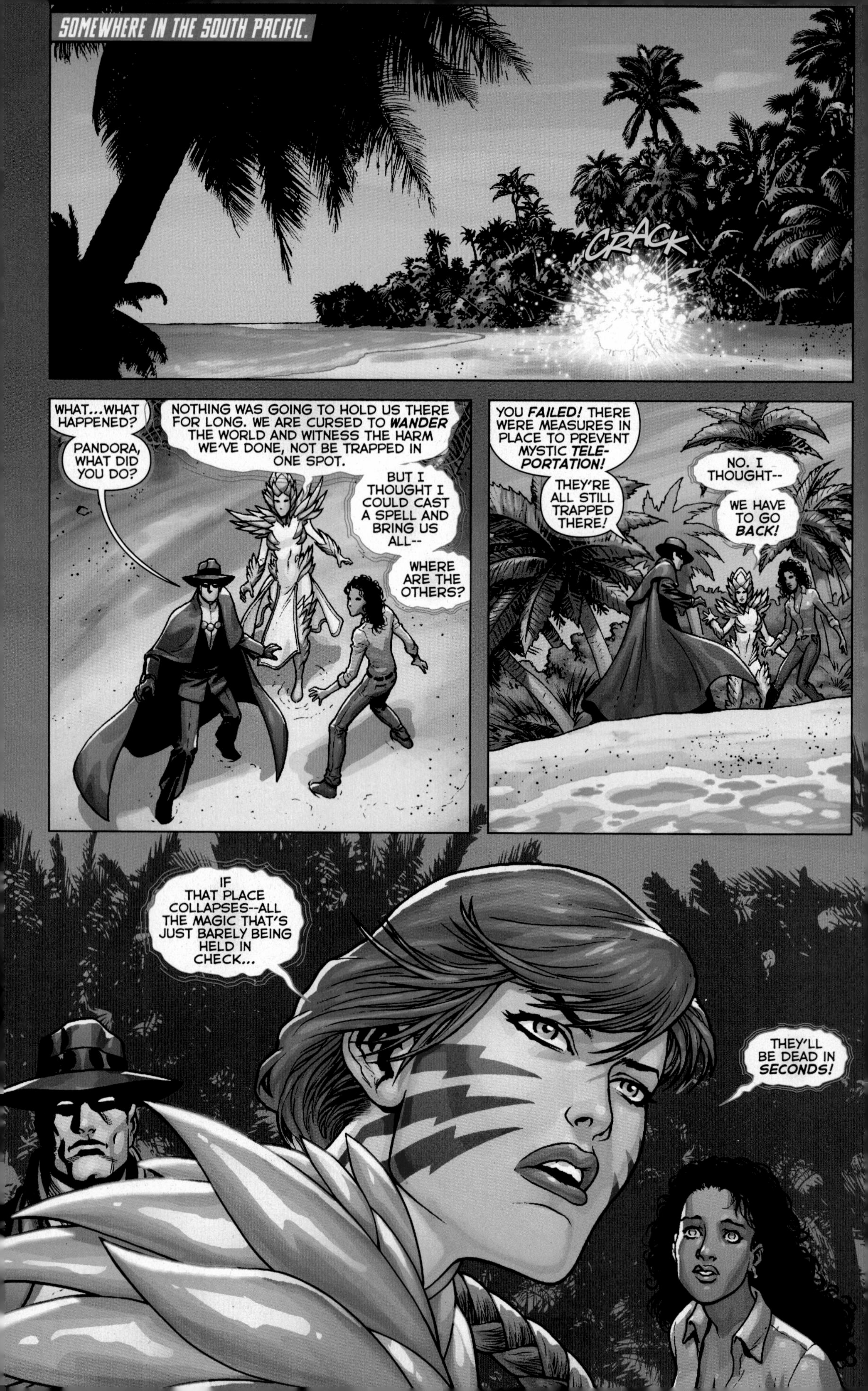
SOMEWHERE IN THE SOUTH PACIFIC.
CRACK
WHAT...WHAT HAPPENED?
PANDORA, WHAT DID YOU DO?
NOTHING WAS GOING TO HOLD US THERE FOR LONG. WE ARE CURSED TO WANDER THE WORLD AND WITNESS THE HARM WE'VE DONE, NOT BE TRAPPED IN ONE SPOT.
BUT I THOUGHT I COULD CAST A SPELL AND BRING US ALL--
WHERE ARE THE OTHERS?
YOU FAILED! THERE WERE MEASURES IN PLACE TO PREVENT MYSTIC TELE-PORTATION!
THEY'RE ALL STILL TRAPPED THERE!
NO. I THOUGHT--
WE HAVE TO GO BACK!
IF THAT PLACE COLLAPSES--ALL THE MAGIC THAT'S JUST BARELY BEING HELD IN CHECK...
THEY'LL BE DEAD IN SECONDS!

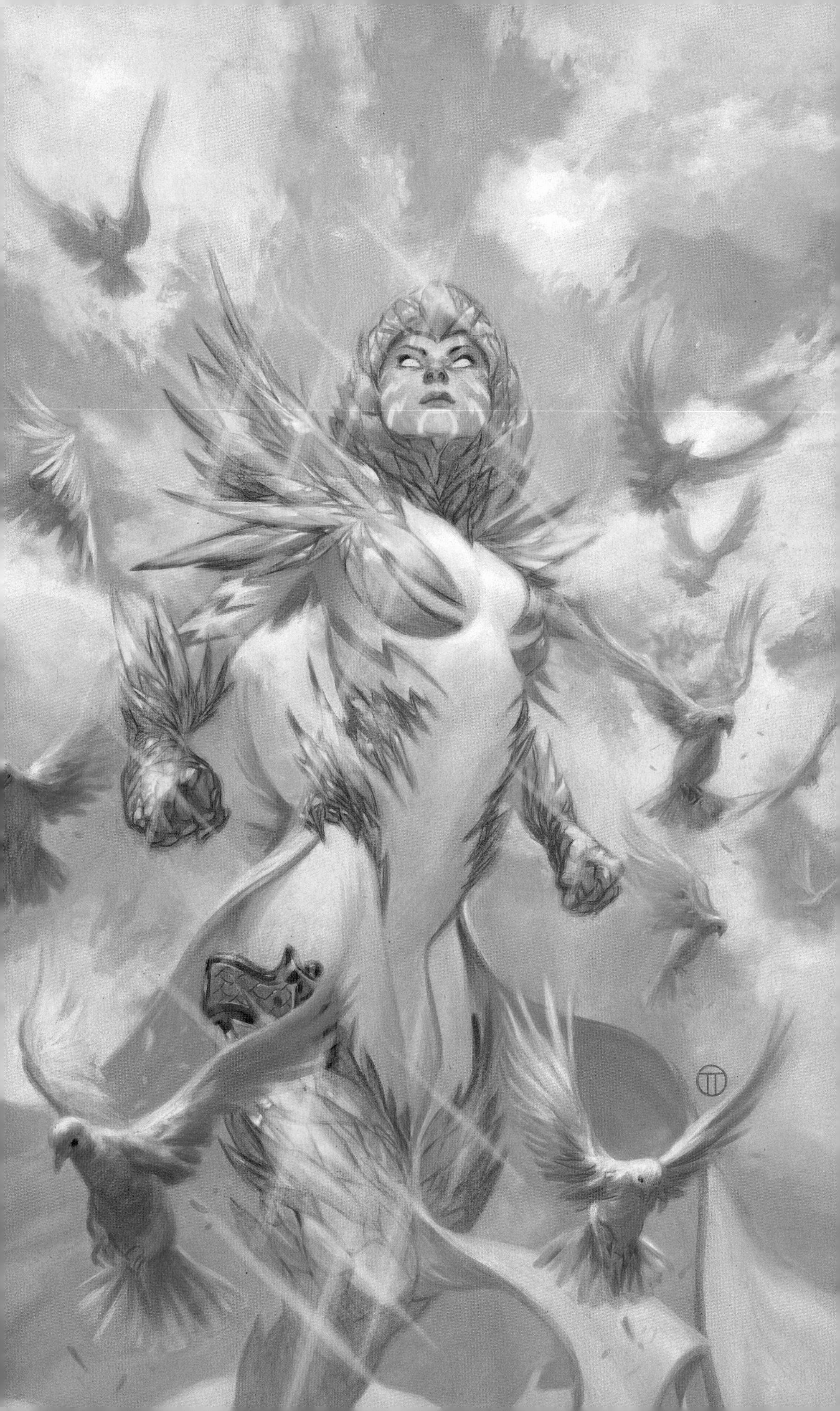

THE BATTLE OF NANDA PARBAT

RAY FAWKES
writer

FRANCIS PORTELA
artist

HI-FI
colorist

DEZI SIENTY
letterer

cover art by
JULIAN TOTINO TEDESCO

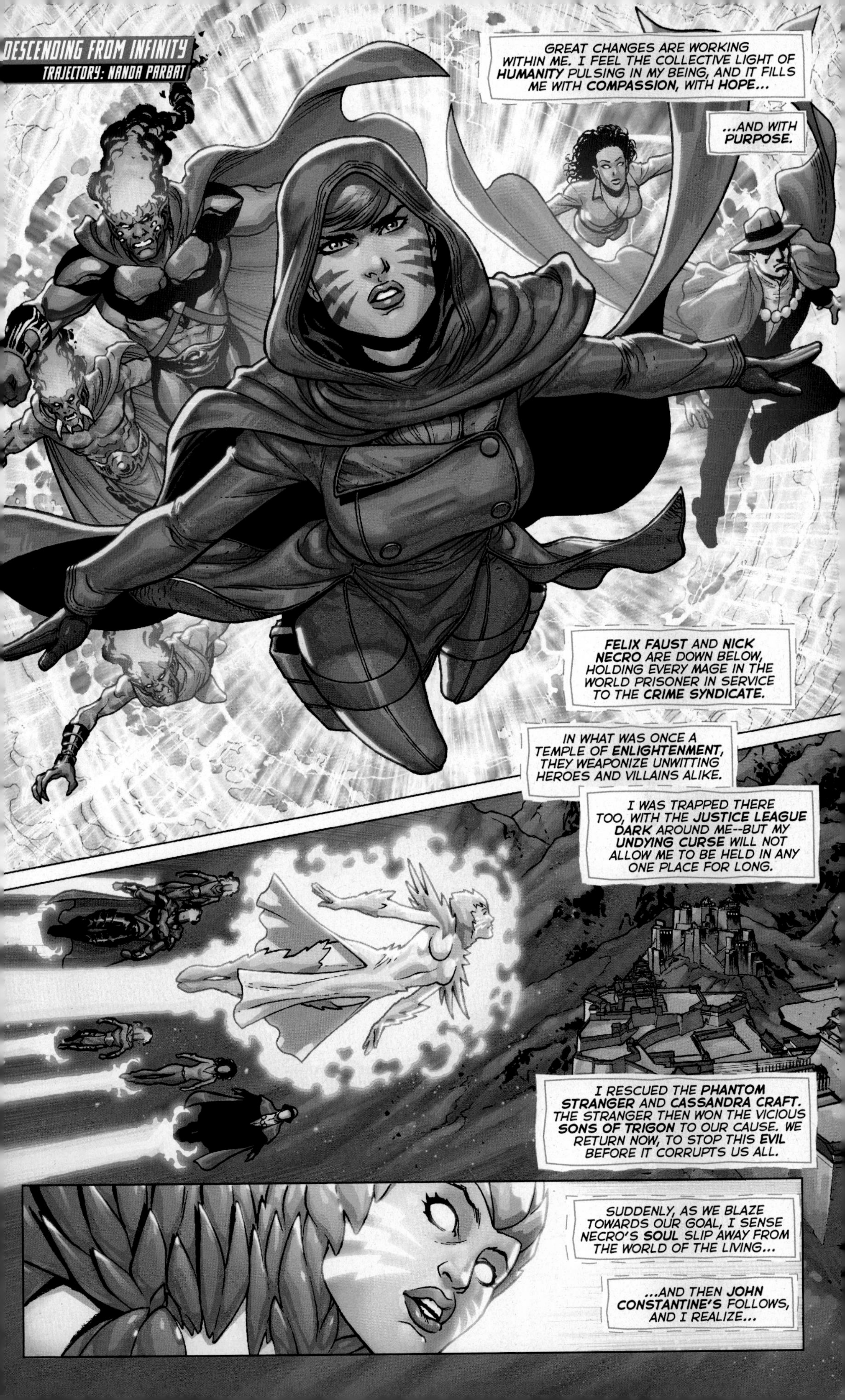
DESCENDING FROM INFINITY
TRAJECTORY: NANDA PARBAT
GREAT CHANGES ARE WORKING WITHIN ME. I FEEL THE COLLECTIVE LIGHT OF HUMANITY PULSING IN MY BEING, AND IT FILLS ME WITH COMPASSION, WITH HOPE...
...AND WITH PURPOSE.
FELIX FAUST AND NICK NECRO ARE DOWN BELOW, HOLDING EVERY MAGE IN THE WORLD PRISONER IN SERVICE TO THE CRIME SYNDICATE.
IN WHAT WAS ONCE A TEMPLE OF ENLIGHTENMENT, THEY WEAPONIZE UNWITTING HEROES AND VILLAINS ALIKE.
I WAS TRAPPED THERE TOO, WITH THE JUSTICE LEAGUE DARK AROUND ME--BUT MY UNDYING CURSE WILL NOT ALLOW ME TO BE HELD IN ANY ONE PLACE FOR LONG.
I RESCUED THE PHANTOM STRANGER AND CASSANDRA CRAFT. THE STRANGER THEN WON THE VICIOUS SONS OF TRIGON TO OUR CAUSE. WE RETURN NOW, TO STOP THIS EVIL BEFORE IT CORRUPTS US ALL.
SUDDENLY, AS WE BLAZE TOWARDS OUR GOAL, I SENSE NECRO'S SOUL SLIP AWAY FROM THE WORLD OF THE LIVING...
...AND THEN JOHN CONSTANTINE'S FOLLOWS, AND I REALIZE...

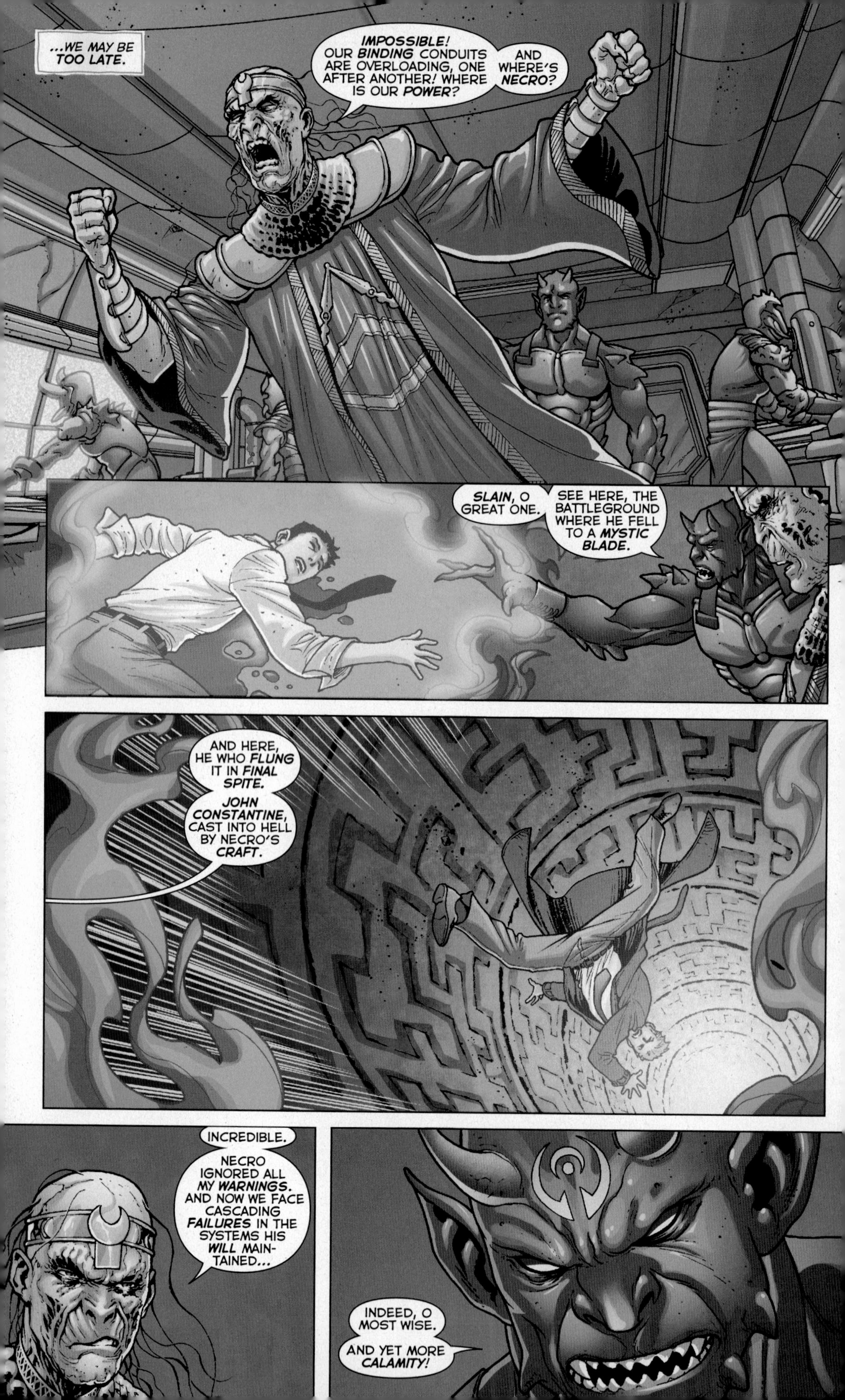
...WE MAY BE TOO LATE.
IMPOSSIBLE! OUR BINDING CONDUITS ARE OVERLOADING, ONE AFTER ANOTHER! WHERE IS OUR POWER?
AND WHERE'S NECRO?
SLAIN, O GREAT ONE.
SEE HERE, THE BATTLEGROUND WHERE HE FELL TO A MYSTIC BLADE.
AND HERE, HE WHO FLUNG IT IN FINAL SPITE.
JOHN CONSTANTINE, CAST INTO HELL BY NECRO'S CRAFT.
INCREDIBLE.
NECRO IGNORED ALL MY WARNINGS. AND NOW WE FACE CASCADING FAILURES IN THE SYSTEMS HIS WILL MAIN-TAINED...
INDEED, O MOST WISE.
AND YET MORE CALAMITY!

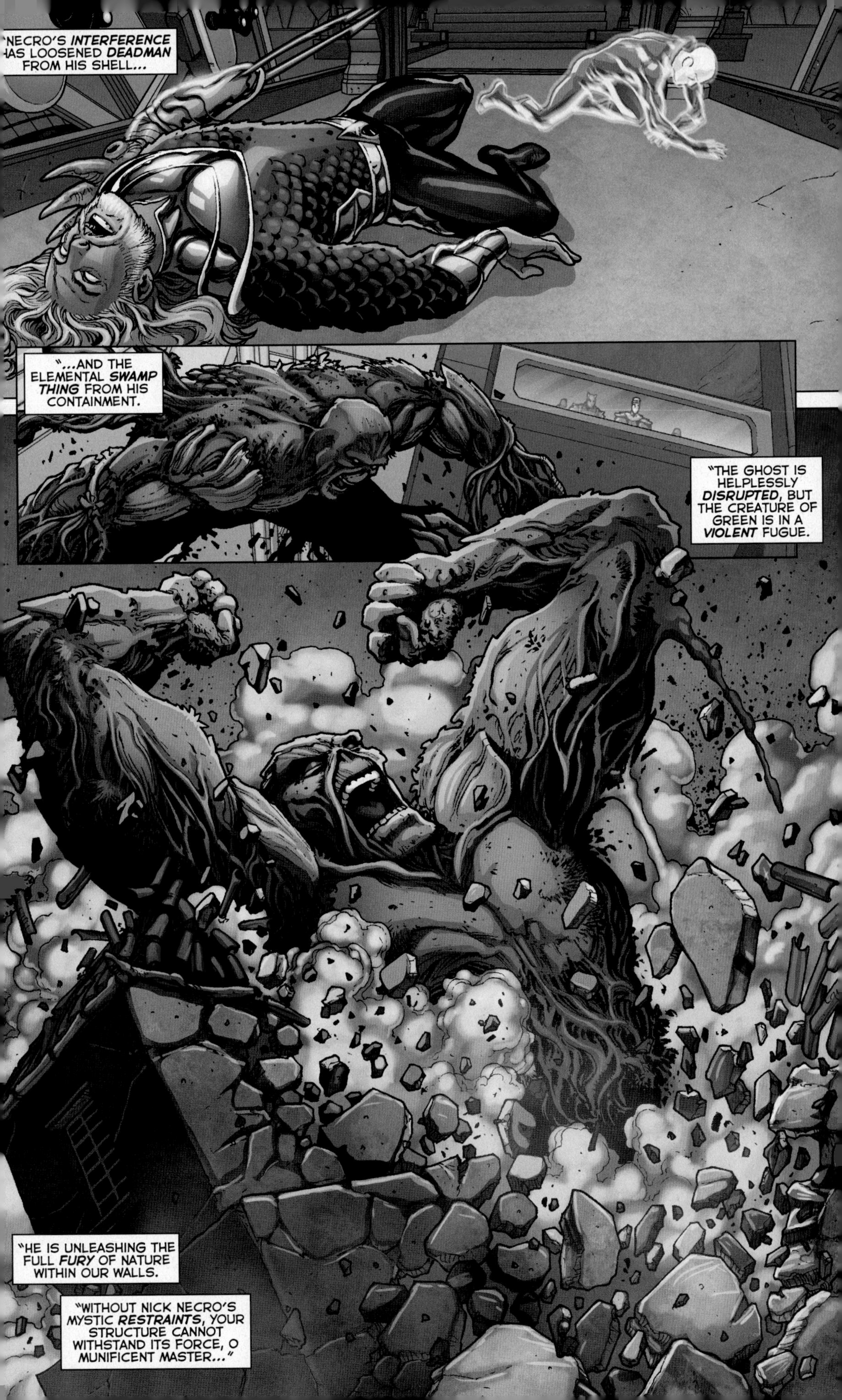
"NECRO'S INTERFERENCE HAS LOOSENED DEADMAN FROM HIS SHELL...
"...AND THE ELEMENTAL SWAMP THING FROM HIS CONTAINMENT.
"THE GHOST IS HELPLESSLY DISRUPTED, BUT THE CREATURE OF GREEN IS IN A VIOLENT FUGUE.
"HE IS UNLEASHING THE FULL FURY OF NATURE WITHIN OUR WALLS.
"WITHOUT NICK NECRO'S MYSTIC RESTRAINTS, YOUR STRUCTURE CANNOT WITHSTAND ITS FORCE, O MUNIFICENT MASTER..."

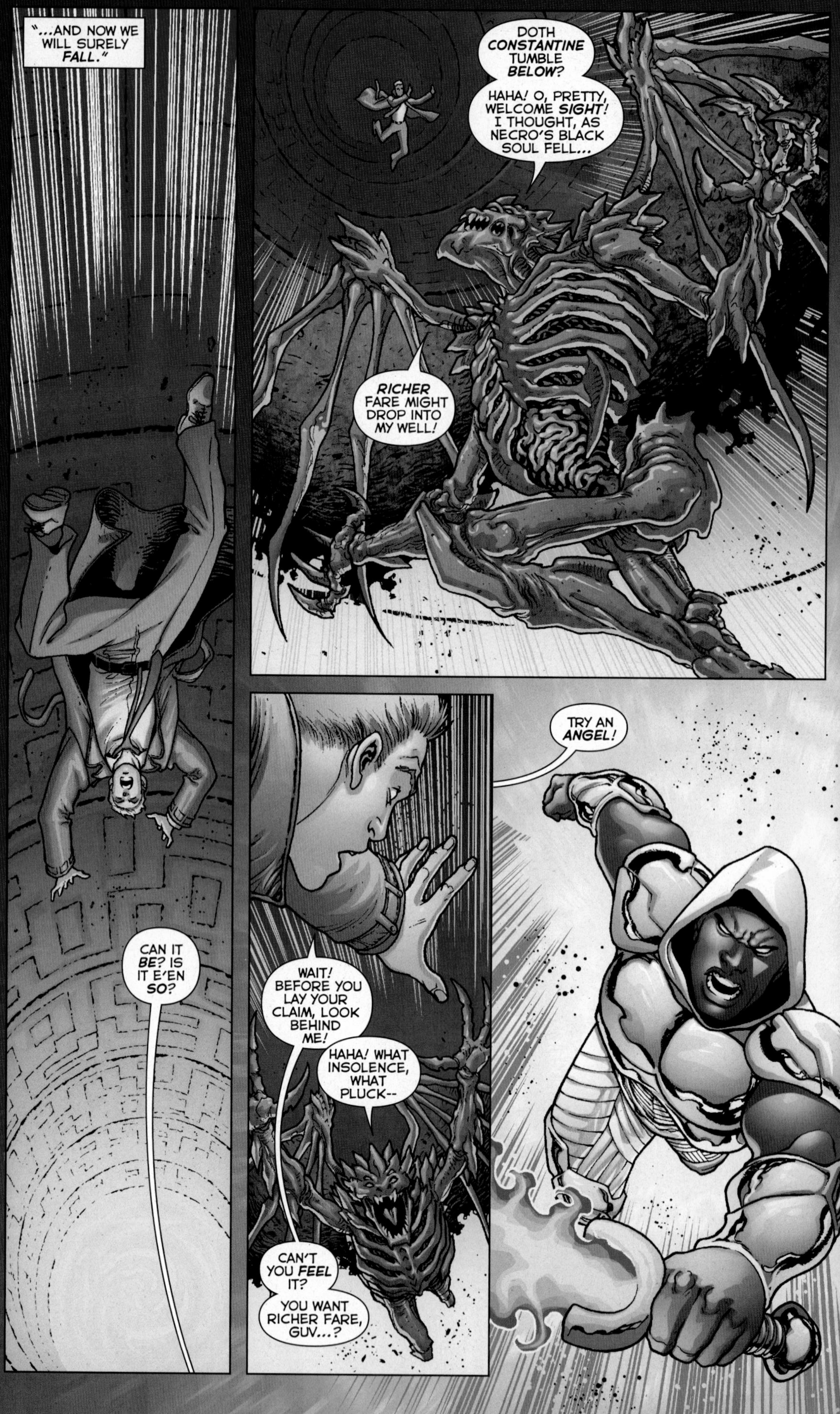
"...AND NOW WE WILL SURELY FALL."
DOTH CONSTANTINE TUMBLE BELOW?
HAHA! O, PRETTY, WELCOME SIGHT! I THOUGHT, AS NECRO'S BLACK SOUL FELL...
RICHER FARE MIGHT DROP INTO MY WELL!
CAN IT BE? IS IT E'EN SO?
WAIT! BEFORE YOU LAY YOUR CLAIM, LOOK BEHIND ME!
HAHA! WHAT INSOLENCE, WHAT PLUCK--
CAN'T YOU FEEL IT?
YOU WANT RICHER FARE, GUV...?
TRY AN ANGEL!

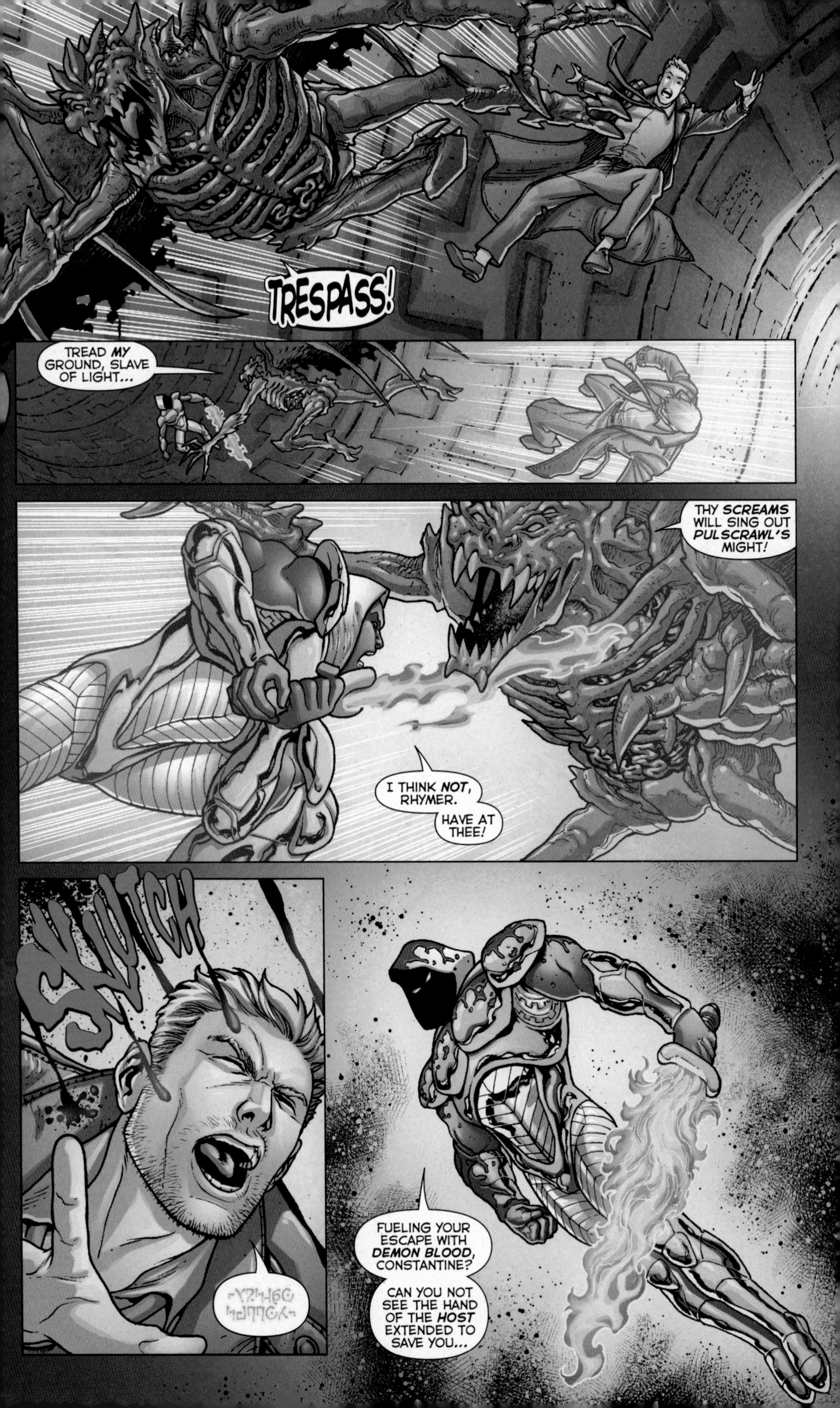
TRESPASS!
TREAD MY GROUND, SLAVE OF LIGHT...
THY SCREAMS WILL SING OUT PULSCRAWL'S MIGHT!
I THINK NOT, RHYMER.
HAVE AT THEE!
SKLUTCH
FUELING YOUR ESCAPE WITH DEMON BLOOD, CONSTANTINE?
CAN YOU NOT SEE THE HAND OF THE HOST EXTENDED TO SAVE YOU...

"...OR HAVE YOU SLIPPED *BEYOND* TRUST?"

SO BE IT! FELIX FAUST CAN WIN THIS DAY *ALONE!*

THE ELEMENTAL IS OUR PRIMARY THREAT!

LOAD *BLACK ORCHID* INTO THE FIRING CHAMBER AND INITIATE THE SEQUENCE!

I'LL DRAW THE ENEMY INTO OUR SIGHTS WITH A SIMPLE *FOCUS* SPELL!

ROOOAAAARRR

BBBBRRROOPPPPPAACCHHHH

WE *PERISH,* O GREAT ONE!

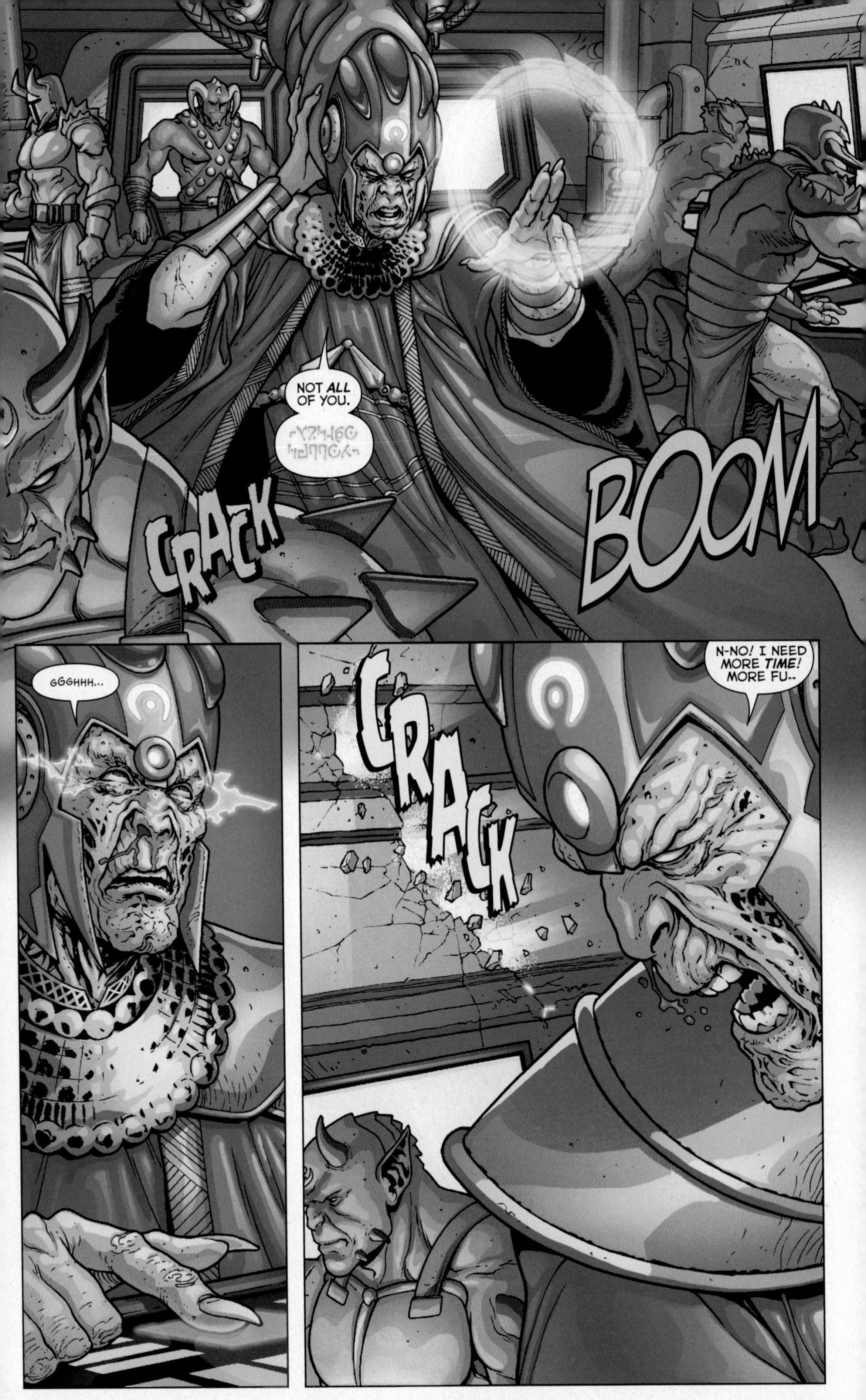

NOT ALL OF YOU.
CRACK
BOOM
GGGHHH...
CRACK
N-NO! I NEED MORE TIME! MORE FU--

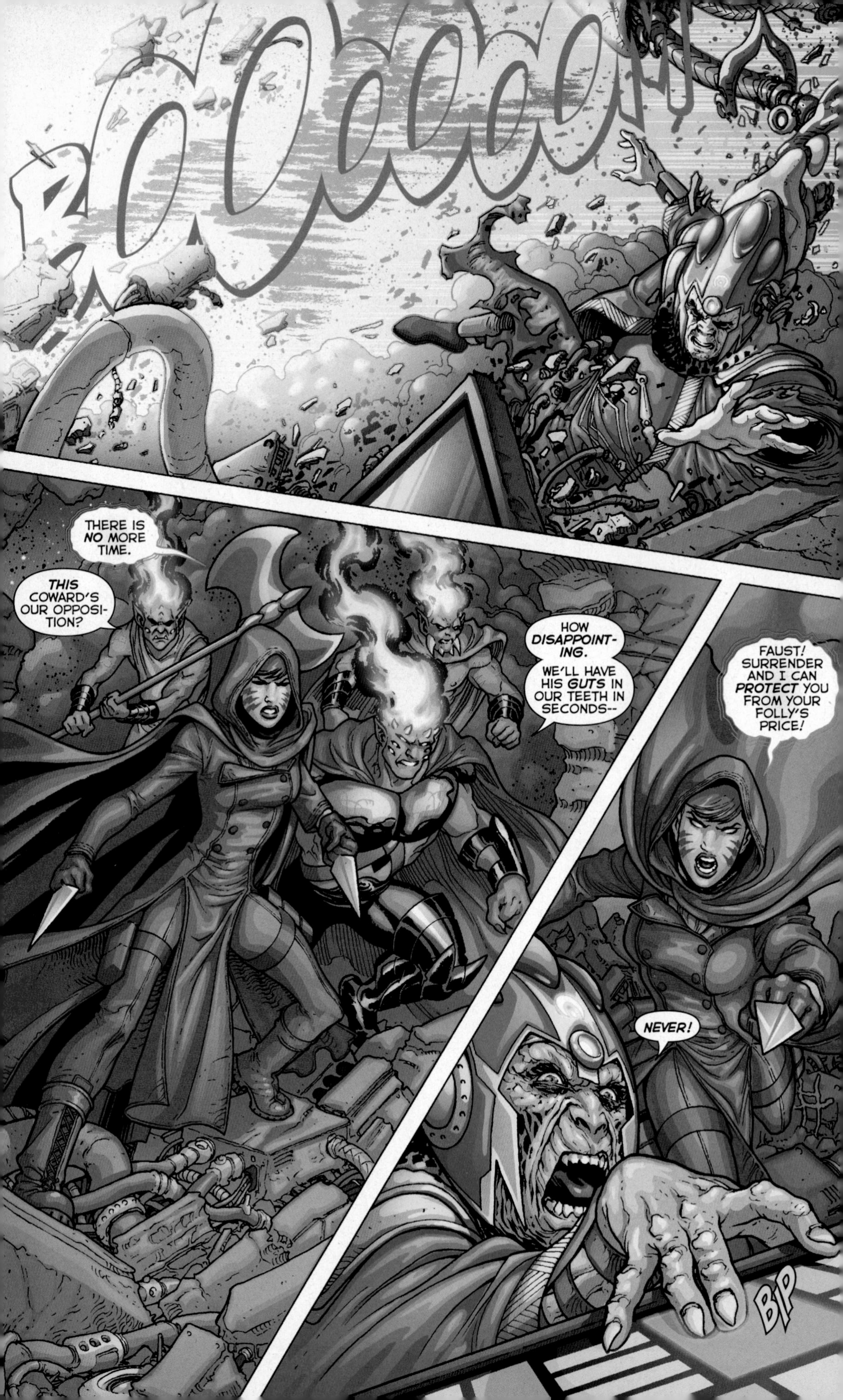

THERE IS NO MORE TIME.
THIS COWARD'S OUR OPPOSITION?
HOW DISAPPOINTING. WE'LL HAVE HIS GUTS IN OUR TEETH IN SECONDS--
FAUST! SURRENDER AND I CAN PROTECT YOU FROM YOUR FOLLY'S PRICE!
NEVER!

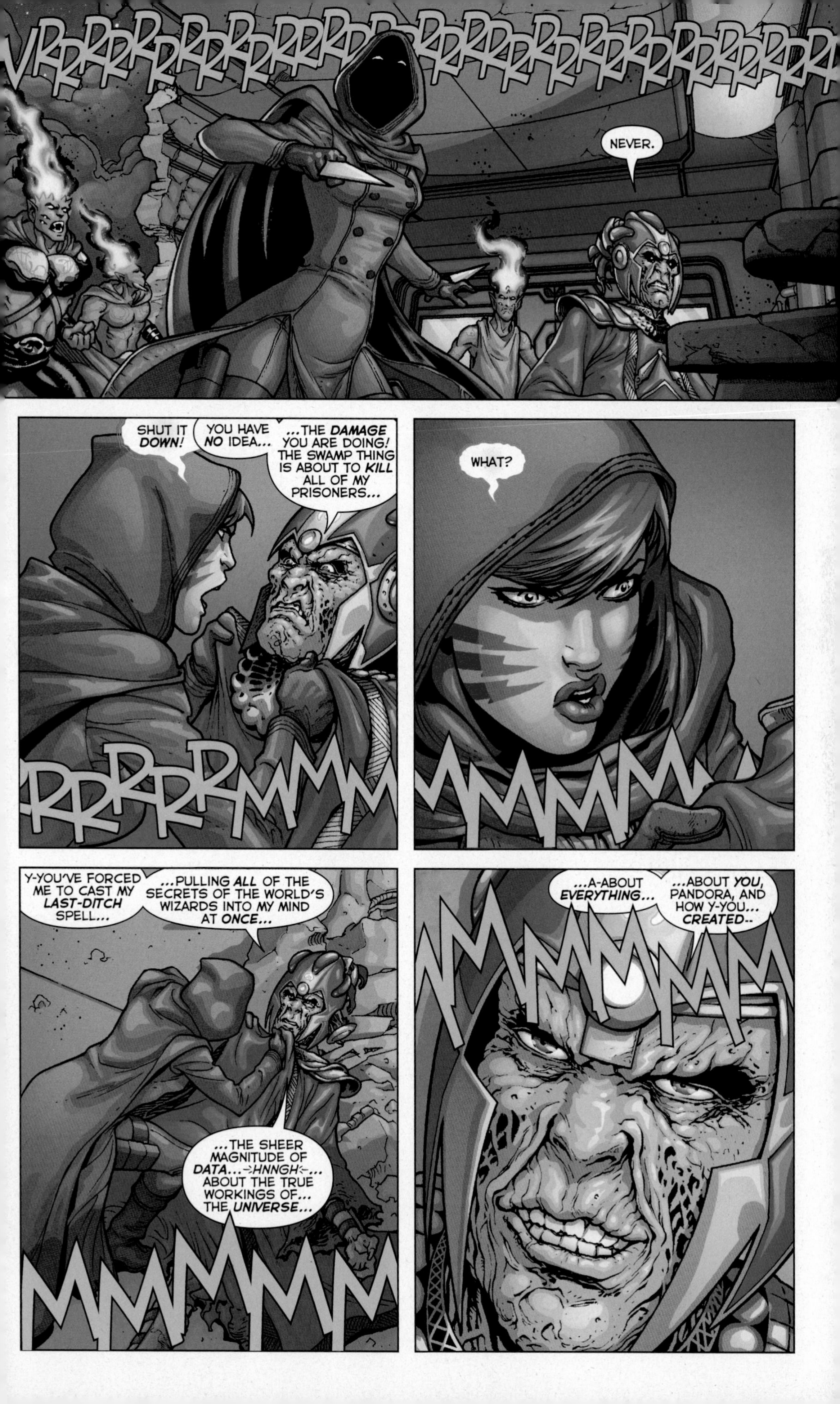

VRRRRRRRRRRRRRRRRRRRRRRRRRRRRRRRRRRRRRRRRRRRRRRRRRRRRRRRRRRRRRRRRRRRRR
NEVER.
SHUT IT DOWN!
YOU HAVE NO IDEA...
...THE DAMAGE YOU ARE DOING! THE SWAMP THING IS ABOUT TO KILL ALL OF MY PRISONERS...
RRRRRMMMM
WHAT?
MMMMMM
Y-YOU'VE FORCED ME TO CAST MY LAST-DITCH SPELL...
...PULLING ALL OF THE SECRETS OF THE WORLD'S WIZARDS INTO MY MIND AT ONCE...
...THE SHEER MAGNITUDE OF DATA... HNNGH... ABOUT THE TRUE WORKINGS OF... THE UNIVERSE...
MMMMMMM
...A-ABOUT EVERYTHING...
...ABOUT YOU, PANDORA, AND HOW Y-YOU... CREATED--
MMMMMMMM

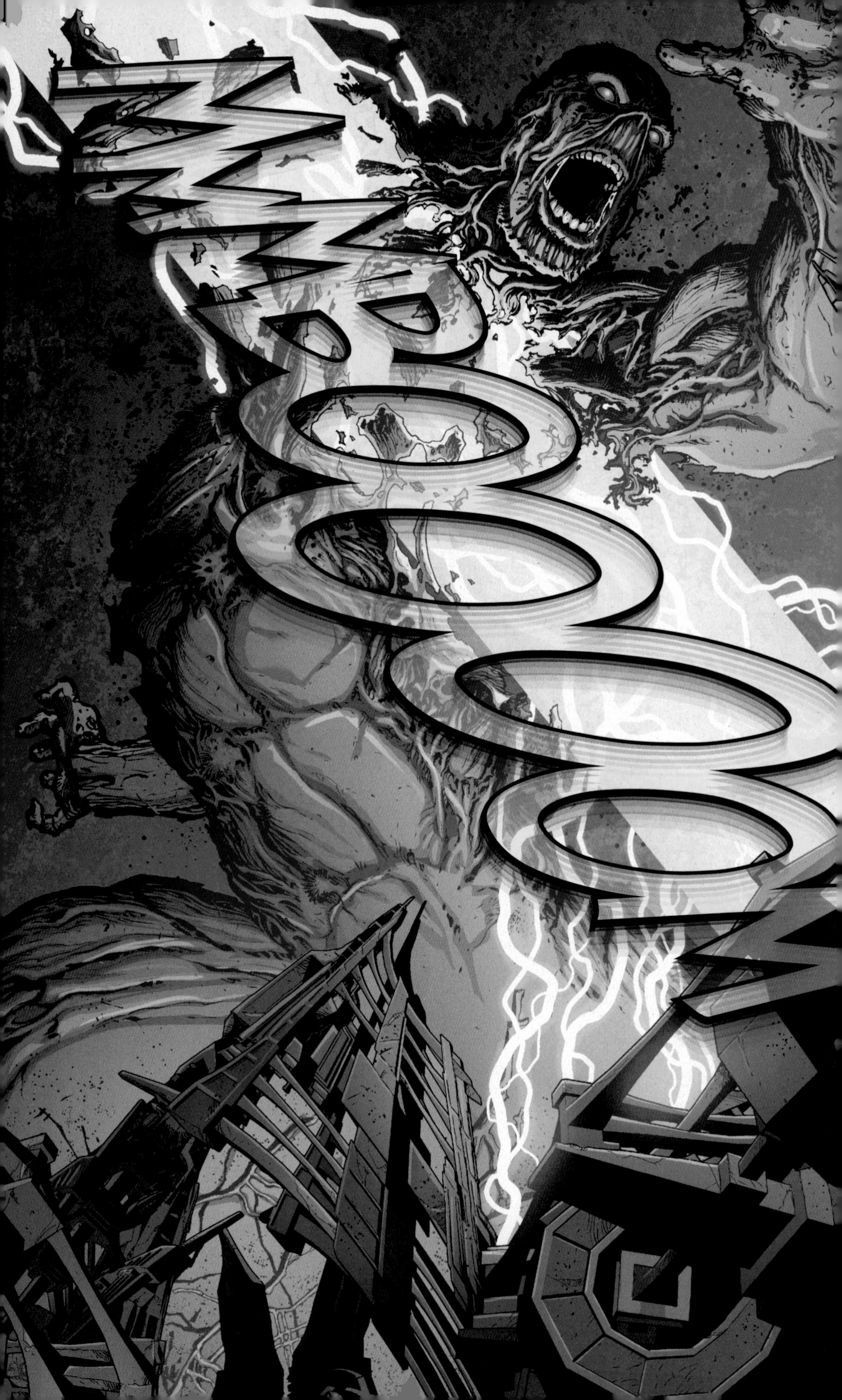

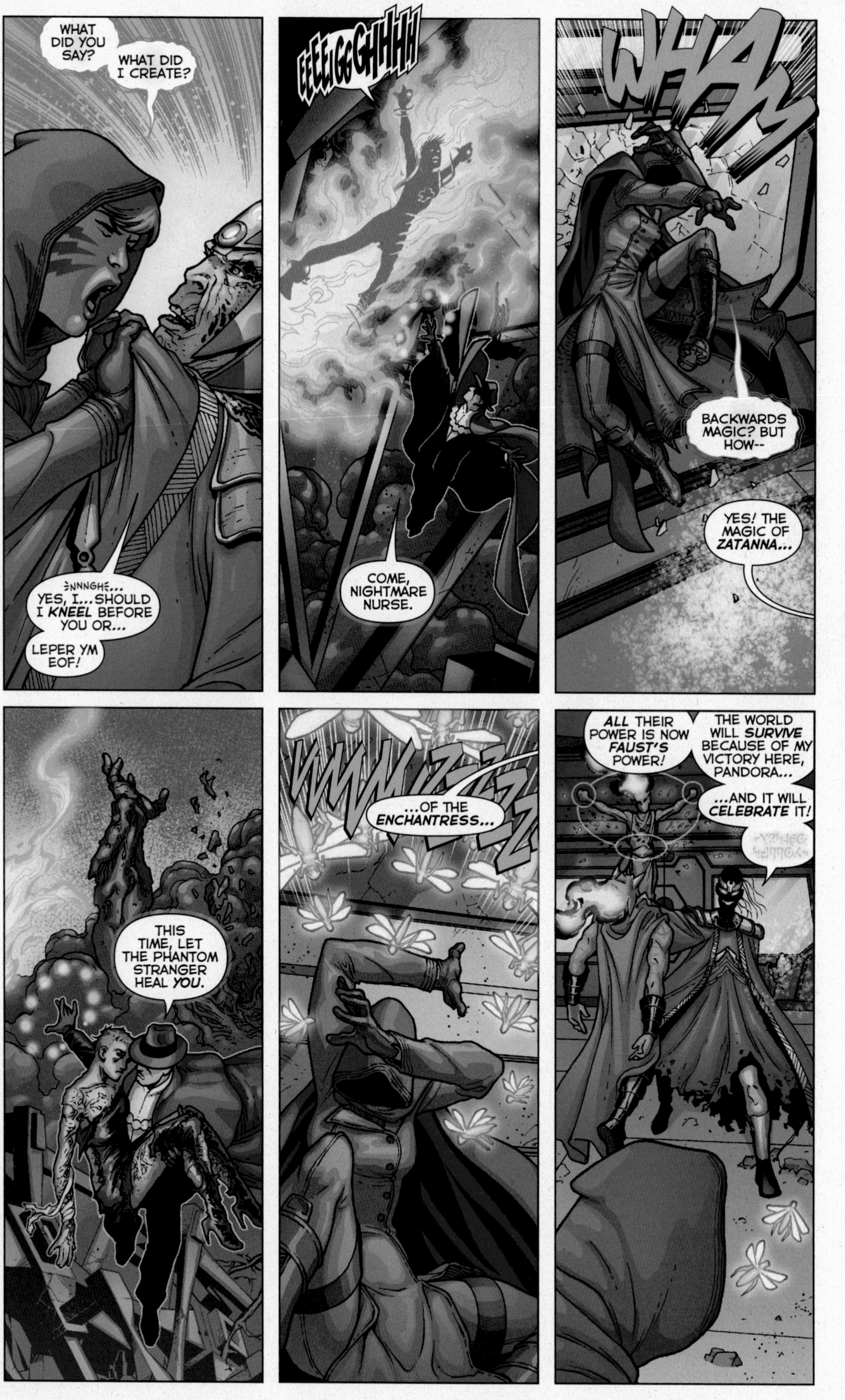
WHAT DID YOU SAY?
WHAT DID I CREATE?
NNNGH... YES, I...SHOULD I KNEEL BEFORE YOU OR...
LEPER YM EOF!
EEEEIGGHHHH
COME, NIGHTMARE NURSE.
WHAM
BACKWARDS MAGIC? BUT HOW--
YES! THE MAGIC OF ZATANNA...
THIS TIME, LET THE PHANTOM STRANGER HEAL YOU.
VVMMZZZZZ
...OF THE ENCHANTRESS...
ALL THEIR POWER IS NOW FAUST'S POWER!
THE WORLD WILL SURVIVE BECAUSE OF MY VICTORY HERE, PANDORA...
...AND IT WILL CELEBRATE IT!

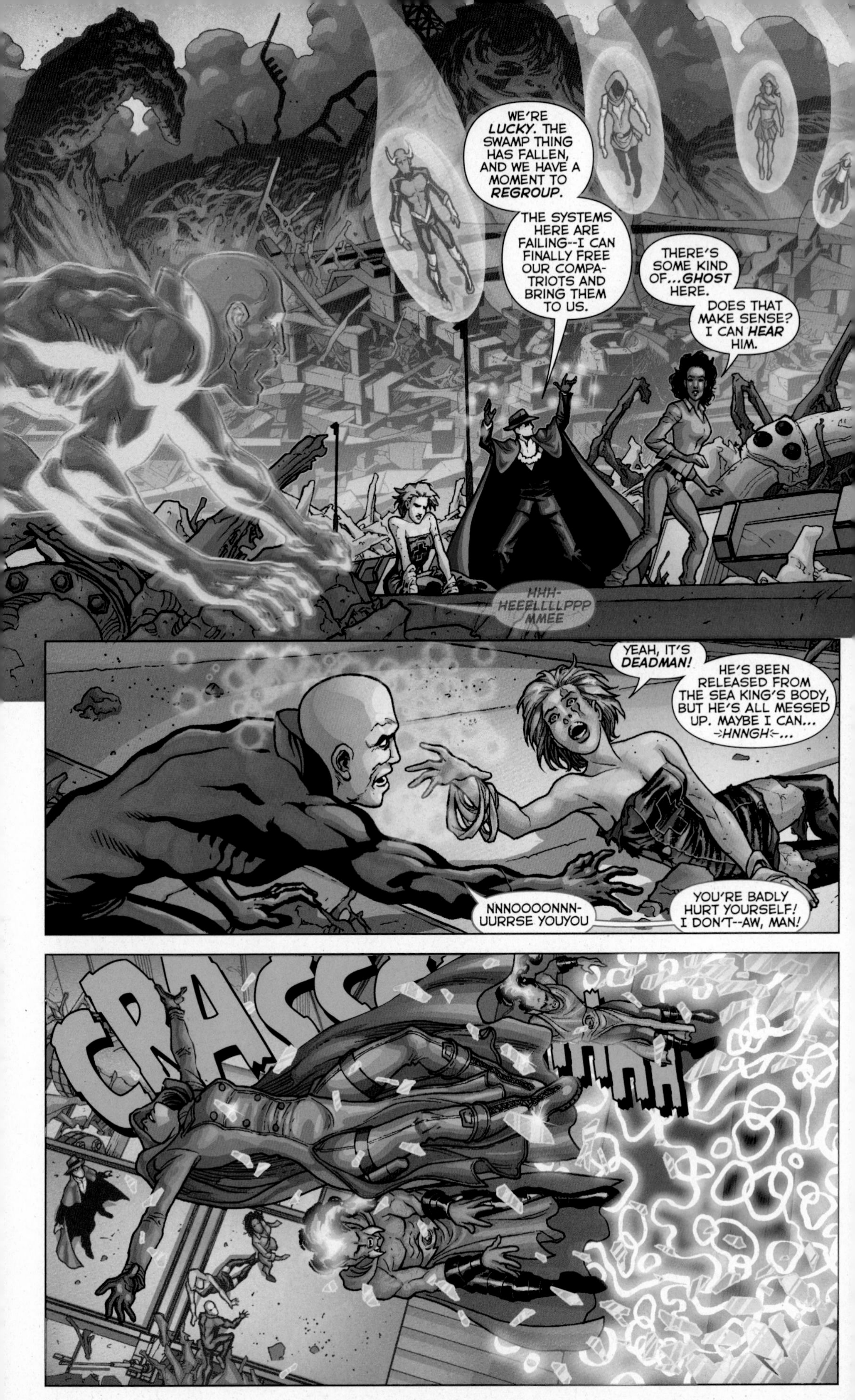

WE'RE LUCKY. THE SWAMP THING HAS FALLEN, AND WE HAVE A MOMENT TO REGROUP.
THE SYSTEMS HERE ARE FAILING--I CAN FINALLY FREE OUR COMPATRIOTS AND BRING THEM TO US.
THERE'S SOME KIND OF...GHOST HERE.
DOES THAT MAKE SENSE? I CAN HEAR HIM.
HHH-HEEELLLLPPP MMEE
YEAH, IT'S DEADMAN!
HE'S BEEN RELEASED FROM THE SEA KING'S BODY, BUT HE'S ALL MESSED UP. MAYBE I CAN... HNNGH...
NNNOOOONNN-UURRSE YOUYOU
YOU'RE BADLY HURT YOURSELF! I DON'T--AW, MAN!

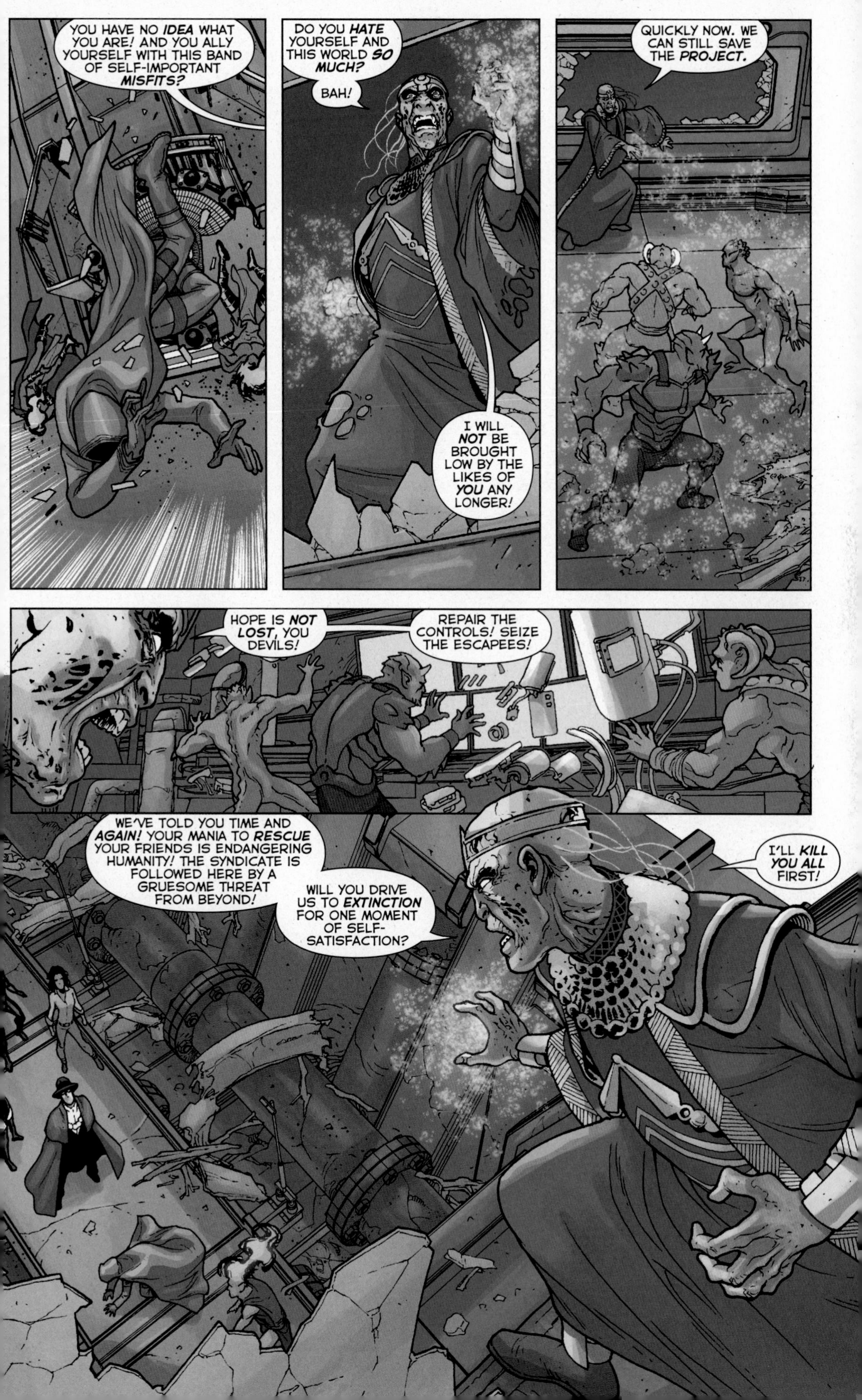

YOU HAVE NO IDEA WHAT YOU ARE! AND YOU ALLY YOURSELF WITH THIS BAND OF SELF-IMPORTANT MISFITS?
DO YOU HATE YOURSELF AND THIS WORLD SO MUCH?
BAH!
I WILL NOT BE BROUGHT LOW BY THE LIKES OF YOU ANY LONGER!
QUICKLY NOW. WE CAN STILL SAVE THE PROJECT.
HOPE IS NOT LOST, YOU DEVILS!
REPAIR THE CONTROLS! SEIZE THE ESCAPEES!
WE'VE TOLD YOU TIME AND AGAIN! YOUR MANIA TO RESCUE YOUR FRIENDS IS ENDANGERING HUMANITY! THE SYNDICATE IS FOLLOWED HERE BY A GRUESOME THREAT FROM BEYOND!
WILL YOU DRIVE US TO EXTINCTION FOR ONE MOMENT OF SELF-SATISFACTION?
I'LL KILL YOU ALL FIRST!

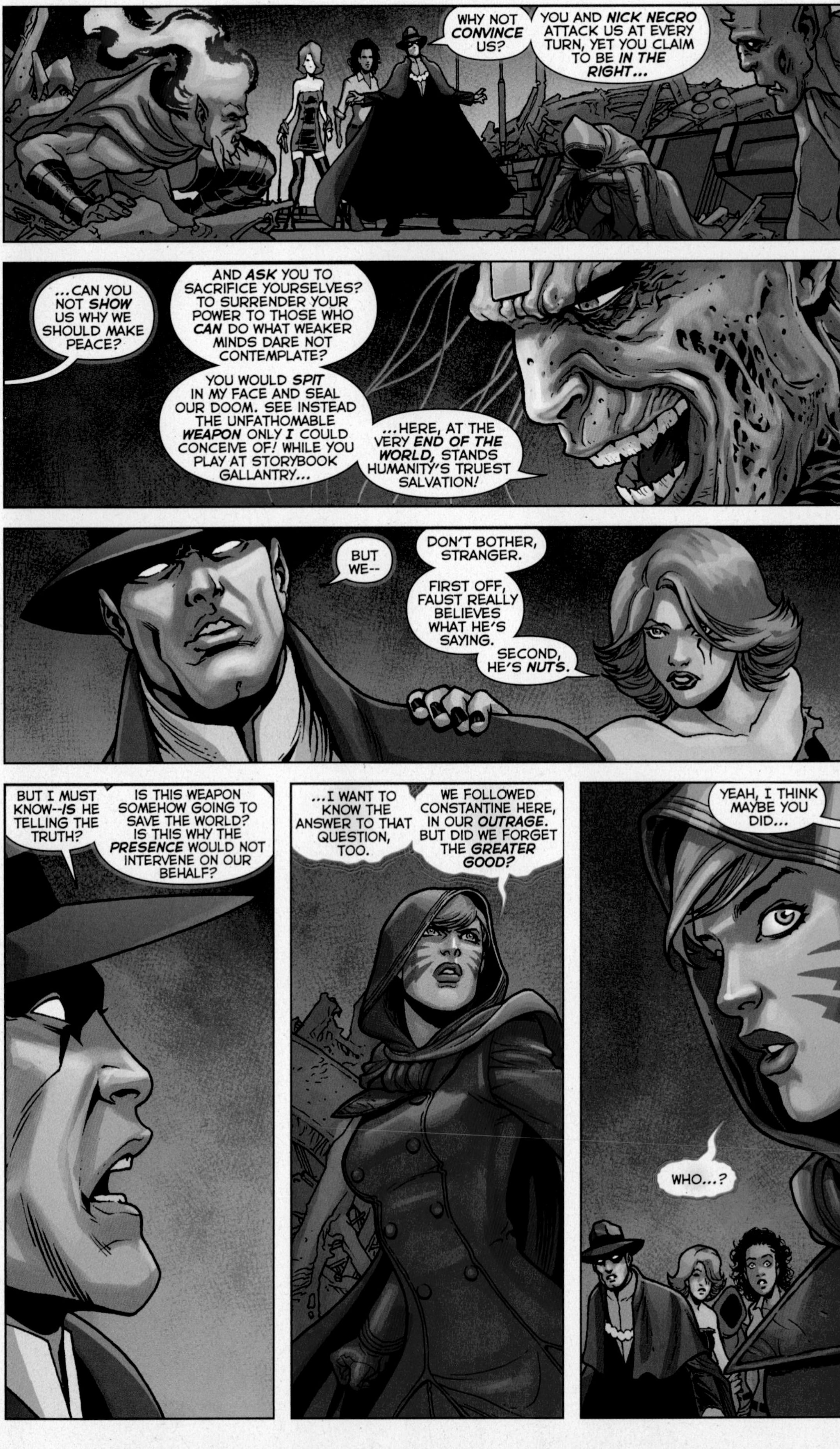

WHY NOT CONVINCE US?
YOU AND NICK NECRO ATTACK US AT EVERY TURN, YET YOU CLAIM TO BE IN THE RIGHT...
...CAN YOU NOT SHOW US WHY WE SHOULD MAKE PEACE?
AND ASK YOU TO SACRIFICE YOURSELVES? TO SURRENDER YOUR POWER TO THOSE WHO CAN DO WHAT WEAKER MINDS DARE NOT CONTEMPLATE?
YOU WOULD SPIT IN MY FACE AND SEAL OUR DOOM. SEE INSTEAD THE UNFATHOMABLE WEAPON ONLY I COULD CONCEIVE OF! WHILE YOU PLAY AT STORYBOOK GALLANTRY...
...HERE, AT THE VERY END OF THE WORLD, STANDS HUMANITY'S TRUEST SALVATION!
BUT WE--
DON'T BOTHER, STRANGER.
FIRST OFF, FAUST REALLY BELIEVES WHAT HE'S SAYING.
SECOND, HE'S NUTS.
BUT I MUST KNOW--IS HE TELLING THE TRUTH?
IS THIS WEAPON SOMEHOW GOING TO SAVE THE WORLD? IS THIS WHY THE PRESENCE WOULD NOT INTERVENE ON OUR BEHALF?
...I WANT TO KNOW THE ANSWER TO THAT QUESTION, TOO.
WE FOLLOWED CONSTANTINE HERE, IN OUR OUTRAGE. BUT DID WE FORGET THE GREATER GOOD?
YEAH, I THINK MAYBE YOU DID...
WHO...?

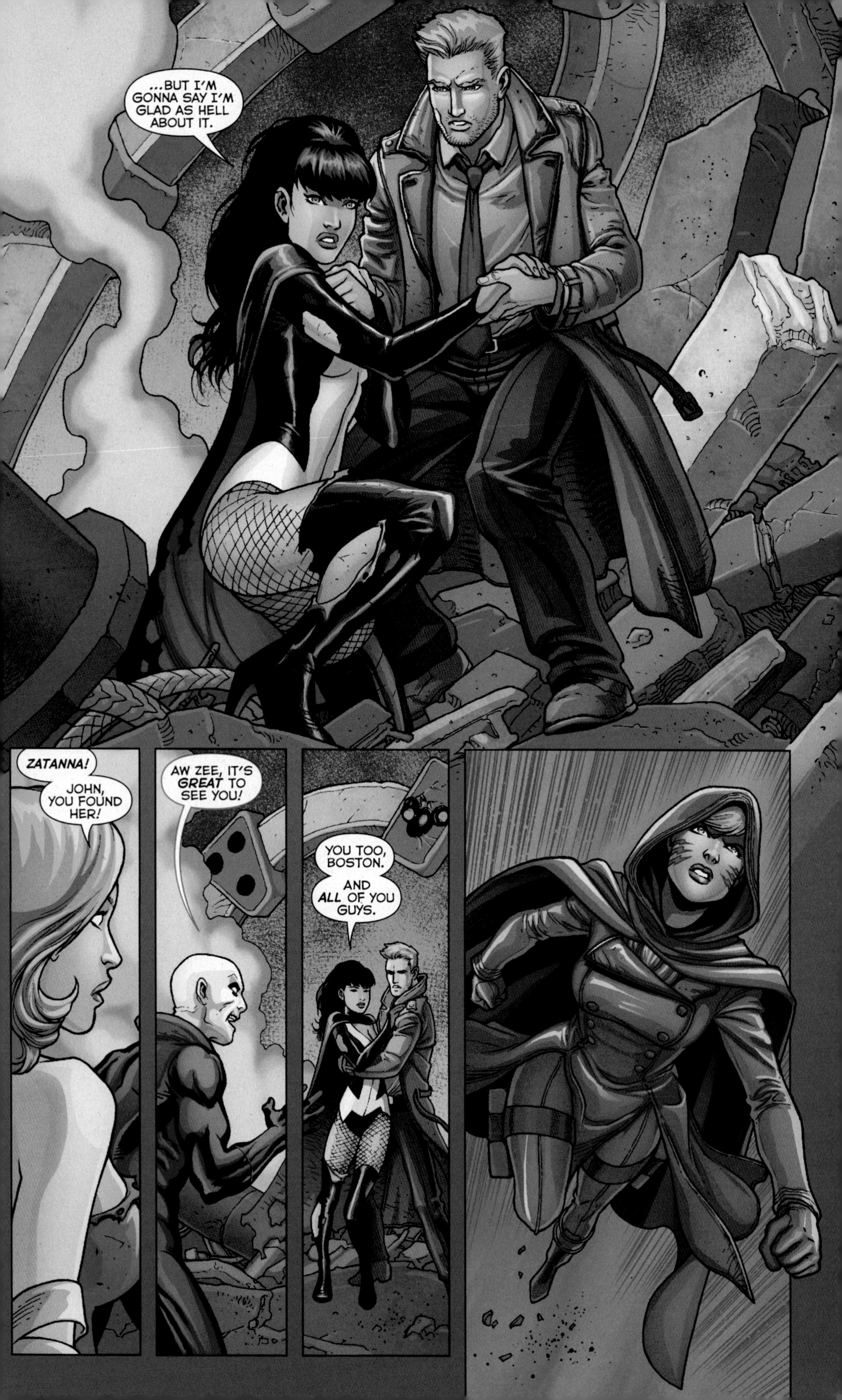
...BUT I'M GONNA SAY I'M GLAD AS HELL ABOUT IT.
ZATANNA!
JOHN, YOU FOUND HER!
AW ZEE, IT'S GREAT TO SEE YOU!
YOU TOO, BOSTON.
AND ALL OF YOU GUYS.

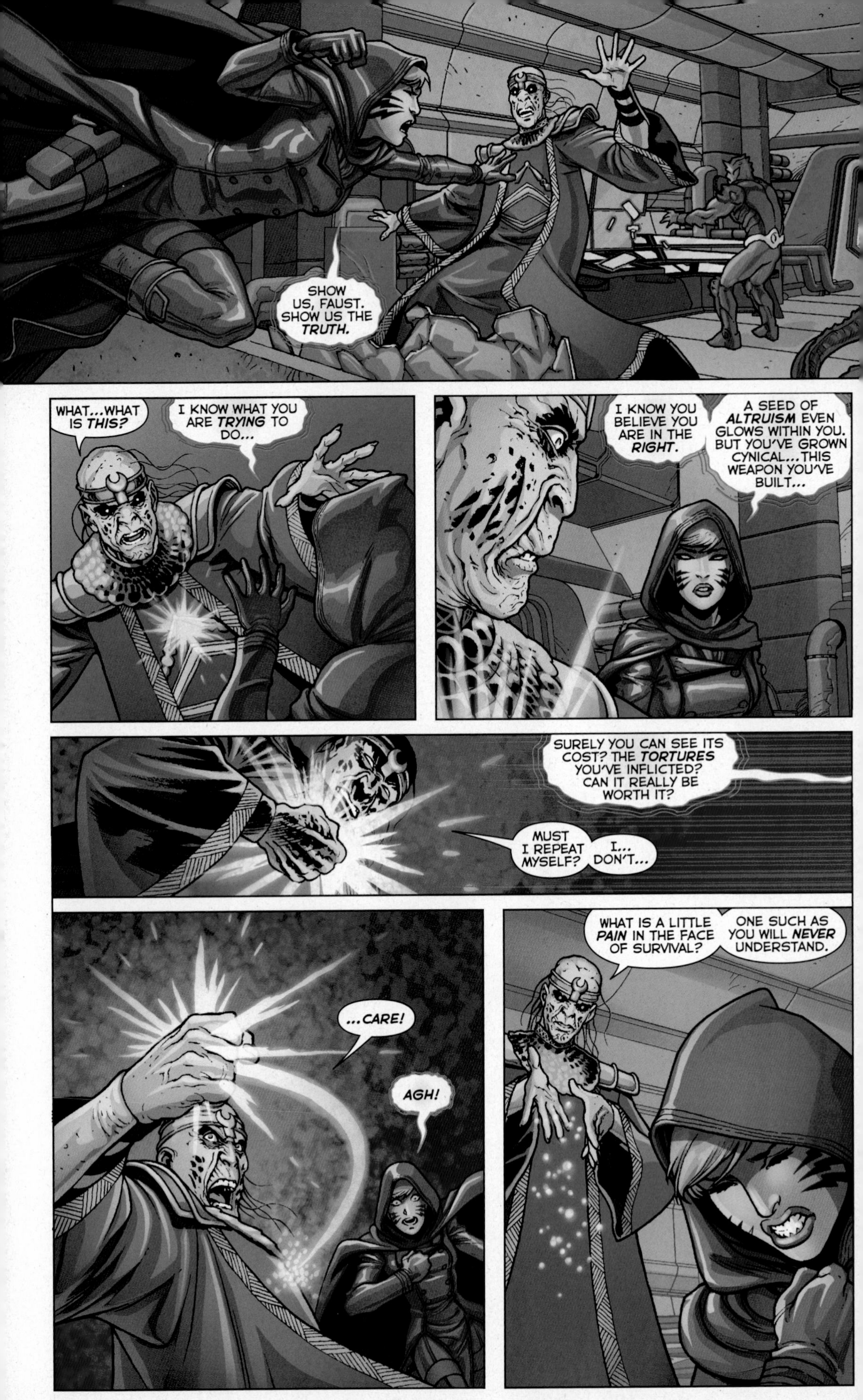
SHOW US, FAUST. SHOW US THE TRUTH.
WHAT...WHAT IS THIS?
I KNOW WHAT YOU ARE TRYING TO DO...
I KNOW YOU BELIEVE YOU ARE IN THE RIGHT.
A SEED OF ALTRUISM EVEN GLOWS WITHIN YOU. BUT YOU'VE GROWN CYNICAL...THIS WEAPON YOU'VE BUILT...
SURELY YOU CAN SEE ITS COST? THE TORTURES YOU'VE INFLICTED? CAN IT REALLY BE WORTH IT?
MUST I REPEAT MYSELF?
I... DON'T...
...CARE!
AGH!
WHAT IS A LITTLE PAIN IN THE FACE OF SURVIVAL?
ONE SUCH AS YOU WILL NEVER UNDERSTAND.

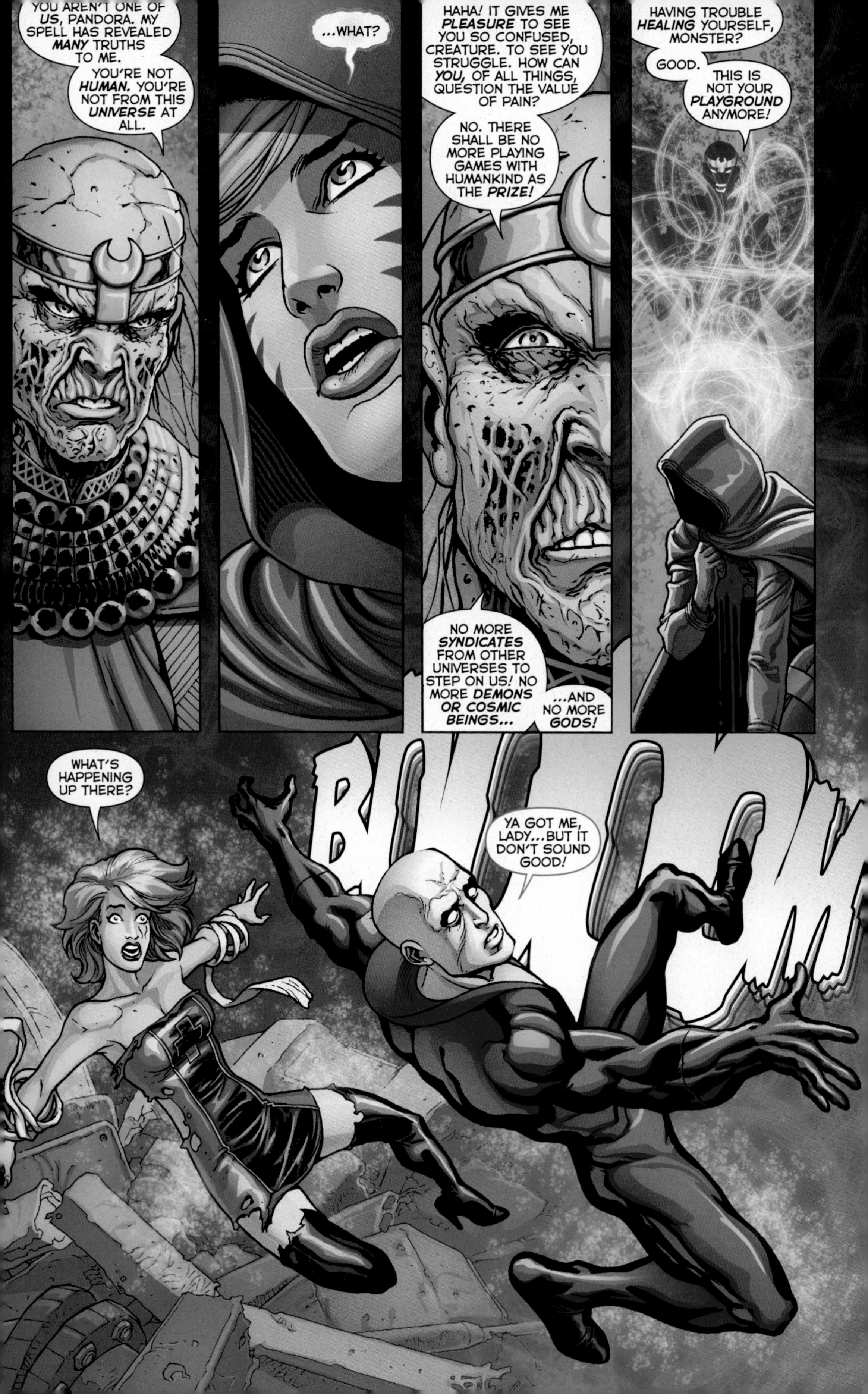
YOU AREN'T ONE OF US, PANDORA. MY SPELL HAS REVEALED MANY TRUTHS TO ME.
YOU'RE NOT HUMAN. YOU'RE NOT FROM THIS UNIVERSE AT ALL.
...WHAT?
HAHA! IT GIVES ME PLEASURE TO SEE YOU SO CONFUSED, CREATURE. TO SEE YOU STRUGGLE. HOW CAN YOU, OF ALL THINGS, QUESTION THE VALUE OF PAIN?
NO. THERE SHALL BE NO MORE PLAYING GAMES WITH HUMANKIND AS THE PRIZE!
NO MORE SYNDICATES FROM OTHER UNIVERSES TO STEP ON US! NO MORE DEMONS OR COSMIC BEINGS...
...AND NO MORE GODS!
HAVING TROUBLE HEALING YOURSELF, MONSTER?
GOOD.
THIS IS NOT YOUR PLAYGROUND ANYMORE!
WHAT'S HAPPENING UP THERE?
YA GOT ME, LADY...BUT IT DON'T SOUND GOOD!

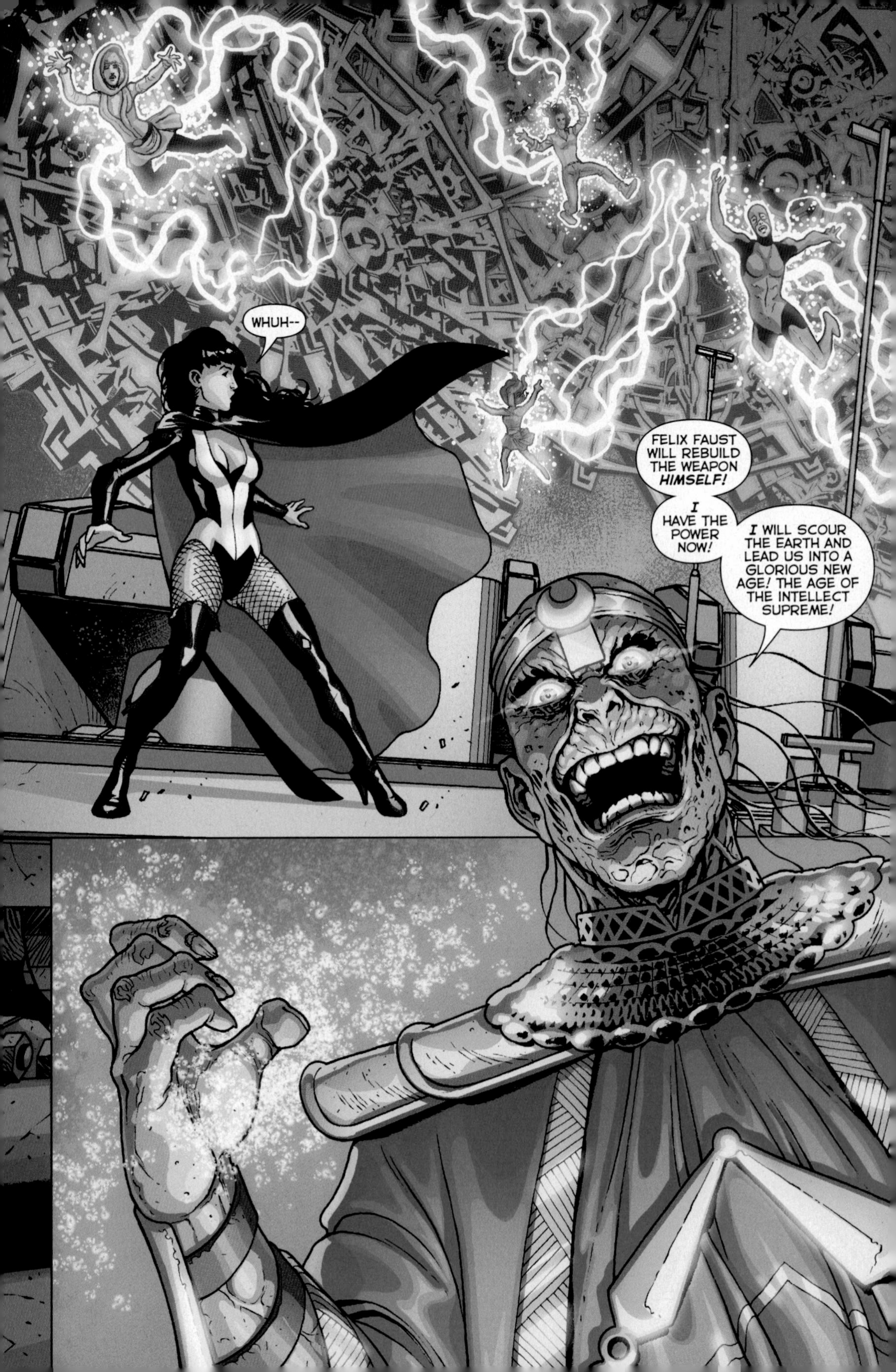
WHUH--
FELIX FAUST WILL REBUILD THE WEAPON HIMSELF!
I HAVE THE POWER NOW!
I WILL SCOUR THE EARTH AND LEAD US INTO A GLORIOUS NEW AGE! THE AGE OF THE INTELLECT SUPREME!

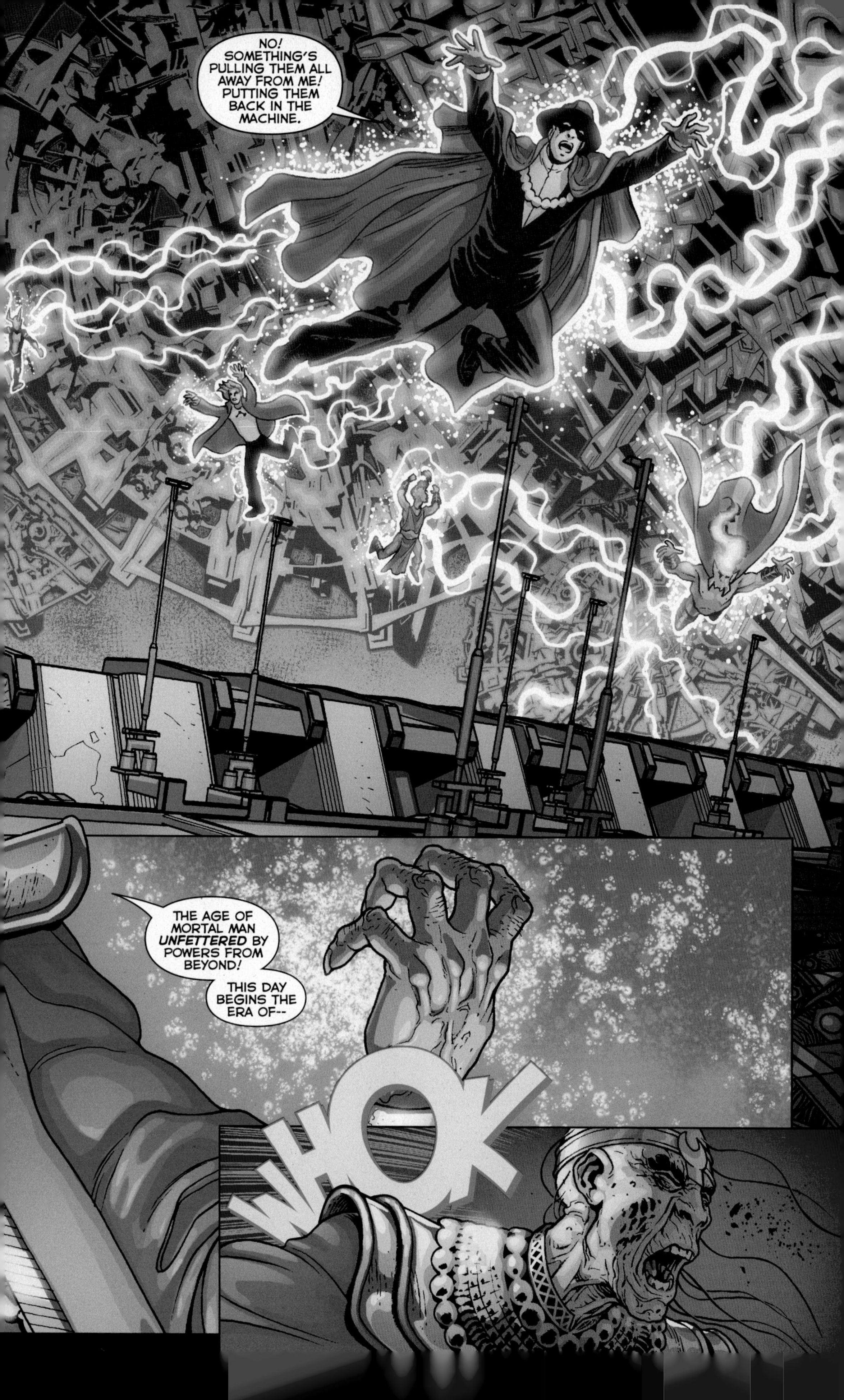
NO! SOMETHING'S PULLING THEM ALL AWAY FROM ME! PUTTING THEM BACK IN THE MACHINE.
THE AGE OF MORTAL MAN UNFETTERED BY POWERS FROM BEYOND!
THIS DAY BEGINS THE ERA OF--
WHOK

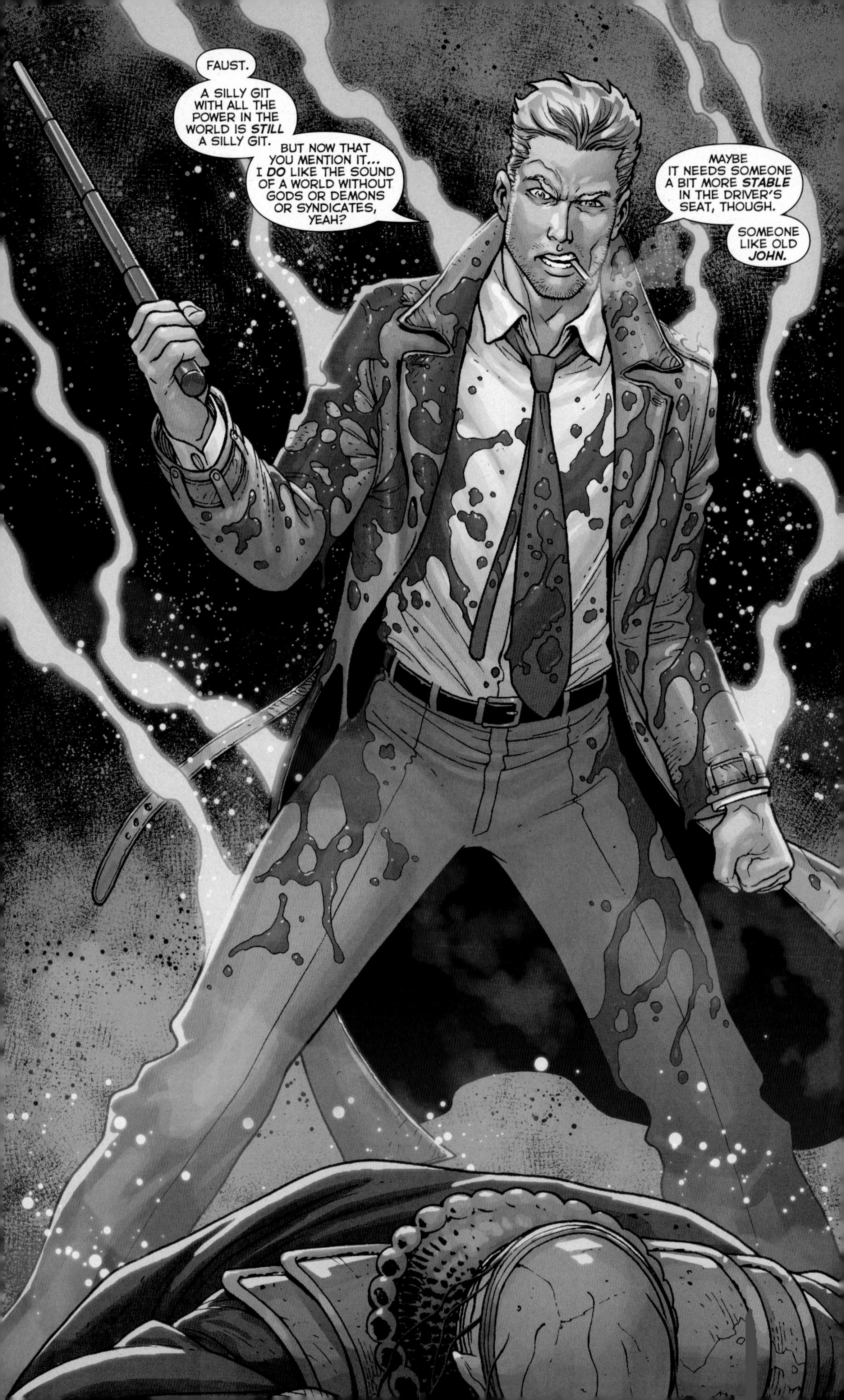
FAUST.
A SILLY GIT WITH ALL THE POWER IN THE WORLD IS *STILL* A SILLY GIT.
BUT NOW THAT YOU MENTION IT... I *DO* LIKE THE SOUND OF A WORLD WITHOUT GODS OR DEMONS OR SYNDICATES, YEAH?
MAYBE IT NEEDS SOMEONE A BIT MORE *STABLE* IN THE DRIVER'S SEAT, THOUGH.
SOMEONE LIKE OLD *JOHN.*

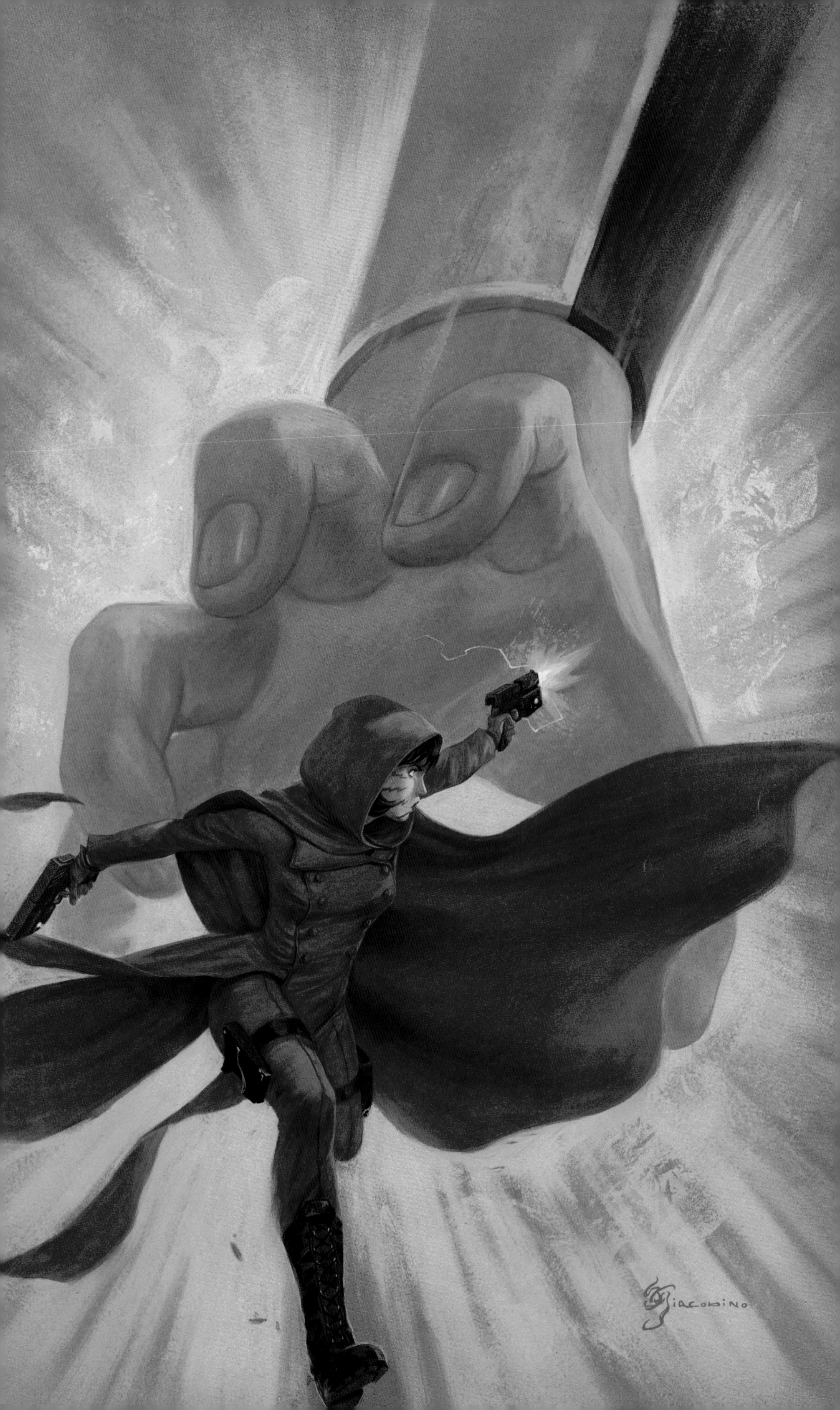

SUNRISE ON THE BATTLEFIELD

RAY FAWKES
writer

IG GUARA
penciller

RUY JOSE
inker

HI-FI
colorist

TRAVIS LANHAM
letterer

cover art by
JULIAN TOTINO TEDESCO

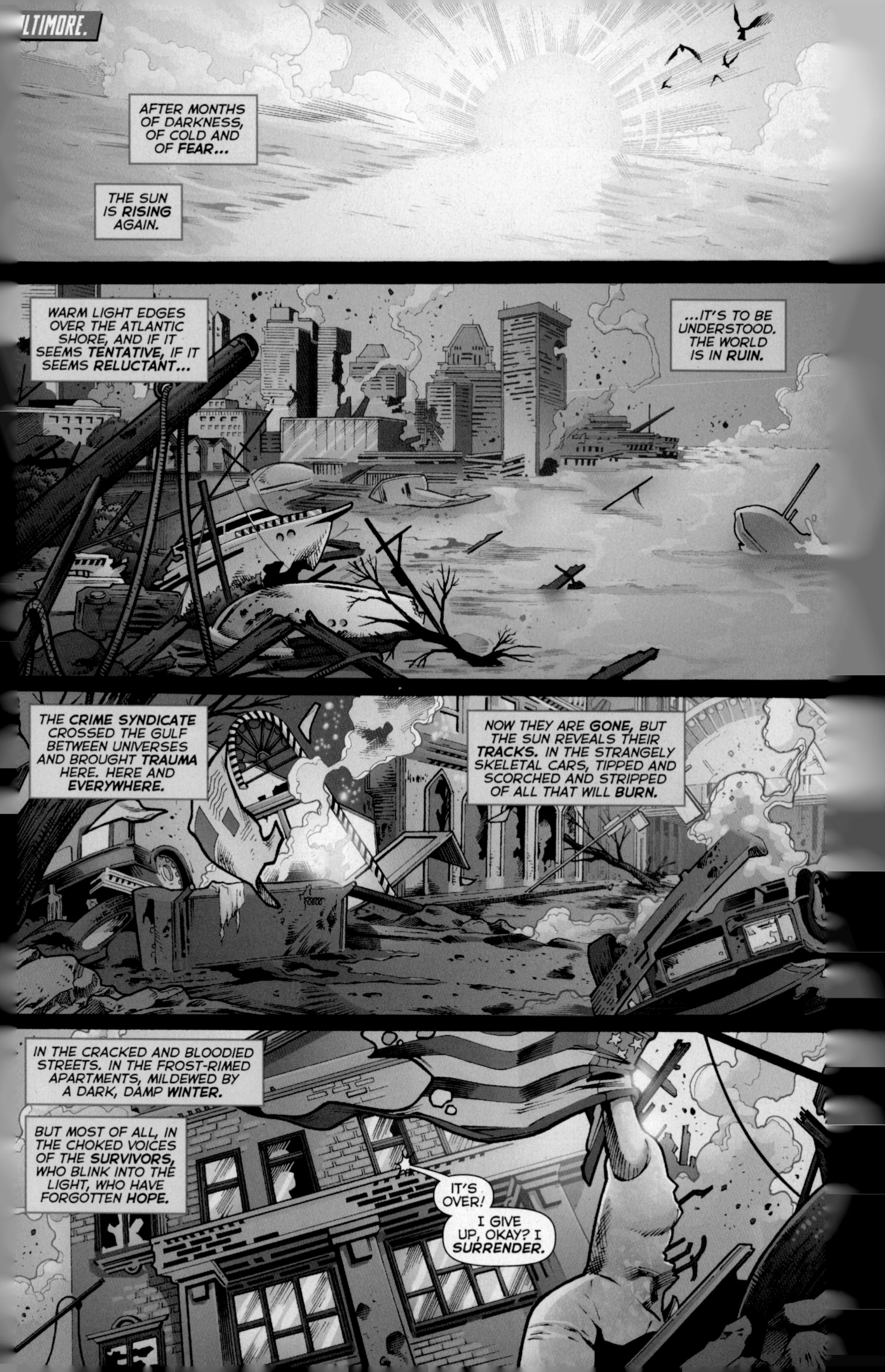
LTIMORE.
AFTER MONTHS OF DARKNESS, OF COLD AND OF FEAR...
THE SUN IS RISING AGAIN.
WARM LIGHT EDGES OVER THE ATLANTIC SHORE, AND IF IT SEEMS TENTATIVE, IF IT SEEMS RELUCTANT...
...IT'S TO BE UNDERSTOOD. THE WORLD IS IN RUIN.
THE CRIME SYNDICATE CROSSED THE GULF BETWEEN UNIVERSES AND BROUGHT TRAUMA HERE. HERE AND EVERYWHERE.
NOW THEY ARE GONE, BUT THE SUN REVEALS THEIR TRACKS. IN THE STRANGELY SKELETAL CARS, TIPPED AND SCORCHED AND STRIPPED OF ALL THAT WILL BURN.
IN THE CRACKED AND BLOODIED STREETS. IN THE FROST-RIMED APARTMENTS, MILDEWED BY A DARK, DAMP WINTER.
BUT MOST OF ALL, IN THE CHOKED VOICES OF THE SURVIVORS, WHO BLINK INTO THE LIGHT, WHO HAVE FORGOTTEN HOPE.
IT'S OVER!
I GIVE UP, OKAY? I SURRENDER.

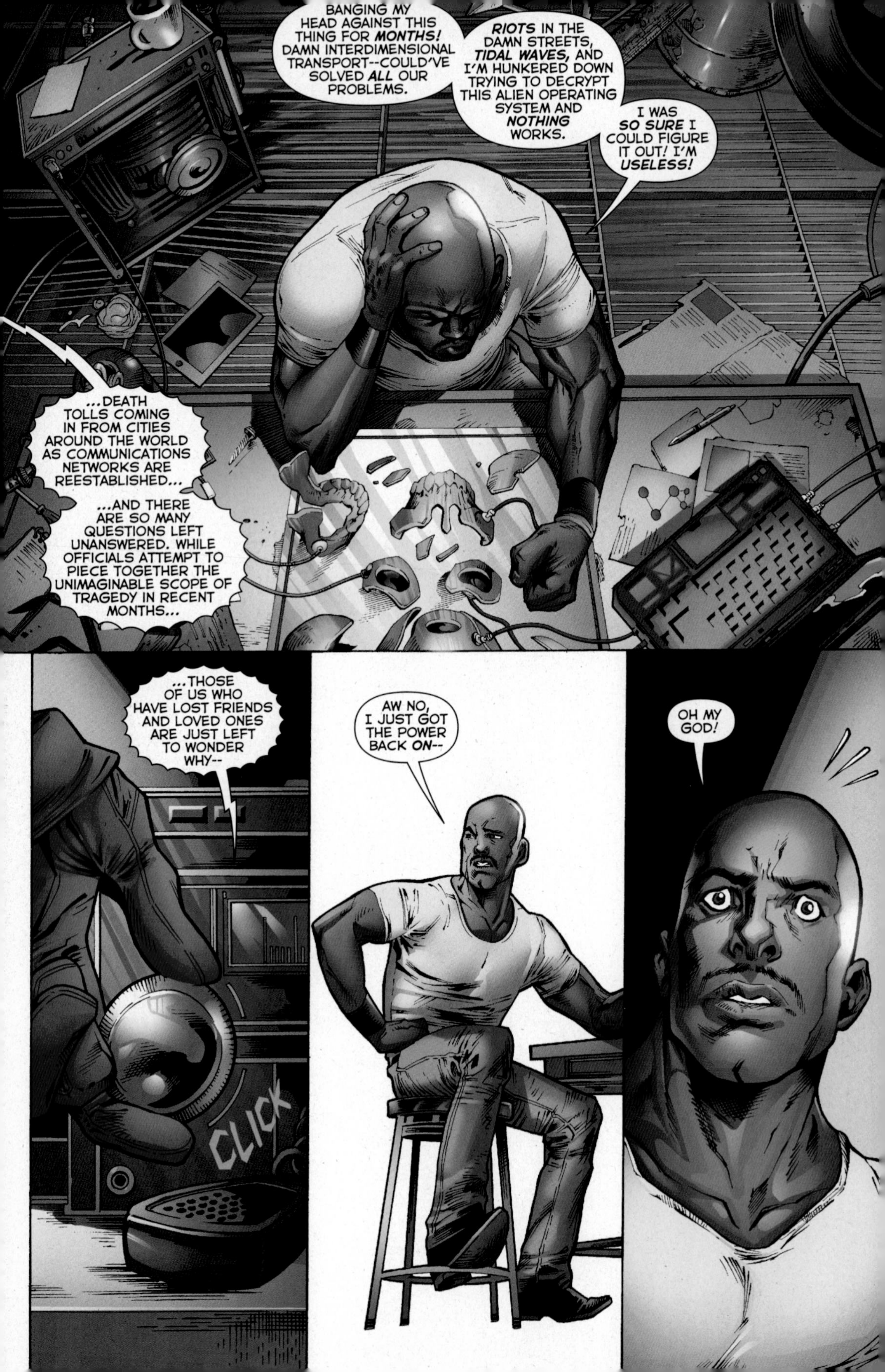
BANGING MY HEAD AGAINST THIS THING FOR MONTHS! DAMN INTERDIMENSIONAL TRANSPORT--COULD'VE SOLVED ALL OUR PROBLEMS.
RIOTS IN THE DAMN STREETS, TIDAL WAVES, AND I'M HUNKERED DOWN TRYING TO DECRYPT THIS ALIEN OPERATING SYSTEM AND NOTHING WORKS.
I WAS SO SURE I COULD FIGURE IT OUT! I'M USELESS!
...DEATH TOLLS COMING IN FROM CITIES AROUND THE WORLD AS COMMUNICATIONS NETWORKS ARE REESTABLISHED...
...AND THERE ARE SO MANY QUESTIONS LEFT UNANSWERED. WHILE OFFICIALS ATTEMPT TO PIECE TOGETHER THE UNIMAGINABLE SCOPE OF TRAGEDY IN RECENT MONTHS...
...THOSE OF US WHO HAVE LOST FRIENDS AND LOVED ONES ARE JUST LEFT TO WONDER WHY--
CLICK
AW NO, I JUST GOT THE POWER BACK ON--
OH MY GOD!

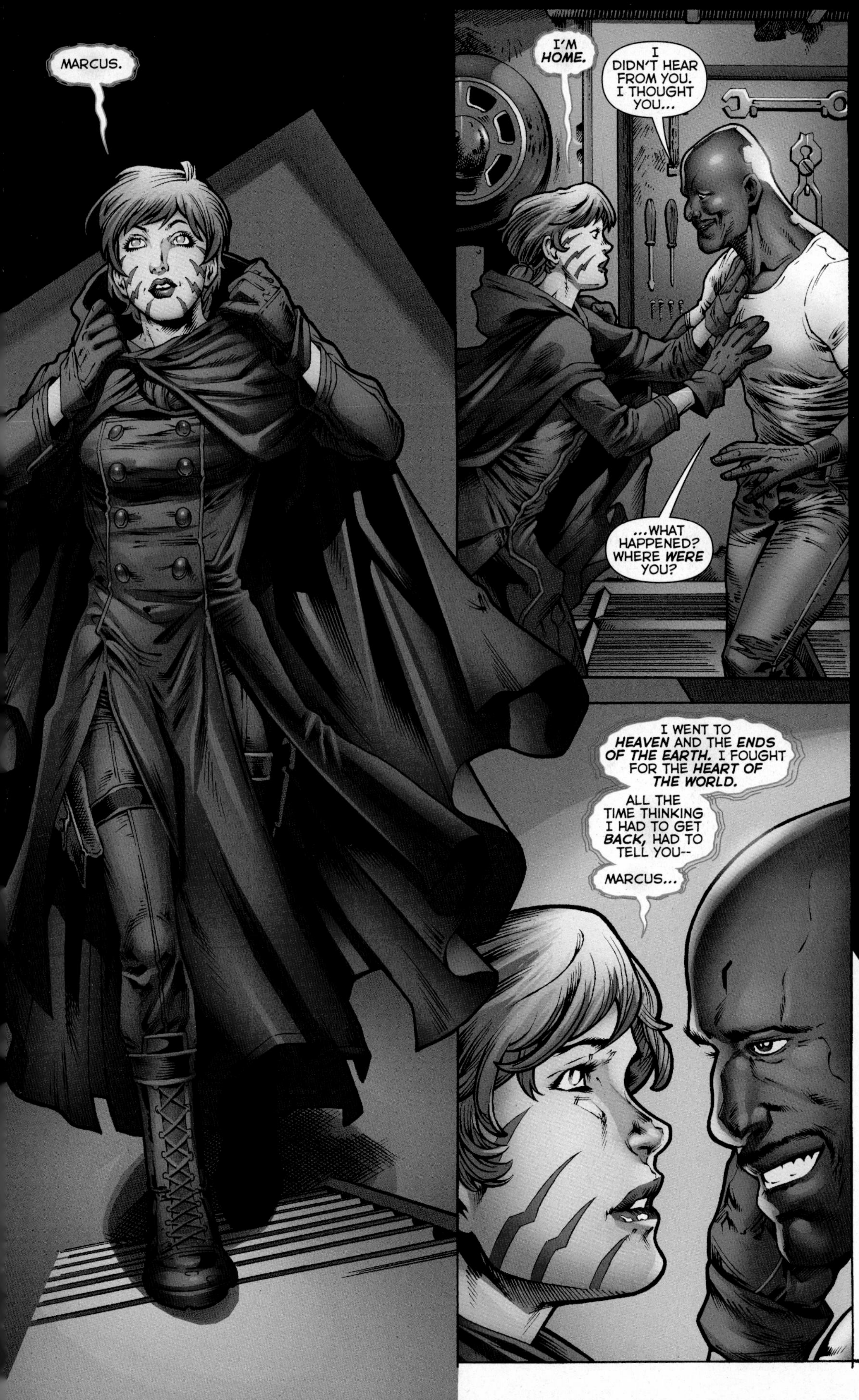
MARCUS.
I'M HOME.
I DIDN'T HEAR FROM YOU. I THOUGHT YOU...
...WHAT HAPPENED? WHERE WERE YOU?
I WENT TO HEAVEN AND THE ENDS OF THE EARTH. I FOUGHT FOR THE HEART OF THE WORLD.
ALL THE TIME THINKING I HAD TO GET BACK, HAD TO TELL YOU--
MARCUS...

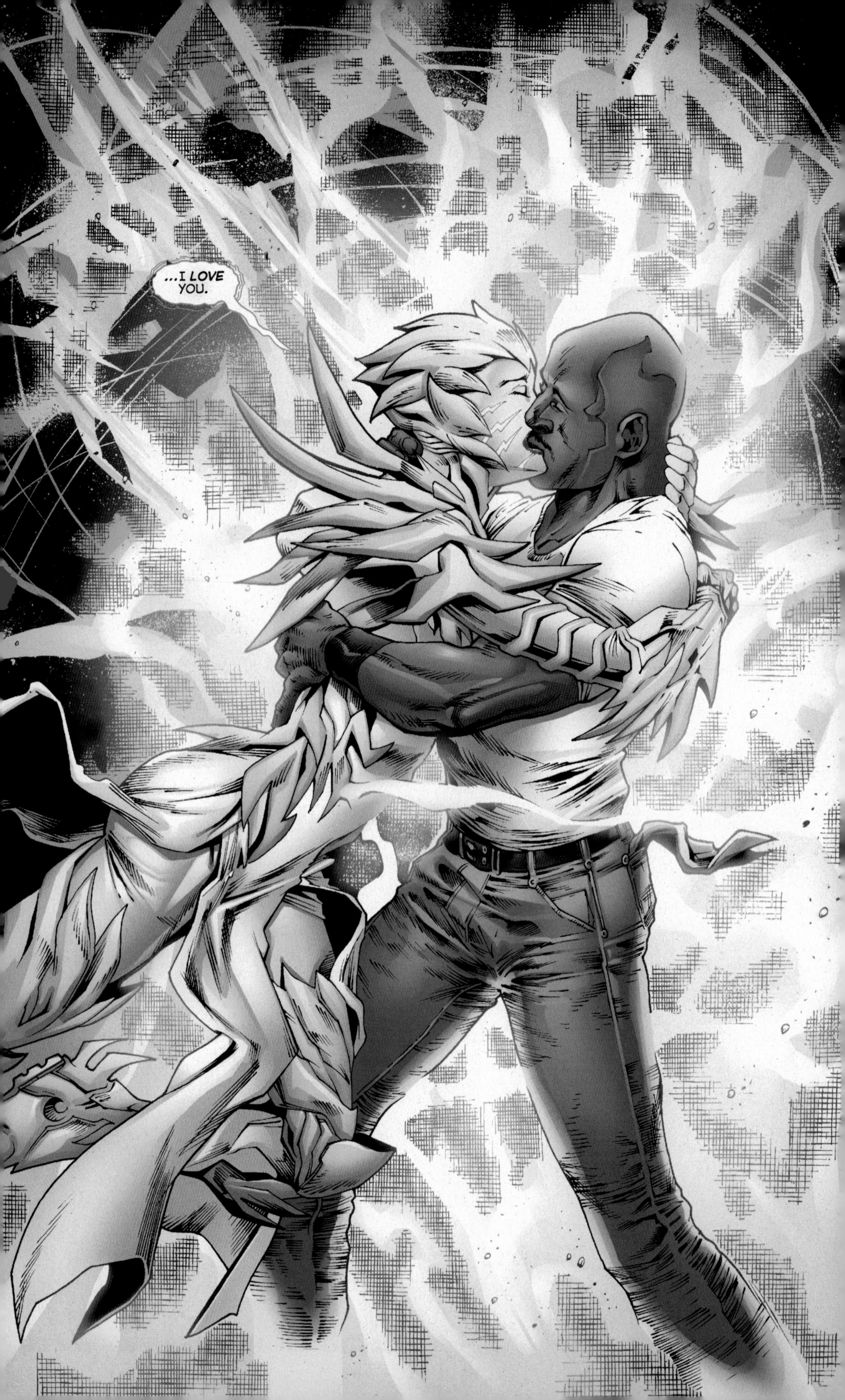
...I LOVE YOU.

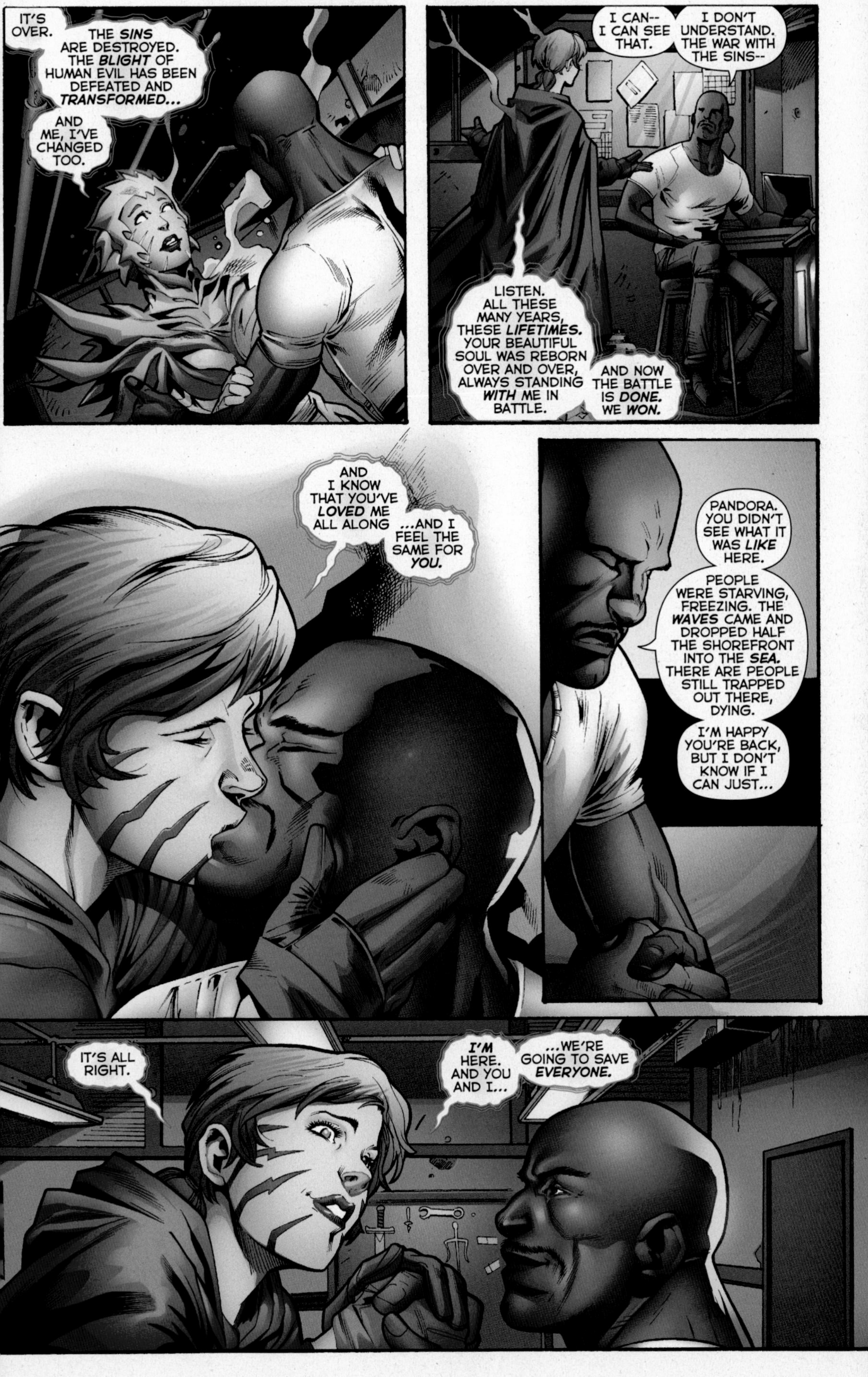
IT'S OVER.
THE SINS ARE DESTROYED. THE BLIGHT OF HUMAN EVIL HAS BEEN DEFEATED AND TRANSFORMED...
AND ME, I'VE CHANGED TOO.
I CAN-- I CAN SEE THAT.
I DON'T UNDERSTAND. THE WAR WITH THE SINS--
LISTEN. ALL THESE MANY YEARS, THESE LIFETIMES. YOUR BEAUTIFUL SOUL WAS REBORN OVER AND OVER, ALWAYS STANDING WITH ME IN BATTLE.
AND NOW THE BATTLE IS DONE. WE WON.
AND I KNOW THAT YOU'VE LOVED ME ALL ALONG
...AND I FEEL THE SAME FOR YOU.
PANDORA. YOU DIDN'T SEE WHAT IT WAS LIKE HERE.
PEOPLE WERE STARVING, FREEZING. THE WAVES CAME AND DROPPED HALF THE SHOREFRONT INTO THE SEA. THERE ARE PEOPLE STILL TRAPPED OUT THERE, DYING.
I'M HAPPY YOU'RE BACK, BUT I DON'T KNOW IF I CAN JUST...
IT'S ALL RIGHT.
I'M HERE. AND YOU AND I...
...WE'RE GOING TO SAVE EVERYONE.

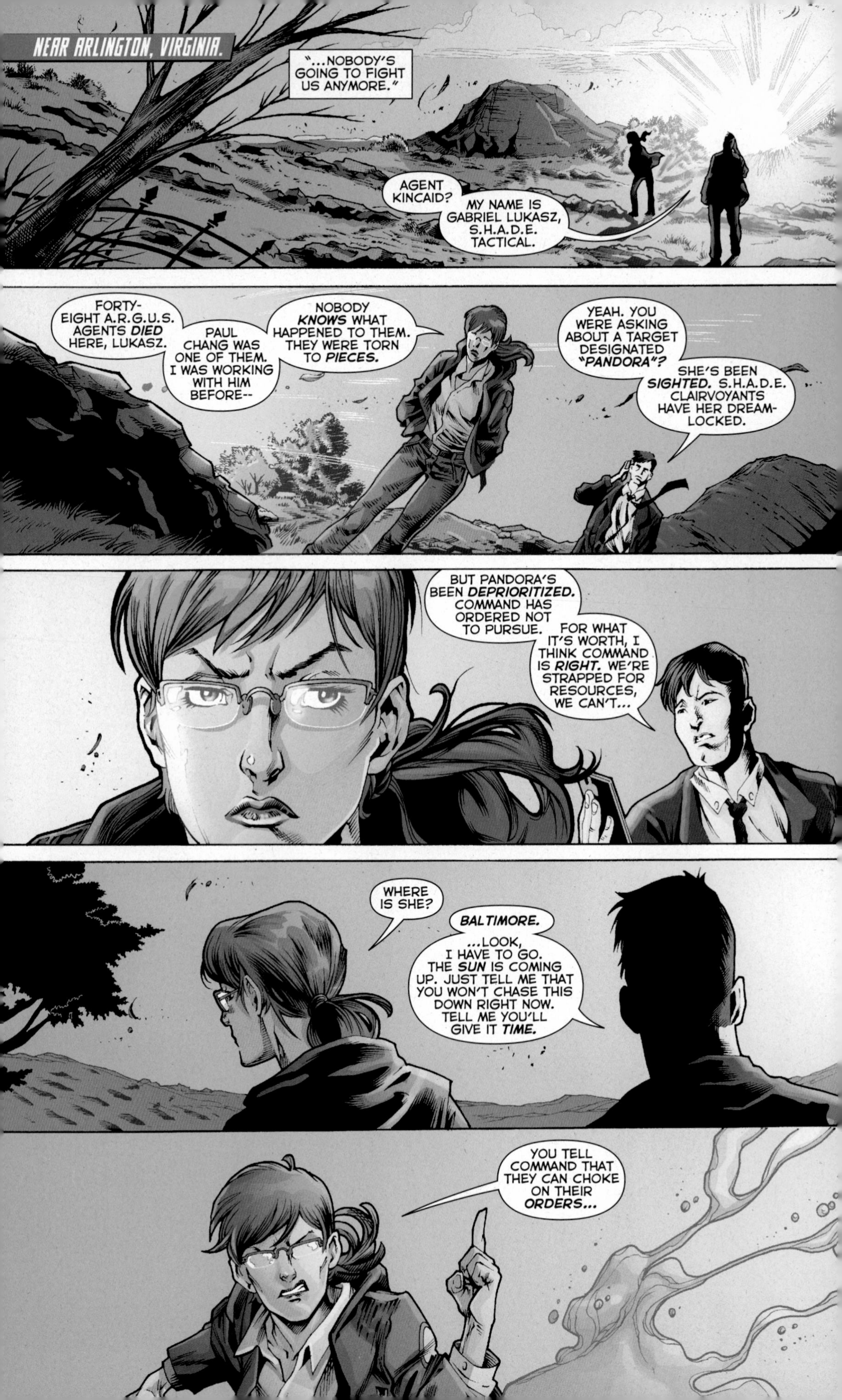

NEAR ARLINGTON, VIRGINIA.
"...NOBODY'S GOING TO FIGHT US ANYMORE."
AGENT KINCAID?
MY NAME IS GABRIEL LUKASZ, S.H.A.D.E. TACTICAL.
FORTY-EIGHT A.R.G.U.S. AGENTS DIED HERE, LUKASZ.
PAUL CHANG WAS ONE OF THEM. I WAS WORKING WITH HIM BEFORE--
NOBODY KNOWS WHAT HAPPENED TO THEM. THEY WERE TORN TO PIECES.
YEAH. YOU WERE ASKING ABOUT A TARGET DESIGNATED "PANDORA"?
SHE'S BEEN SIGHTED. S.H.A.D.E. CLAIRVOYANTS HAVE HER DREAM-LOCKED.
BUT PANDORA'S BEEN DEPRIORITIZED. COMMAND HAS ORDERED NOT TO PURSUE.
FOR WHAT IT'S WORTH, I THINK COMMAND IS RIGHT. WE'RE STRAPPED FOR RESOURCES, WE CAN'T...
WHERE IS SHE?
BALTIMORE.
...LOOK, I HAVE TO GO. THE SUN IS COMING UP. JUST TELL ME THAT YOU WON'T CHASE THIS DOWN RIGHT NOW. TELL ME YOU'LL GIVE IT TIME.
YOU TELL COMMAND THAT THEY CAN CHOKE ON THEIR ORDERS...

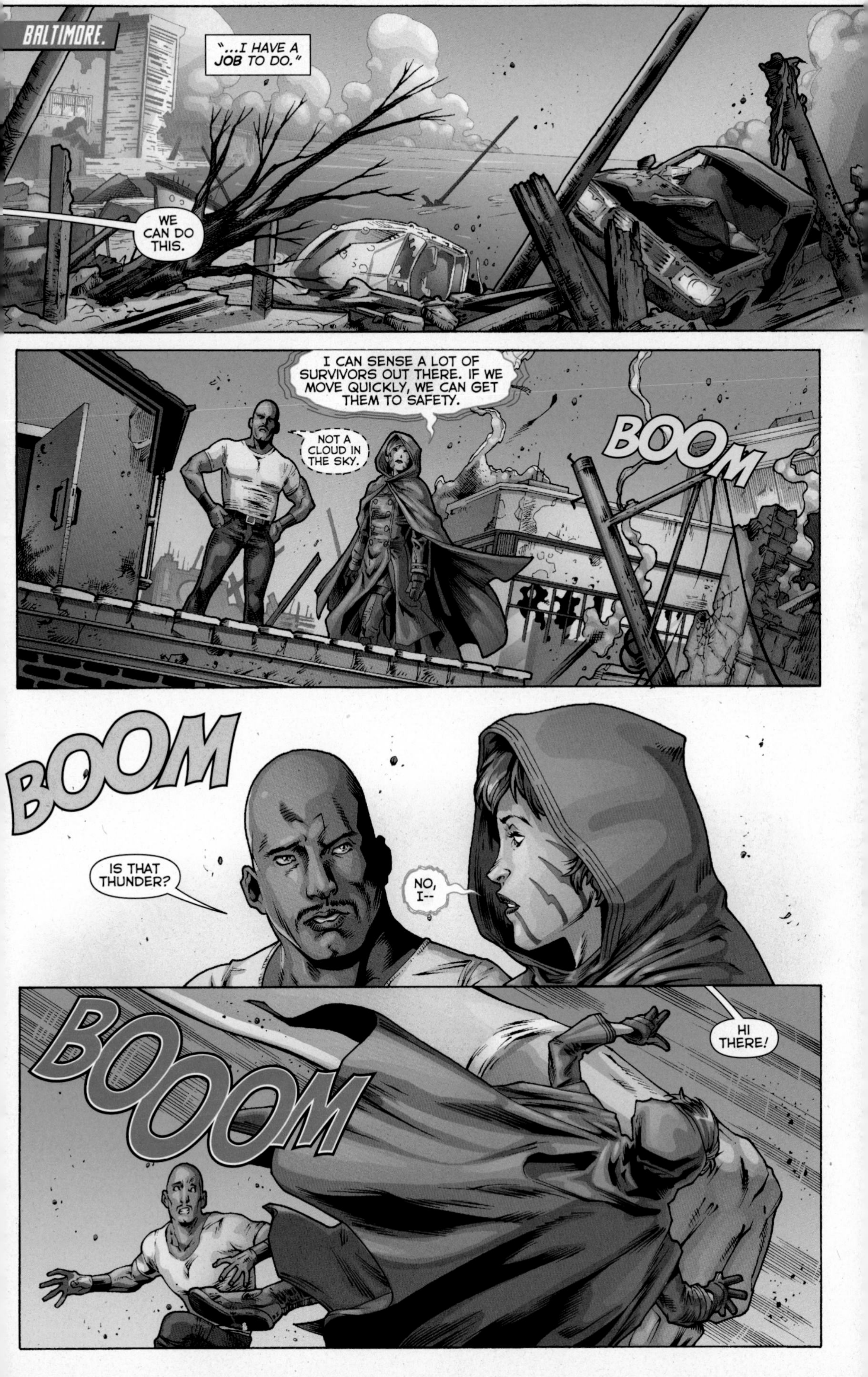
BALTIMORE.
"...I HAVE A JOB TO DO."
WE CAN DO THIS.
I CAN SENSE A LOT OF SURVIVORS OUT THERE. IF WE MOVE QUICKLY, WE CAN GET THEM TO SAFETY.
NOT A CLOUD IN THE SKY.
BOOM
BOOM
IS THAT THUNDER?
NO, I--
BOOOM
HI THERE!

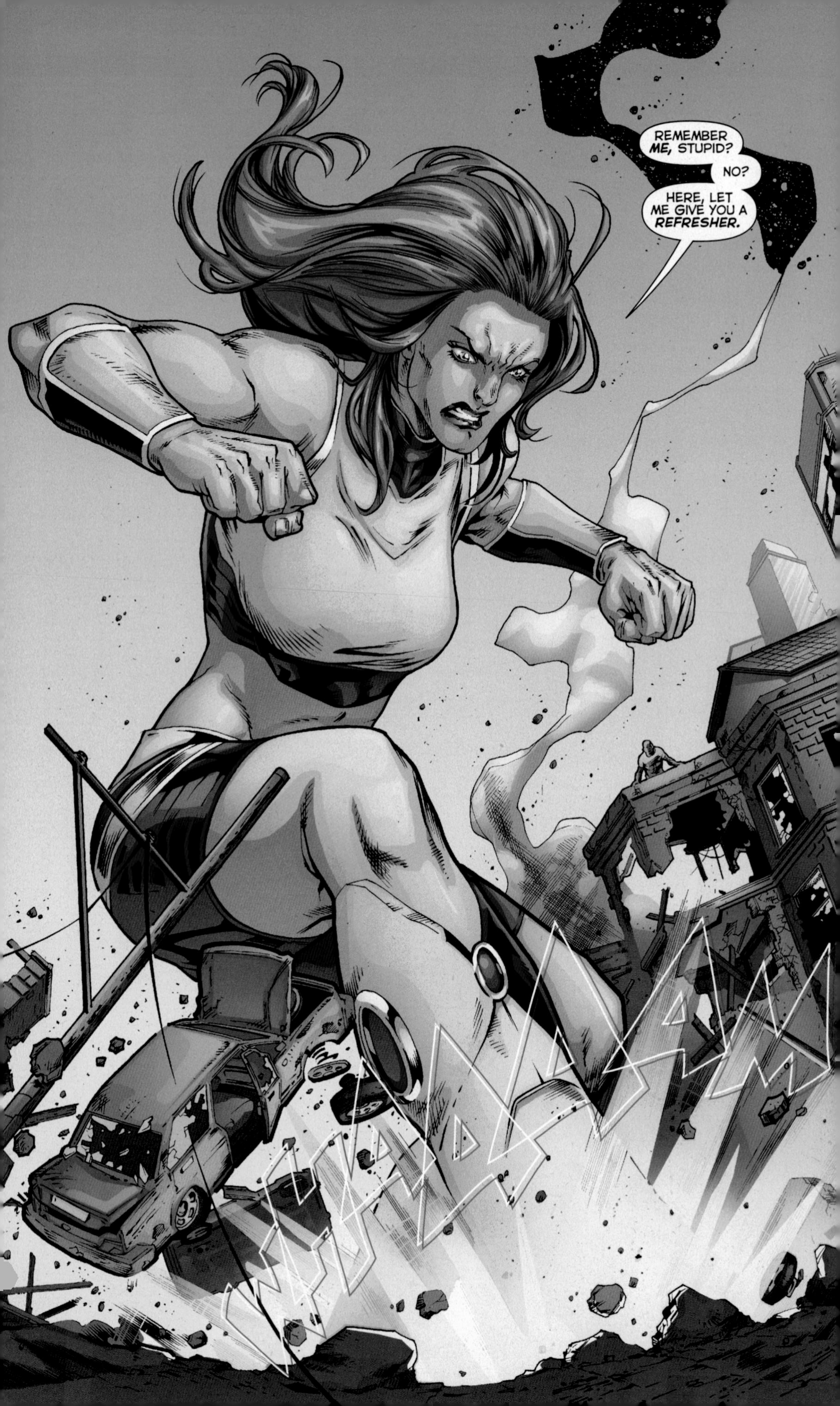
REMEMBER ME, STUPID?
NO?
HERE, LET ME GIVE YOU A REFRESHER.

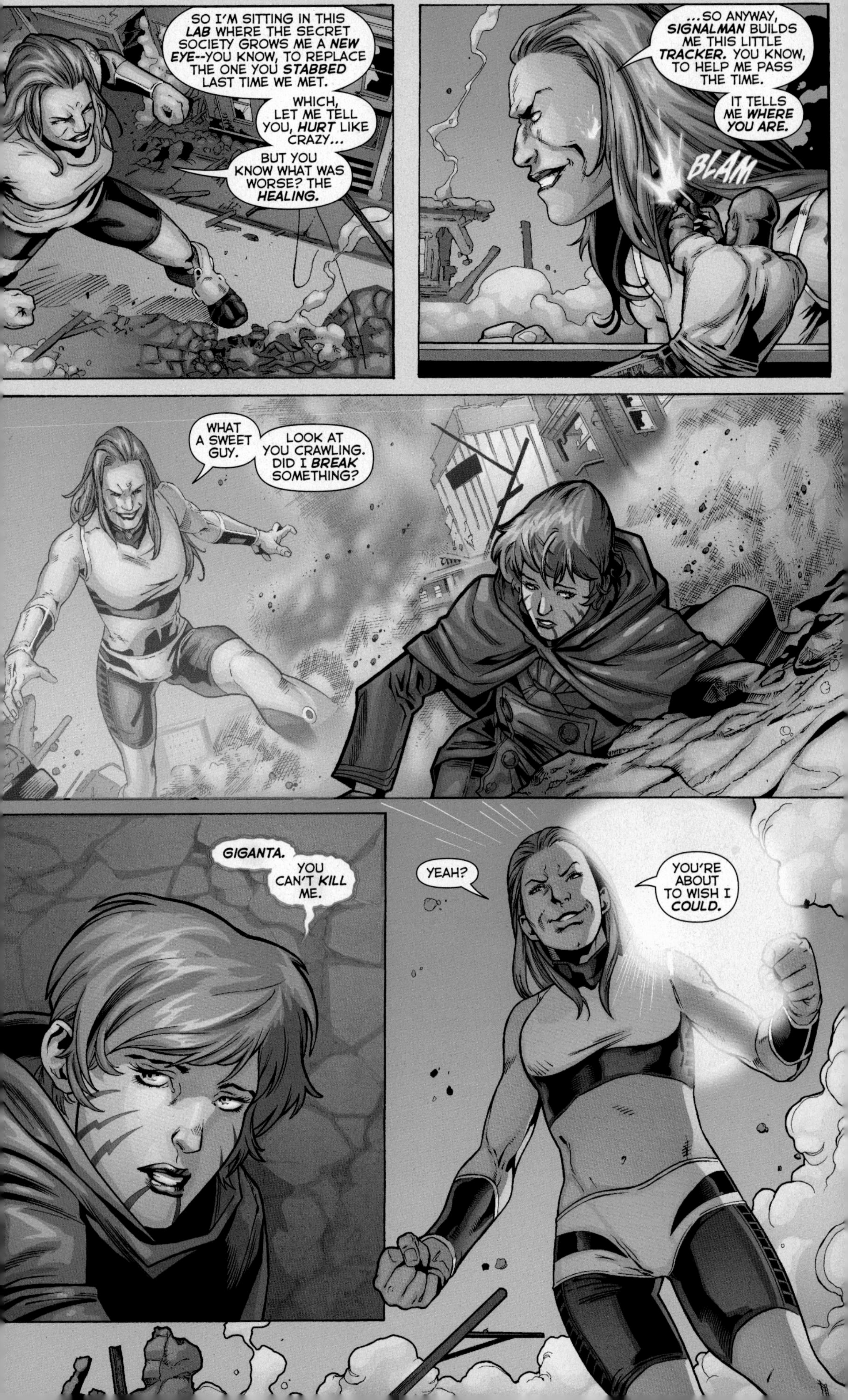
SO I'M SITTING IN THIS LAB WHERE THE SECRET SOCIETY GROWS ME A NEW EYE--YOU KNOW, TO REPLACE THE ONE YOU STABBED LAST TIME WE MET.
WHICH, LET ME TELL YOU, HURT LIKE CRAZY...
BUT YOU KNOW WHAT WAS WORSE? THE HEALING.
...SO ANYWAY, SIGNALMAN BUILDS ME THIS LITTLE TRACKER. YOU KNOW, TO HELP ME PASS THE TIME.
IT TELLS ME WHERE YOU ARE.
BLAM
WHAT A SWEET GUY.
LOOK AT YOU CRAWLING. DID I BREAK SOMETHING?
GIGANTA.
YOU CAN'T KILL ME.
YEAH?
YOU'RE ABOUT TO WISH I COULD.

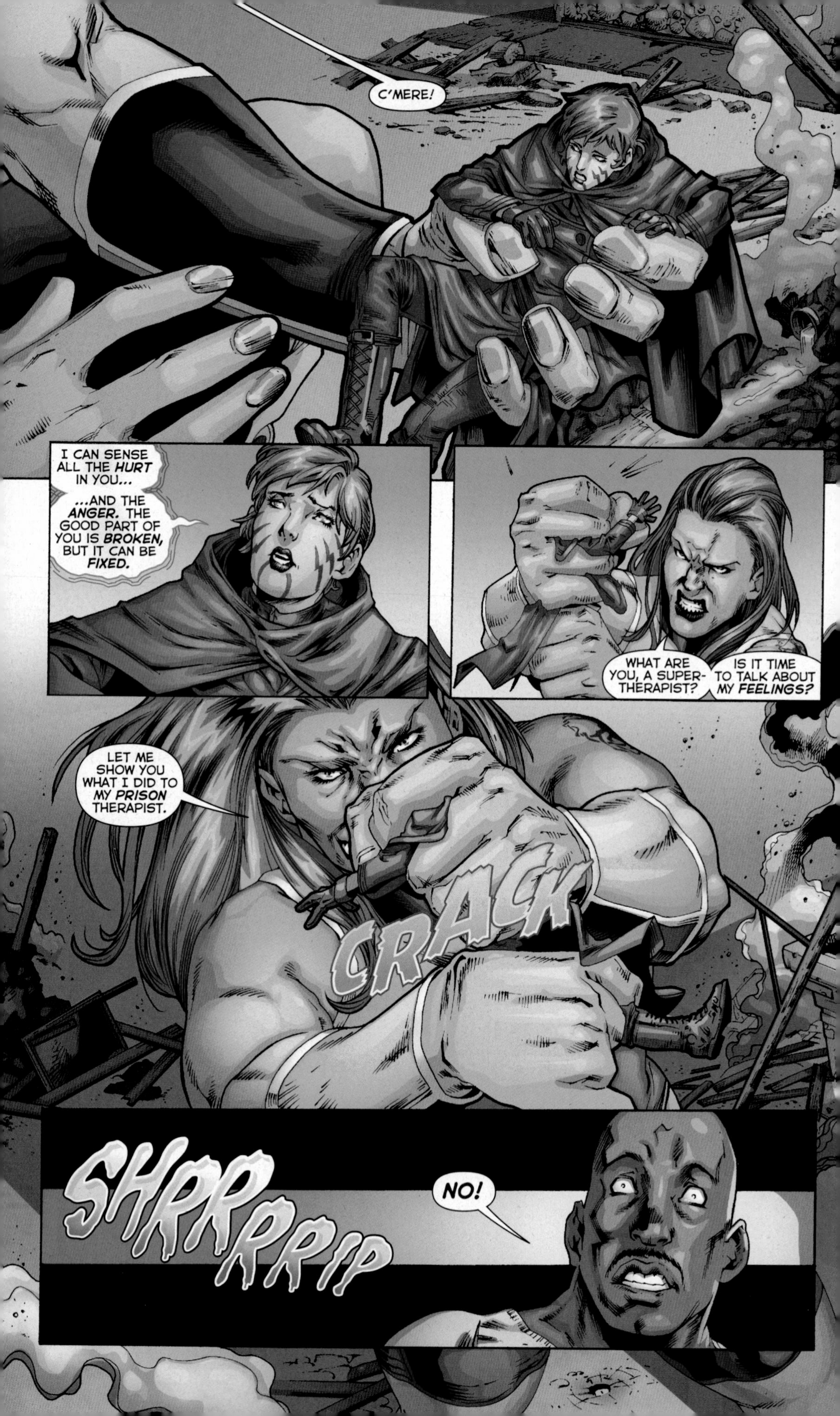
C'MERE!
I CAN SENSE ALL THE *HURT* IN YOU...
...AND THE *ANGER.* THE GOOD PART OF YOU IS *BROKEN,* BUT IT CAN BE *FIXED.*
WHAT ARE YOU, A SUPER-THERAPIST?
IS IT TIME TO TALK ABOUT MY *FEELINGS?*
LET ME SHOW YOU WHAT I DID TO MY *PRISON* THERAPIST.
CRACK
SHRRRRIP
NO!

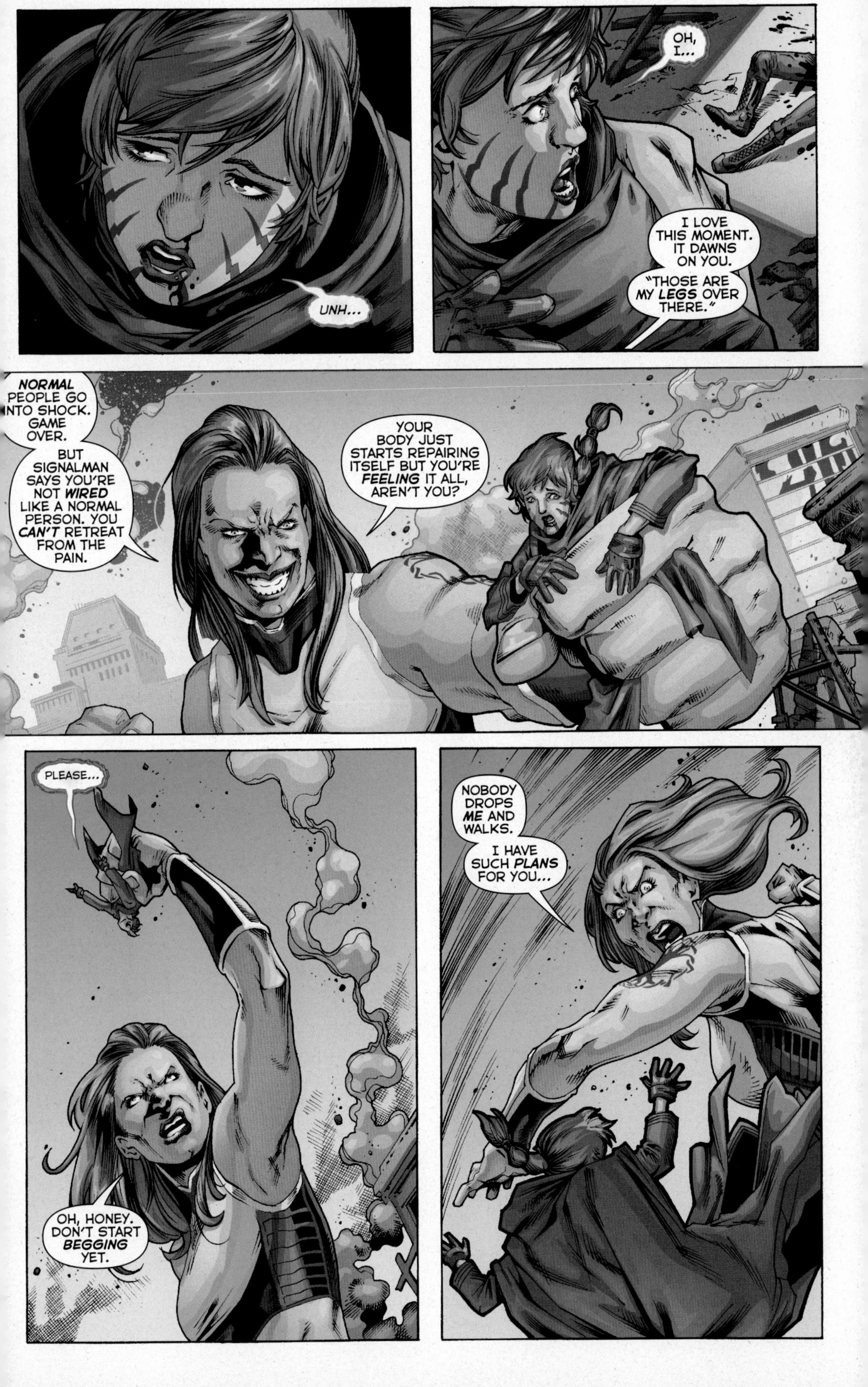

UNH...
OH, I...
I LOVE THIS MOMENT. IT DAWNS ON YOU.
"THOSE ARE MY LEGS OVER THERE."
NORMAL PEOPLE GO INTO SHOCK. GAME OVER.
BUT SIGNALMAN SAYS YOU'RE NOT WIRED LIKE A NORMAL PERSON. YOU CAN'T RETREAT FROM THE PAIN.
YOUR BODY JUST STARTS REPAIRING ITSELF BUT YOU'RE FEELING IT ALL, AREN'T YOU?
PLEASE...
OH, HONEY. DON'T START BEGGING YET.
NOBODY DROPS ME AND WALKS.
I HAVE SUCH PLANS FOR YOU...

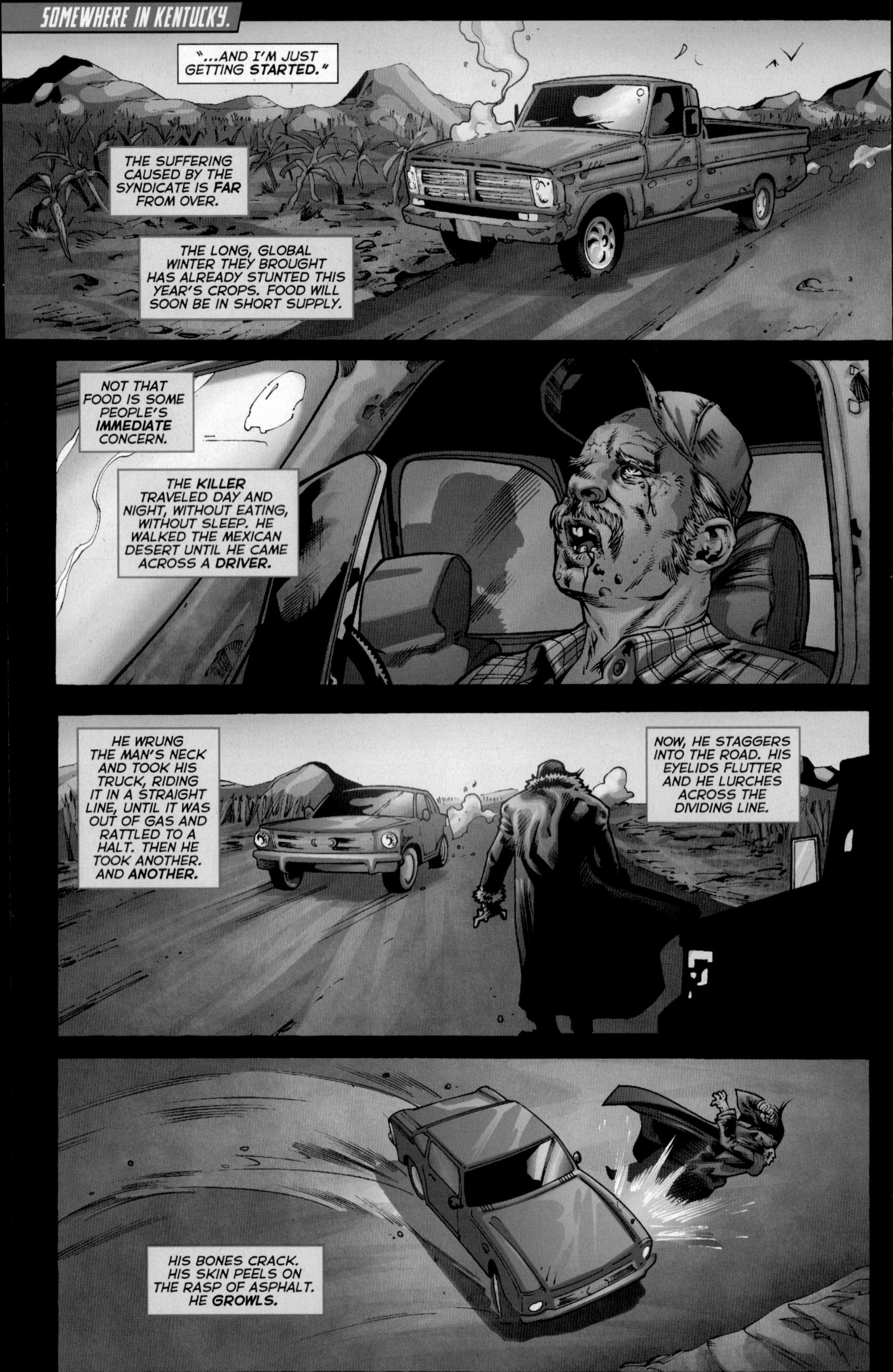
SOMEWHERE IN KENTUCKY.
"...AND I'M JUST GETTING STARTED."
THE SUFFERING CAUSED BY THE SYNDICATE IS FAR FROM OVER.
THE LONG, GLOBAL WINTER THEY BROUGHT HAS ALREADY STUNTED THIS YEAR'S CROPS. FOOD WILL SOON BE IN SHORT SUPPLY.
NOT THAT FOOD IS SOME PEOPLE'S IMMEDIATE CONCERN.
THE KILLER TRAVELED DAY AND NIGHT, WITHOUT EATING, WITHOUT SLEEP. HE WALKED THE MEXICAN DESERT UNTIL HE CAME ACROSS A DRIVER.
HE WRUNG THE MAN'S NECK AND TOOK HIS TRUCK, RIDING IT IN A STRAIGHT LINE, UNTIL IT WAS OUT OF GAS AND RATTLED TO A HALT. THEN HE TOOK ANOTHER. AND ANOTHER.
NOW, HE STAGGERS INTO THE ROAD. HIS EYELIDS FLUTTER AND HE LURCHES ACROSS THE DIVIDING LINE.
HIS BONES CRACK. HIS SKIN PEELS ON THE RASP OF ASPHALT. HE GROWLS.

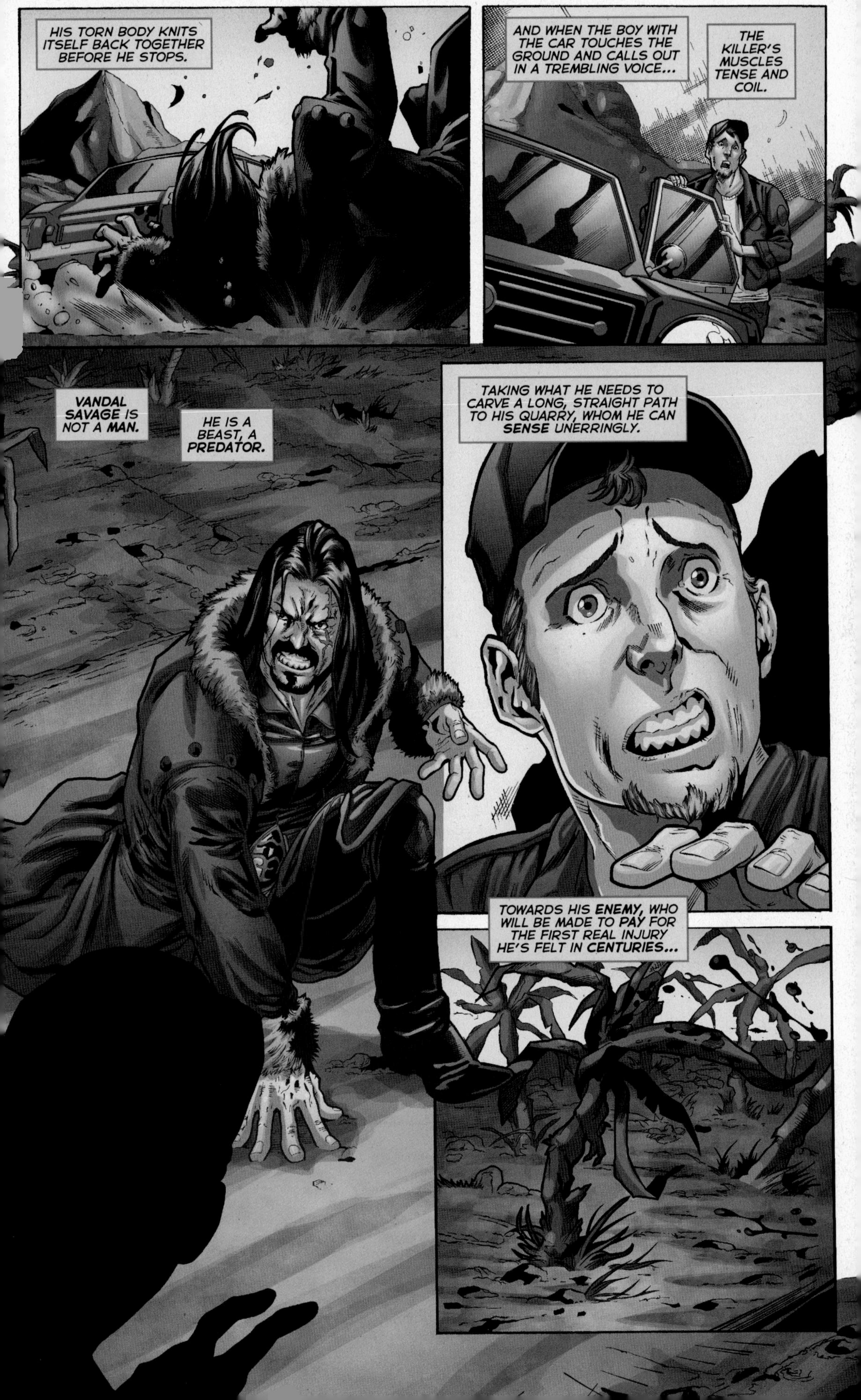
HIS TORN BODY KNITS ITSELF BACK TOGETHER BEFORE HE STOPS.
AND WHEN THE BOY WITH THE CAR TOUCHES THE GROUND AND CALLS OUT IN A TREMBLING VOICE...
THE KILLER'S MUSCLES TENSE AND COIL.
VANDAL SAVAGE IS NOT A MAN.
HE IS A BEAST, A PREDATOR.
TAKING WHAT HE NEEDS TO CARVE A LONG, STRAIGHT PATH TO HIS QUARRY, WHOM HE CAN SENSE UNERRINGLY.
TOWARDS HIS ENEMY, WHO WILL BE MADE TO PAY FOR THE FIRST REAL INJURY HE'S FELT IN CENTURIES...

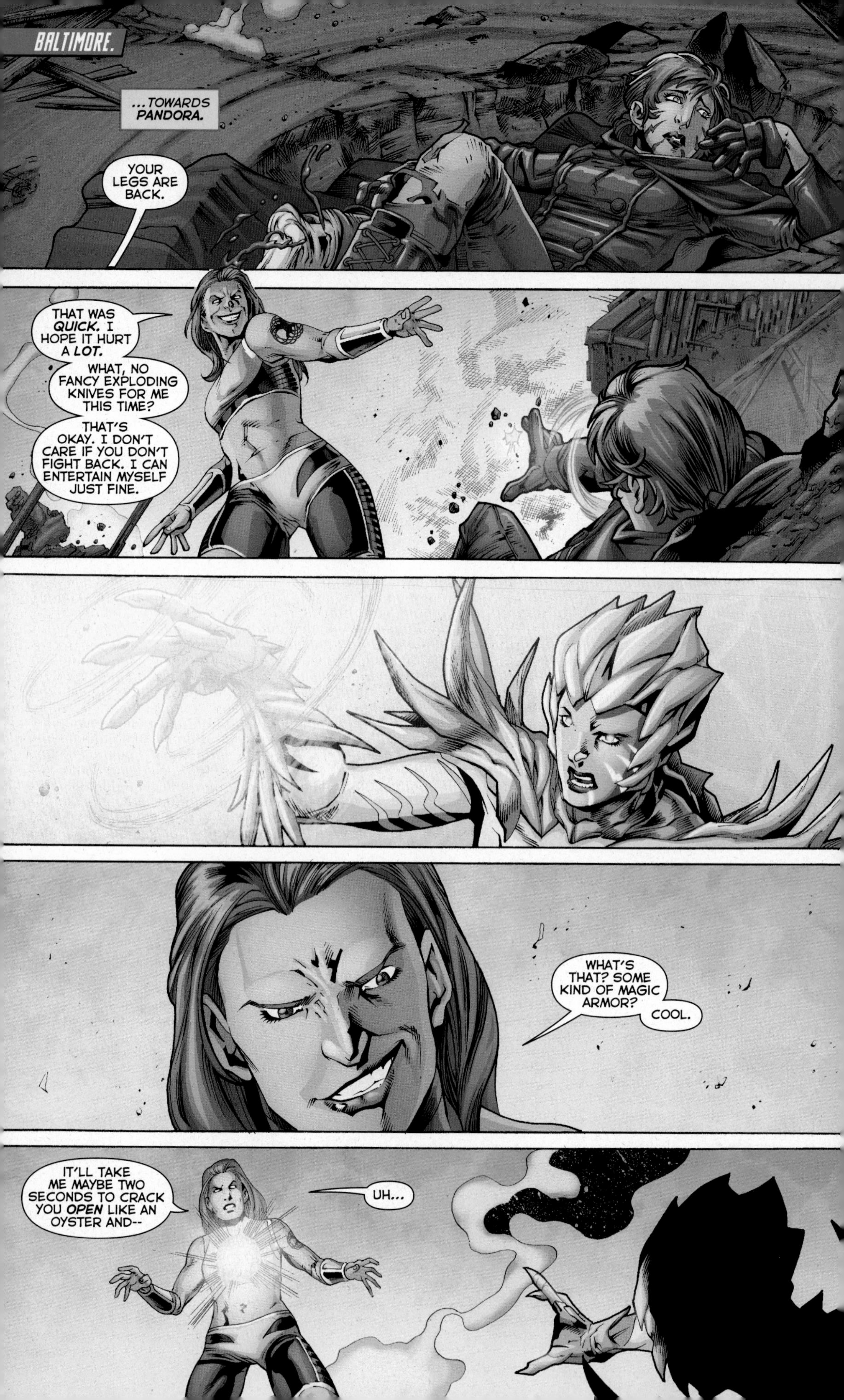

BALTIMORE.
...TOWARDS PANDORA.
YOUR LEGS ARE BACK.
THAT WAS QUICK. I HOPE IT HURT A LOT.
WHAT, NO FANCY EXPLODING KNIVES FOR ME THIS TIME?
THAT'S OKAY. I DON'T CARE IF YOU DON'T FIGHT BACK. I CAN ENTERTAIN MYSELF JUST FINE.
WHAT'S THAT? SOME KIND OF MAGIC ARMOR?
COOL.
IT'LL TAKE ME MAYBE TWO SECONDS TO CRACK YOU OPEN LIKE AN OYSTER AND--
UH...

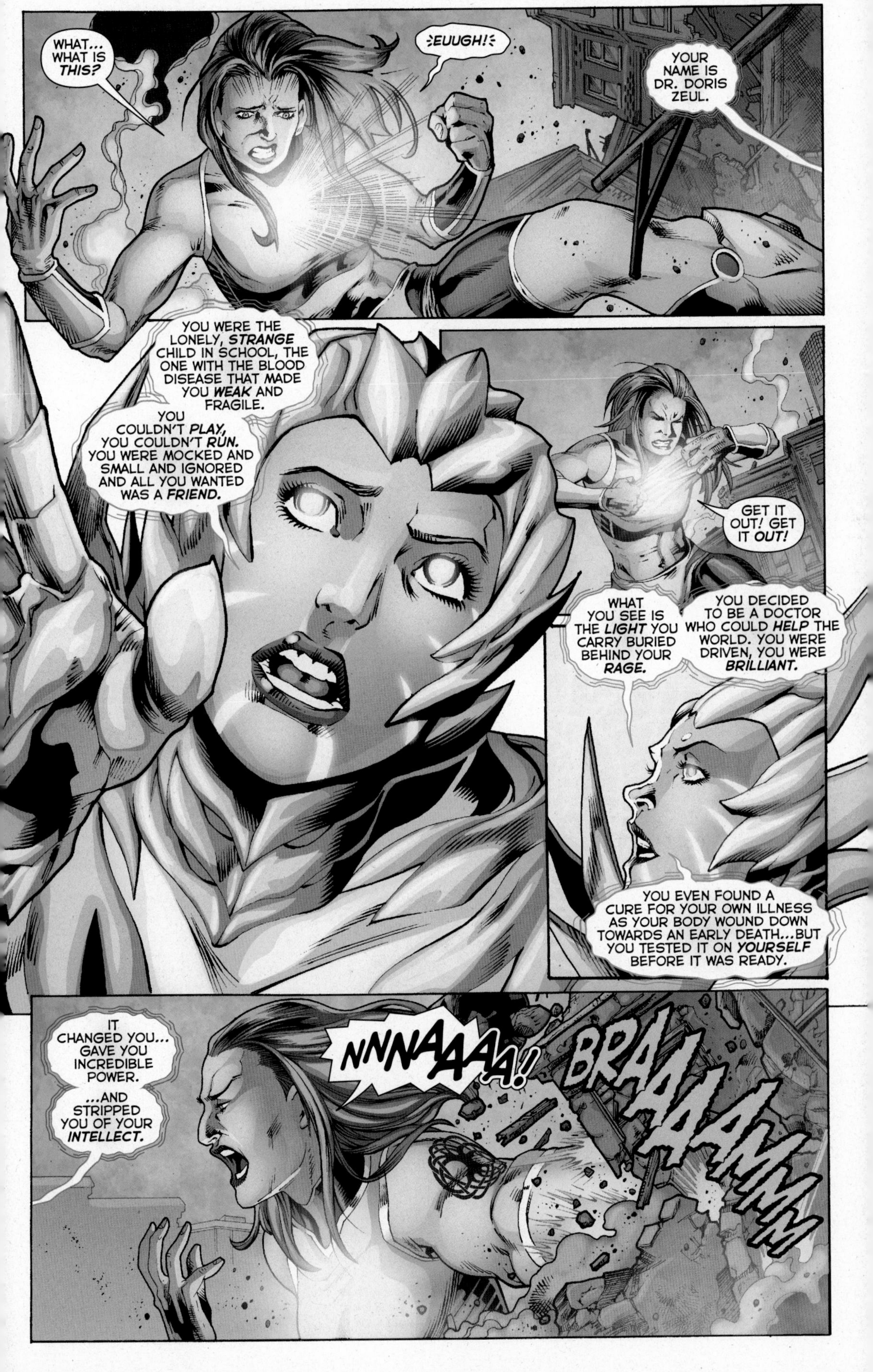

WHAT... WHAT IS THIS?
EUUGH!
YOUR NAME IS DR. DORIS ZEUL.
YOU WERE THE LONELY, STRANGE CHILD IN SCHOOL, THE ONE WITH THE BLOOD DISEASE THAT MADE YOU WEAK AND FRAGILE.
YOU COULDN'T PLAY, YOU COULDN'T RUN. YOU WERE MOCKED AND SMALL AND IGNORED AND ALL YOU WANTED WAS A FRIEND.
GET IT OUT! GET IT OUT!
WHAT YOU SEE IS THE LIGHT YOU CARRY BURIED BEHIND YOUR RAGE.
YOU DECIDED TO BE A DOCTOR WHO COULD HELP THE WORLD. YOU WERE DRIVEN, YOU WERE BRILLIANT.
YOU EVEN FOUND A CURE FOR YOUR OWN ILLNESS AS YOUR BODY WOUND DOWN TOWARDS AN EARLY DEATH...BUT YOU TESTED IT ON YOURSELF BEFORE IT WAS READY.
IT CHANGED YOU... GAVE YOU INCREDIBLE POWER.
...AND STRIPPED YOU OF YOUR INTELLECT.
NNNAAAAA!
BRAAAAMM

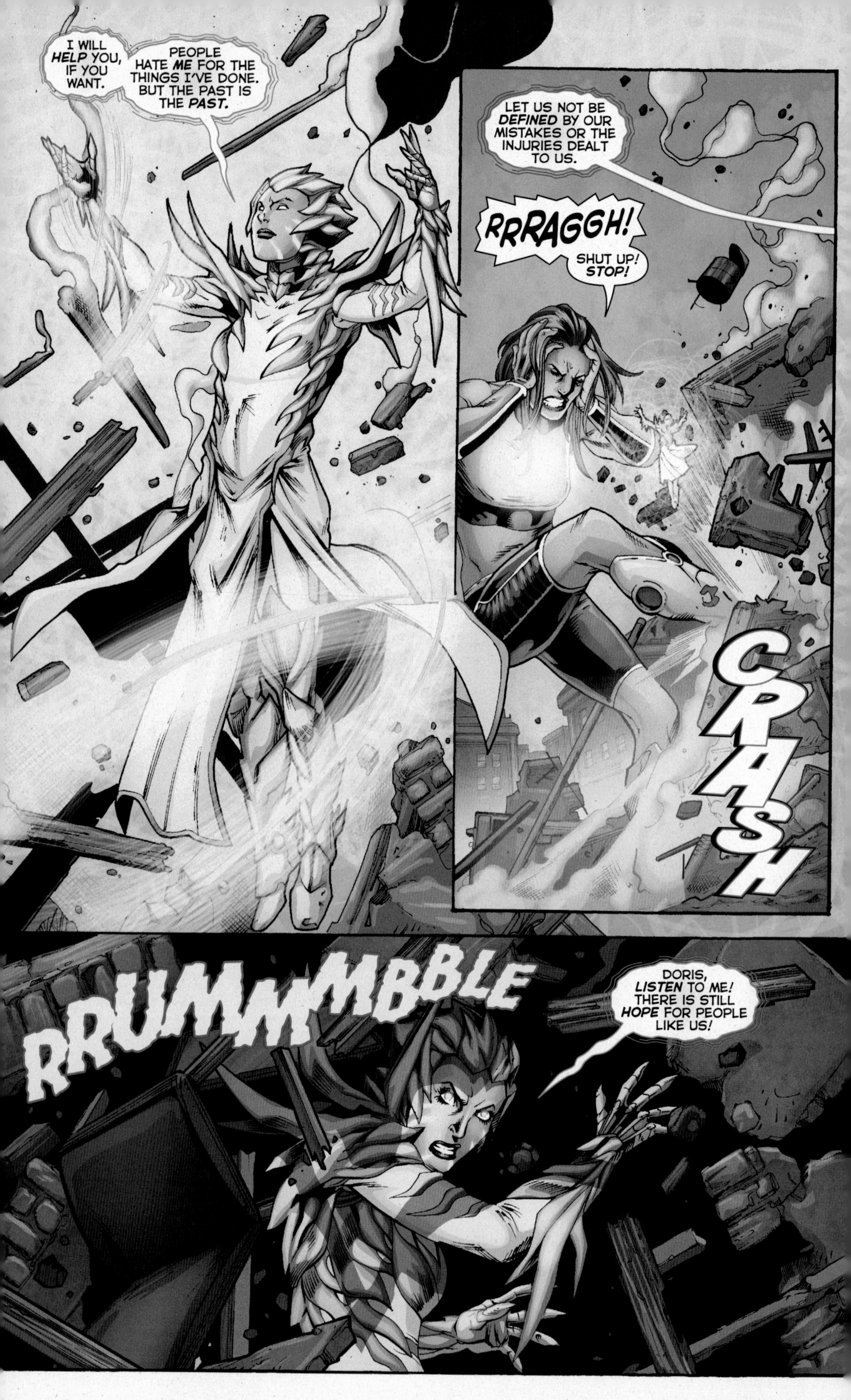
I WILL HELP YOU, IF YOU WANT.
PEOPLE HATE ME FOR THE THINGS I'VE DONE. BUT THE PAST IS THE PAST.
LET US NOT BE DEFINED BY OUR MISTAKES OR THE INJURIES DEALT TO US.
RRRAGGH!
SHUT UP! STOP!
CRASH
RRUMMMBBLE
DORIS, LISTEN TO ME! THERE IS STILL HOPE FOR PEOPLE LIKE US!

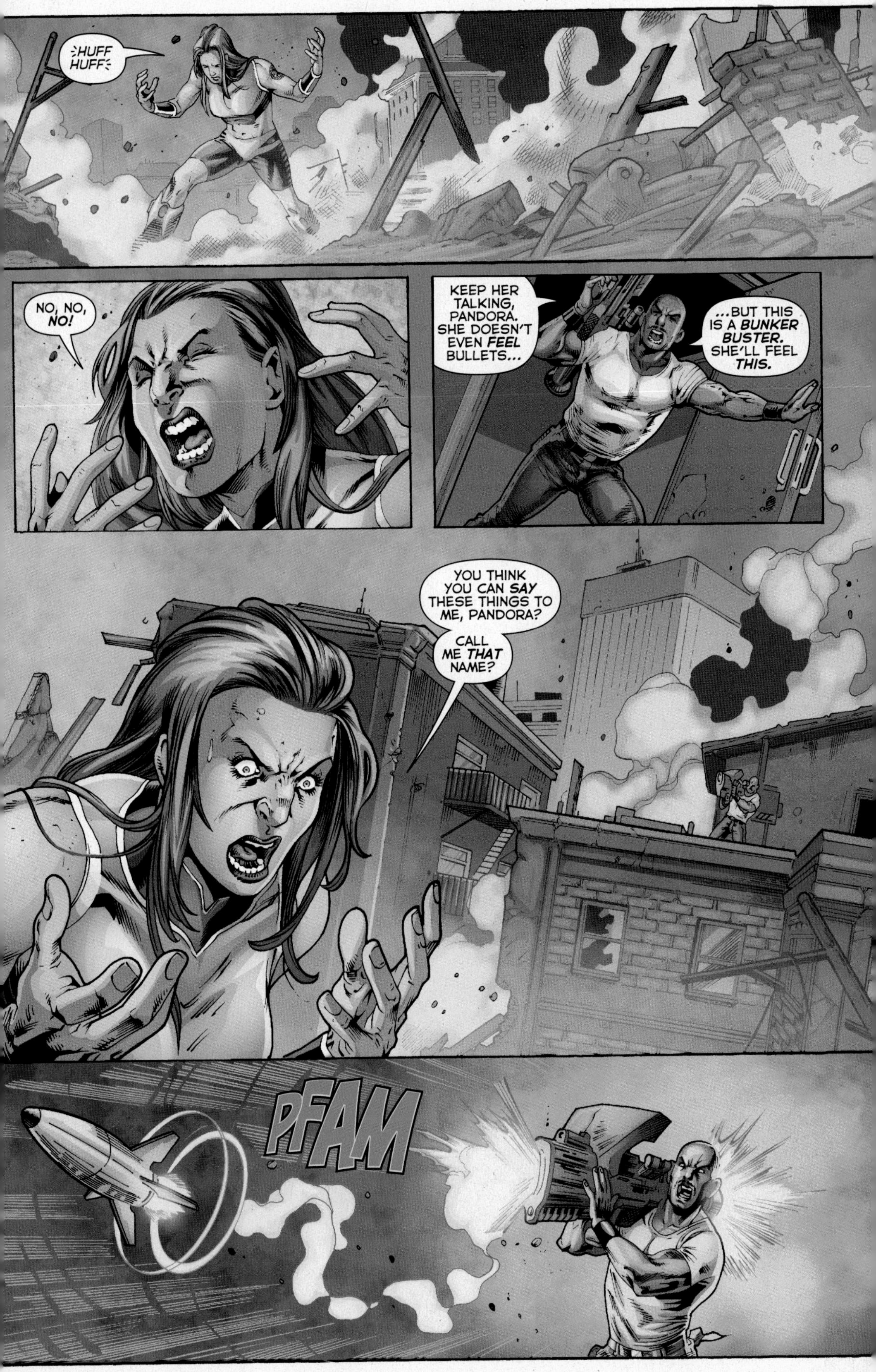
HUFF HUFF
NO, NO, NO!
KEEP HER TALKING, PANDORA. SHE DOESN'T EVEN FEEL BULLETS...
...BUT THIS IS A BUNKER BUSTER. SHE'LL FEEL THIS.
YOU THINK YOU CAN SAY THESE THINGS TO ME, PANDORA?
CALL ME THAT NAME?
PFAM

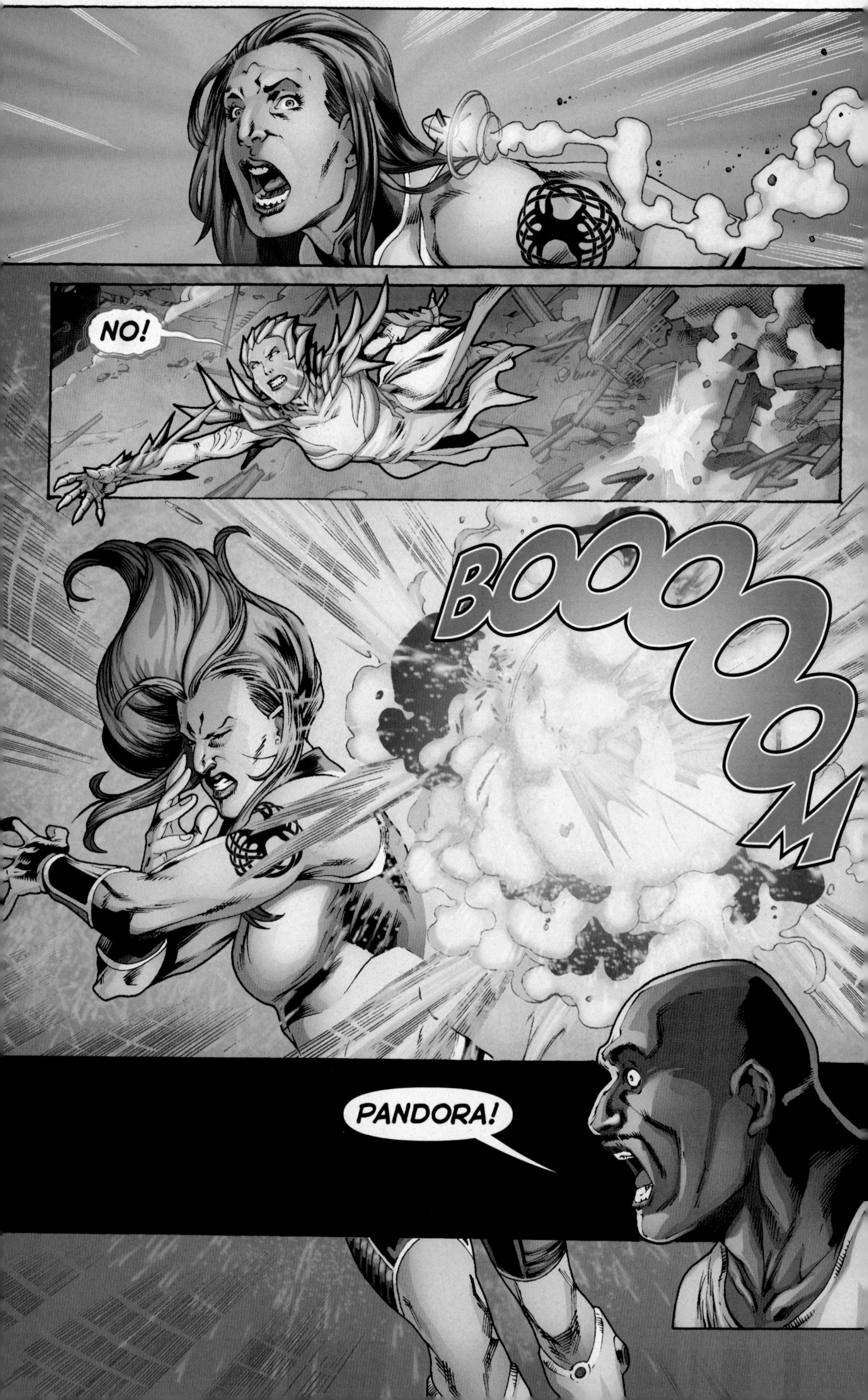
NO!
BOOOOOOM
PANDORA!

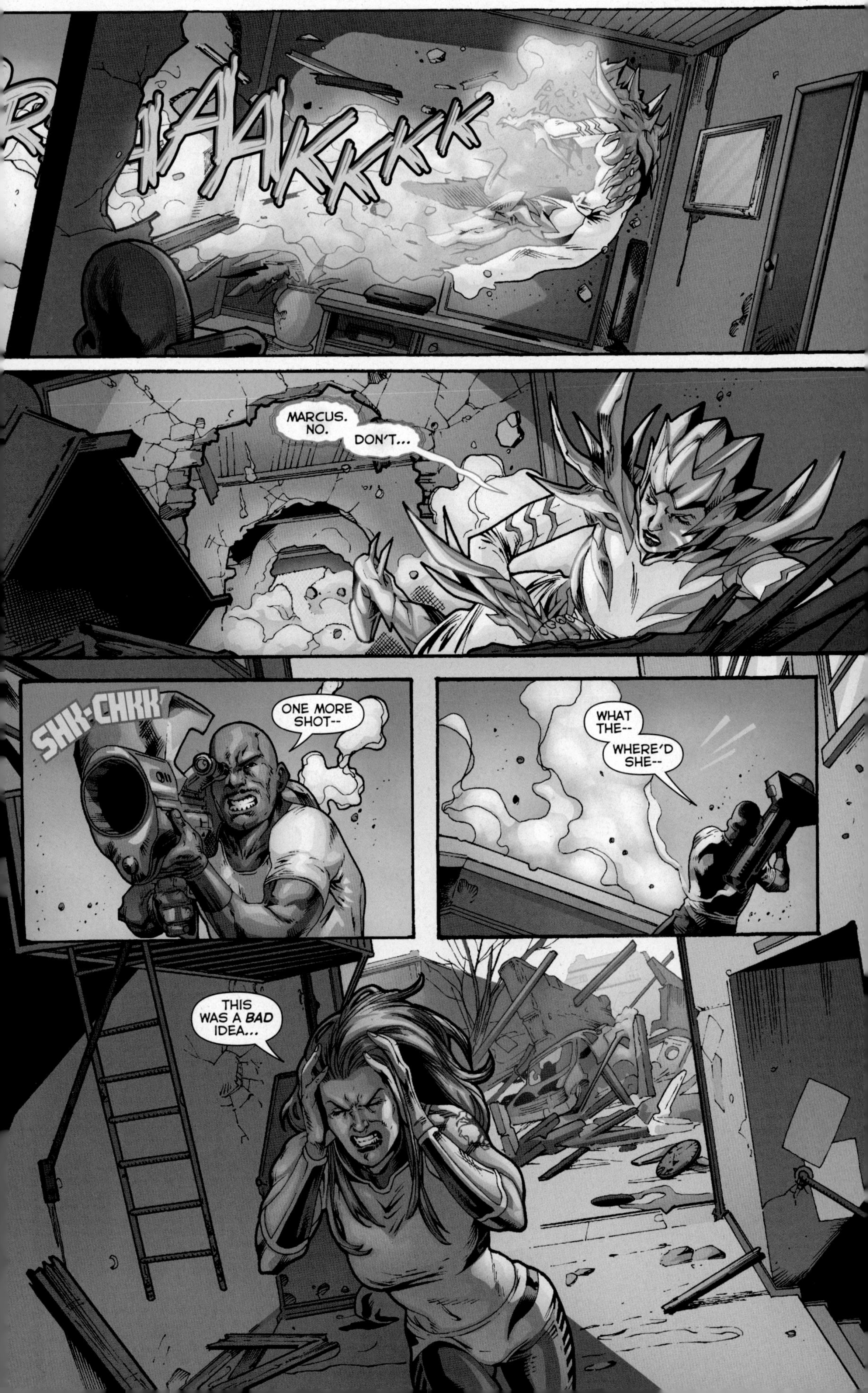
RAAAAKKKKK
MARCUS. NO.
DON'T...
SHK-CHKK
ONE MORE SHOT--
WHAT THE--
WHERE'D SHE--
THIS WAS A *BAD* IDEA...

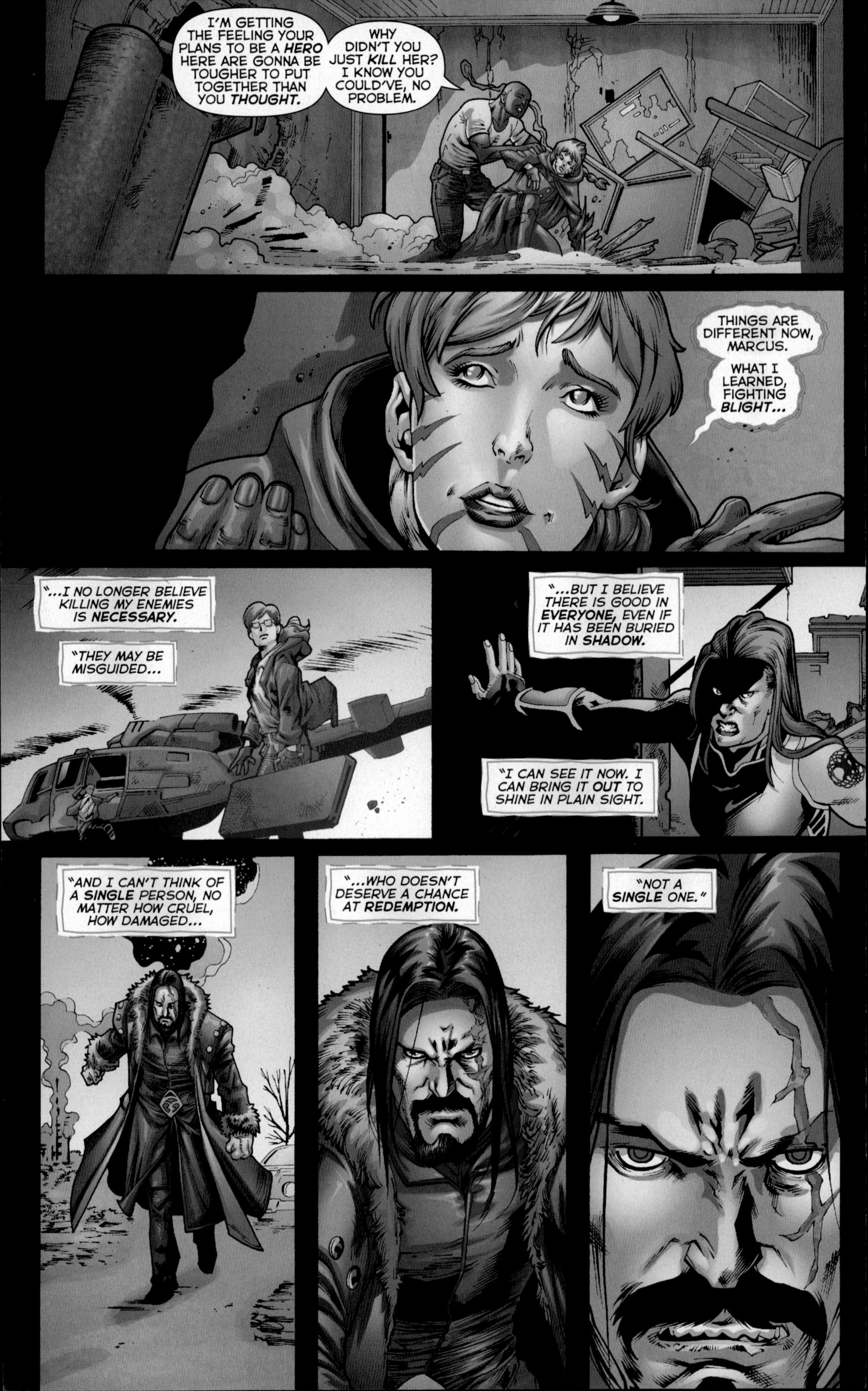
I'M GETTING THE FEELING YOUR PLANS TO BE A HERO HERE ARE GONNA BE TOUGHER TO PUT TOGETHER THAN YOU THOUGHT.
WHY DIDN'T YOU JUST KILL HER? I KNOW YOU COULD'VE, NO PROBLEM.
THINGS ARE DIFFERENT NOW, MARCUS.
WHAT I LEARNED, FIGHTING BLIGHT...
"...I NO LONGER BELIEVE KILLING MY ENEMIES IS NECESSARY.
"THEY MAY BE MISGUIDED...
"...BUT I BELIEVE THERE IS GOOD IN EVERYONE, EVEN IF IT HAS BEEN BURIED IN SHADOW.
"I CAN SEE IT NOW. I CAN BRING IT OUT TO SHINE IN PLAIN SIGHT.
"AND I CAN'T THINK OF A SINGLE PERSON, NO MATTER HOW CRUEL, HOW DAMAGED...
"...WHO DOESN'T DESERVE A CHANCE AT REDEMPTION.
"NOT A SINGLE ONE."

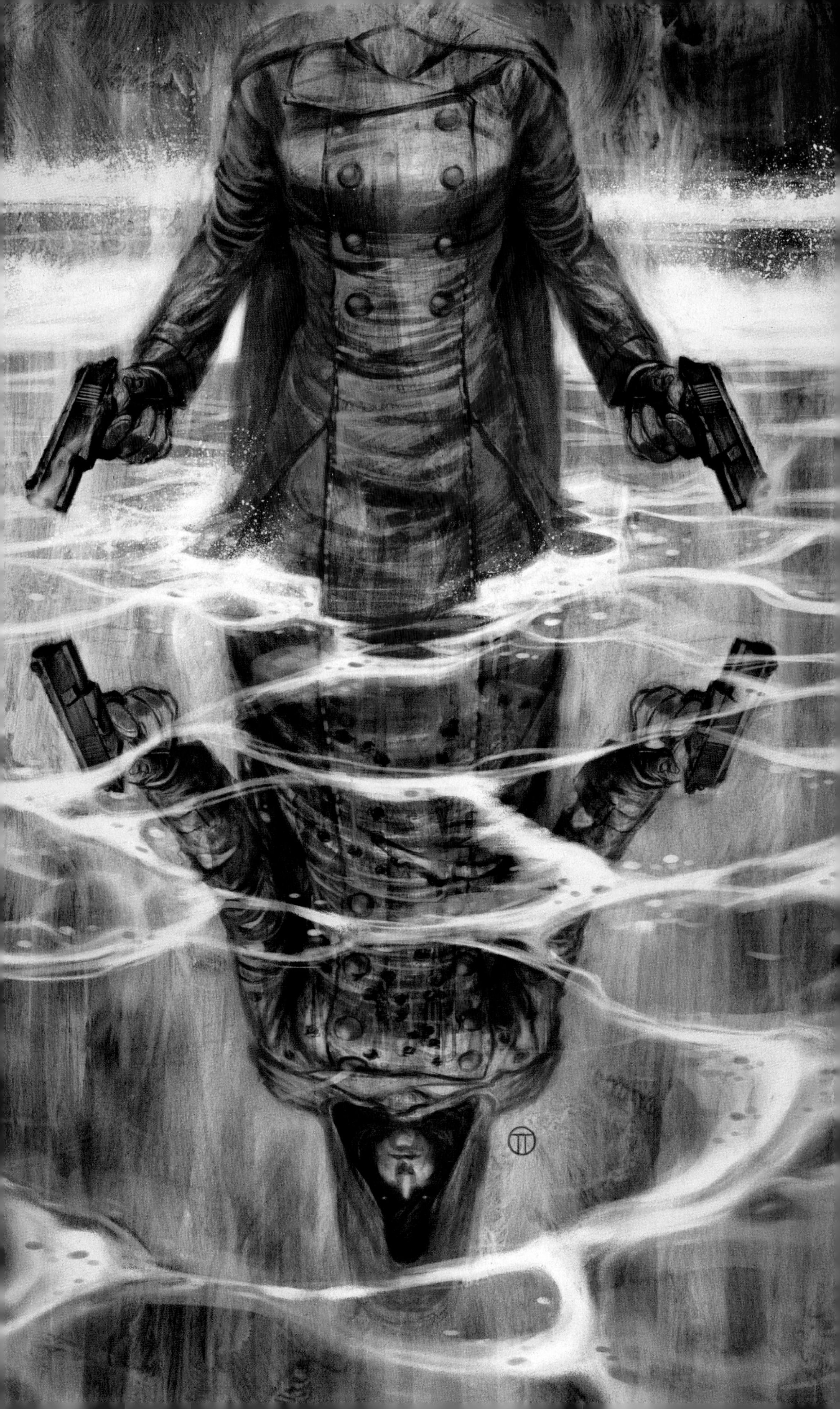

CHOICES

RAY FAWKES
writer

TOM DERENICK
breakdowns

FRANCIS PORTELA
artist

ANDEW DALHOUSE
colorist

TAYLOR ESPOSITO
letterer

cover art by
VICTOR IBAÑEZ

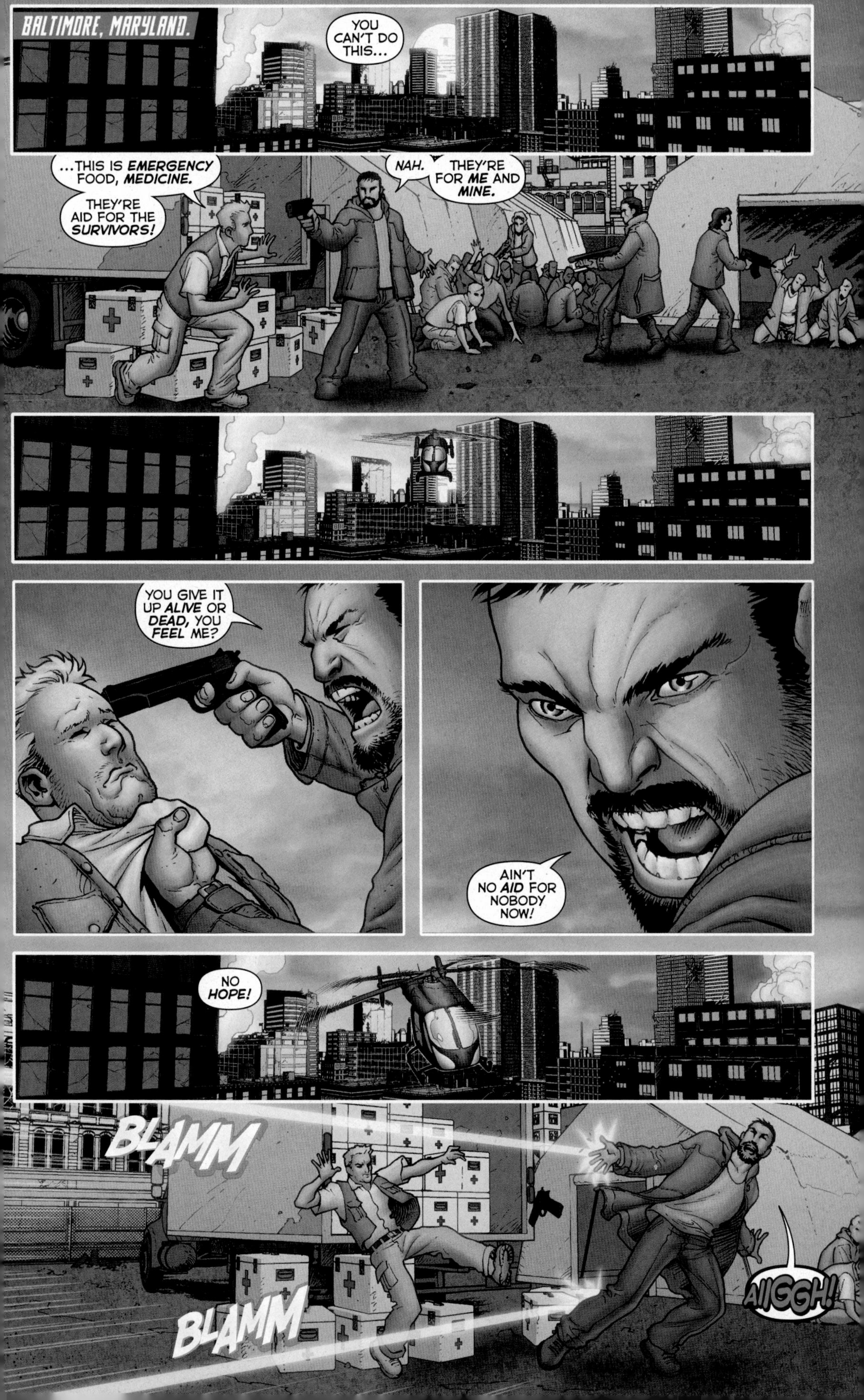

BALTIMORE, MARYLAND.
YOU CAN'T DO THIS...
...THIS IS EMERGENCY FOOD, MEDICINE.
THEY'RE AID FOR THE SURVIVORS!
NAH.
THEY'RE FOR ME AND MINE.
YOU GIVE IT UP ALIVE OR DEAD, YOU FEEL ME?
AIN'T NO AID FOR NOBODY NOW!
NO HOPE!
BLAMM
BLAMM
AIIGGH!

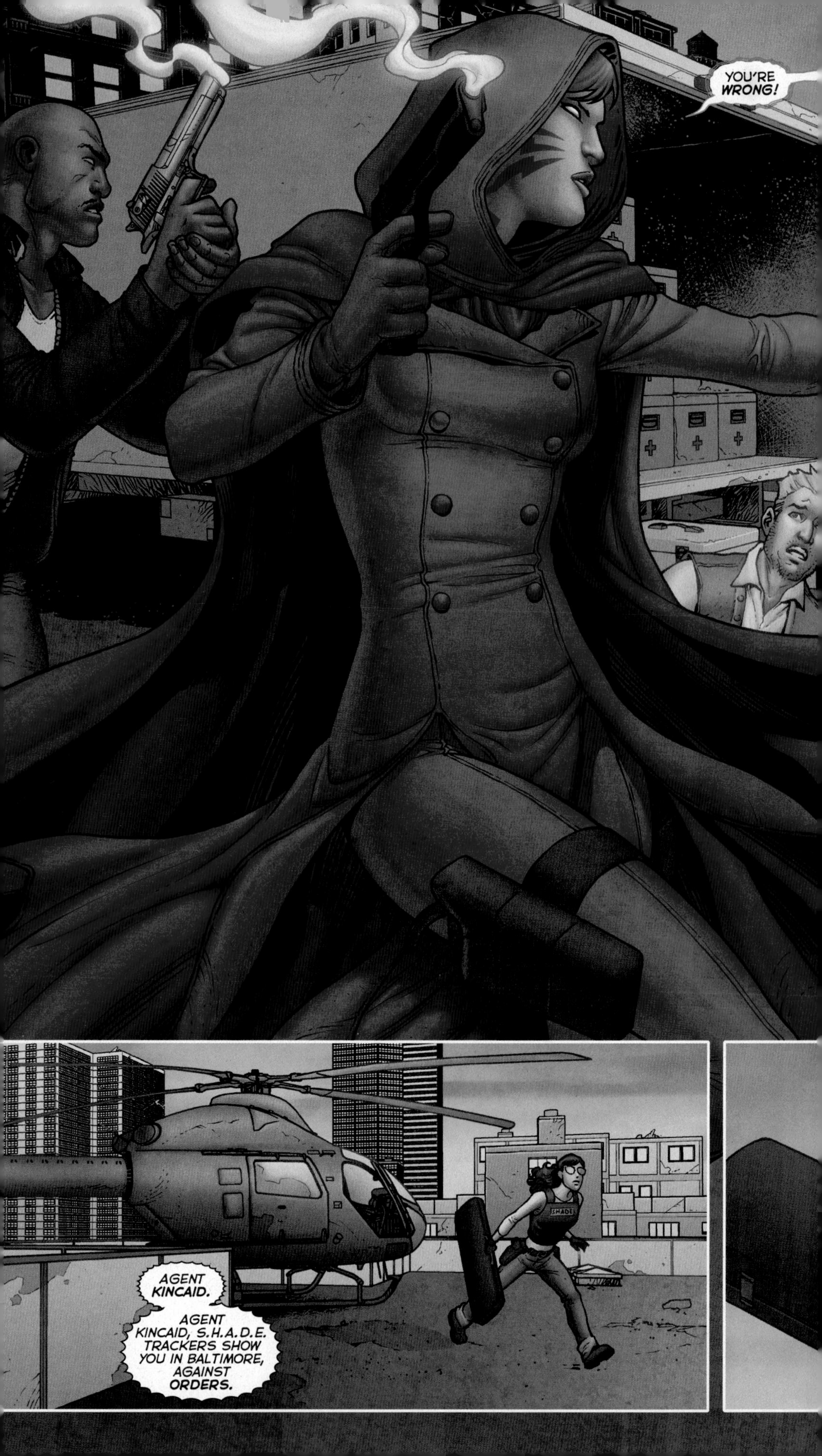
YOU'RE WRONG!
AGENT KINCAID.
AGENT KINCAID, S.H.A.D.E. TRACKERS SHOW YOU IN BALTIMORE, AGAINST ORDERS.

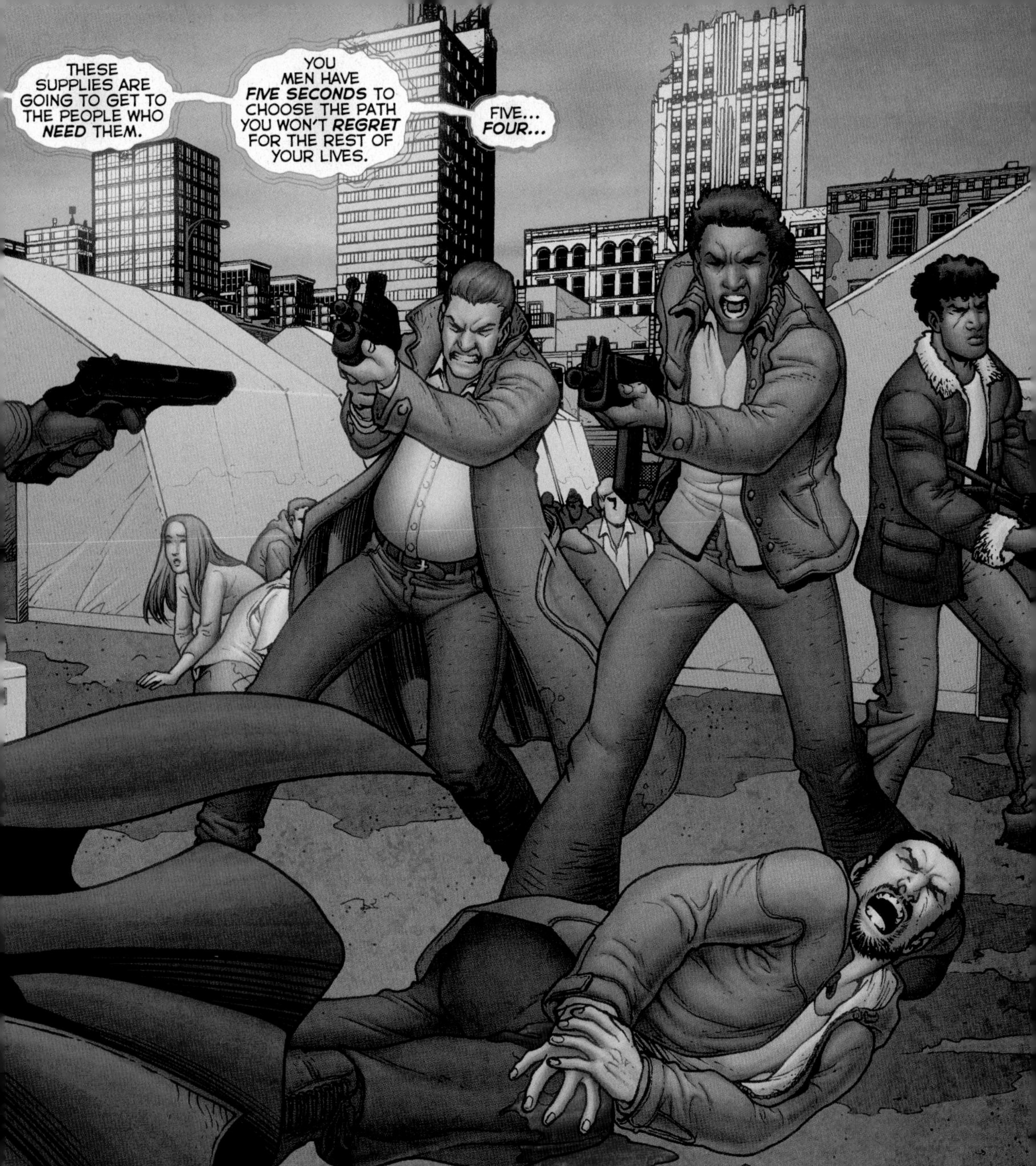
THESE SUPPLIES ARE GOING TO GET TO THE PEOPLE WHO NEED THEM.
YOU MEN HAVE FIVE SECONDS TO CHOOSE THE PATH YOU WON'T REGRET FOR THE REST OF YOUR LIVES.
FIVE... FOUR...

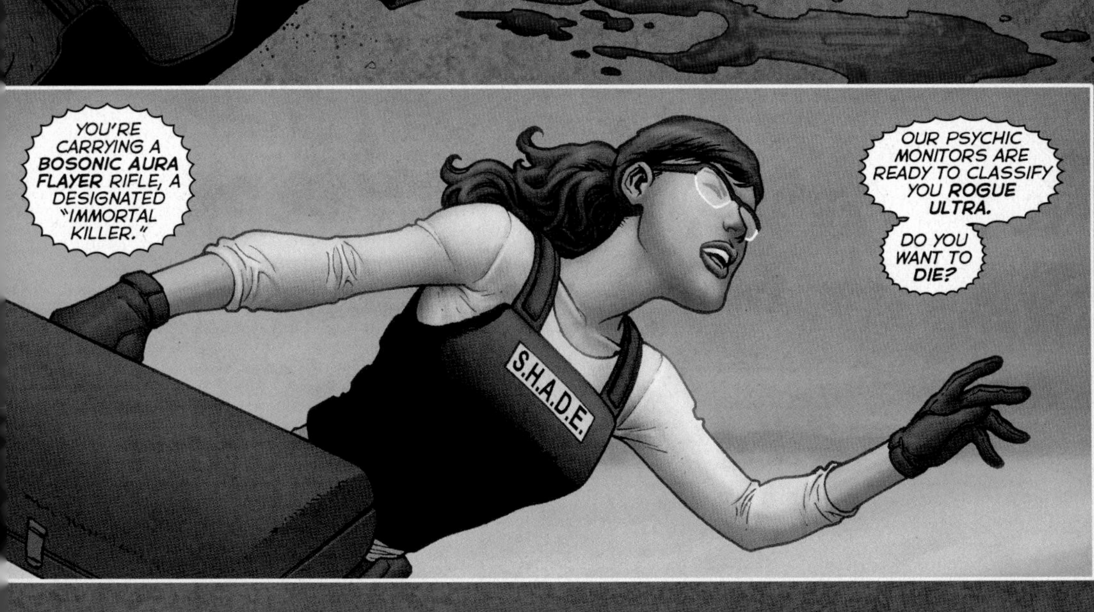
YOU'RE CARRYING A BOSONIC AURA FLAYER RIFLE, A DESIGNATED "IMMORTAL KILLER."
OUR PSYCHIC MONITORS ARE READY TO CLASSIFY YOU ROGUE ULTRA.
DO YOU WANT TO DIE?
S.H.A.D.E.

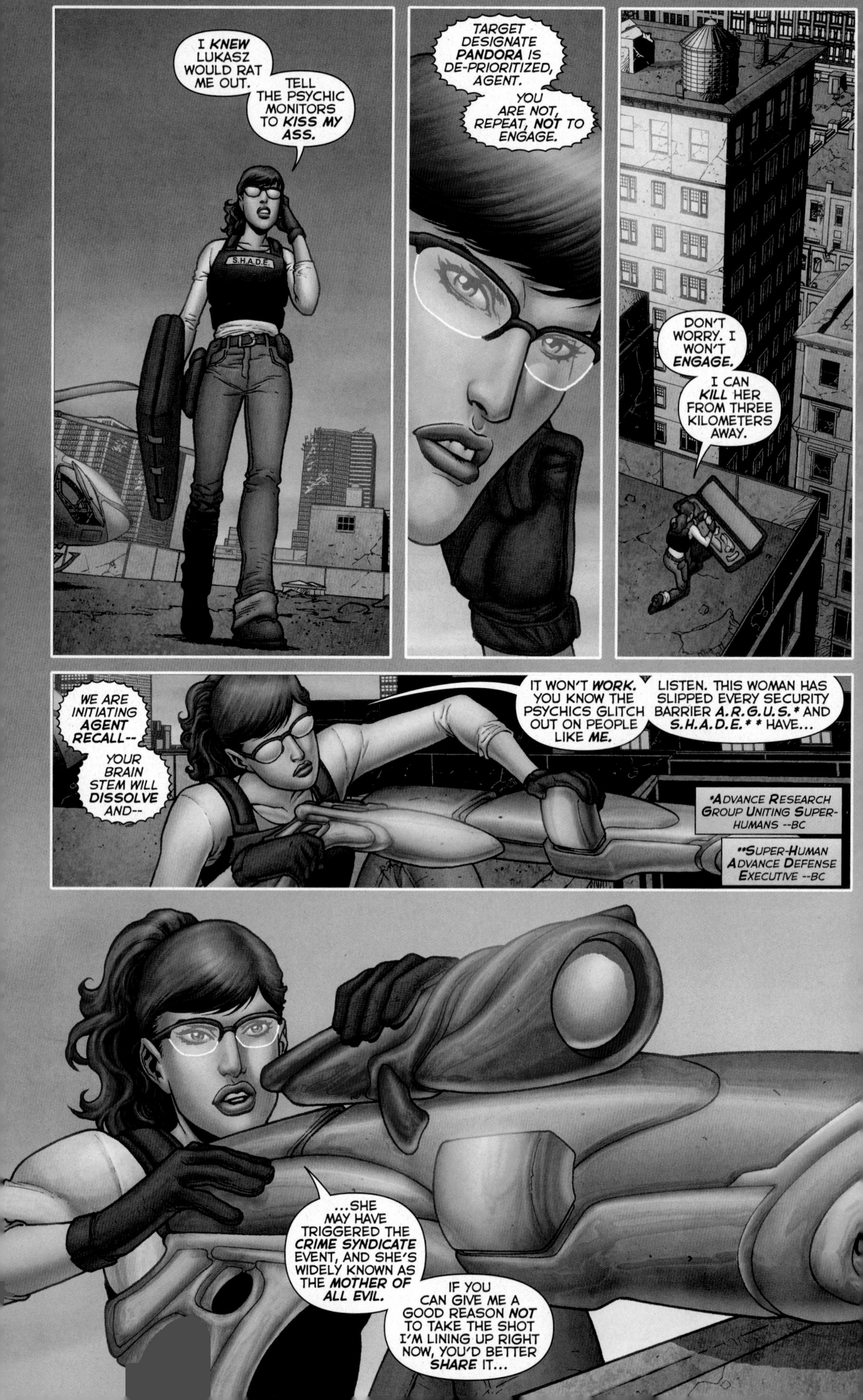
I KNEW LUKASZ WOULD RAT ME OUT.
TELL THE PSYCHIC MONITORS TO KISS MY ASS.
S.H.A.D.E.
TARGET DESIGNATE PANDORA IS DE-PRIORITIZED, AGENT.
YOU ARE NOT, REPEAT, NOT TO ENGAGE.
DON'T WORRY. I WON'T ENGAGE.
I CAN KILL HER FROM THREE KILOMETERS AWAY.
WE ARE INITIATING AGENT RECALL--
YOUR BRAIN STEM WILL DISSOLVE AND--
IT WON'T WORK. YOU KNOW THE PSYCHICS GLITCH OUT ON PEOPLE LIKE ME.
LISTEN. THIS WOMAN HAS SLIPPED EVERY SECURITY BARRIER A.R.G.U.S.* AND S.H.A.D.E.** HAVE...
*ADVANCE RESEARCH GROUP UNITING SUPER-HUMANS --BC
**SUPER-HUMAN ADVANCE DEFENSE EXECUTIVE --BC
...SHE MAY HAVE TRIGGERED THE CRIME SYNDICATE EVENT, AND SHE'S WIDELY KNOWN AS THE MOTHER OF ALL EVIL.
IF YOU CAN GIVE ME A GOOD REASON NOT TO TAKE THE SHOT I'M LINING UP RIGHT NOW, YOU'D BETTER SHARE IT...

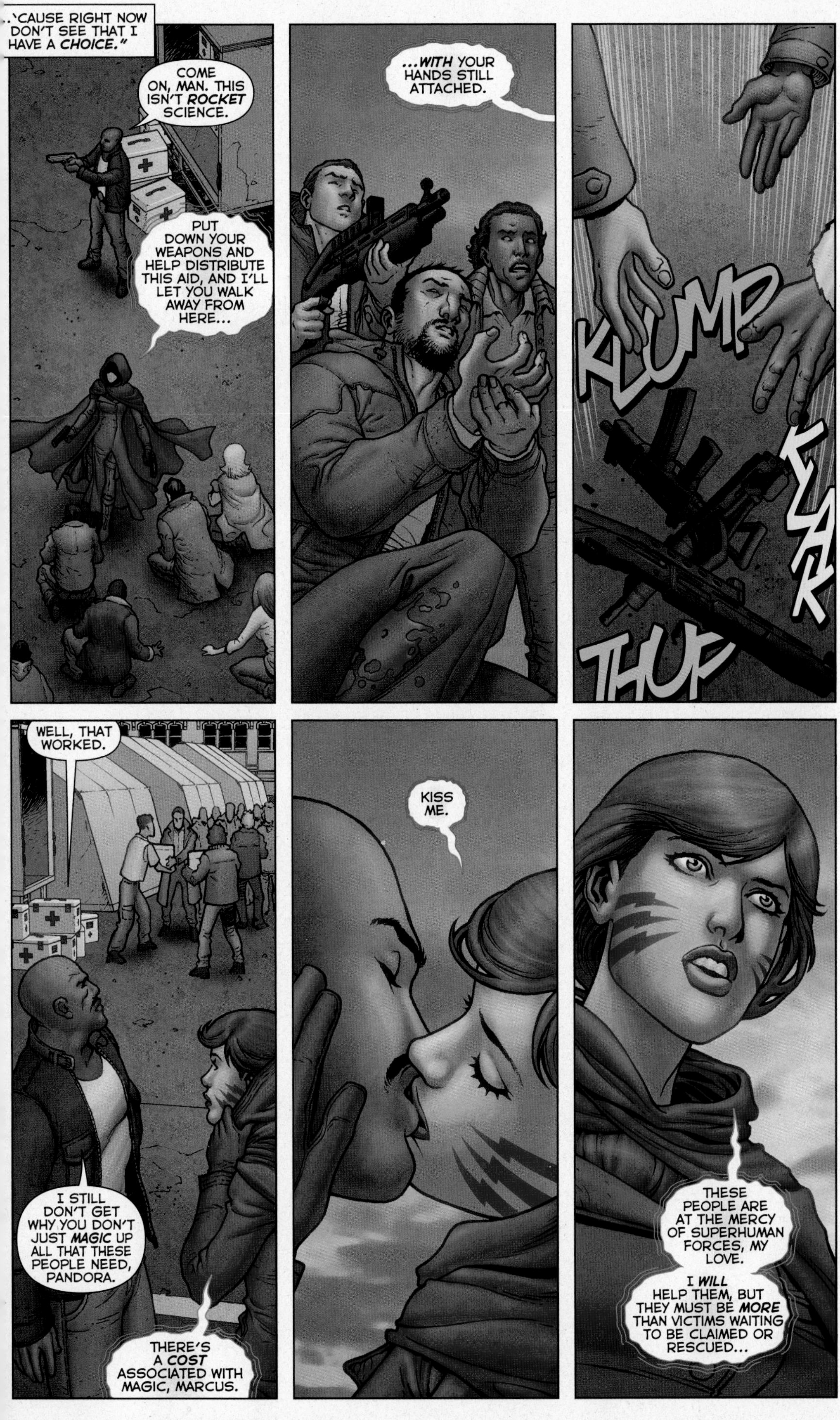

..'CAUSE RIGHT NOW DON'T SEE THAT I HAVE A *CHOICE."*
COME ON, MAN. THIS ISN'T *ROCKET* SCIENCE.
PUT DOWN YOUR WEAPONS AND HELP DISTRIBUTE THIS AID, AND I'LL LET YOU WALK AWAY FROM HERE...
...WITH YOUR HANDS STILL ATTACHED.
KLUMP
KLAK
THUP
WELL, THAT WORKED.
I STILL DON'T GET WHY YOU DON'T JUST *MAGIC* UP ALL THAT THESE PEOPLE NEED, PANDORA.
THERE'S A *COST* ASSOCIATED WITH MAGIC, MARCUS.
KISS ME.
THESE PEOPLE ARE AT THE MERCY OF SUPERHUMAN FORCES, MY LOVE.
I *WILL* HELP THEM, BUT THEY MUST BE *MORE* THAN VICTIMS WAITING TO BE CLAIMED OR RESCUED...

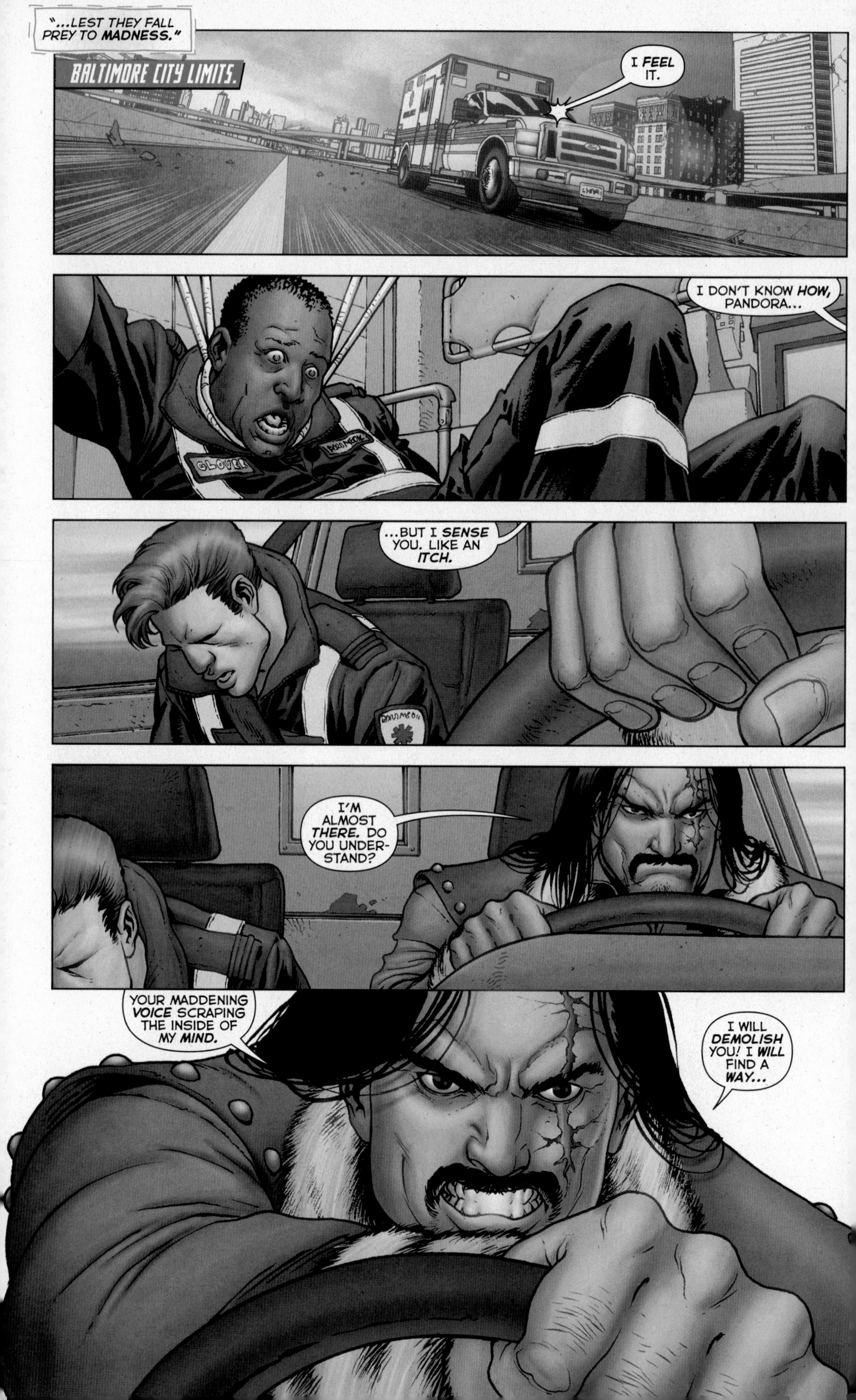
"...LEST THEY FALL PREY TO MADNESS."
BALTIMORE CITY LIMITS.
I FEEL IT.
GLOVER
I DON'T KNOW HOW, PANDORA...
...BUT I SENSE YOU. LIKE AN ITCH.
I'M ALMOST THERE. DO YOU UNDERSTAND?
YOUR MADDENING VOICE SCRAPING THE INSIDE OF MY MIND.
I WILL DEMOLISH YOU! I WILL FIND A WAY...

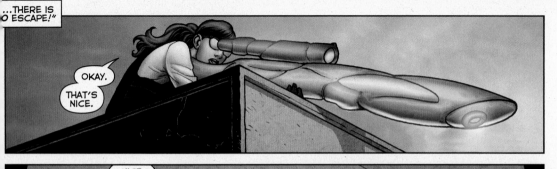

OKAY.

THAT'S
NICE.

NICE
TARGET.

JUST
STAND UP FOR
ME. CLEAR THE BY-
STANDERS.

STAND
UP.

OH,
GOOD.

PARAMEDICS.
WE COULD USE
THE HELP.

KKCHOW

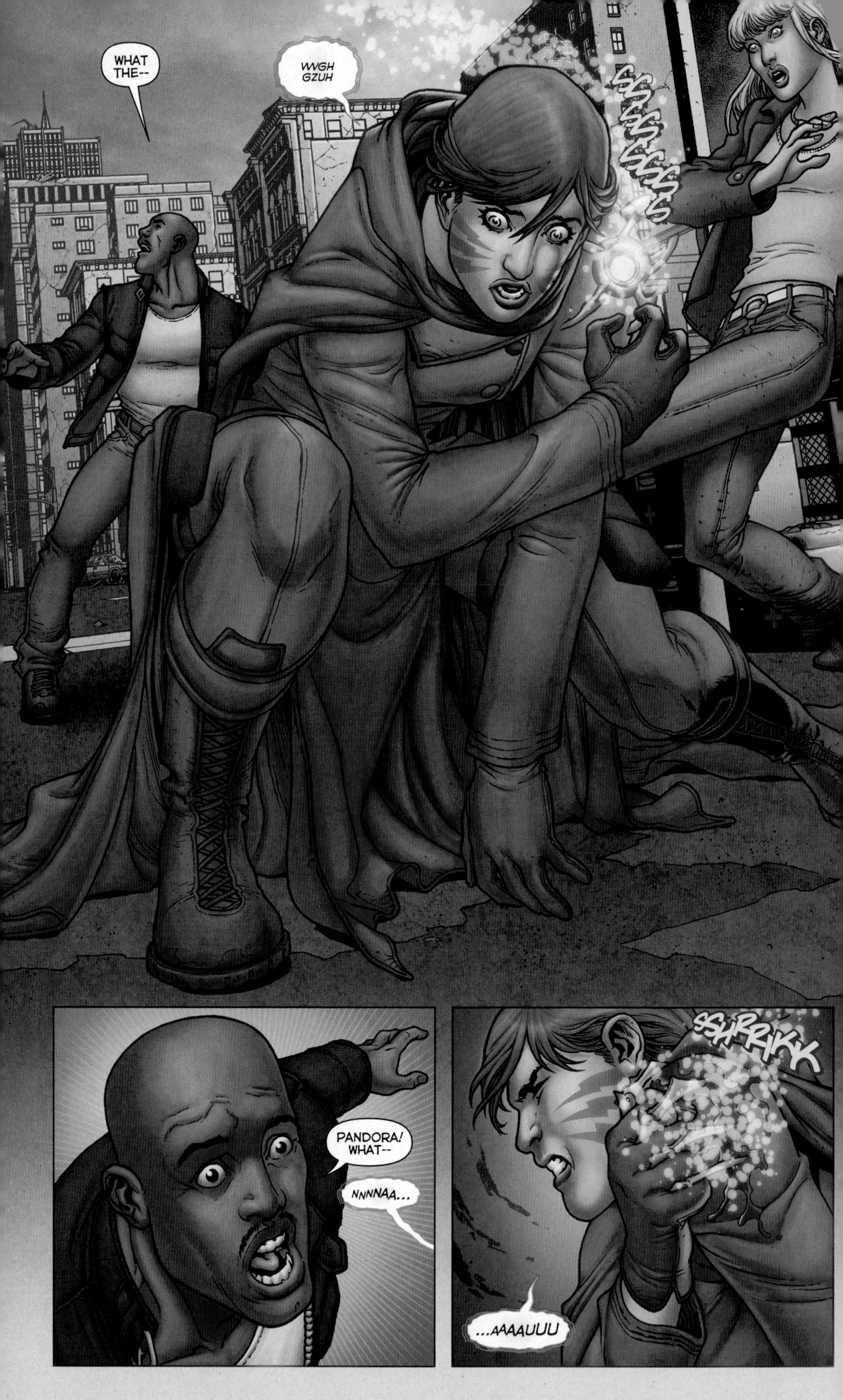
WHAT THE--
WWGH GZUH
SSSSSSSSS
PANDORA! WHAT--
NNNNAA...
SSHRRIKK
...AAAAUUU

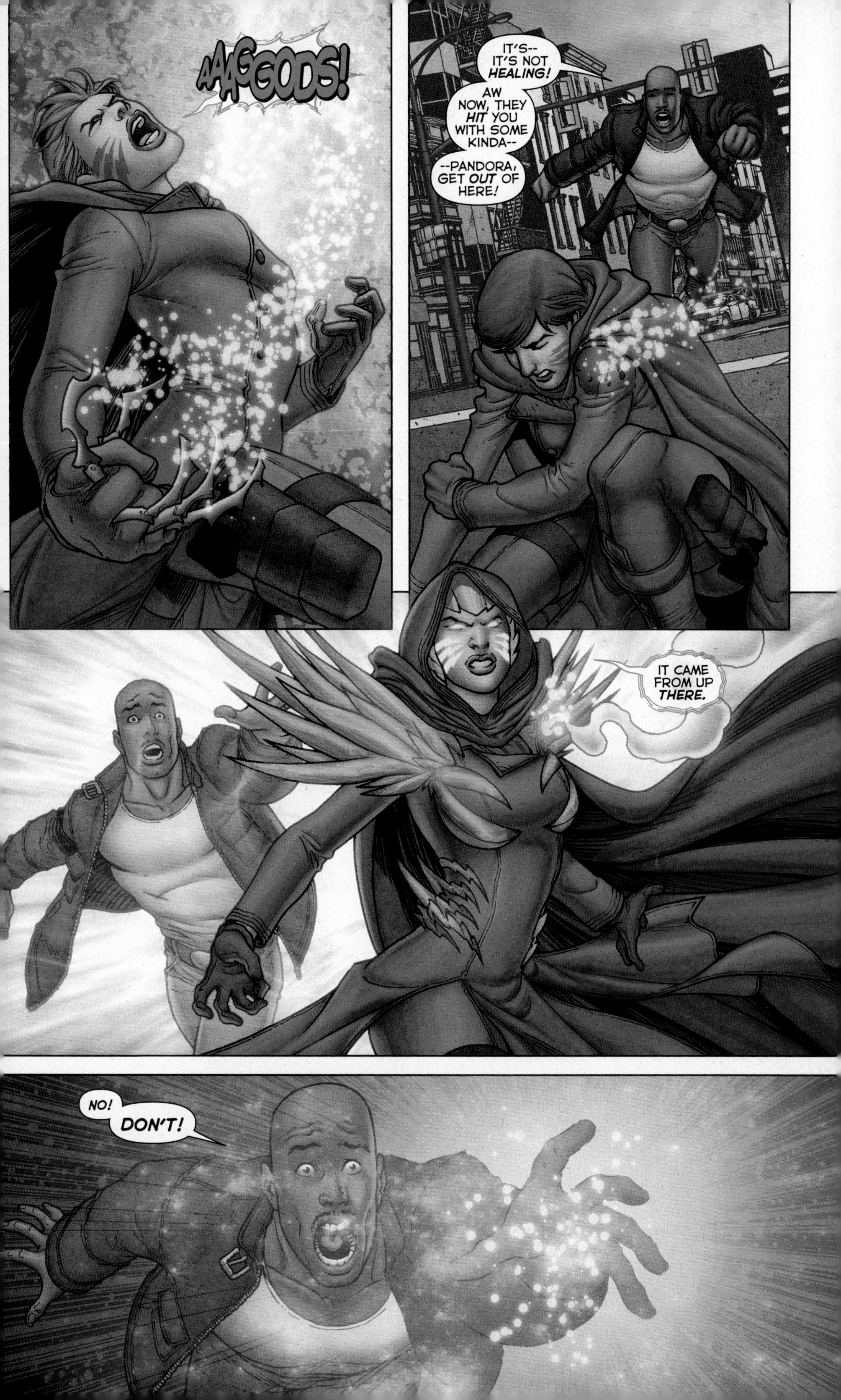
AAAGGODS!
IT'S-- IT'S NOT HEALING!
AW NOW, THEY HIT YOU WITH SOME KINDA--
--PANDORA, GET OUT OF HERE!
IT CAME FROM UP THERE.
NO! DON'T!

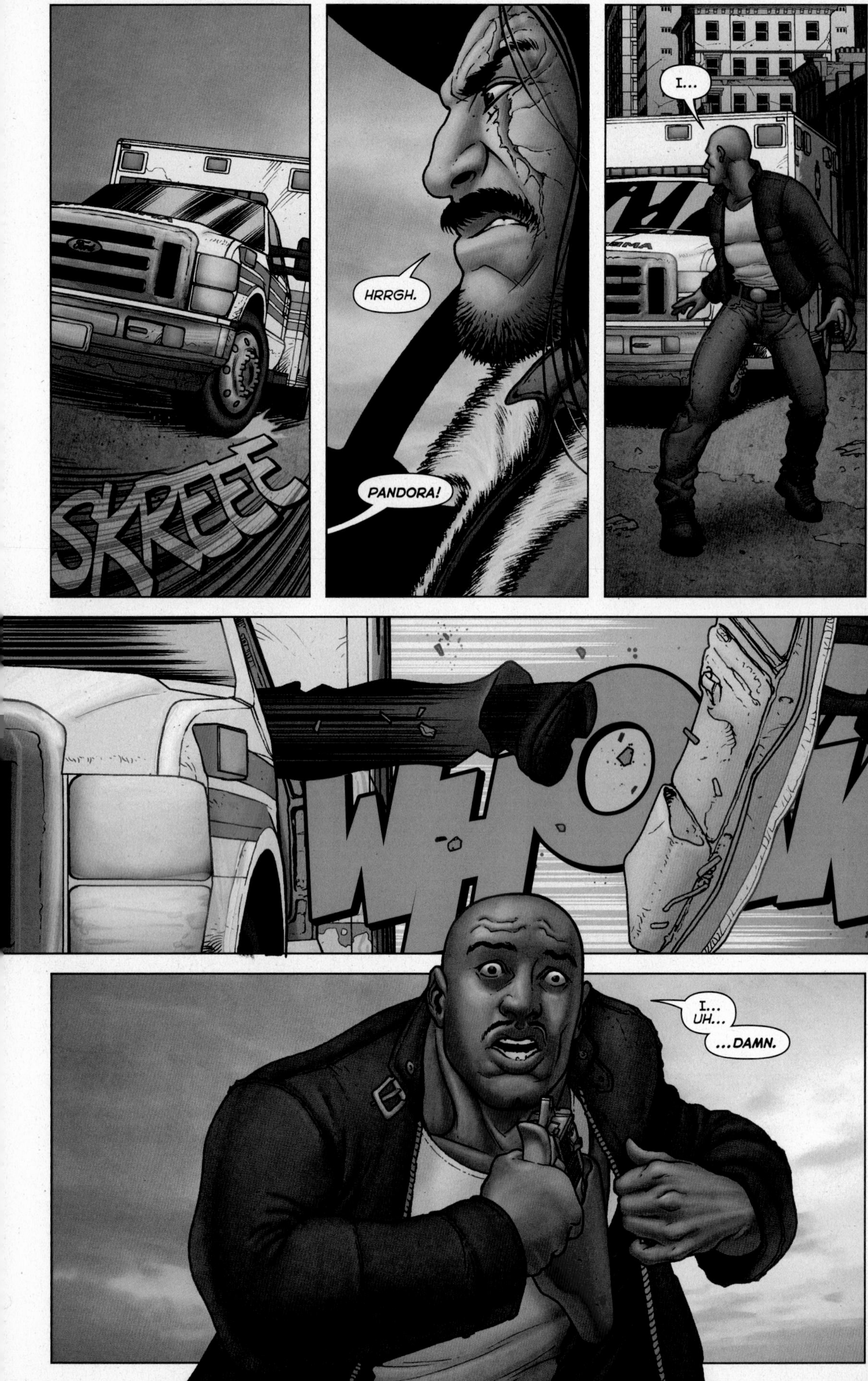
SKREEE
HRRGH.
PANDORA!
I...
WHOOM
I... UH...
...DAMN.

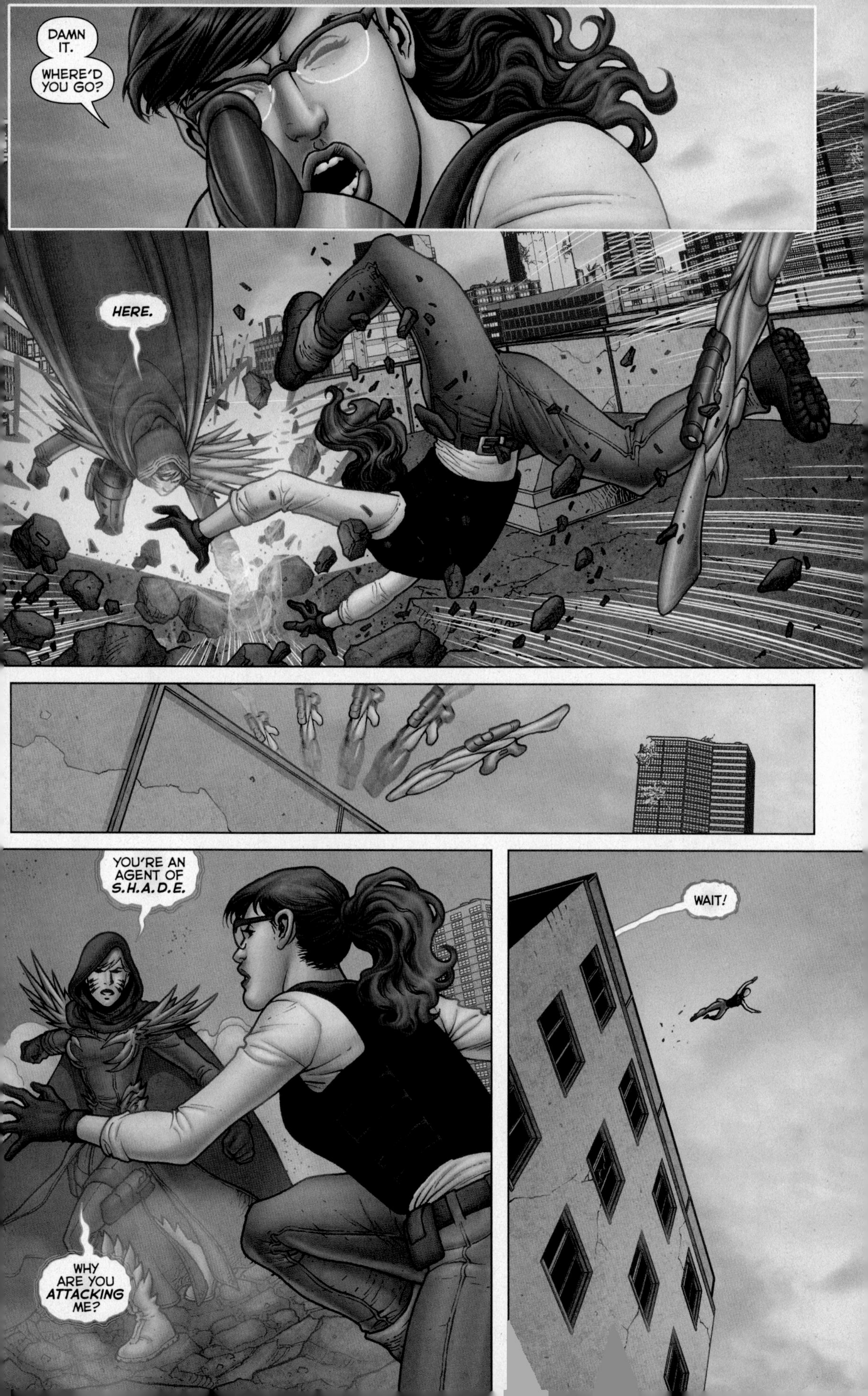
DAMN IT.
WHERE'D YOU GO?
HERE.
YOU'RE AN AGENT OF S.H.A.D.E.
WHY ARE YOU ATTACKING ME?
WAIT!

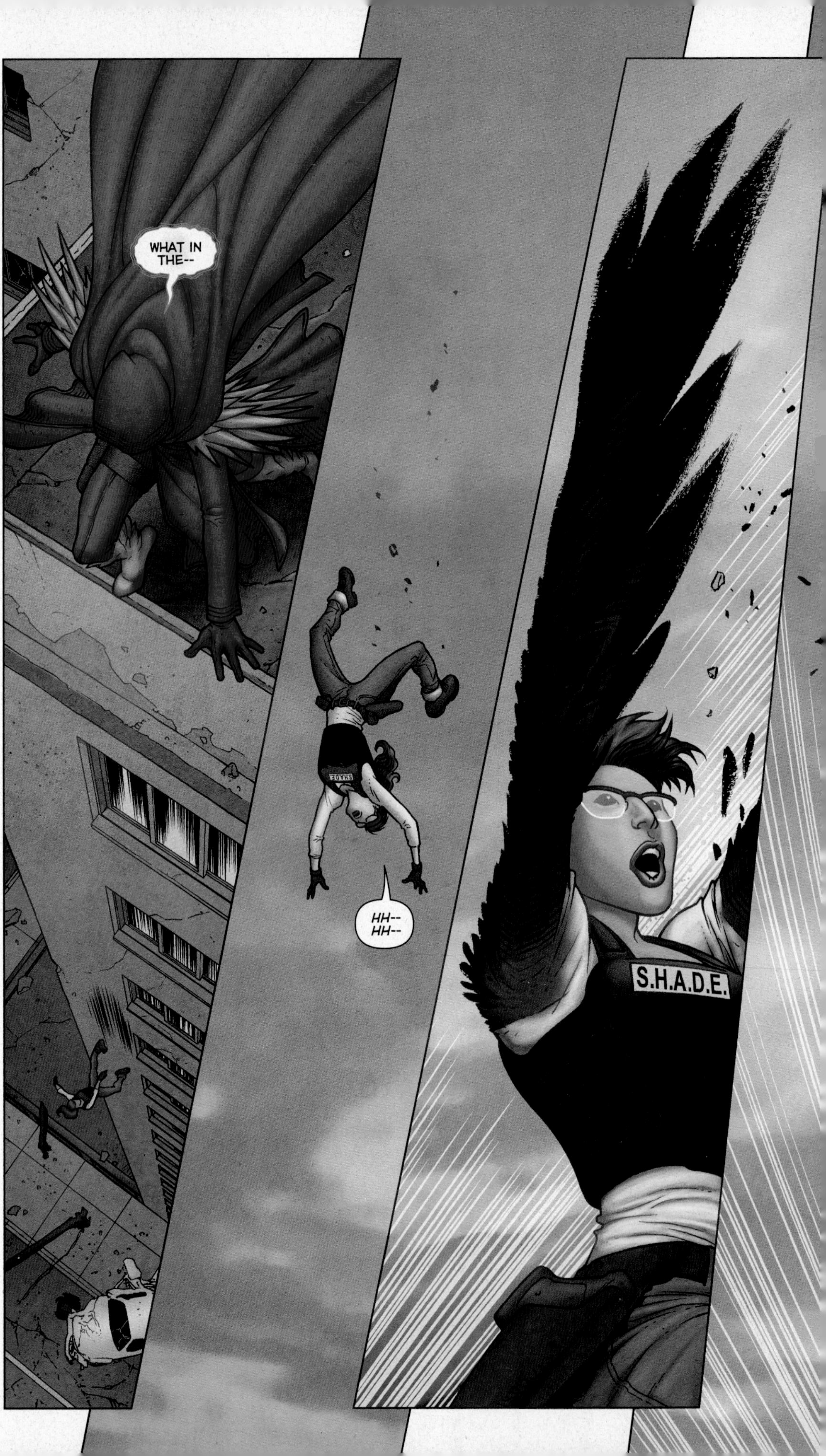
WHAT IN THE--
HH-- HH--
S.H.A.D.E.

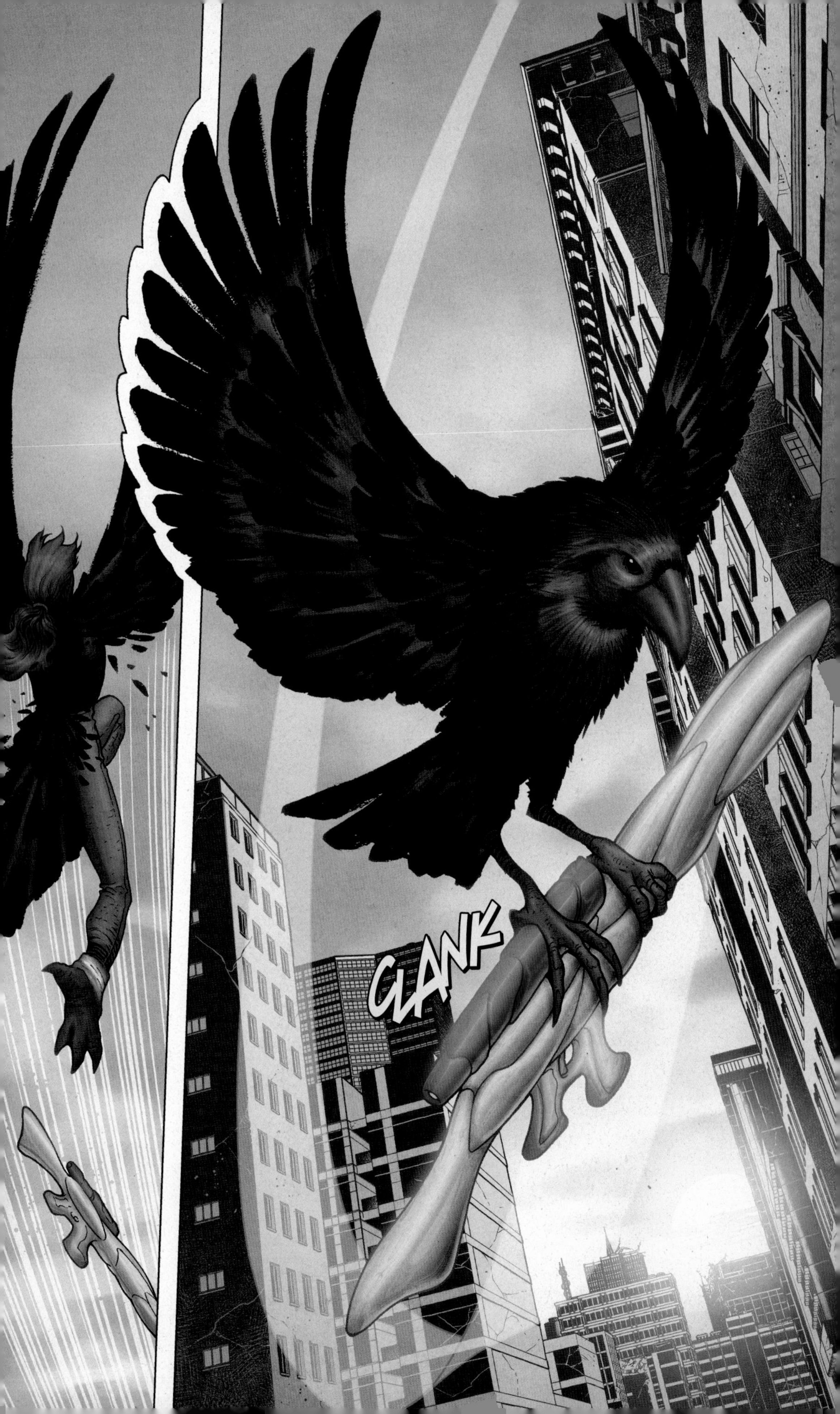
CLANK

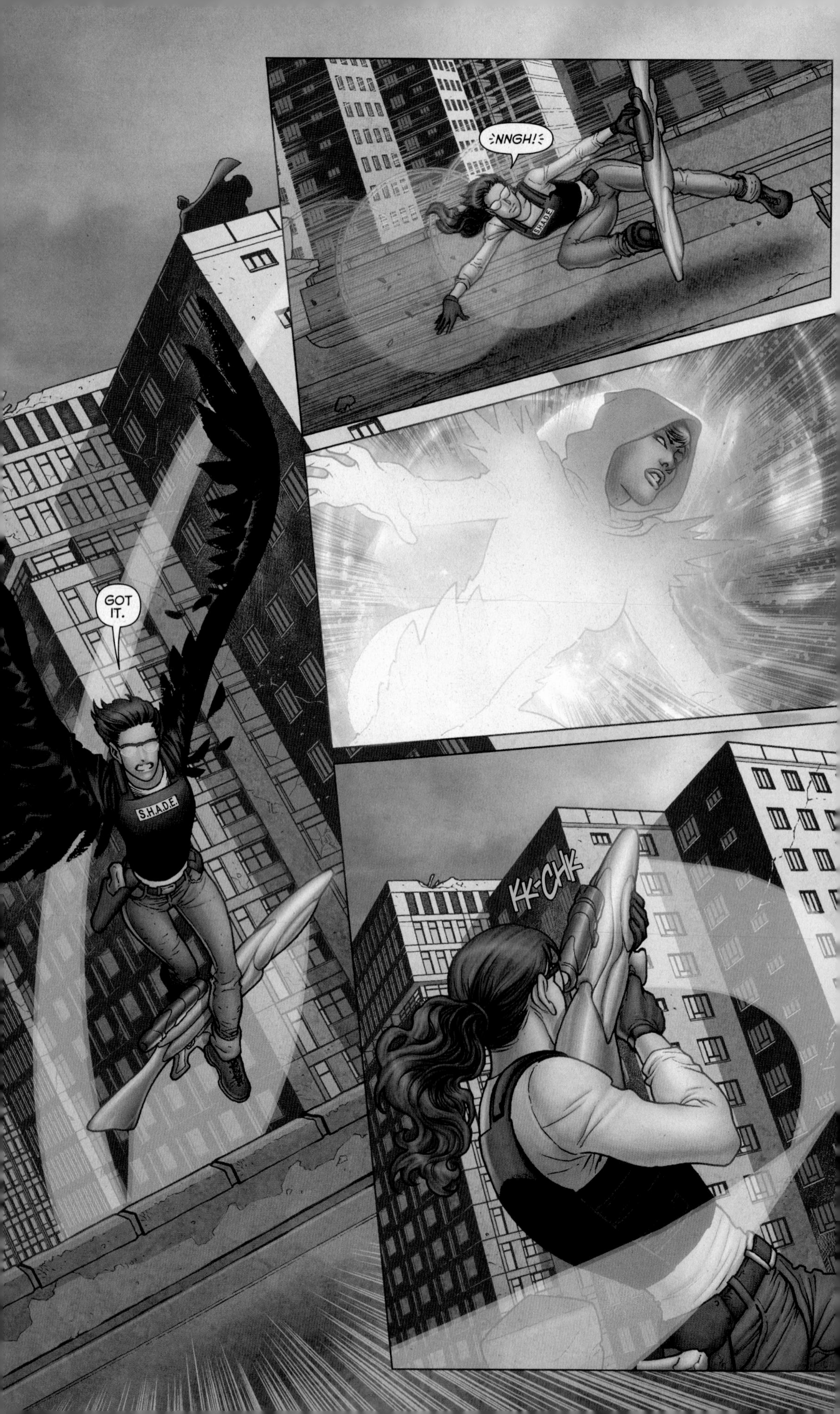
NNGH!
GOT IT.
KK-CHK

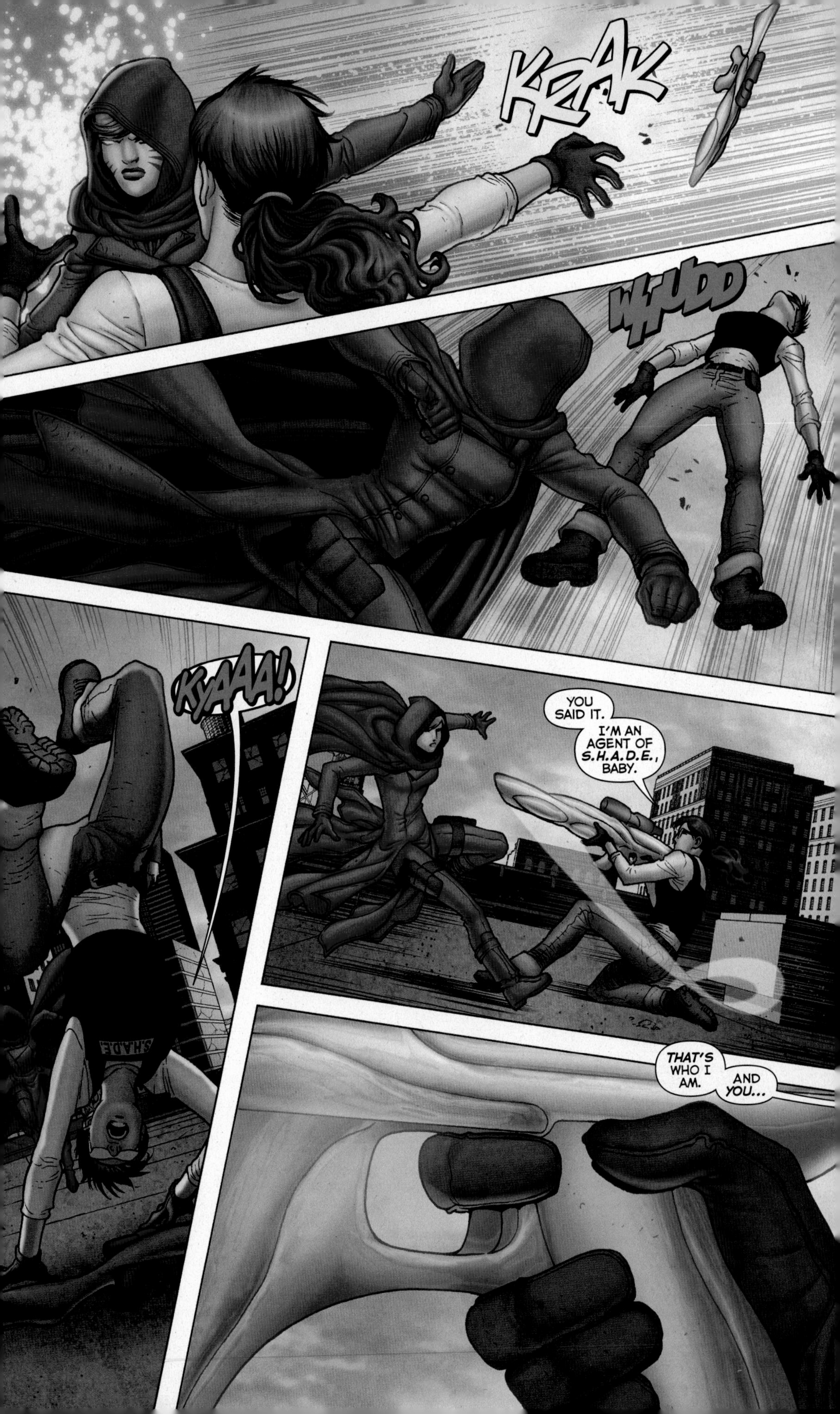
KRAK
WHUDD
KYAAA!
YOU SAID IT. I'M AN AGENT OF S.H.A.D.E., BABY.
THAT'S WHO I AM.
AND YOU...

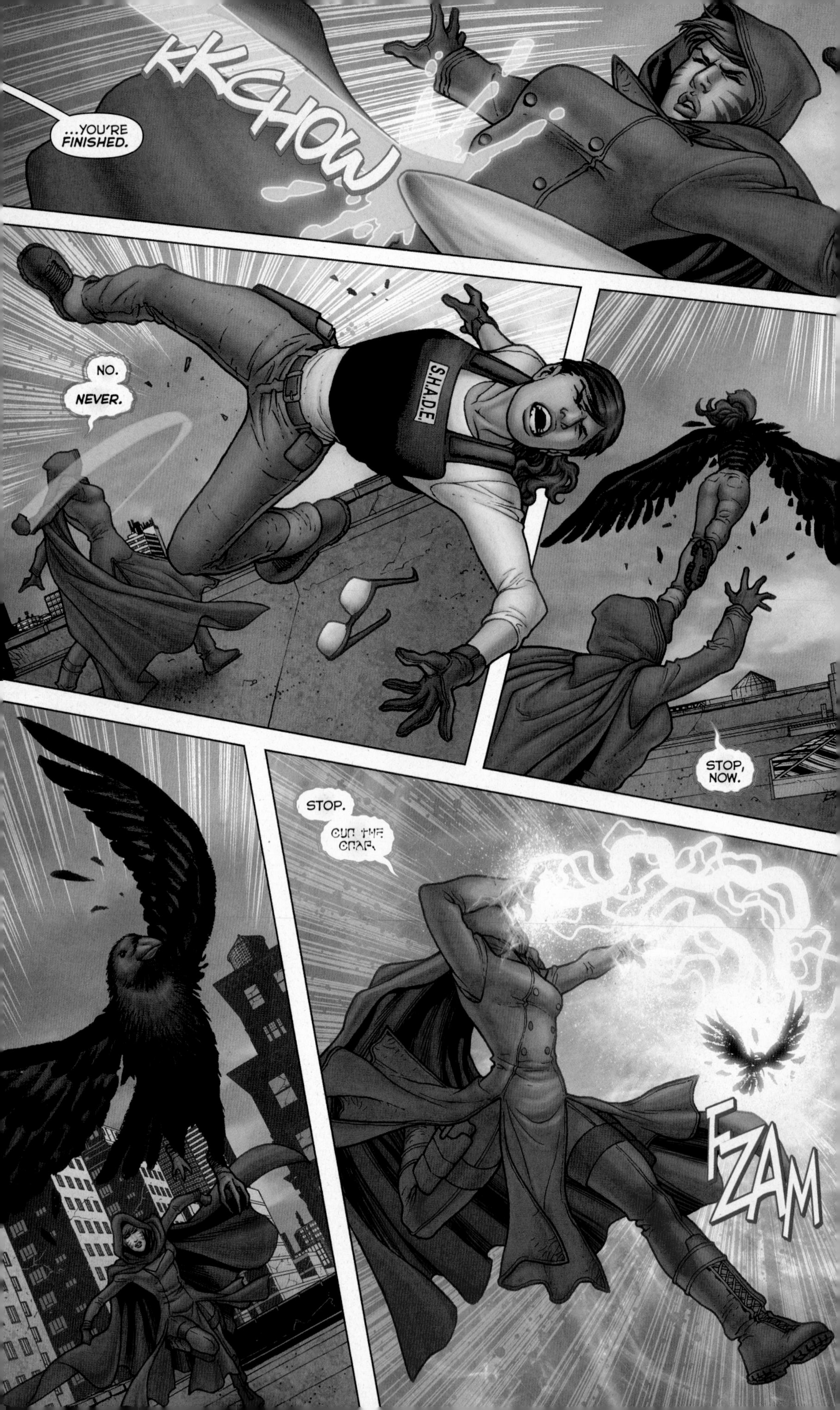
KKCHOW
...YOU'RE FINISHED.
NO.
NEVER.
STOP, NOW.
STOP.
CUT THE CRAP.
FZAM

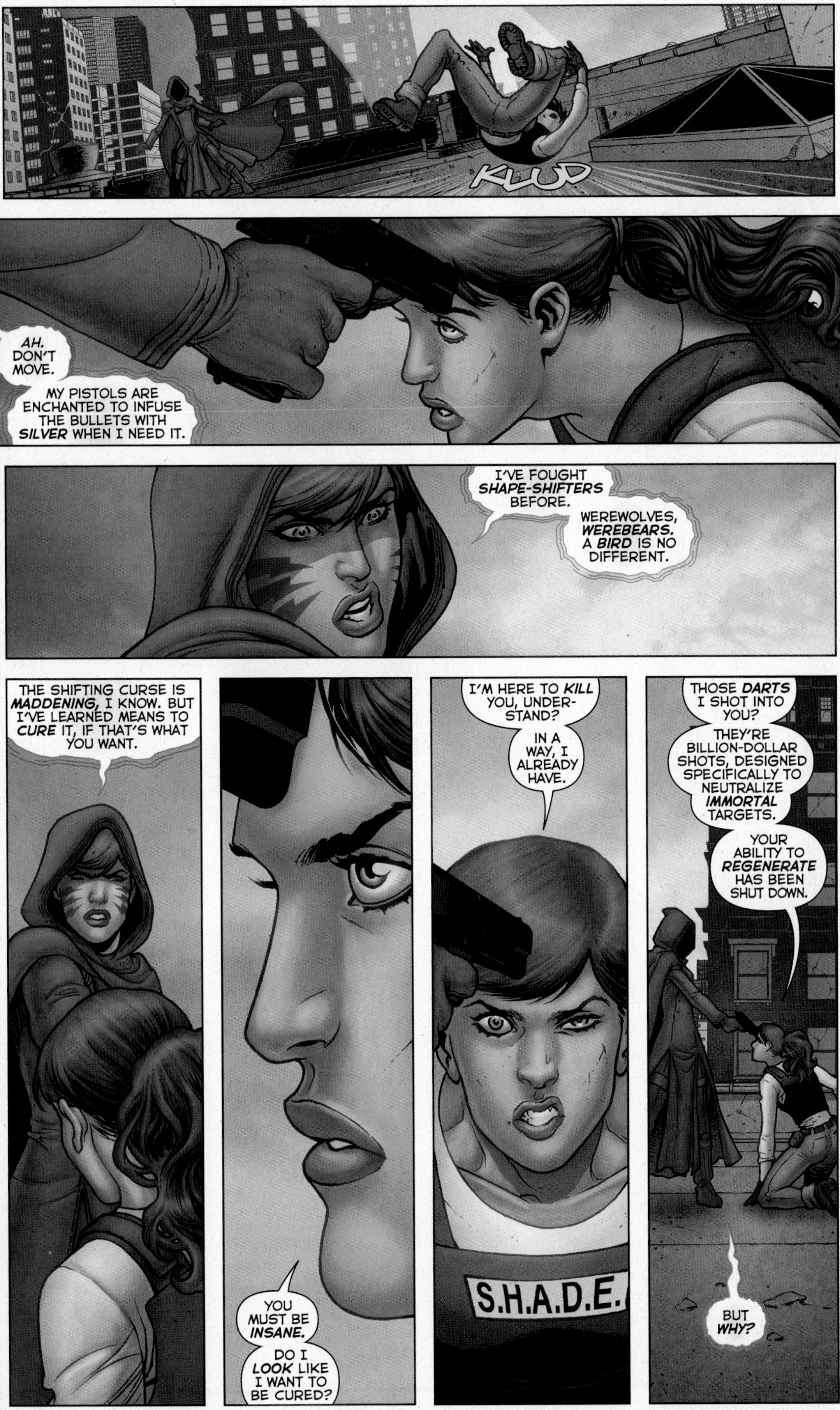
KLUD
AH. DON'T MOVE.
MY PISTOLS ARE ENCHANTED TO INFUSE THE BULLETS WITH SILVER WHEN I NEED IT.
I'VE FOUGHT SHAPE-SHIFTERS BEFORE.
WEREWOLVES, WEREBEARS. A BIRD IS NO DIFFERENT.
THE SHIFTING CURSE IS MADDENING, I KNOW. BUT I'VE LEARNED MEANS TO CURE IT, IF THAT'S WHAT YOU WANT.
YOU MUST BE INSANE.
DO I LOOK LIKE I WANT TO BE CURED?
I'M HERE TO KILL YOU, UNDERSTAND?
IN A WAY, I ALREADY HAVE.
S.H.A.D.E.
THOSE DARTS I SHOT INTO YOU?
THEY'RE BILLION-DOLLAR SHOTS, DESIGNED SPECIFICALLY TO NEUTRALIZE IMMORTAL TARGETS.
YOUR ABILITY TO REGENERATE HAS BEEN SHUT DOWN.
BUT WHY?

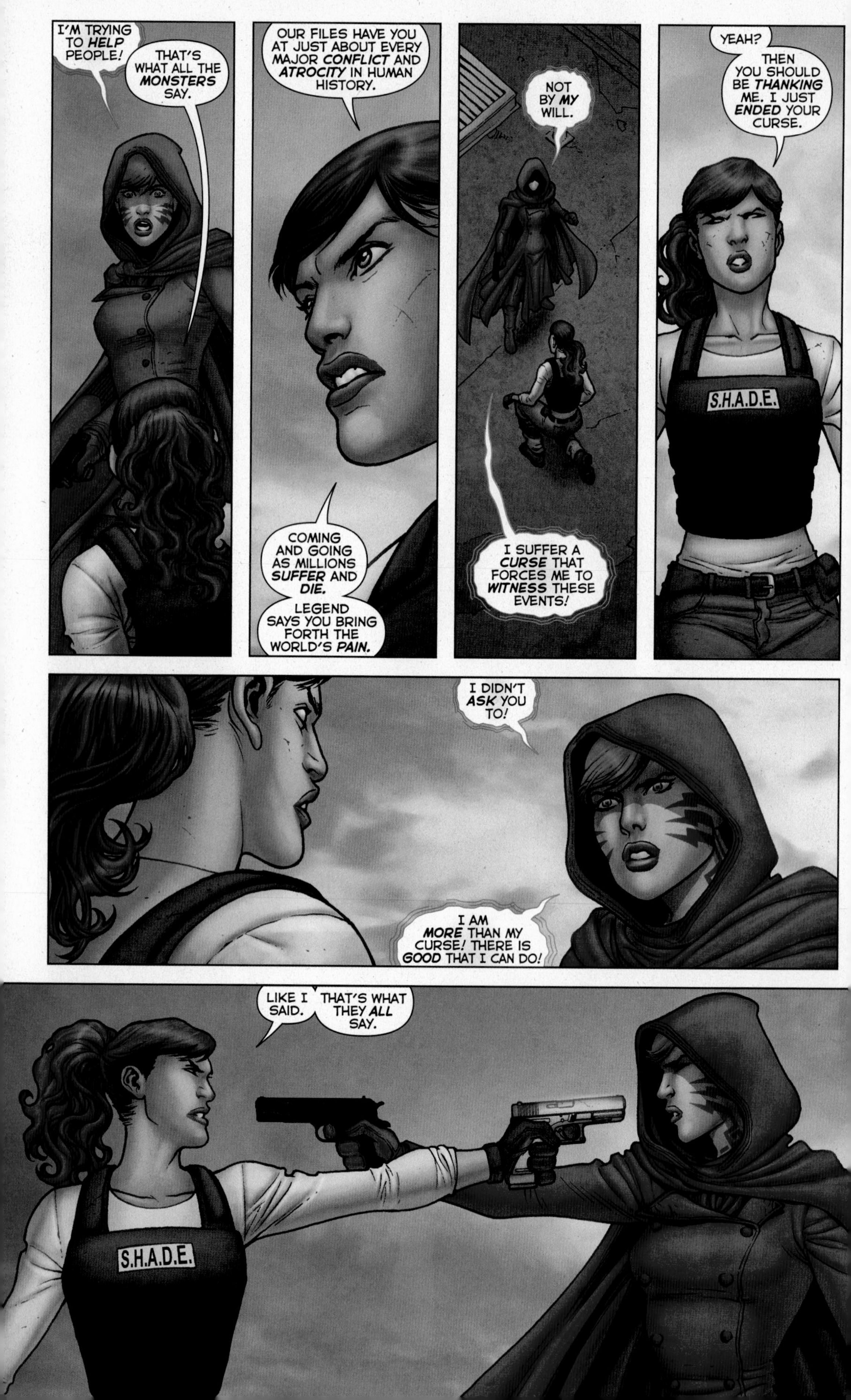
I'M TRYING TO HELP PEOPLE!
THAT'S WHAT ALL THE MONSTERS SAY.
OUR FILES HAVE YOU AT JUST ABOUT EVERY MAJOR CONFLICT AND ATROCITY IN HUMAN HISTORY.
COMING AND GOING AS MILLIONS SUFFER AND DIE.
LEGEND SAYS YOU BRING FORTH THE WORLD'S PAIN.
NOT BY MY WILL.
I SUFFER A CURSE THAT FORCES ME TO WITNESS THESE EVENTS!
YEAH?
THEN YOU SHOULD BE THANKING ME. I JUST ENDED YOUR CURSE.
S.H.A.D.E.
I DIDN'T ASK YOU TO!
I AM MORE THAN MY CURSE! THERE IS GOOD THAT I CAN DO!
LIKE I SAID.
THAT'S WHAT THEY ALL SAY.
S.H.A.D.E.

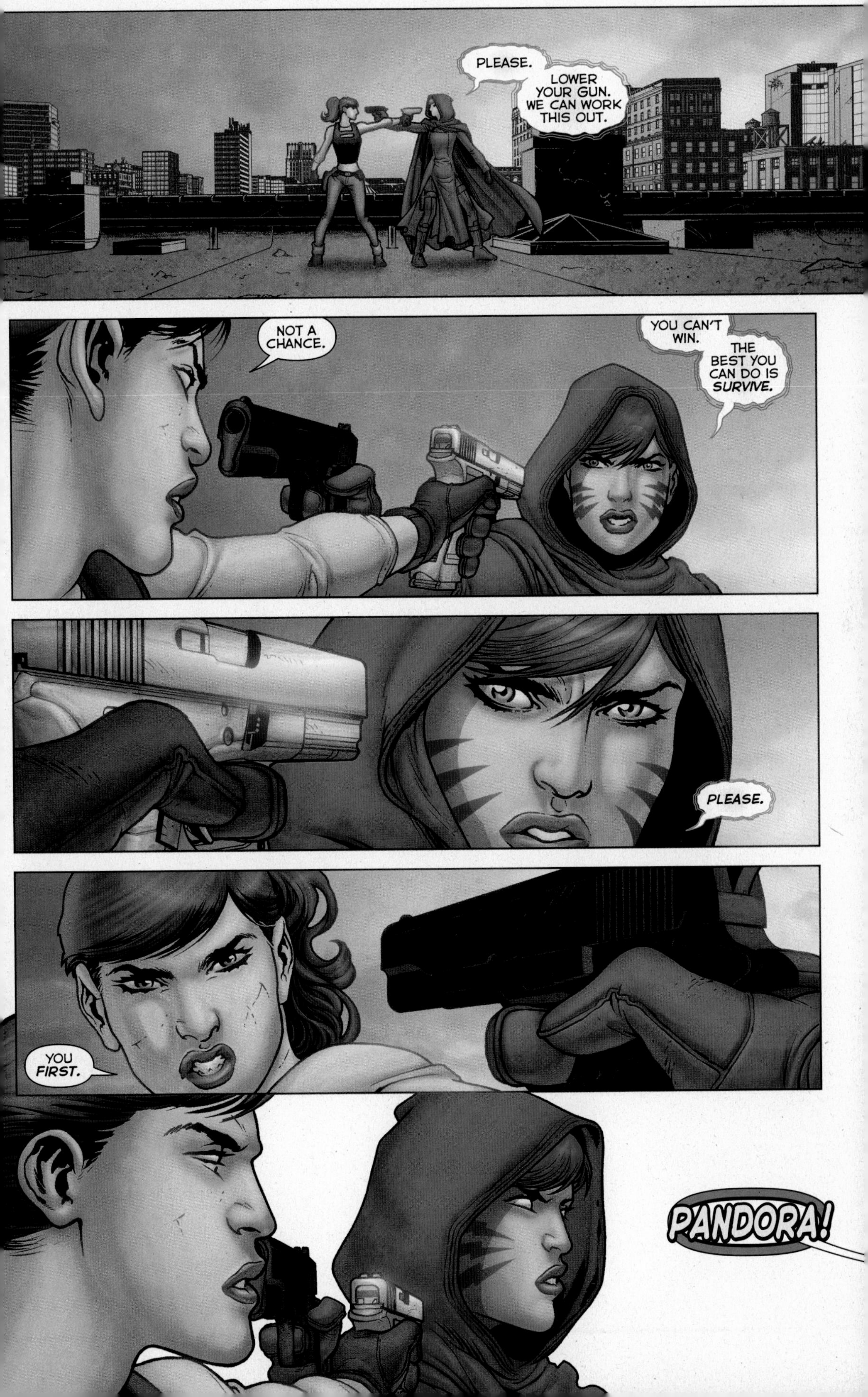
PLEASE.
LOWER YOUR GUN. WE CAN WORK THIS OUT.
NOT A CHANCE.
YOU CAN'T WIN.
THE BEST YOU CAN DO IS *SURVIVE.*
PLEASE.
YOU *FIRST.*
PANDORA!

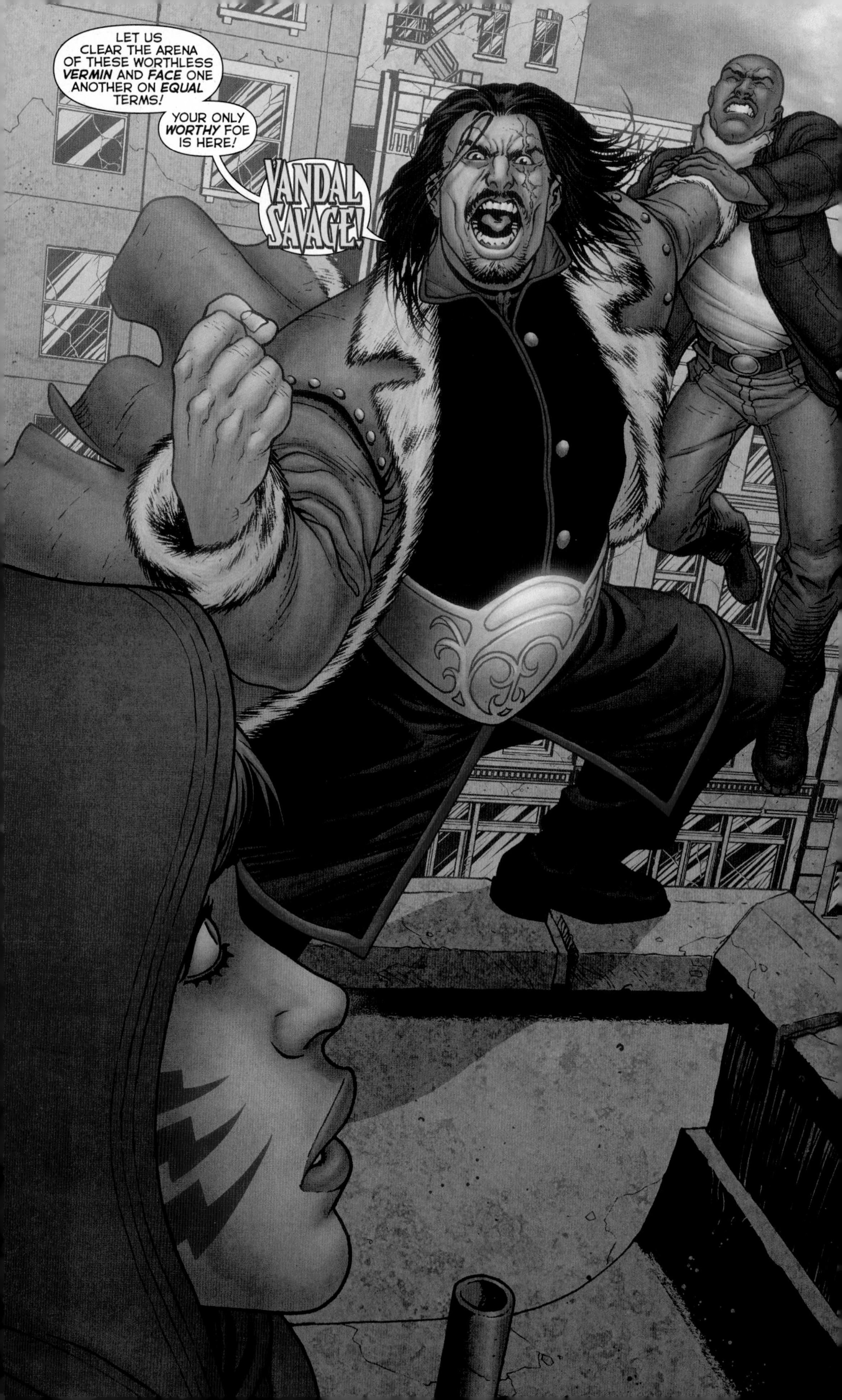

LET US CLEAR THE ARENA OF THESE WORTHLESS *VERMIN* AND *FACE* ONE ANOTHER ON *EQUAL* TERMS!
YOUR ONLY *WORTHY* FOE IS HERE!
VANDAL SAVAGE!

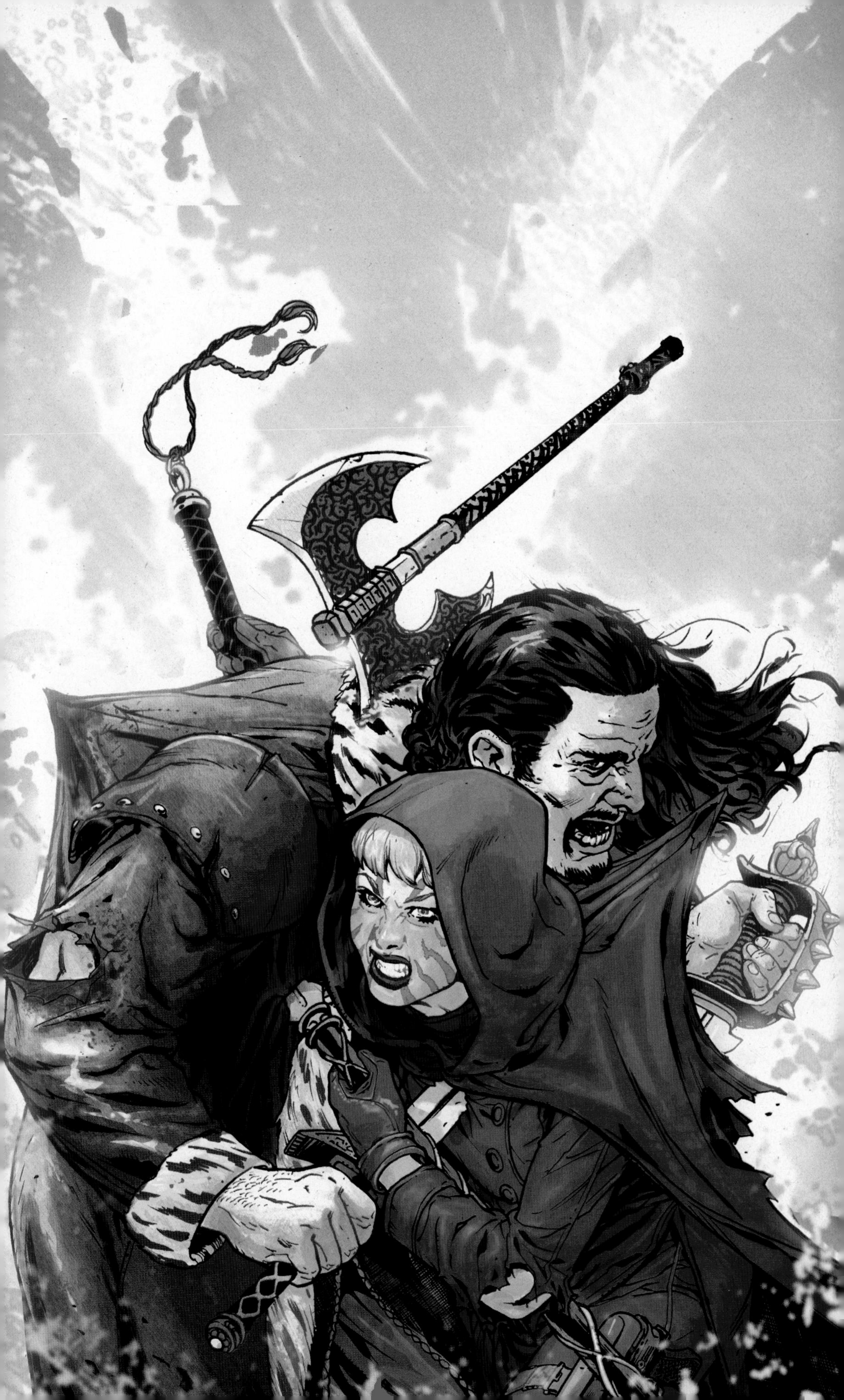

ONE IN TEN BILLION

RAY FAWKES
writer

TOM DERENICK
breakdowns

FRANCIS PORTELA
artist

ANDEW DALHOUSE
colorist

DEZI SIENTY
TAYLOR ESPOSITO
letterers

cover art by
VICTOR IBAÑEZ

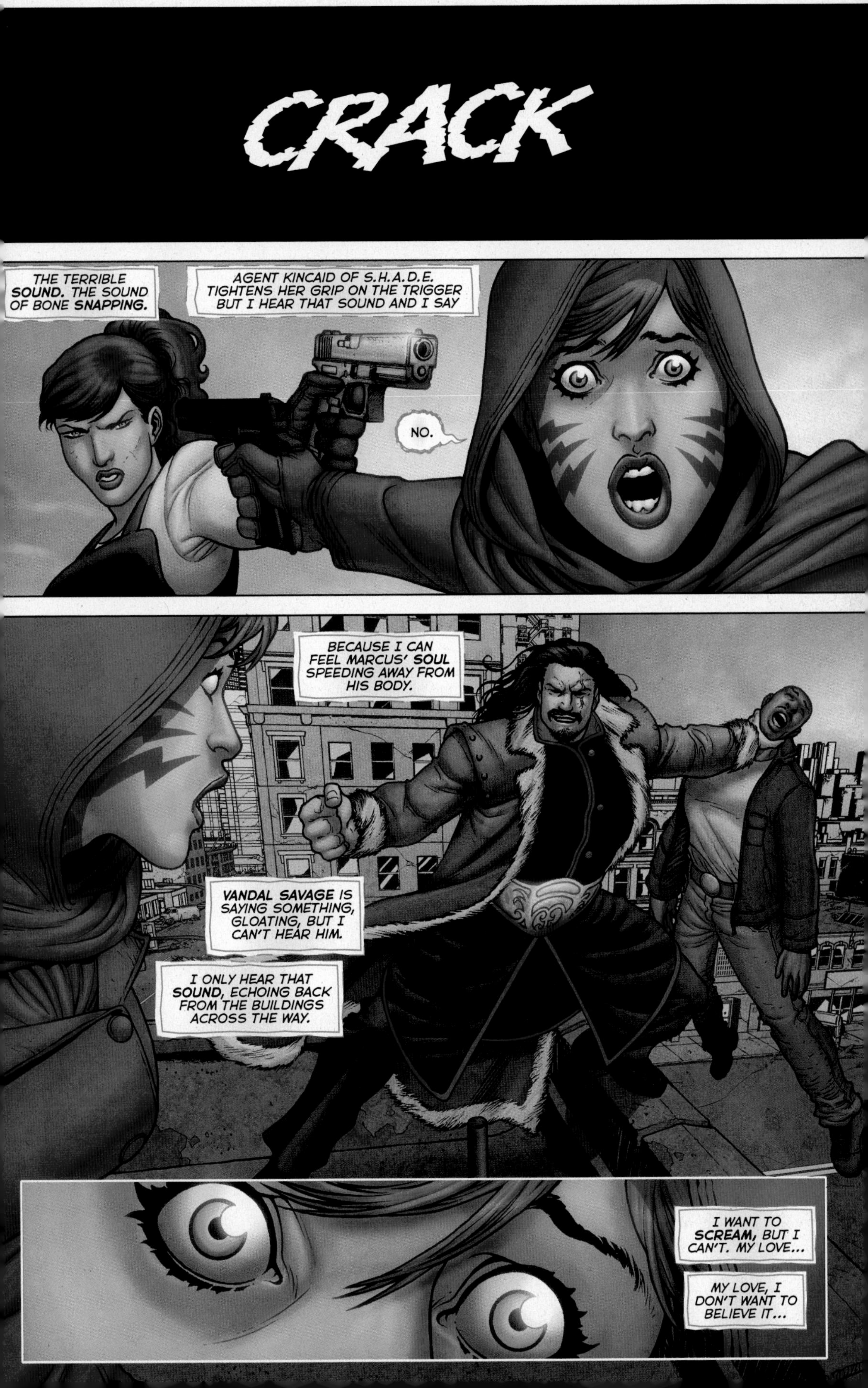
CRACK
THE TERRIBLE SOUND. THE SOUND OF BONE SNAPPING.
AGENT KINCAID OF S.H.A.D.E. TIGHTENS HER GRIP ON THE TRIGGER BUT I HEAR THAT SOUND AND I SAY
NO.
BECAUSE I CAN FEEL MARCUS' SOUL SPEEDING AWAY FROM HIS BODY.
VANDAL SAVAGE IS SAYING SOMETHING, GLOATING, BUT I CAN'T HEAR HIM.
I ONLY HEAR THAT SOUND, ECHOING BACK FROM THE BUILDINGS ACROSS THE WAY.
I WANT TO SCREAM, BUT I CAN'T. MY LOVE...
MY LOVE, I DON'T WANT TO BELIEVE IT...

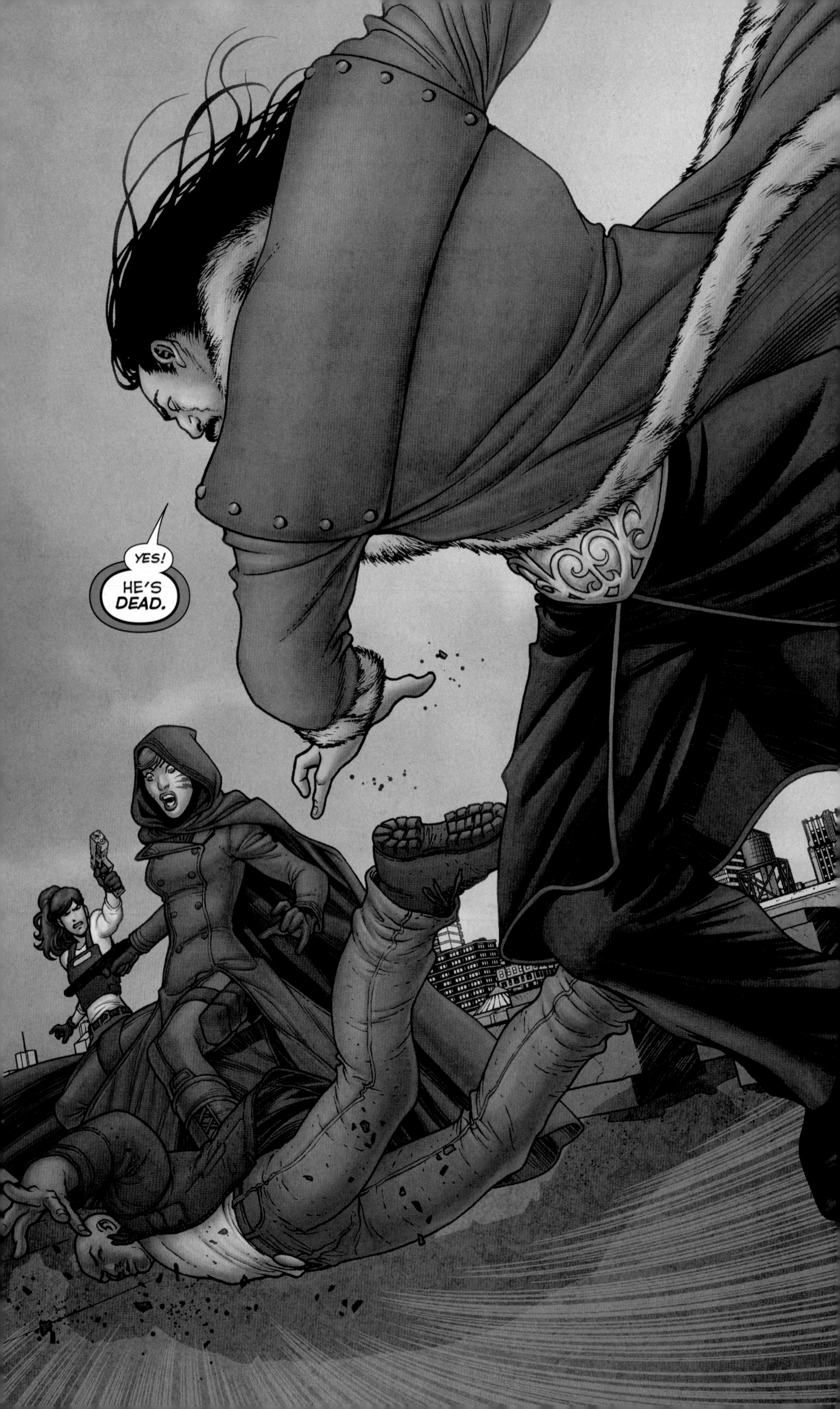
YES!
HE'S DEAD.

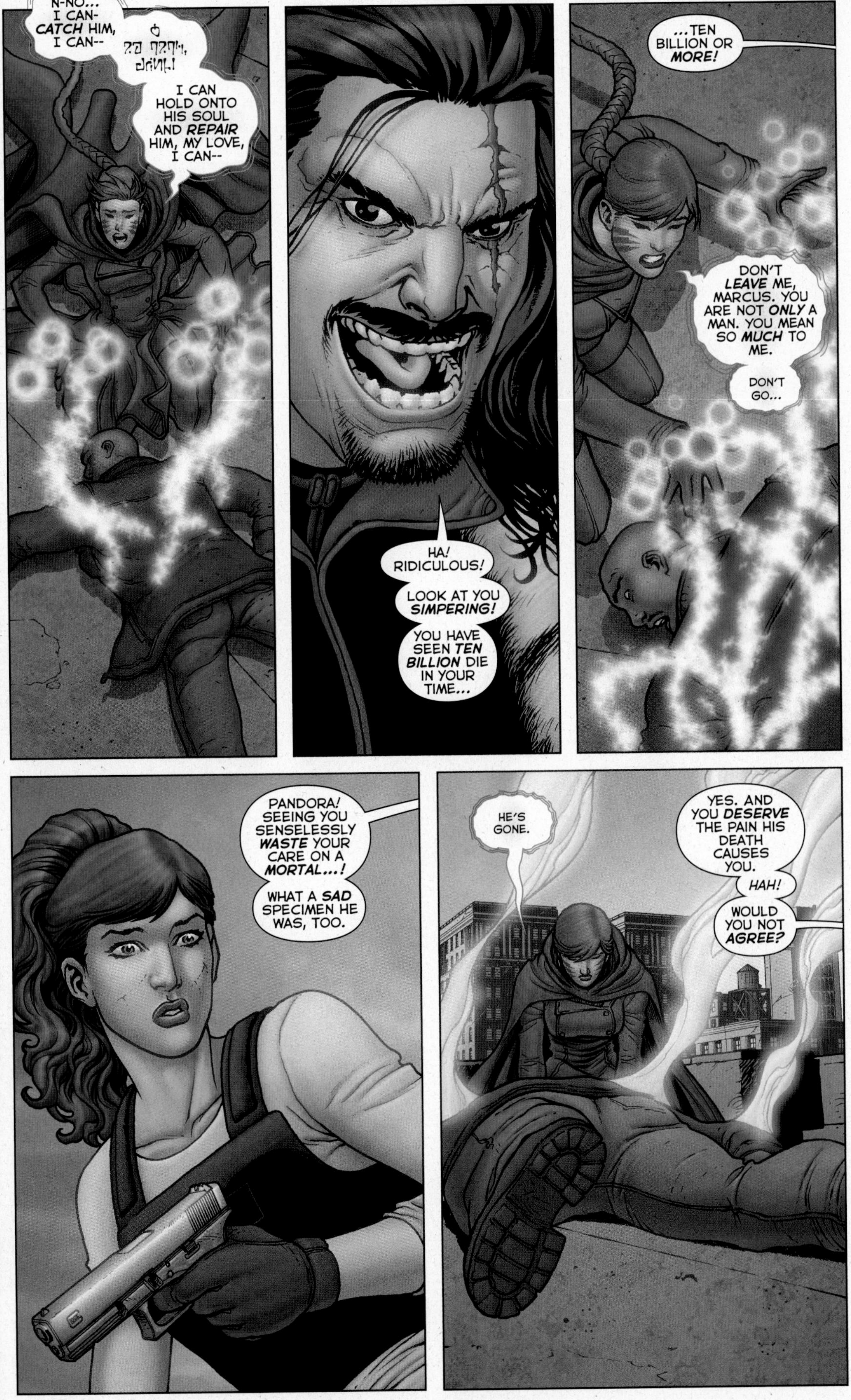
N-NO... I CAN-CATCH HIM, I CAN--
I CAN HOLD ONTO HIS SOUL AND REPAIR HIM, MY LOVE, I CAN--
HA! RIDICULOUS!
LOOK AT YOU SIMPERING!
YOU HAVE SEEN TEN BILLION DIE IN YOUR TIME...
...TEN BILLION OR MORE!
DON'T LEAVE ME, MARCUS. YOU ARE NOT ONLY A MAN. YOU MEAN SO MUCH TO ME.
DON'T GO...
PANDORA! SEEING YOU SENSELESSLY WASTE YOUR CARE ON A MORTAL...!
WHAT A SAD SPECIMEN HE WAS, TOO.
HE'S GONE.
YES. AND YOU DESERVE THE PAIN HIS DEATH CAUSES YOU.
HAH!
WOULD YOU NOT AGREE?

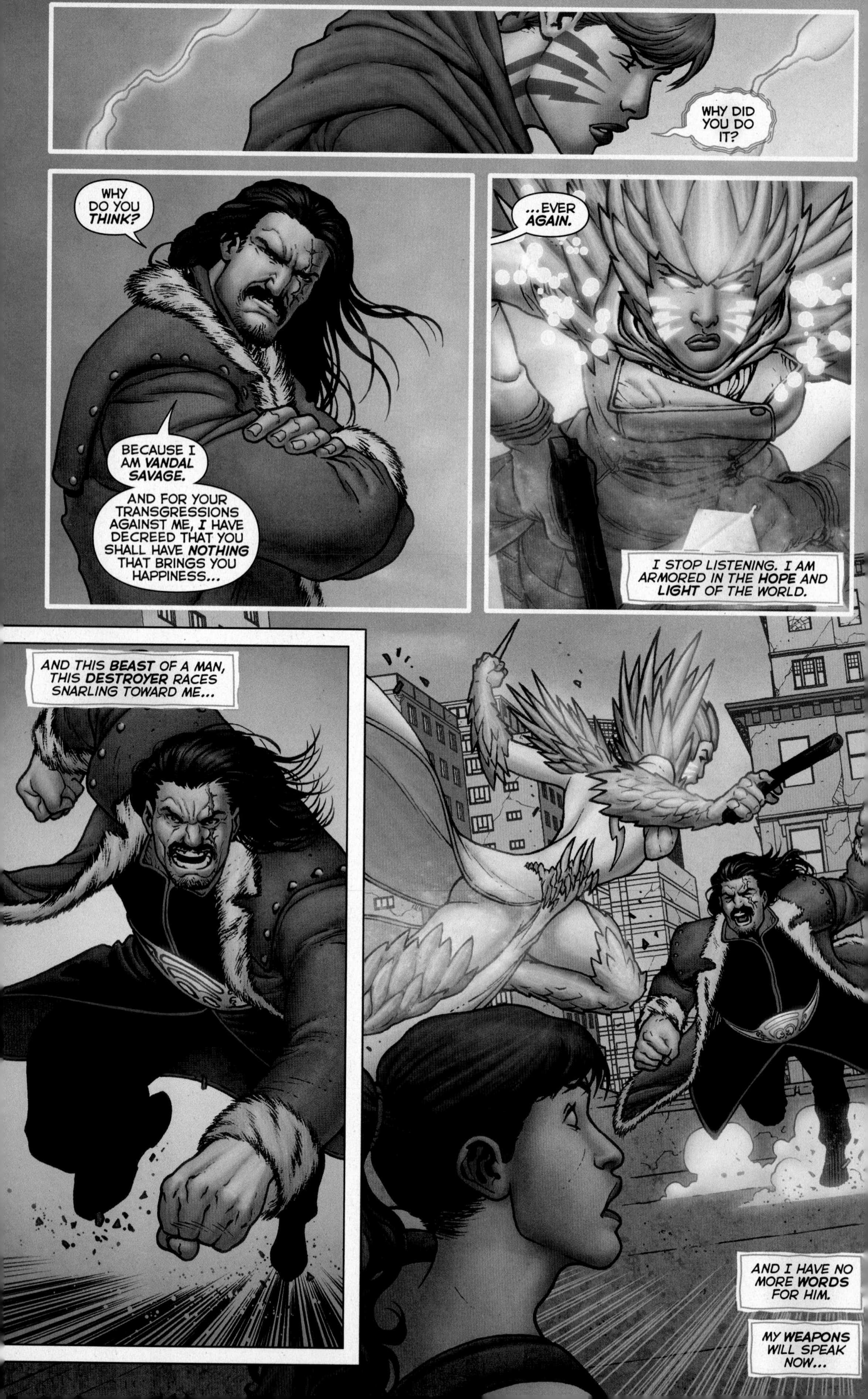

WHY DID YOU DO IT?
WHY DO YOU THINK?
BECAUSE I AM VANDAL SAVAGE.
AND FOR YOUR TRANSGRESSIONS AGAINST ME, I HAVE DECREED THAT YOU SHALL HAVE NOTHING THAT BRINGS YOU HAPPINESS...
...EVER AGAIN.
I STOP LISTENING. I AM ARMORED IN THE HOPE AND LIGHT OF THE WORLD.
AND THIS BEAST OF A MAN, THIS DESTROYER RACES SNARLING TOWARD ME...
AND I HAVE NO MORE WORDS FOR HIM.
MY WEAPONS WILL SPEAK NOW...

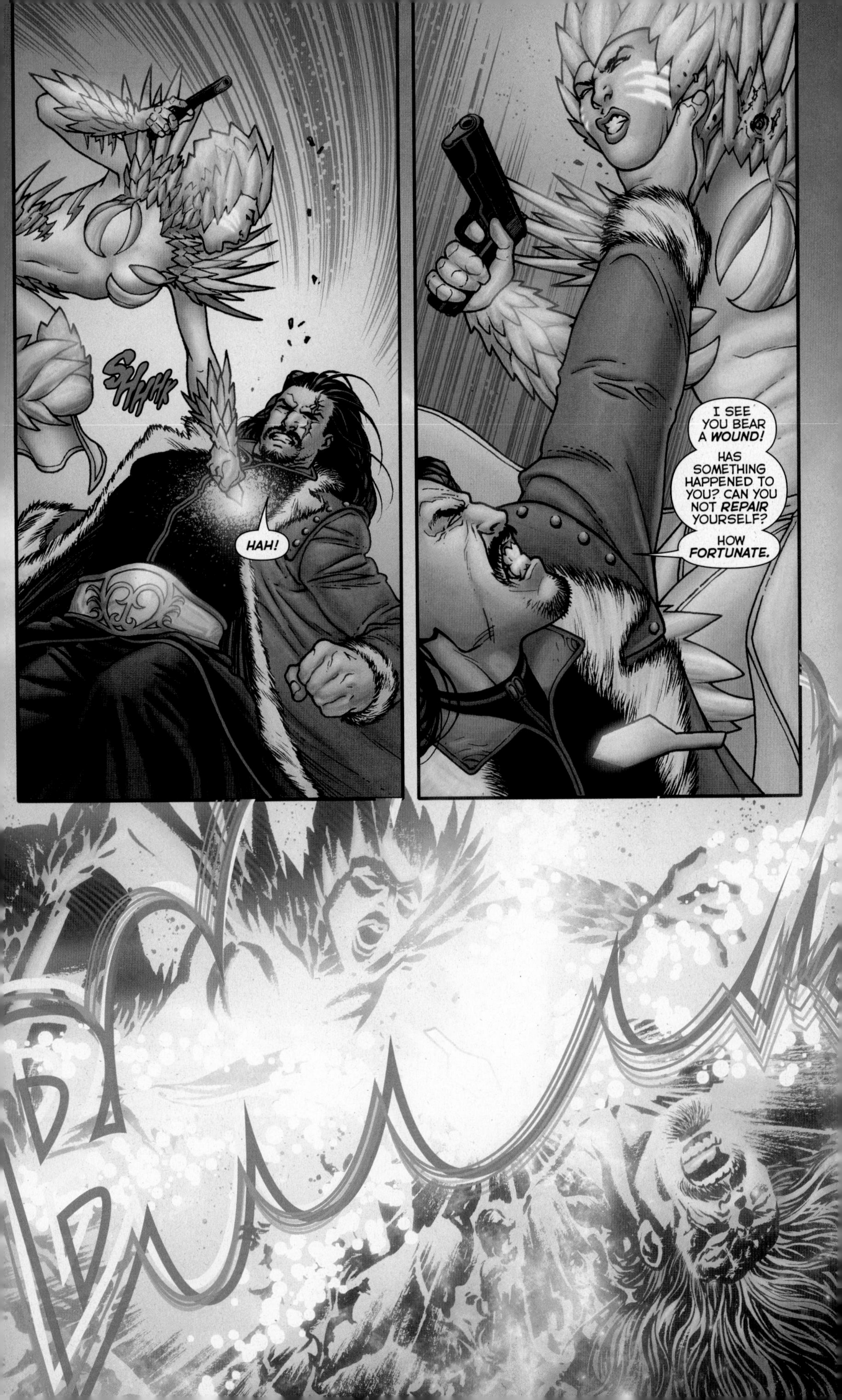
SHHHK
HAH!
I SEE YOU BEAR A WOUND!
HAS SOMETHING HAPPENED TO YOU? CAN YOU NOT REPAIR YOURSELF?
HOW FORTUNATE.

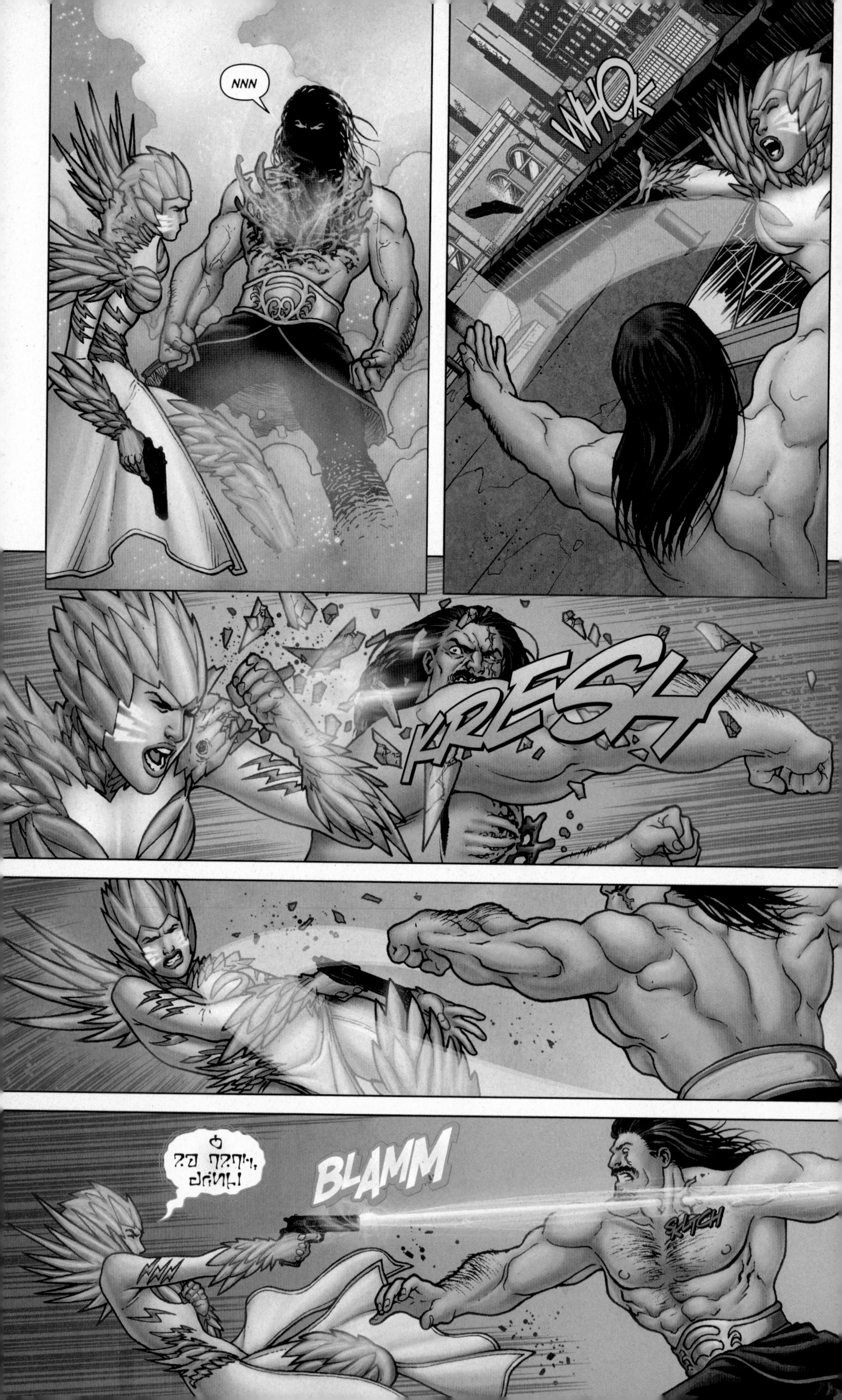
NNN
WHOK
KRESH
BLAMM
SKLTCH

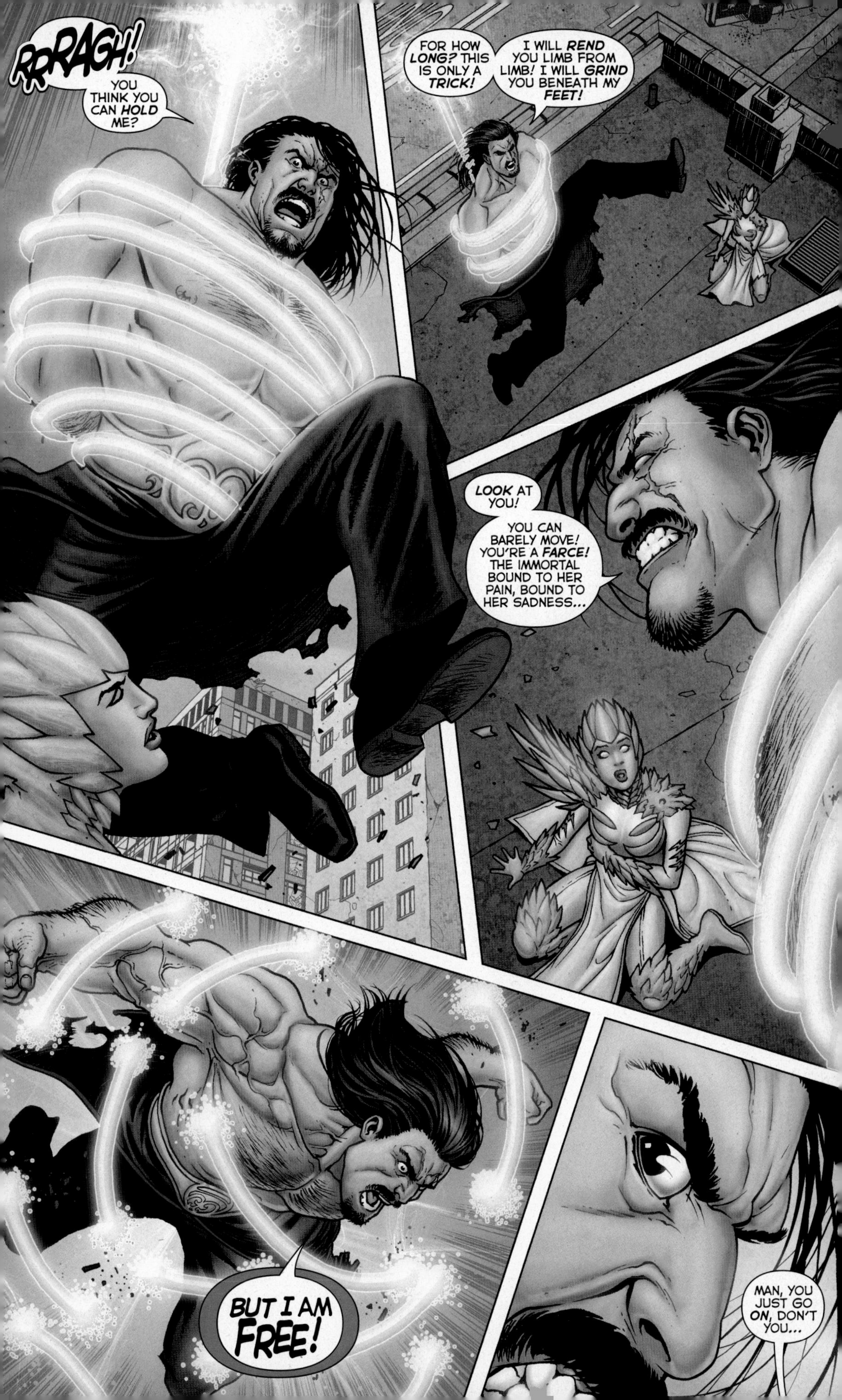
RRRAGH!
YOU THINK YOU CAN HOLD ME?
FOR HOW LONG? THIS IS ONLY A TRICK!
I WILL REND YOU LIMB FROM LIMB! I WILL GRIND YOU BENEATH MY FEET!
LOOK AT YOU!
YOU CAN BARELY MOVE! YOU'RE A FARCE! THE IMMORTAL BOUND TO HER PAIN, BOUND TO HER SADNESS...
BUT I AM FREE!
MAN, YOU JUST GO ON, DON'T YOU...

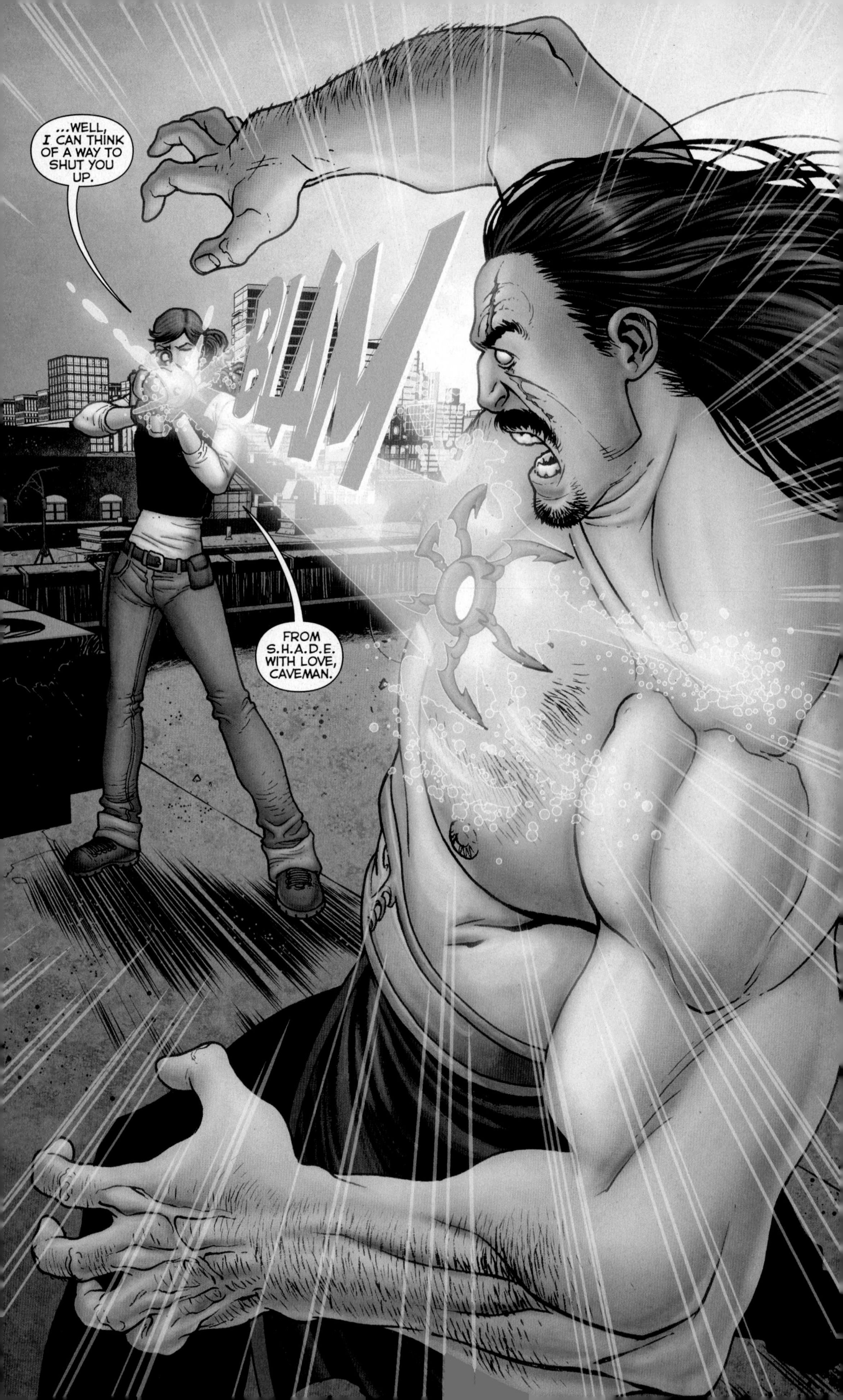
...WELL, I CAN THINK OF A WAY TO SHUT YOU UP.
BLAM
FROM S.H.A.D.E. WITH LOVE, CAVEMAN.

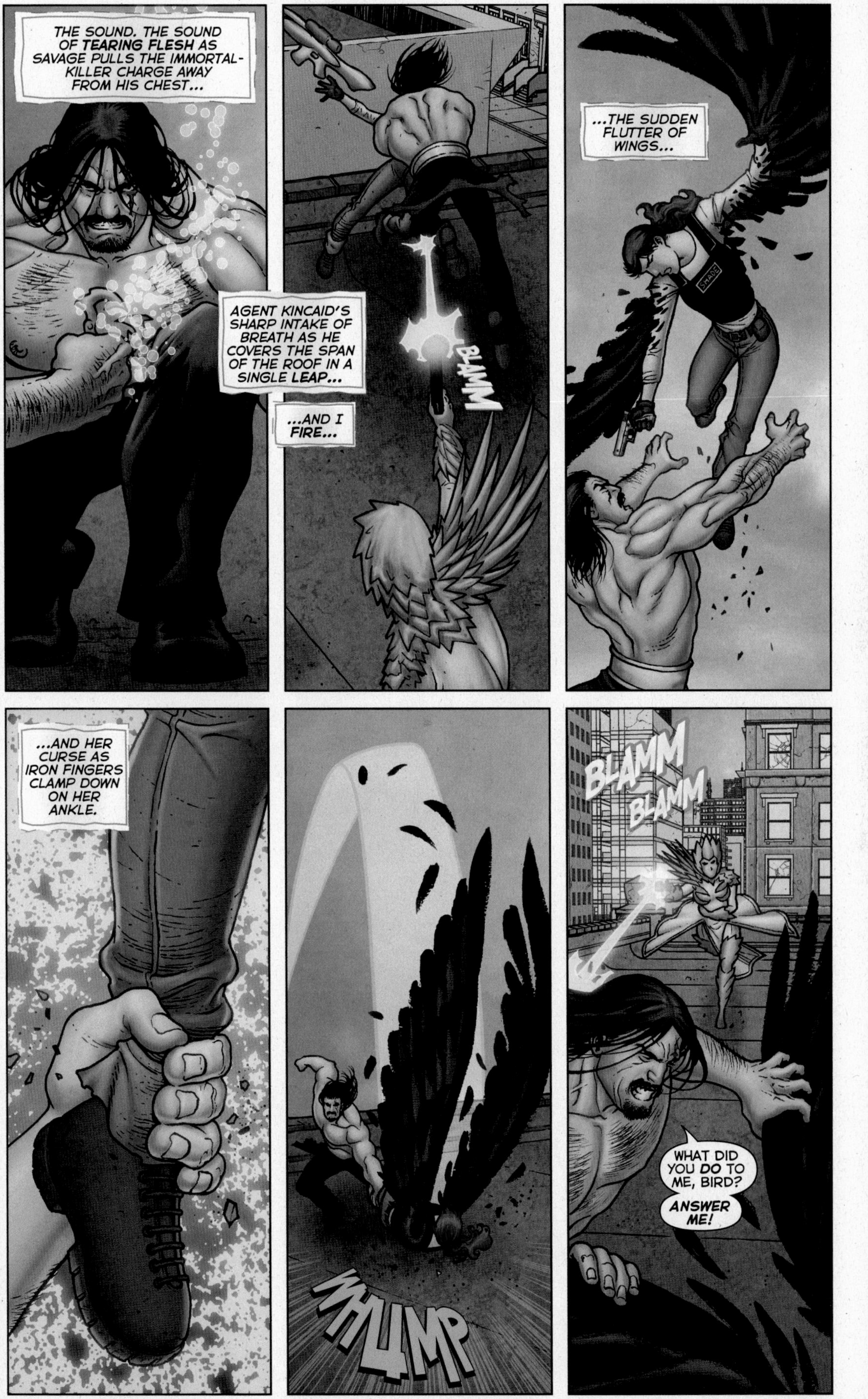
THE SOUND. THE SOUND OF TEARING FLESH AS SAVAGE PULLS THE IMMORTAL-KILLER CHARGE AWAY FROM HIS CHEST...
AGENT KINCAID'S SHARP INTAKE OF BREATH AS HE COVERS THE SPAN OF THE ROOF IN A SINGLE LEAP...
...AND I FIRE...
BLAMM
...THE SUDDEN FLUTTER OF WINGS...
SHADE
...AND HER CURSE AS IRON FINGERS CLAMP DOWN ON HER ANKLE.
WHUMP
BLAMM
BLAMM
WHAT DID YOU DO TO ME, BIRD?
ANSWER ME!

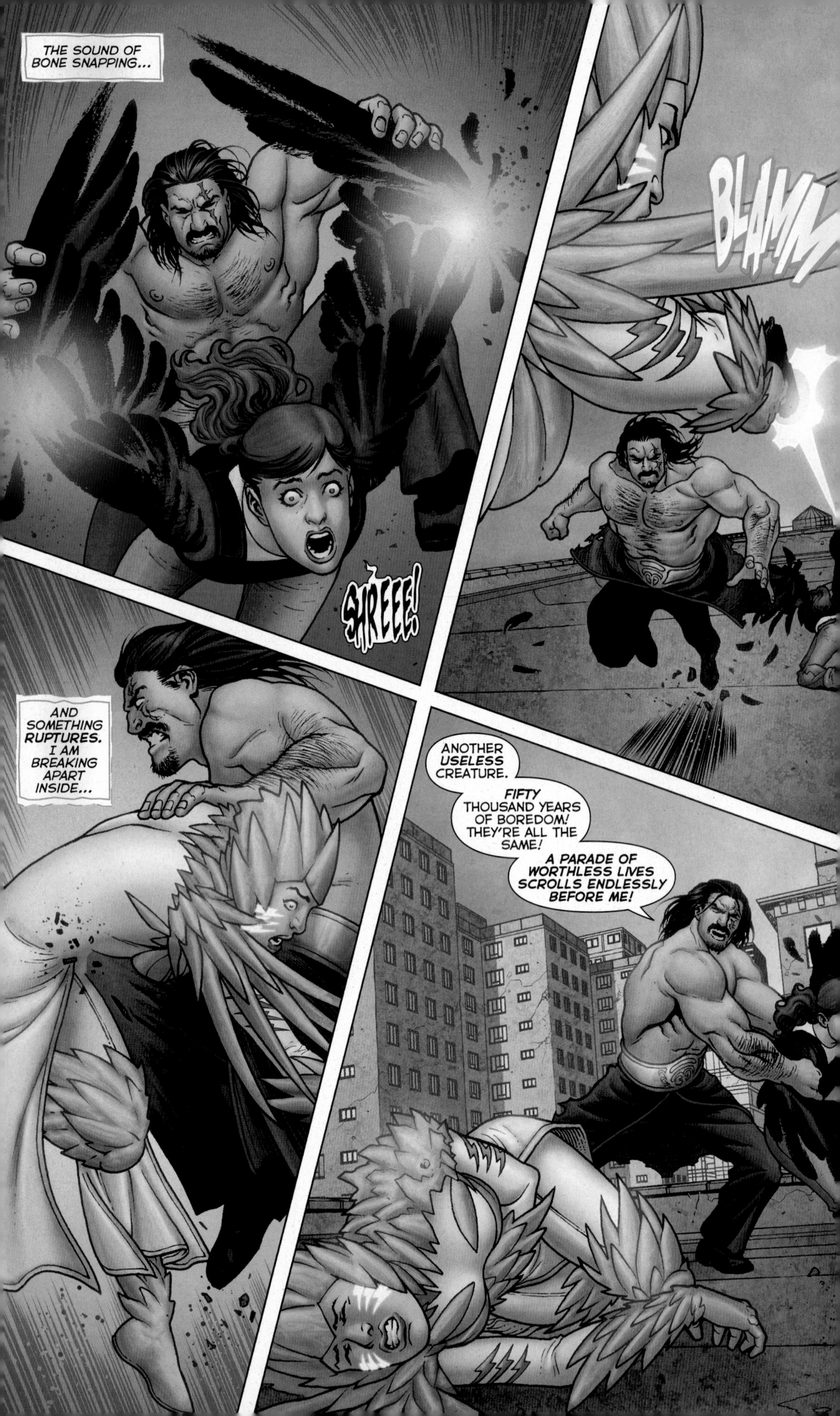
THE SOUND OF BONE SNAPPING...
SHREEE!
BLAMM
AND SOMETHING RUPTURES. I AM BREAKING APART INSIDE...
ANOTHER USELESS CREATURE.
FIFTY THOUSAND YEARS OF BOREDOM! THEY'RE ALL THE SAME!
A PARADE OF WORTHLESS LIVES SCROLLS ENDLESSLY BEFORE ME!

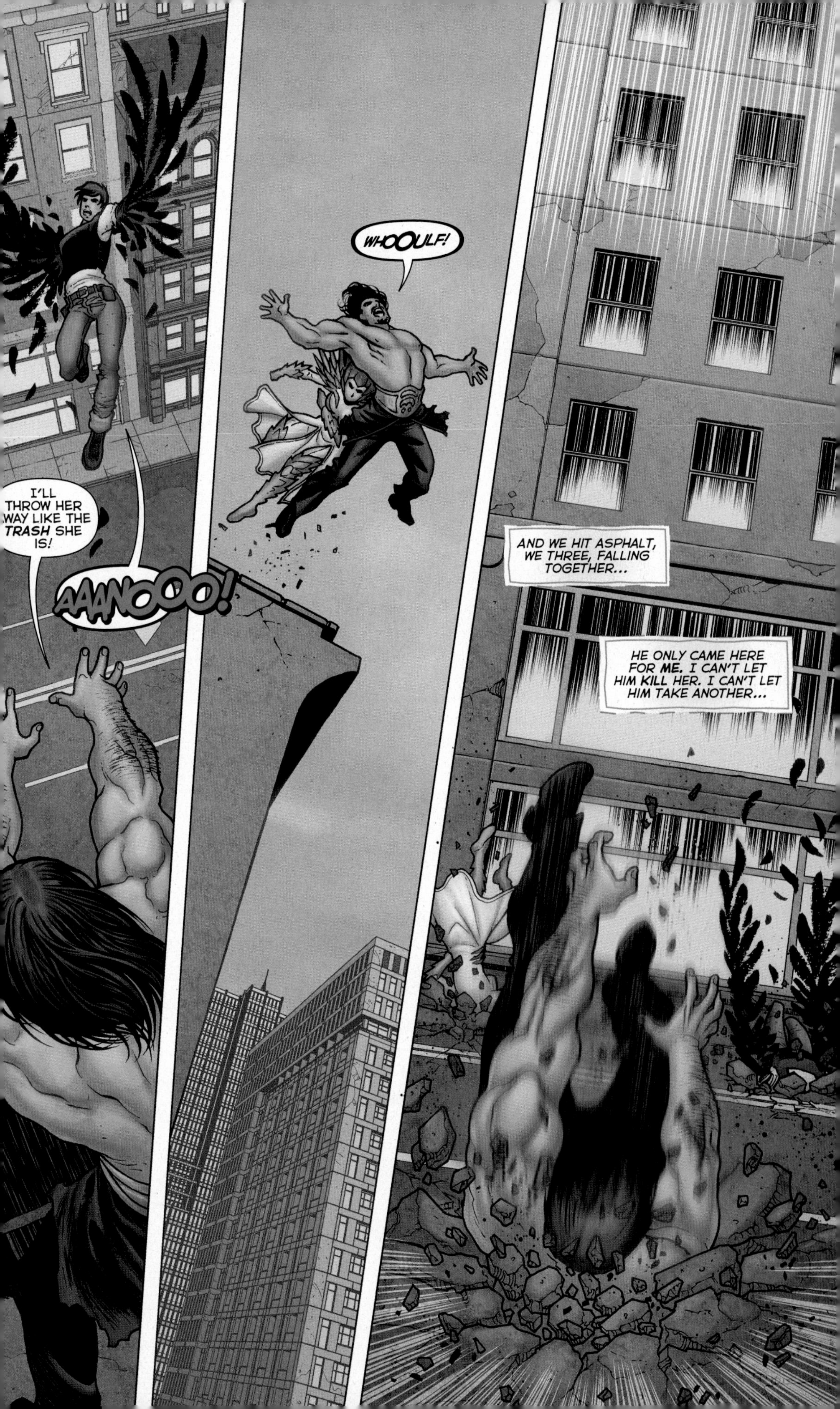

I'LL THROW HER AWAY LIKE THE TRASH SHE IS!
AAANOOO!
WHOOULF!
AND WE HIT ASPHALT, WE THREE, FALLING TOGETHER...
HE ONLY CAME HERE FOR ME. I CAN'T LET HIM KILL HER. I CAN'T LET HIM TAKE ANOTHER...

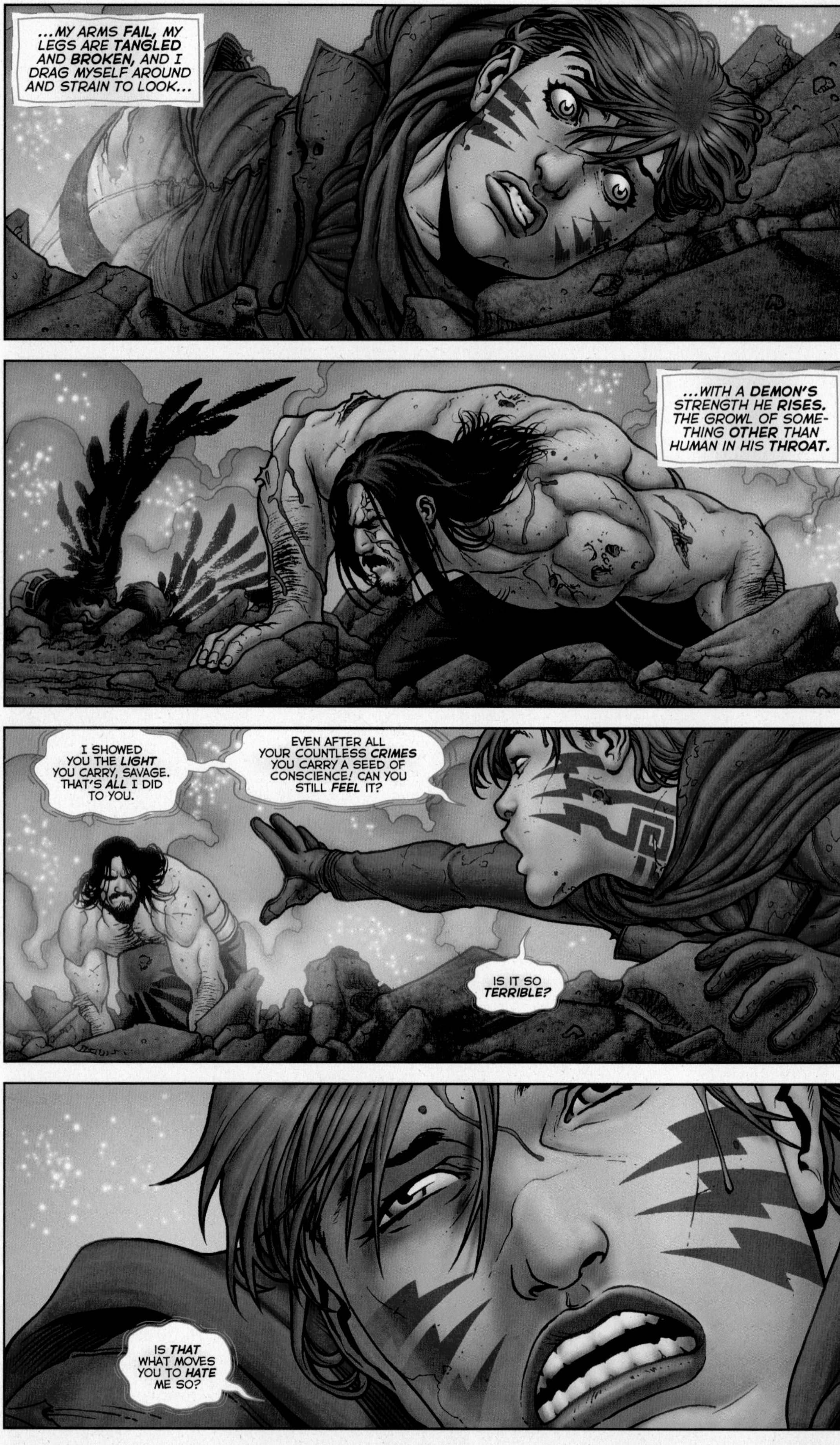
...MY ARMS FAIL, MY LEGS ARE TANGLED AND BROKEN, AND I DRAG MYSELF AROUND AND STRAIN TO LOOK...
...WITH A DEMON'S STRENGTH HE RISES. THE GROWL OF SOMETHING OTHER THAN HUMAN IN HIS THROAT.
I SHOWED YOU THE LIGHT YOU CARRY, SAVAGE. THAT'S ALL I DID TO YOU.
EVEN AFTER ALL YOUR COUNTLESS CRIMES YOU CARRY A SEED OF CONSCIENCE! CAN YOU STILL FEEL IT?
IS IT SO TERRIBLE?
IS THAT WHAT MOVES YOU TO HATE ME SO?

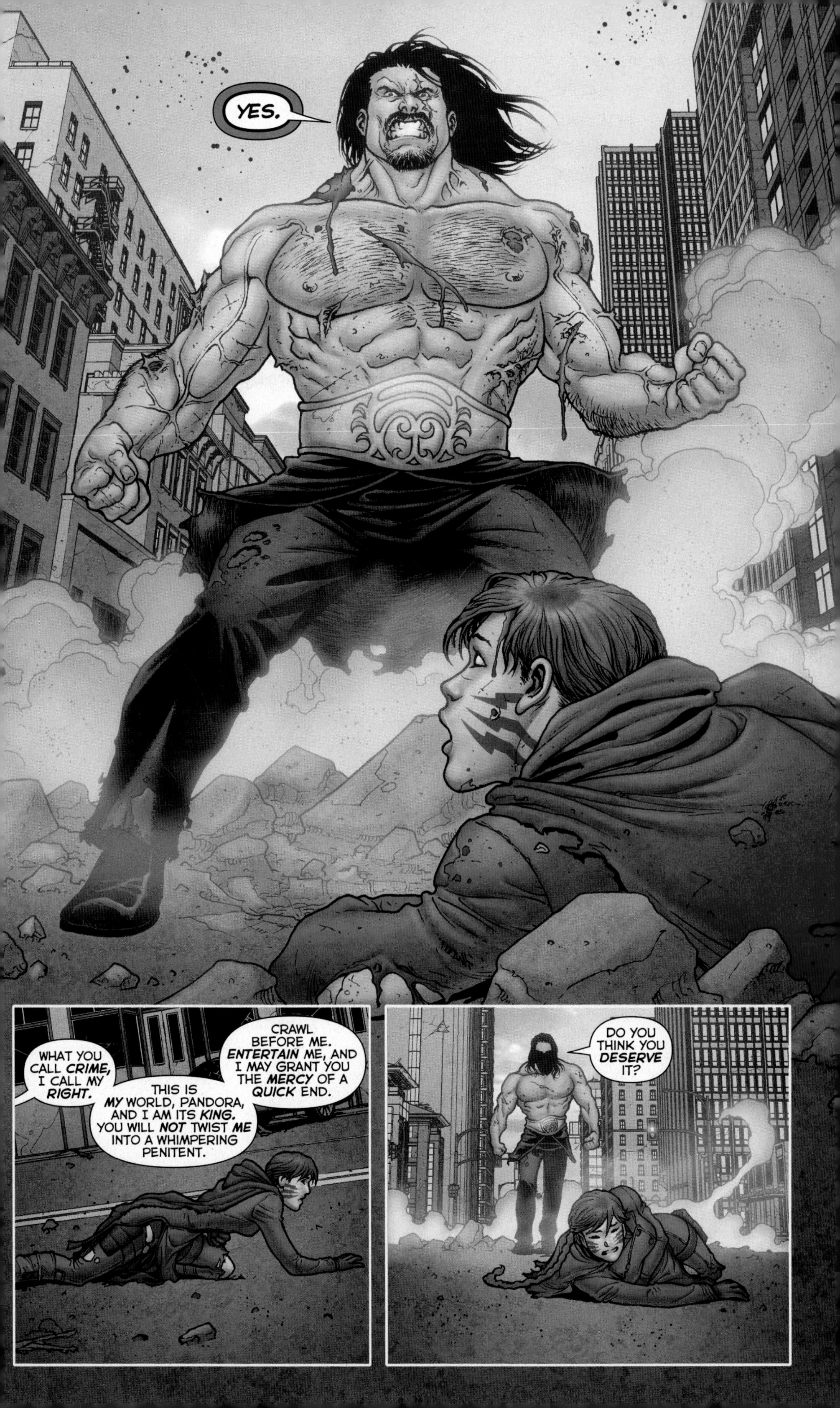
YES.
WHAT YOU CALL CRIME, I CALL MY RIGHT.
THIS IS MY WORLD, PANDORA, AND I AM ITS KING. YOU WILL NOT TWIST ME INTO A WHIMPERING PENITENT.
CRAWL BEFORE ME. ENTERTAIN ME, AND I MAY GRANT YOU THE MERCY OF A QUICK END.
DO YOU THINK YOU DESERVE IT?

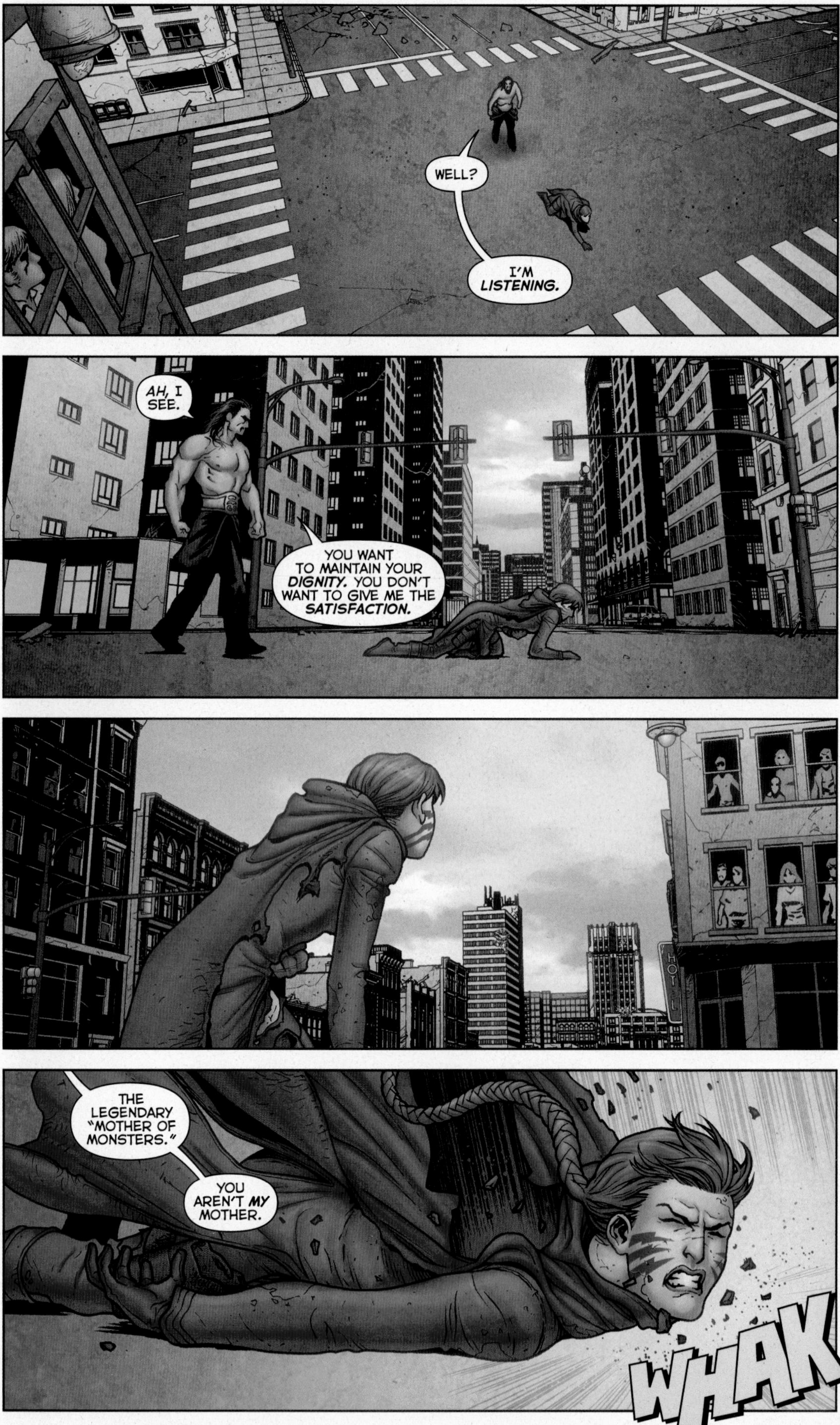
WELL?
I'M LISTENING.
AH, I SEE.
YOU WANT TO MAINTAIN YOUR DIGNITY. YOU DON'T WANT TO GIVE ME THE SATISFACTION.
HOTEL
THE LEGENDARY "MOTHER OF MONSTERS."
YOU AREN'T MY MOTHER.
WHAK

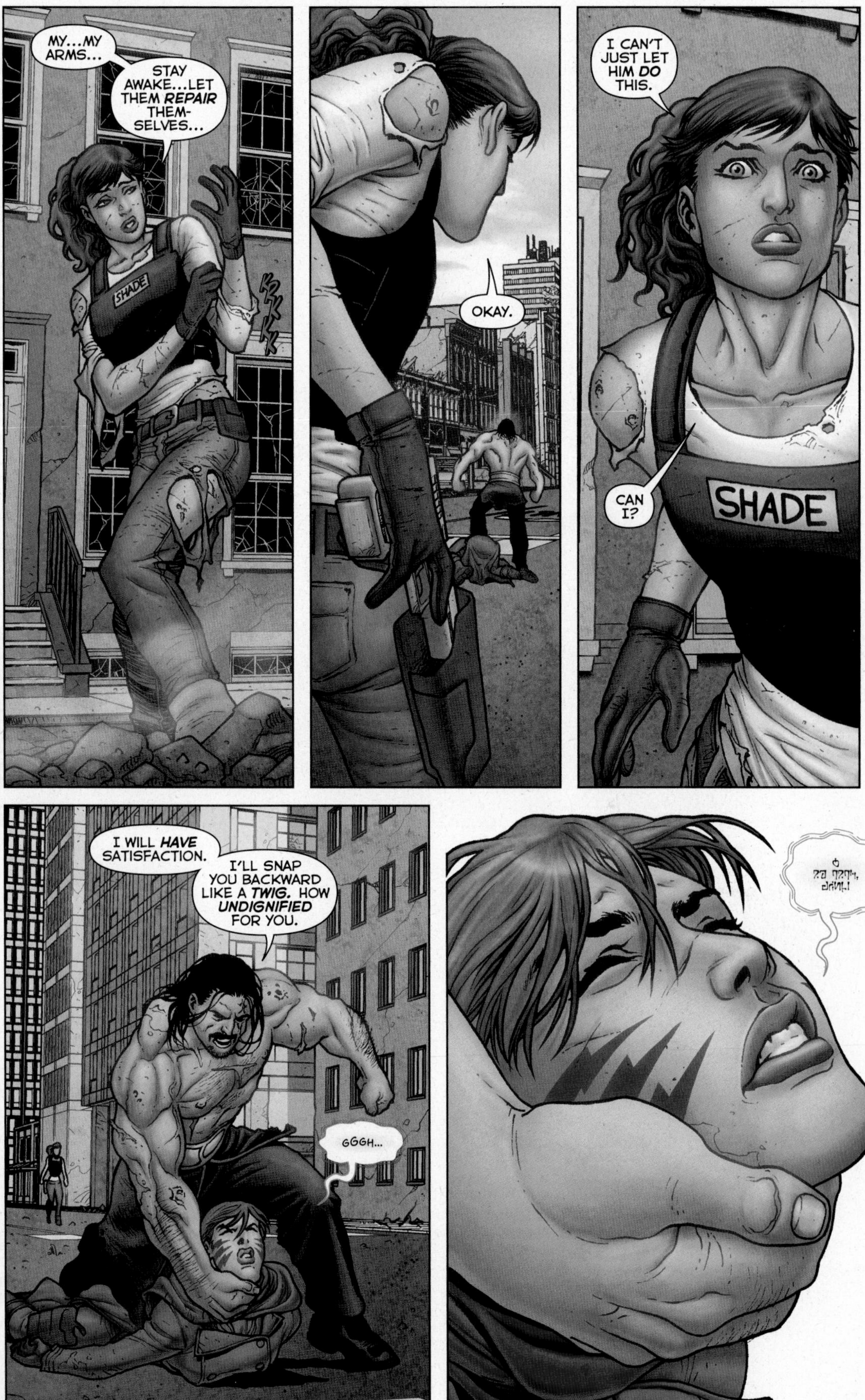

MY...MY ARMS...
STAY AWAKE...LET THEM REPAIR THEM-SELVES...
KKKK
OKAY.
I CAN'T JUST LET HIM DO THIS.
CAN I?
SHADE
I WILL HAVE SATISFACTION.
I'LL SNAP YOU BACKWARD LIKE A TWIG. HOW UNDIGNIFIED FOR YOU.
GGGH...

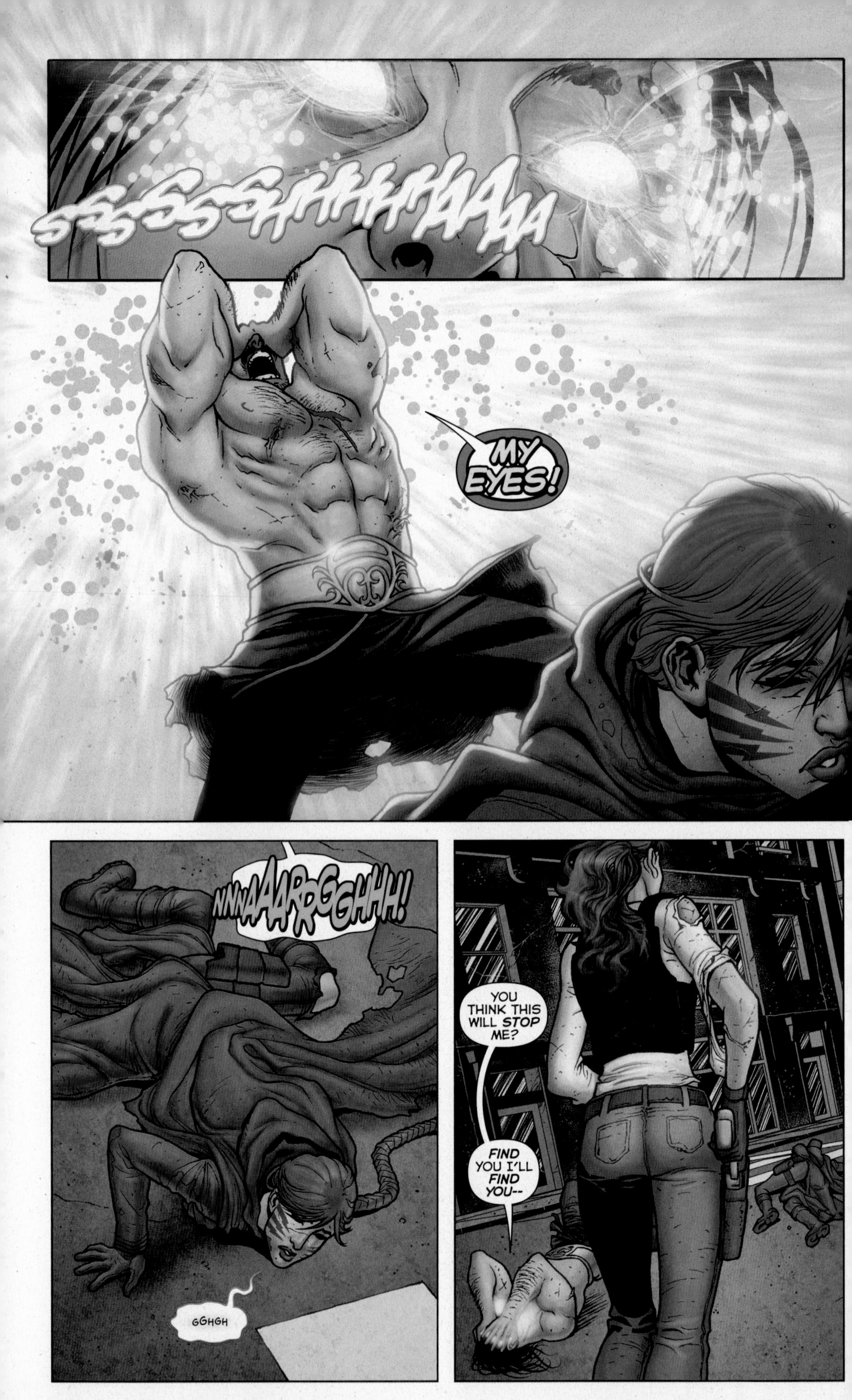
SSSSSHHHHHAAAAA
MY EYES!
NNNAAARRGGHHH!
GGHGH
YOU THINK THIS WILL STOP ME?
FIND YOU I'LL FIND YOU--

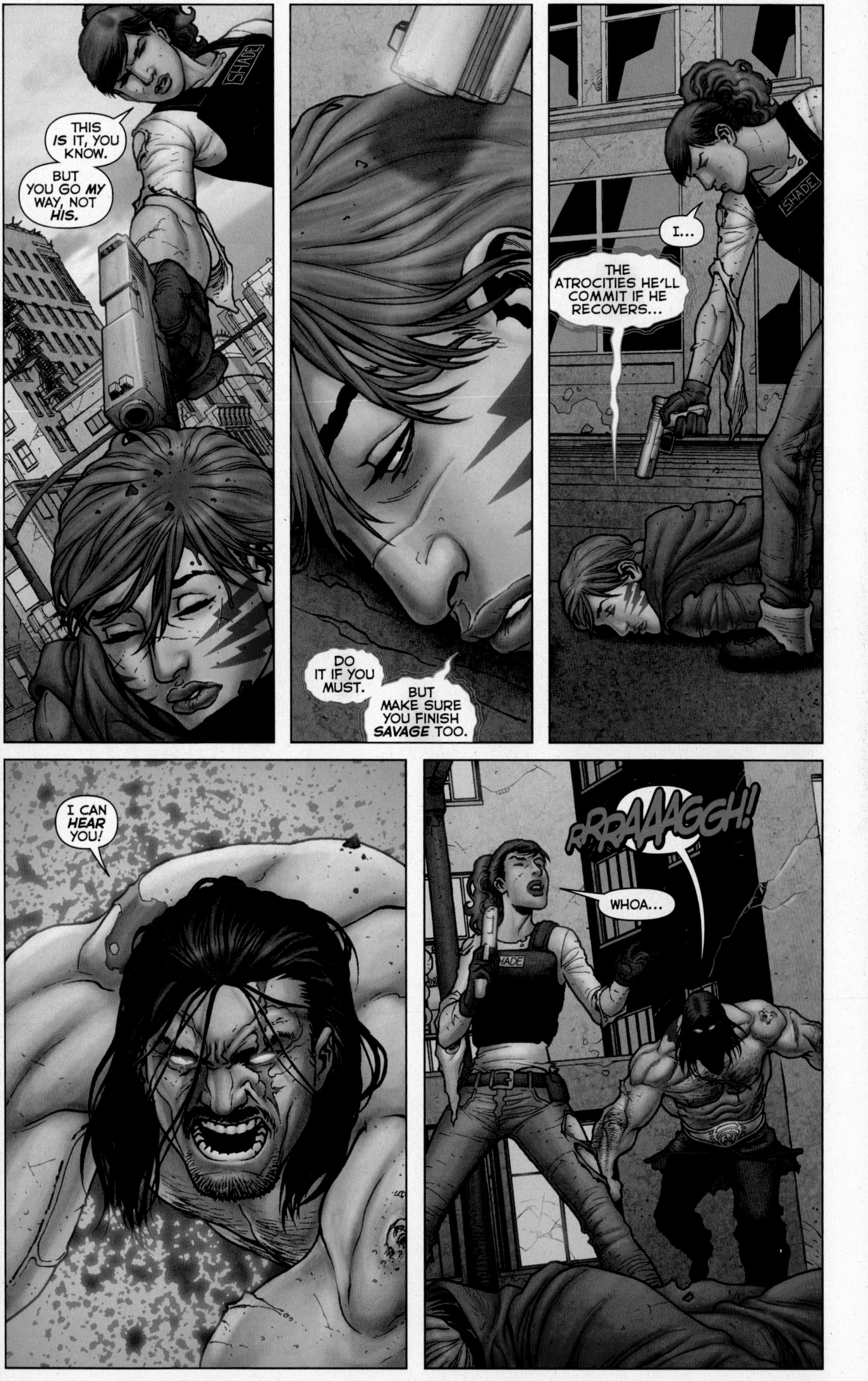
THIS IS IT, YOU KNOW.
BUT YOU GO MY WAY, NOT HIS.
DO IT IF YOU MUST.
BUT MAKE SURE YOU FINISH SAVAGE TOO.
I...
THE ATROCITIES HE'LL COMMIT IF HE RECOVERS...
I CAN HEAR YOU!
RRRAAAAGGH!
WHOA...

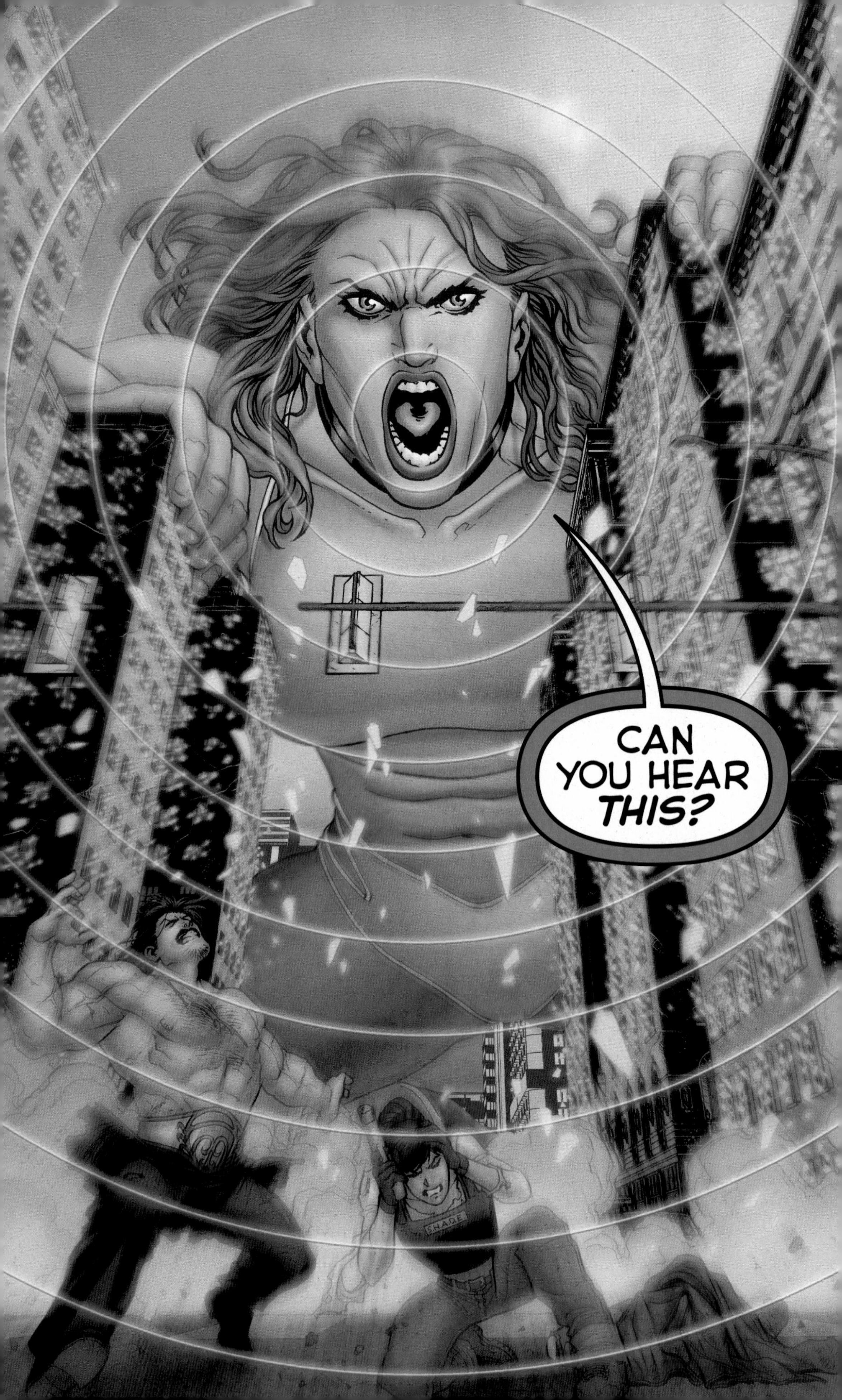
CAN YOU HEAR THIS?
SHADE

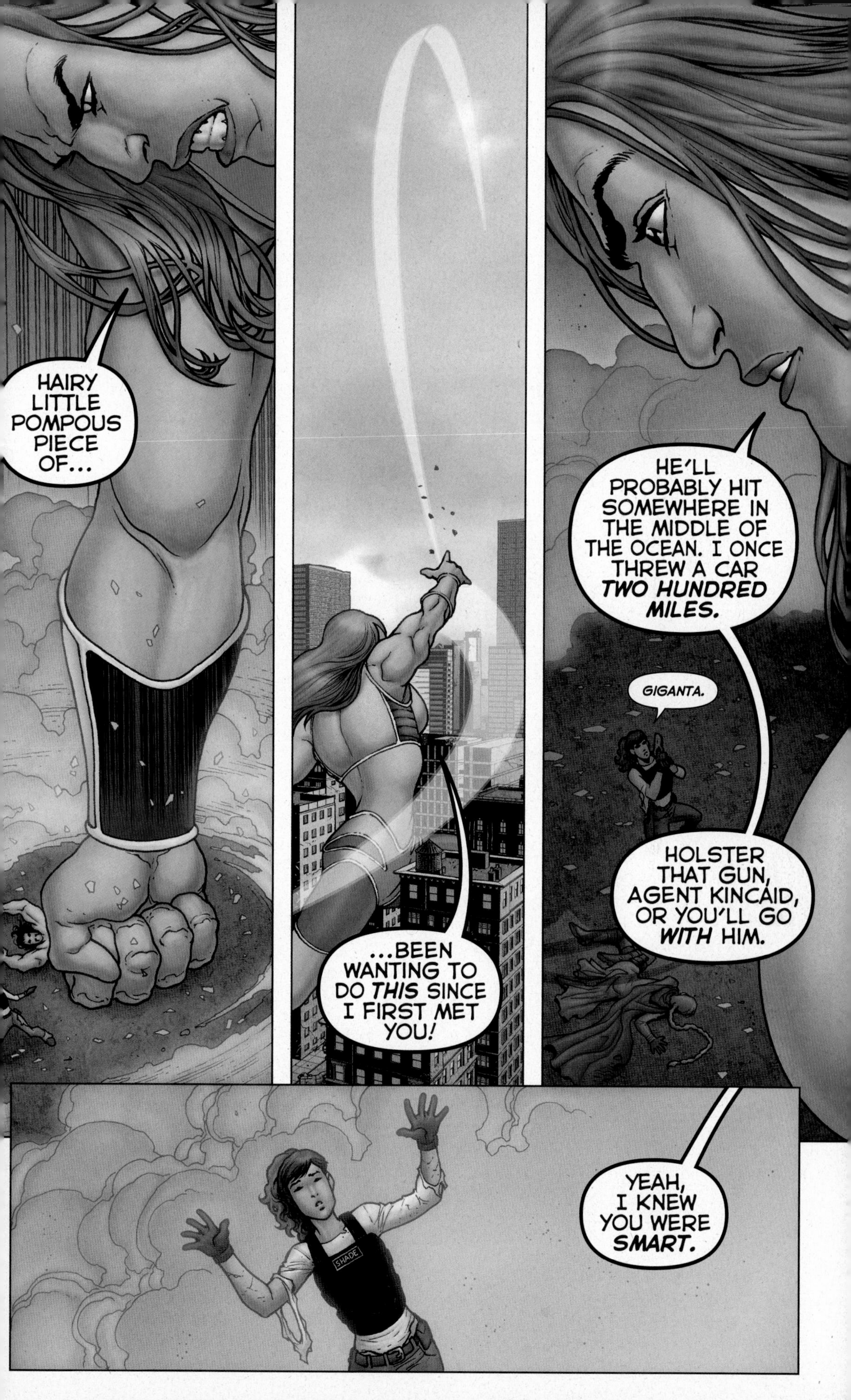
HAIRY LITTLE POMPOUS PIECE OF...
...BEEN WANTING TO DO *THIS* SINCE I FIRST MET YOU!
HE'LL PROBABLY HIT SOMEWHERE IN THE MIDDLE OF THE OCEAN. I ONCE THREW A CAR ***TWO HUNDRED MILES.***
GIGANTA.
HOLSTER THAT GUN, AGENT KINCAID, OR YOU'LL GO ***WITH*** HIM.
SHADE
YEAH, I KNEW YOU WERE ***SMART.***

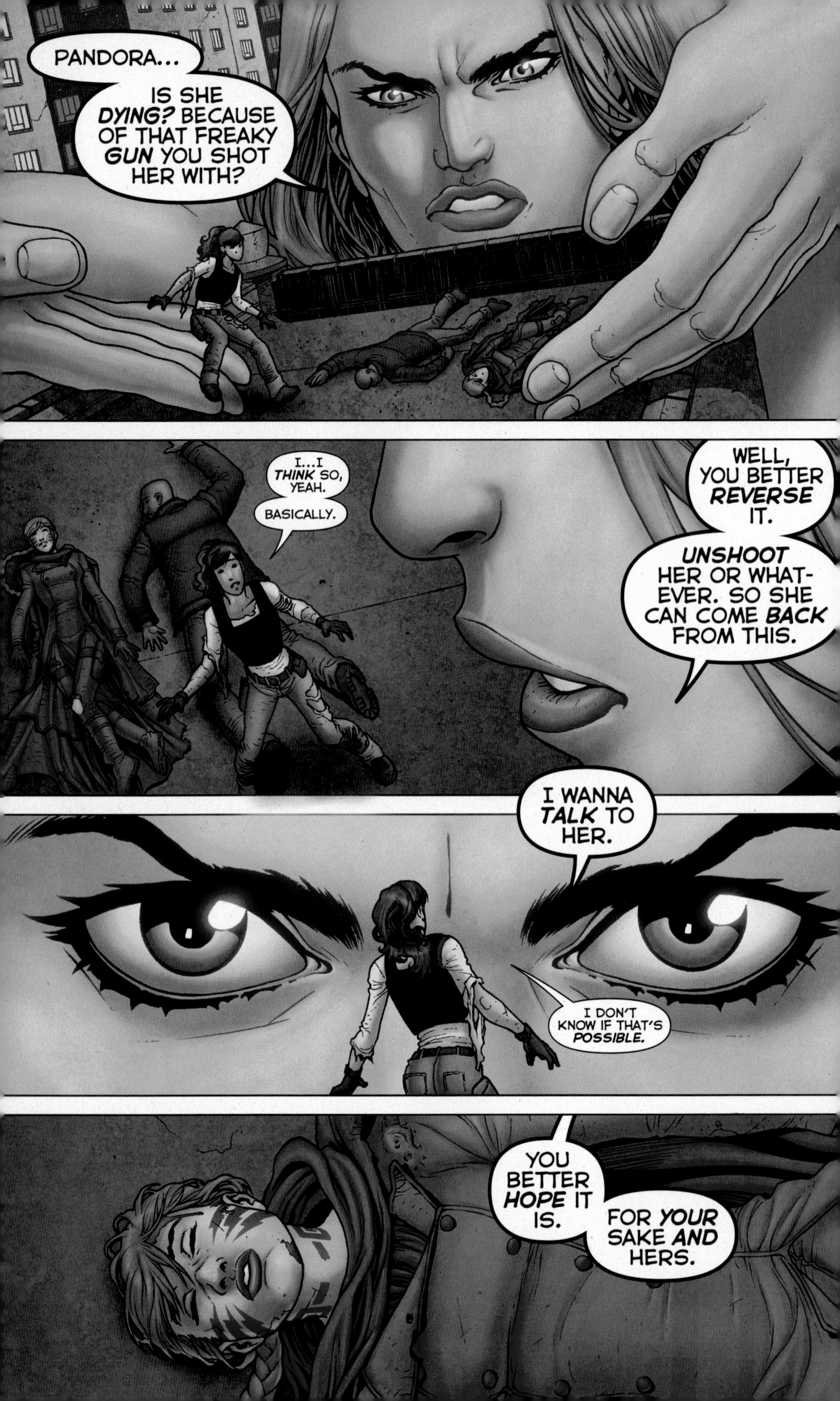
PANDORA...
IS SHE DYING? BECAUSE OF THAT FREAKY GUN YOU SHOT HER WITH?
I...I THINK SO, YEAH.
BASICALLY.
WELL, YOU BETTER REVERSE IT.
UNSHOOT HER OR WHAT-EVER. SO SHE CAN COME BACK FROM THIS.
I WANNA TALK TO HER.
I DON'T KNOW IF THAT'S POSSIBLE.
YOU BETTER HOPE IT IS.
FOR YOUR SAKE AND HERS.

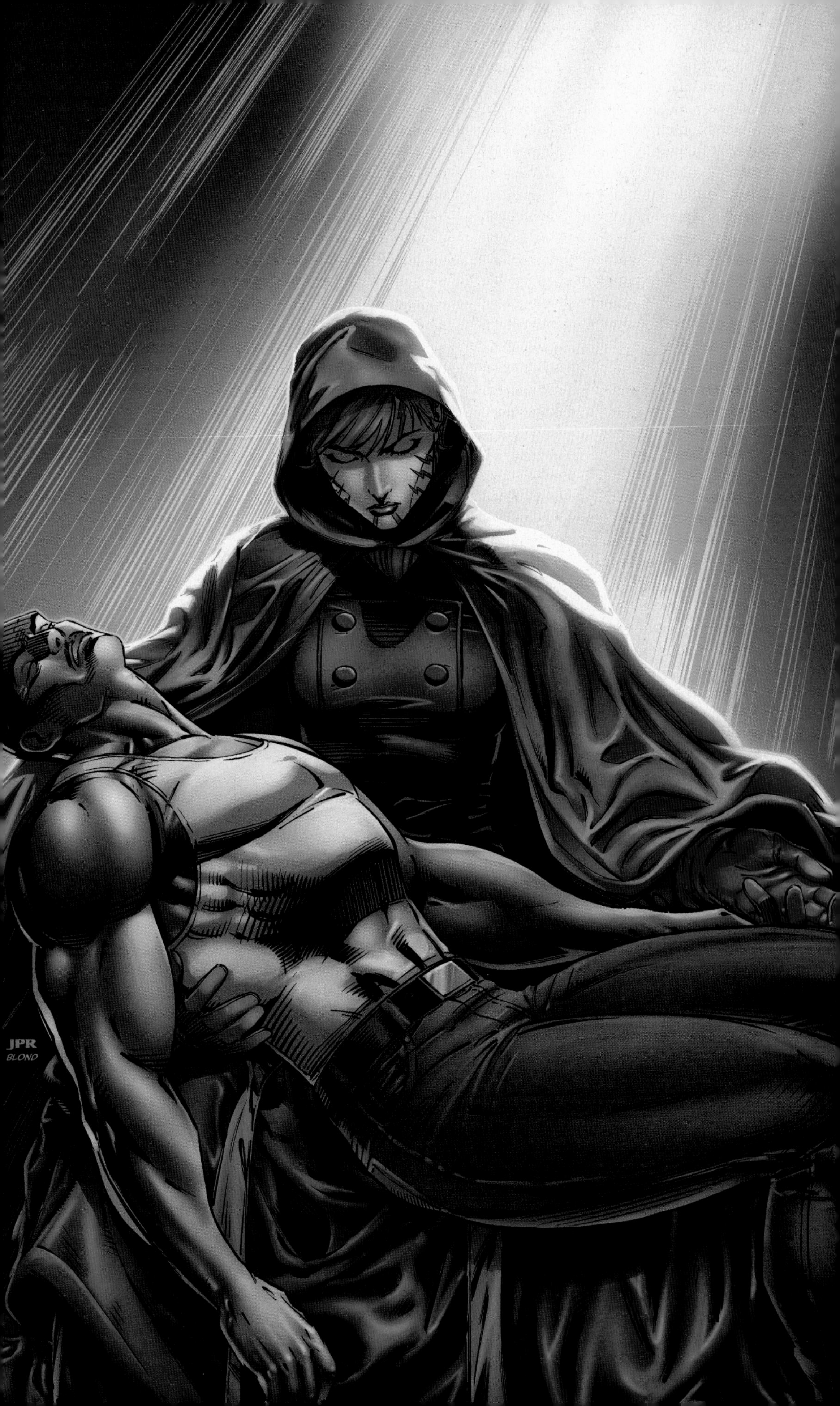
JPR
BLOND

ALL MY NAMES

RAY FAWKES
writer

TOM DERENICK
breakdowns

FRANCIS PORTELA
artist

ANDEW DALHOUSE
colorist

TAYLOR ESPOSITO
letterer

cover art by
JEREMY ROBERTS with BLOND

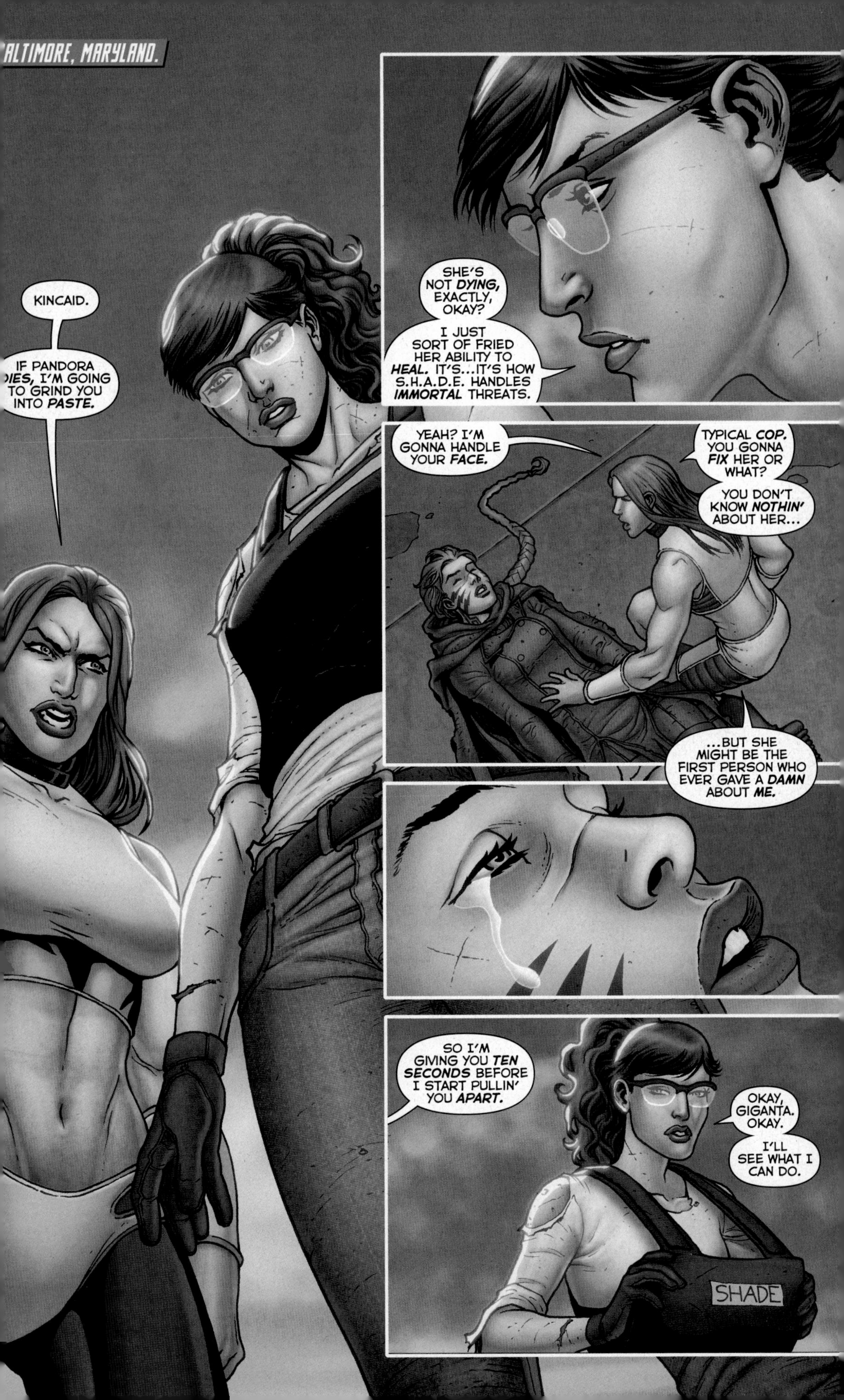
ALTIMORE, MARYLAND.
KINCAID.
IF PANDORA DIES, I'M GOING TO GRIND YOU INTO PASTE.
SHE'S NOT DYING, EXACTLY, OKAY?
I JUST SORT OF FRIED HER ABILITY TO HEAL. IT'S...IT'S HOW S.H.A.D.E. HANDLES IMMORTAL THREATS.
YEAH? I'M GONNA HANDLE YOUR FACE.
TYPICAL COP. YOU GONNA FIX HER OR WHAT?
YOU DON'T KNOW NOTHIN' ABOUT HER...
...BUT SHE MIGHT BE THE FIRST PERSON WHO EVER GAVE A DAMN ABOUT ME.
SO I'M GIVING YOU TEN SECONDS BEFORE I START PULLIN' YOU APART.
OKAY, GIGANTA. OKAY.
I'LL SEE WHAT I CAN DO.
SHADE

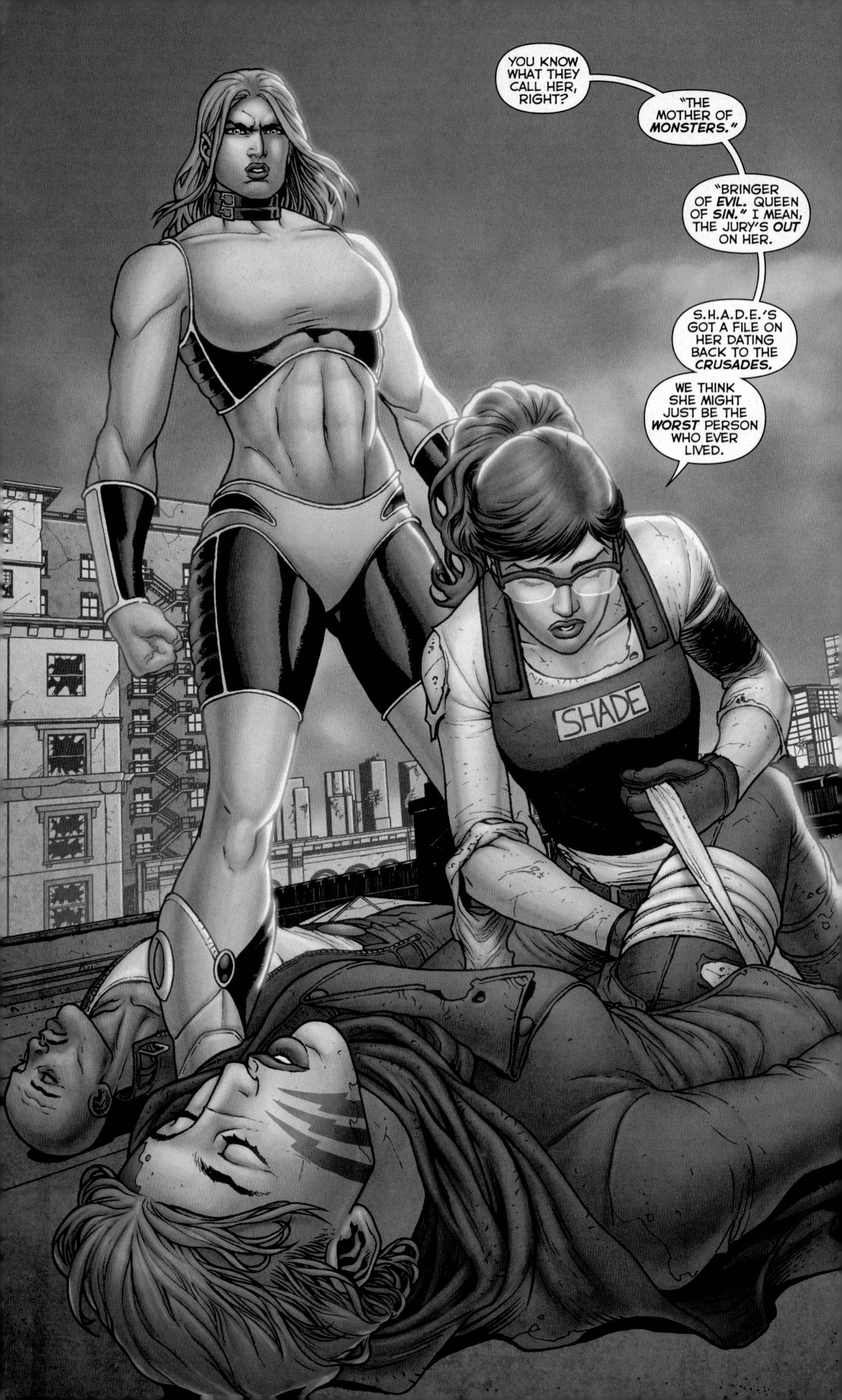
YOU KNOW WHAT THEY CALL HER, RIGHT?
"THE MOTHER OF MONSTERS."
"BRINGER OF EVIL. QUEEN OF SIN." I MEAN, THE JURY'S OUT ON HER.
S.H.A.D.E.'S GOT A FILE ON HER DATING BACK TO THE CRUSADES.
WE THINK SHE MIGHT JUST BE THE WORST PERSON WHO EVER LIVED.
SHADE

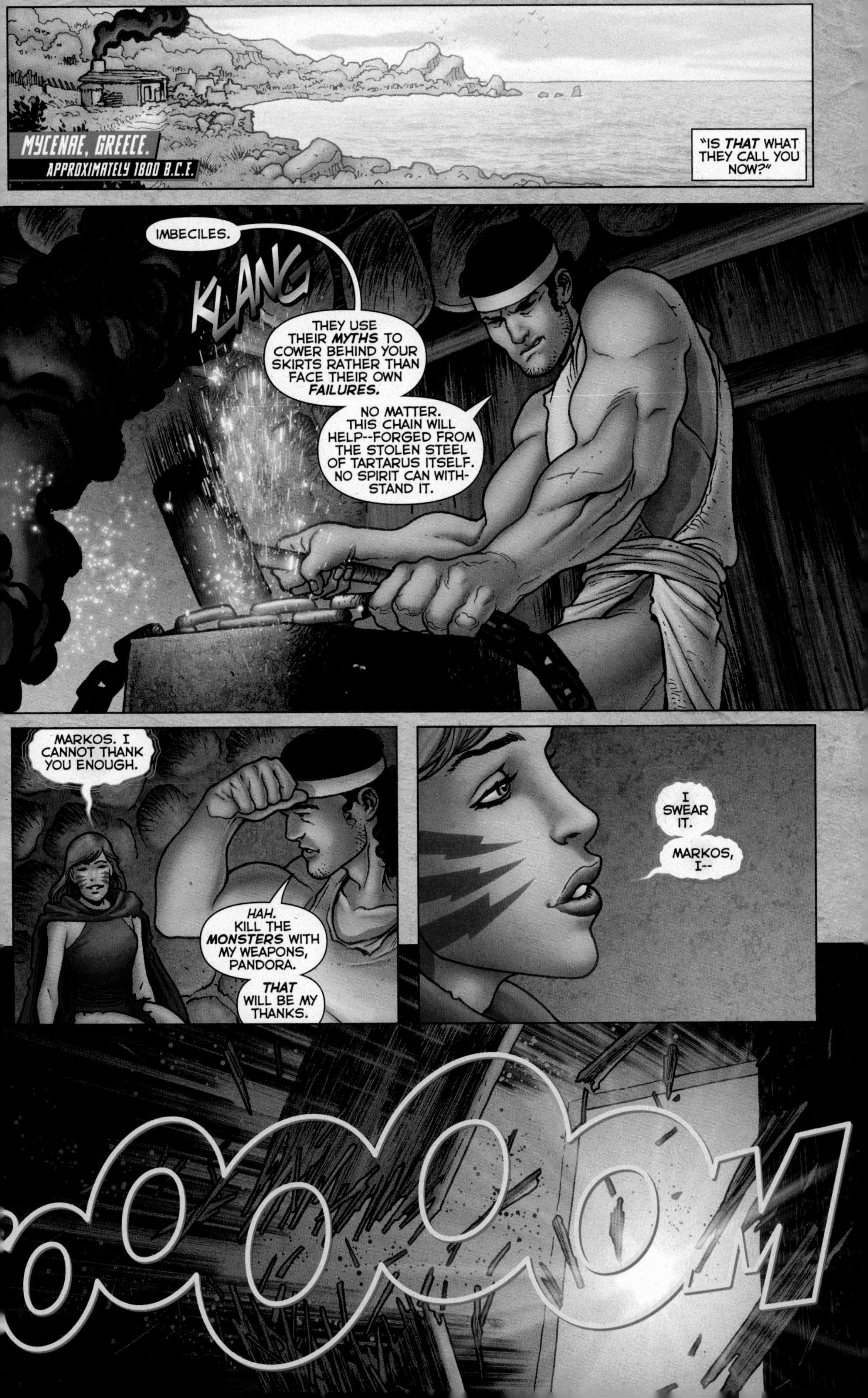
MYCENAE, GREECE.
APPROXIMATELY 1800 B.C.E.
"IS THAT WHAT THEY CALL YOU NOW?"
IMBECILES.
KLANG
THEY USE THEIR MYTHS TO COWER BEHIND YOUR SKIRTS RATHER THAN FACE THEIR OWN FAILURES.
NO MATTER. THIS CHAIN WILL HELP--FORGED FROM THE STOLEN STEEL OF TARTARUS ITSELF. NO SPIRIT CAN WITH-STAND IT.
MARKOS. I CANNOT THANK YOU ENOUGH.
HAH. KILL THE MONSTERS WITH MY WEAPONS, PANDORA.
THAT WILL BE MY THANKS.
I SWEAR IT.
MARKOS, I--
BOOOOOM

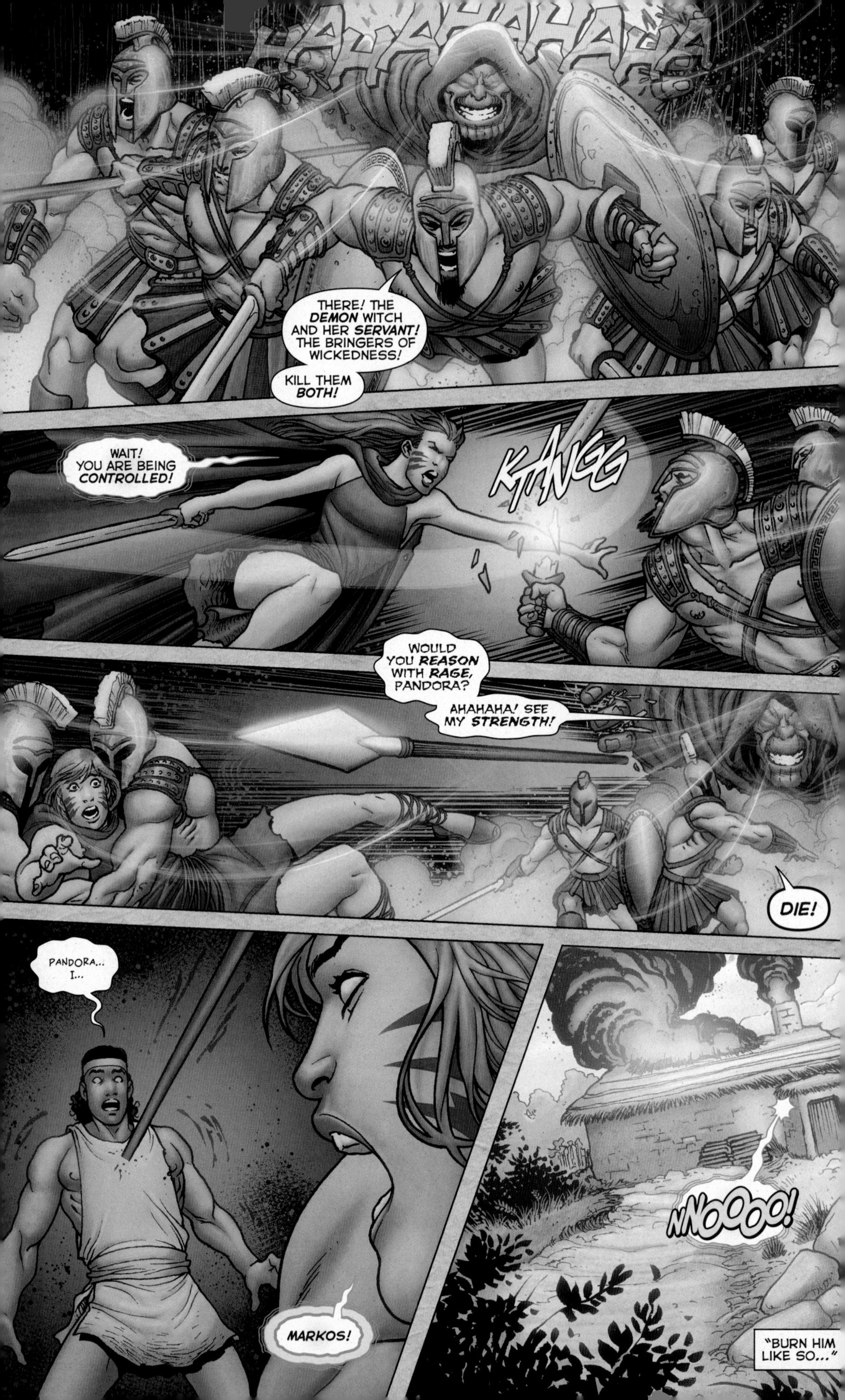
HAHAHAHAHAHA
THERE! THE DEMON WITCH AND HER SERVANT! THE BRINGERS OF WICKEDNESS!
KILL THEM BOTH!
WAIT! YOU ARE BEING CONTROLLED!
KTANGG
WOULD YOU REASON WITH RAGE, PANDORA?
AHAHAHA! SEE MY STRENGTH!
DIE!
PANDORA... I...
MARKOS!
NNOOOOO!
"BURN HIM LIKE SO..."

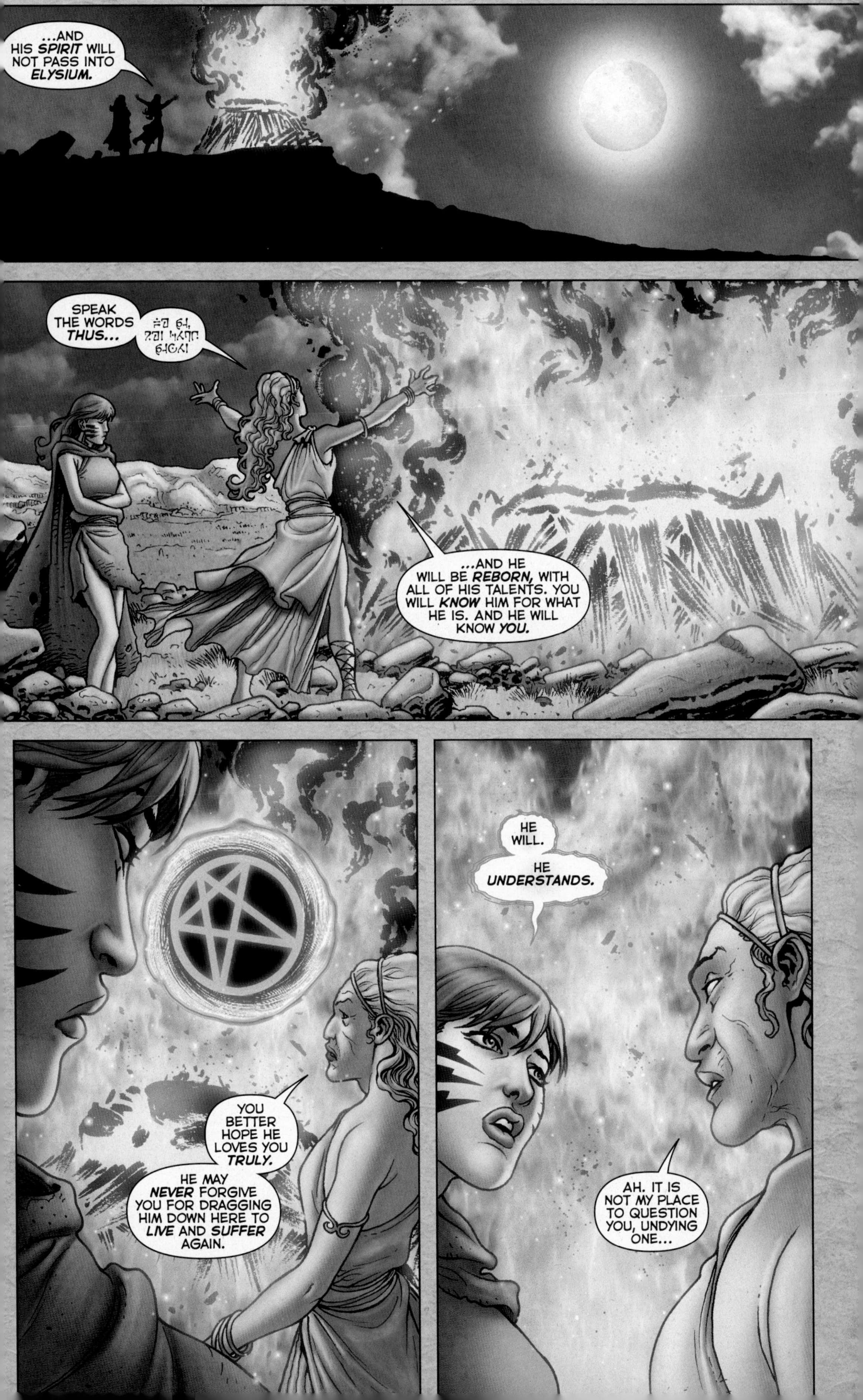
...AND HIS SPIRIT WILL NOT PASS INTO ELYSIUM.
SPEAK THE WORDS THUS...
...AND HE WILL BE REBORN, WITH ALL OF HIS TALENTS. YOU WILL KNOW HIM FOR WHAT HE IS. AND HE WILL KNOW YOU.
YOU BETTER HOPE HE LOVES YOU TRULY.
HE MAY NEVER FORGIVE YOU FOR DRAGGING HIM DOWN HERE TO LIVE AND SUFFER AGAIN.
HE WILL.
HE UNDERSTANDS.
AH. IT IS NOT MY PLACE TO QUESTION YOU, UNDYING ONE...

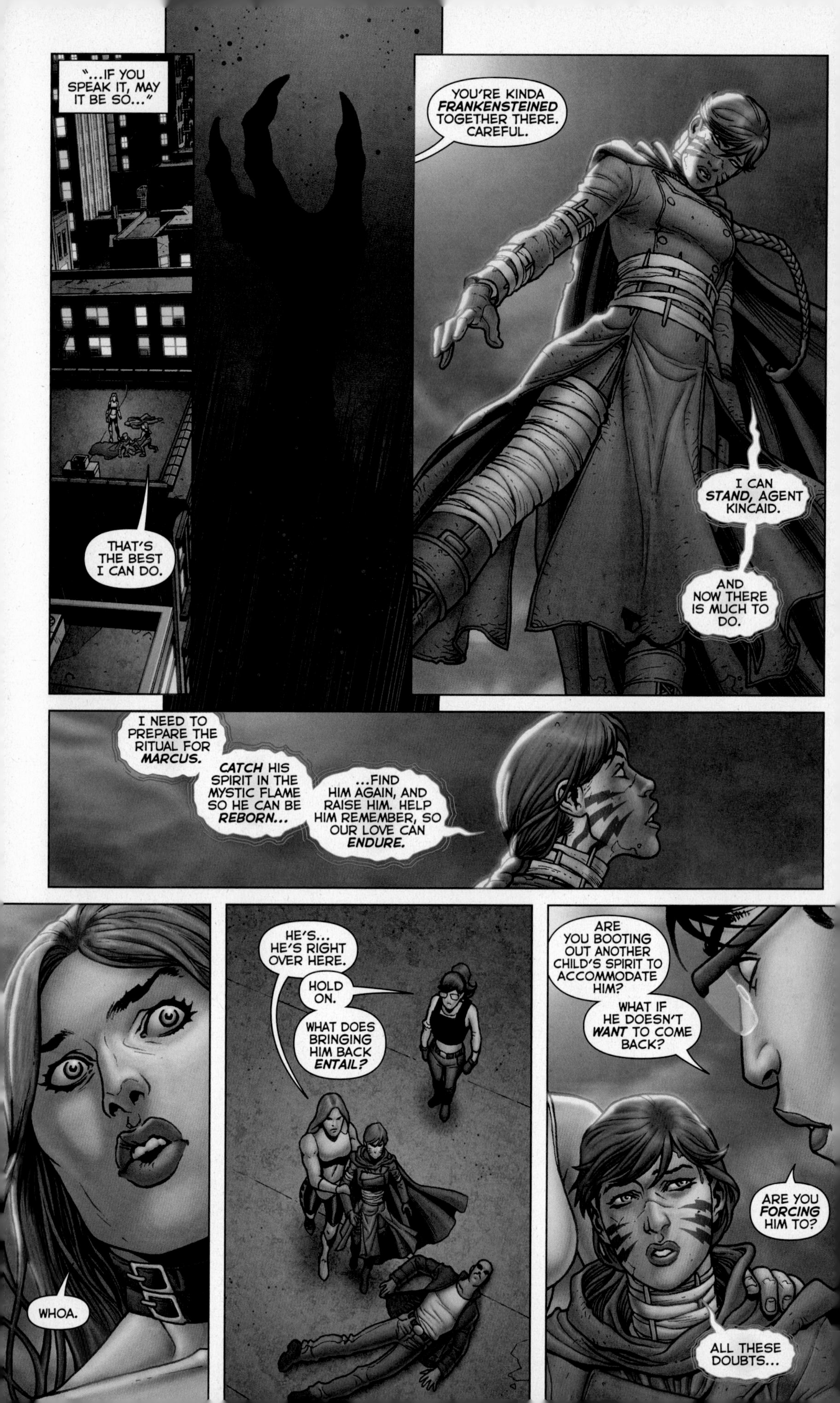
"...IF YOU SPEAK IT, MAY IT BE SO..."
THAT'S THE BEST I CAN DO.
YOU'RE KINDA FRANKENSTEINED TOGETHER THERE. CAREFUL.
I CAN STAND, AGENT KINCAID.
AND NOW THERE IS MUCH TO DO.
I NEED TO PREPARE THE RITUAL FOR MARCUS.
CATCH HIS SPIRIT IN THE MYSTIC FLAME SO HE CAN BE REBORN...
...FIND HIM AGAIN, AND RAISE HIM. HELP HIM REMEMBER, SO OUR LOVE CAN ENDURE.
WHOA.
HE'S... HE'S RIGHT OVER HERE.
HOLD ON.
WHAT DOES BRINGING HIM BACK ENTAIL?
ARE YOU BOOTING OUT ANOTHER CHILD'S SPIRIT TO ACCOMMODATE HIM?
WHAT IF HE DOESN'T WANT TO COME BACK?
ARE YOU FORCING HIM TO?
ALL THESE DOUBTS...

I HAVE ASKED ALL THESE QUESTIONS BEFORE.

THE NATURAL SOUL OF THE CHILD IS PUSHED BACK IN THE *QUEUE* AND BORN NEXT. ELSEWHERE.

THAT SOUNDS... CONVENIENT.

SO YOU BEEN *REINCARNATING* THIS GUY? HOW MANY TIMES?

MARCUS IS MY WEAPON-SMITH AND MY COMPANION, EVER AT MY *SIDE* IN THE *WAR* AGAINST EVIL.

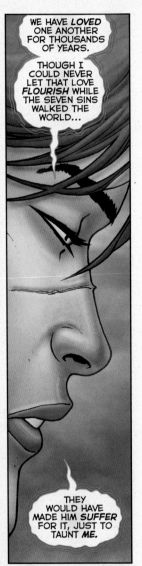

WE HAVE *LOVED* ONE ANOTHER FOR THOUSANDS OF YEARS.

THOUGH I COULD NEVER LET THAT LOVE *FLOURISH* WHILE THE SEVEN SINS WALKED THE WORLD...

THEY WOULD HAVE MADE HIM *SUFFER* FOR IT, JUST TO TAUNT *ME*.

NOW THAT THEY ARE *DESTROYED*, I THOUGHT WE COULD FINALLY BE TOGETHER IN *HAPPINESS*...

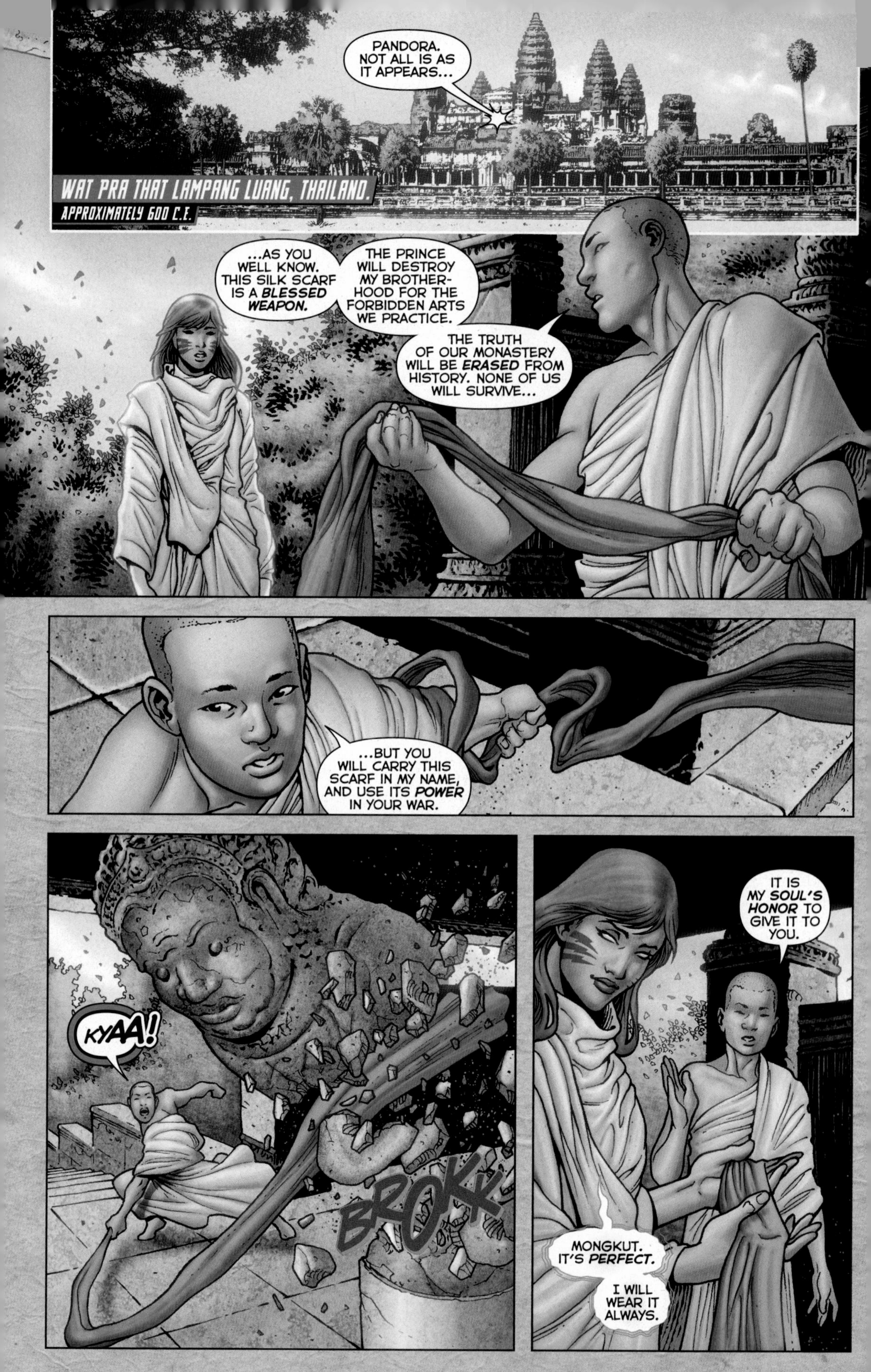
PANDORA. NOT ALL IS AS IT APPEARS...
WAT PRA THAT LAMPANG LUANG, THAILAND.
APPROXIMATELY 600 C.E.
...AS YOU WELL KNOW. THIS SILK SCARF IS A BLESSED WEAPON.
THE PRINCE WILL DESTROY MY BROTHERHOOD FOR THE FORBIDDEN ARTS WE PRACTICE.
THE TRUTH OF OUR MONASTERY WILL BE ERASED FROM HISTORY. NONE OF US WILL SURVIVE...
...BUT YOU WILL CARRY THIS SCARF IN MY NAME, AND USE ITS POWER IN YOUR WAR.
KYAA!
BROKK
IT IS MY SOUL'S HONOR TO GIVE IT TO YOU.
MONGKUT. IT'S PERFECT.
I WILL WEAR IT ALWAYS.

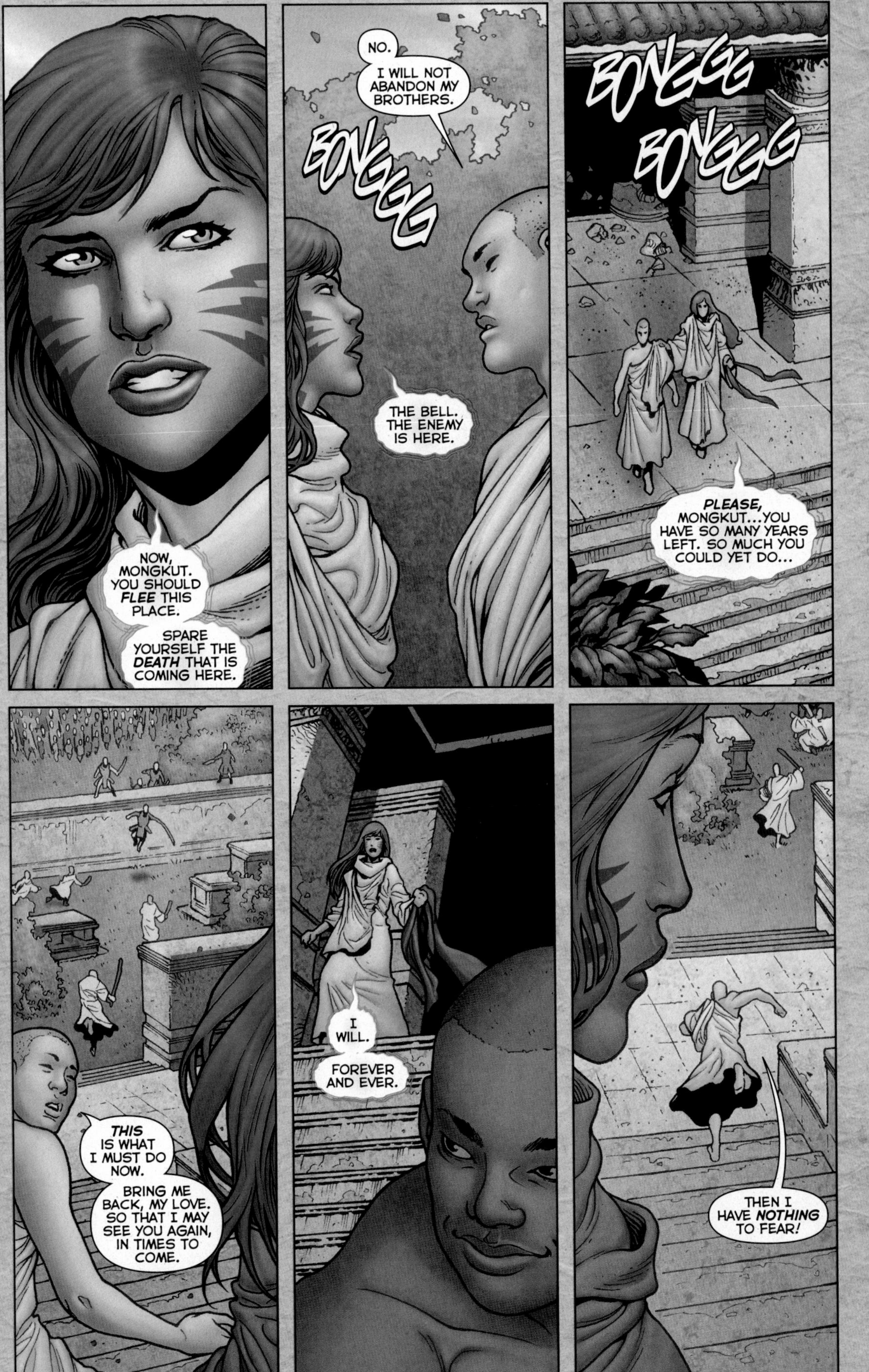
NOW, MONGKUT. YOU SHOULD FLEE THIS PLACE.
SPARE YOURSELF THE DEATH THAT IS COMING HERE.
NO.
I WILL NOT ABANDON MY BROTHERS.
BONGGG
THE BELL. THE ENEMY IS HERE.
BONGGG
BONGGG
PLEASE, MONGKUT...YOU HAVE SO MANY YEARS LEFT. SO MUCH YOU COULD YET DO...
THIS IS WHAT I MUST DO NOW.
BRING ME BACK, MY LOVE. SO THAT I MAY SEE YOU AGAIN, IN TIMES TO COME.
I WILL.
FOREVER AND EVER.
THEN I HAVE NOTHING TO FEAR!

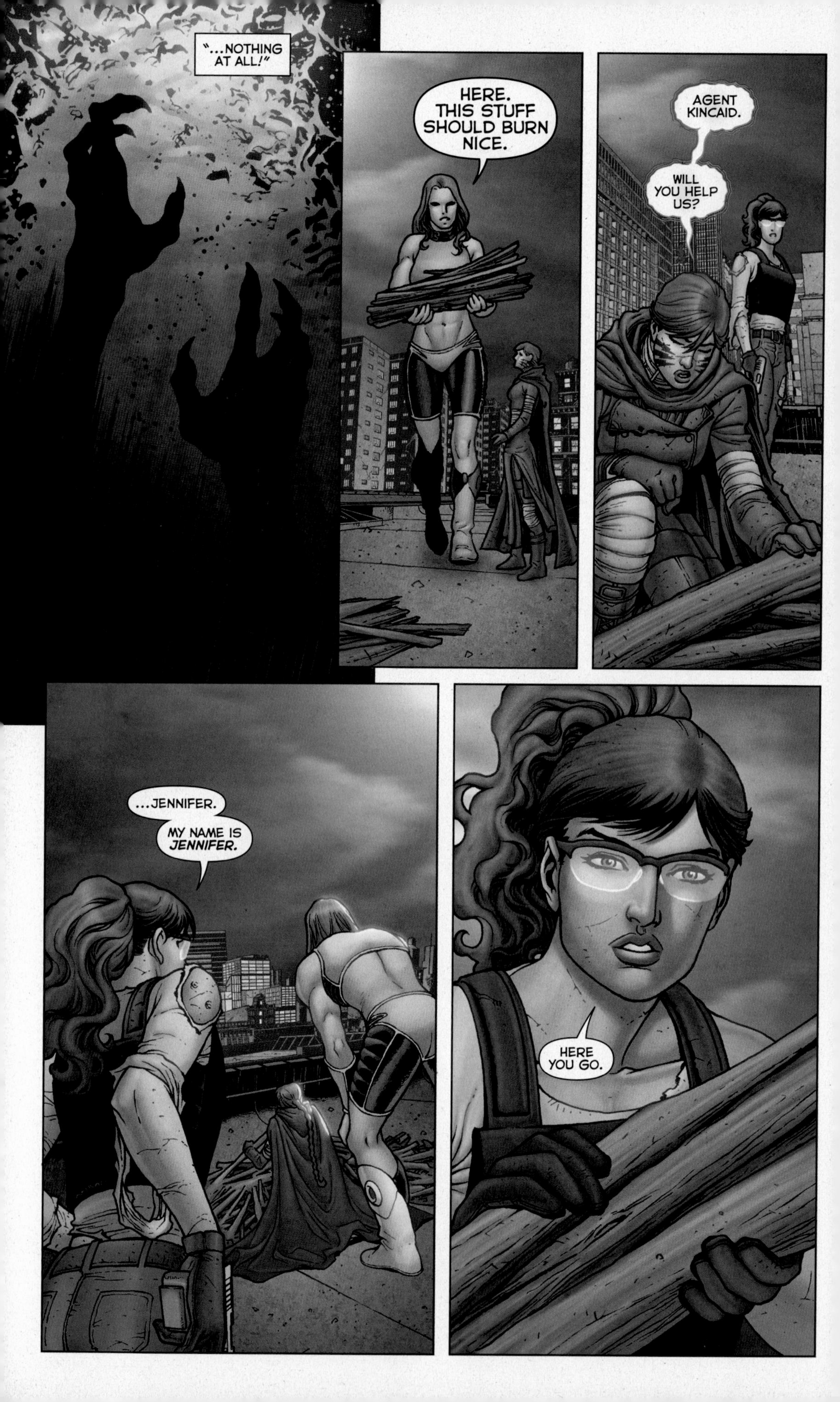
"...NOTHING AT ALL!"
HERE. THIS STUFF SHOULD BURN NICE.
AGENT KINCAID.
WILL YOU HELP US?
...JENNIFER.
MY NAME IS *JENNIFER.*
HERE YOU GO.

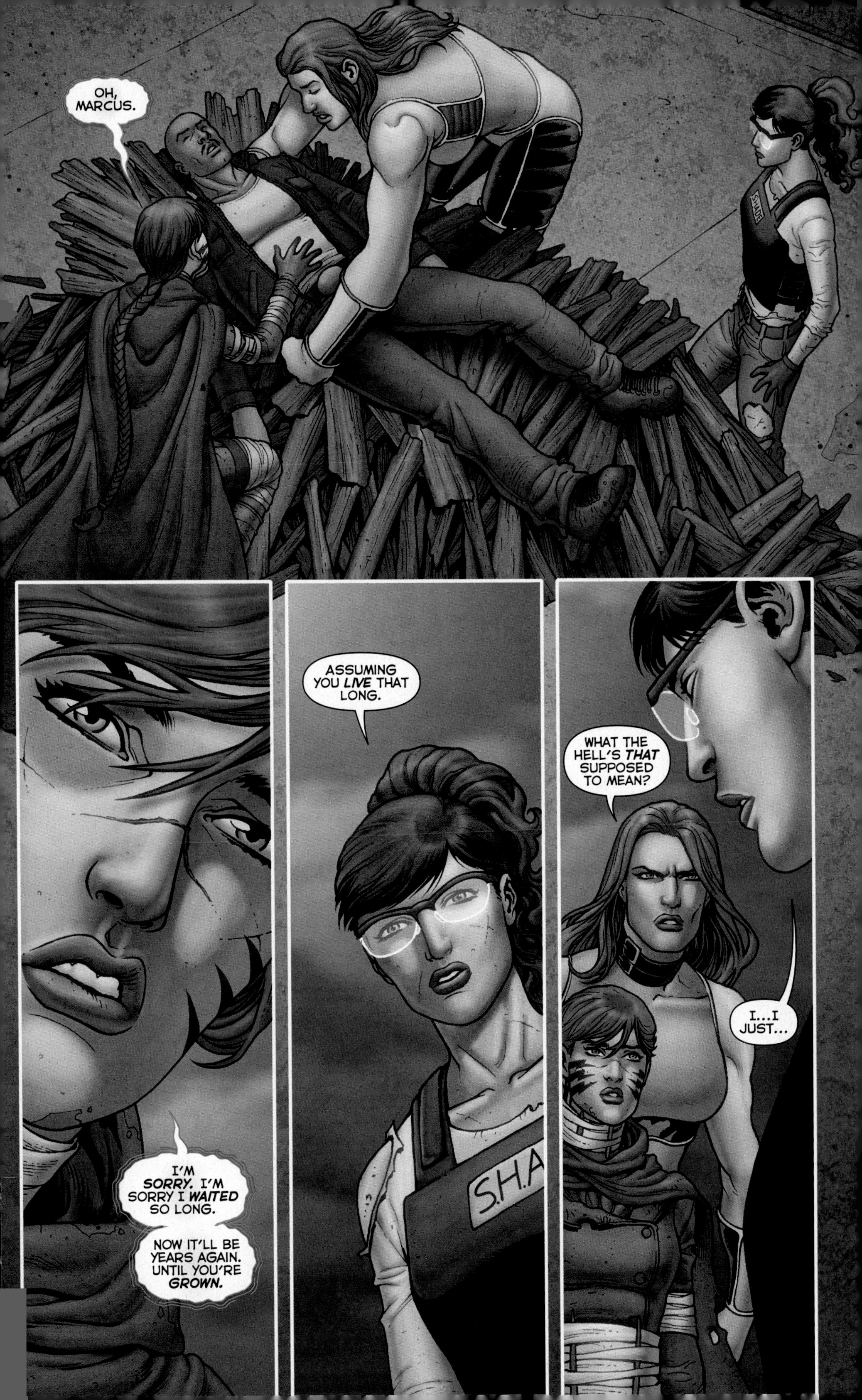
OH, MARCUS.
I'M SORRY. I'M SORRY I WAITED SO LONG.
NOW IT'LL BE YEARS AGAIN. UNTIL YOU'RE GROWN.
ASSUMING YOU LIVE THAT LONG.
WHAT THE HELL'S THAT SUPPOSED TO MEAN?
I...I JUST...

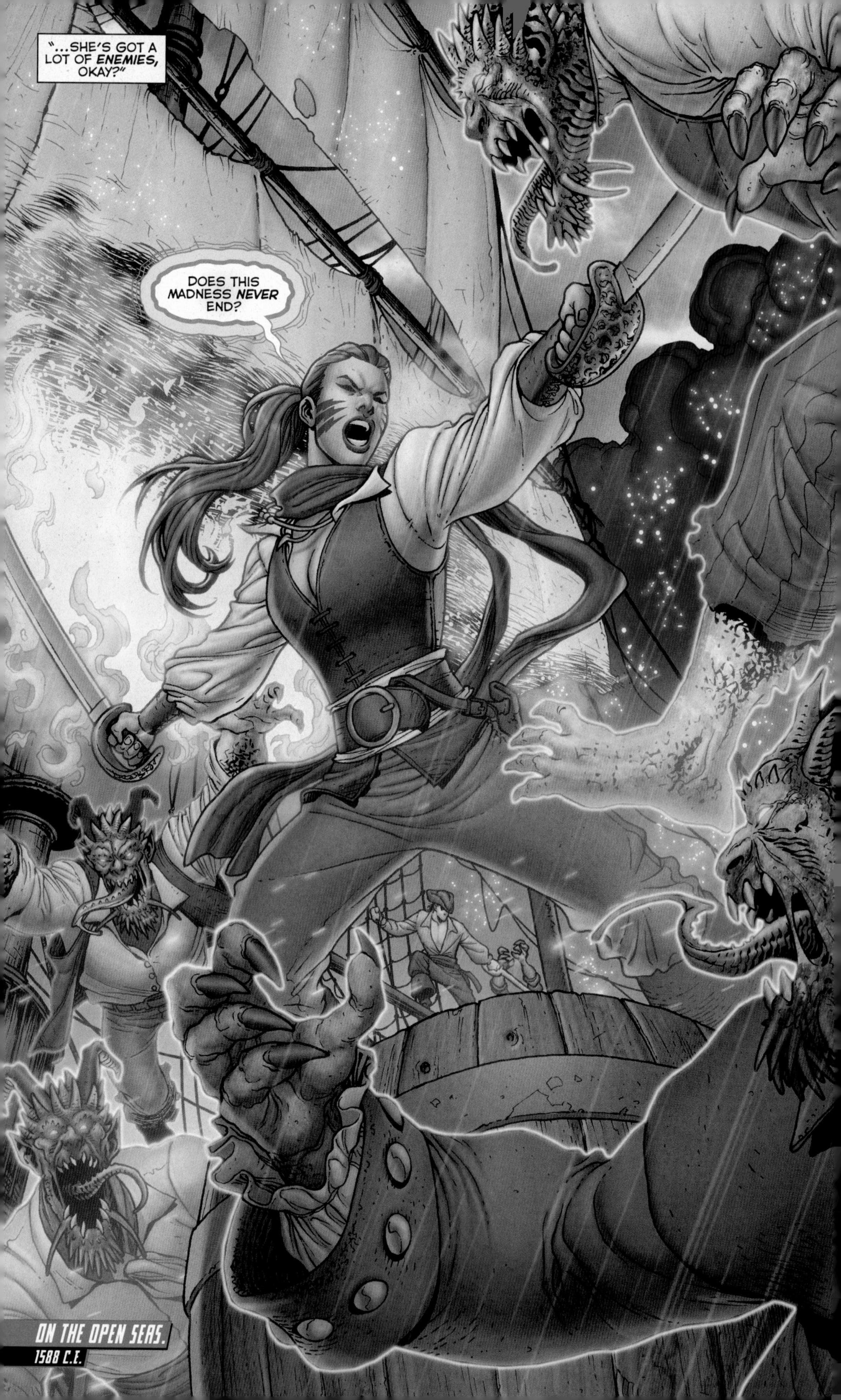
"...SHE'S GOT A LOT OF ENEMIES, OKAY?"
DOES THIS MADNESS NEVER END?
ON THE OPEN SEAS. 1588 C.E.

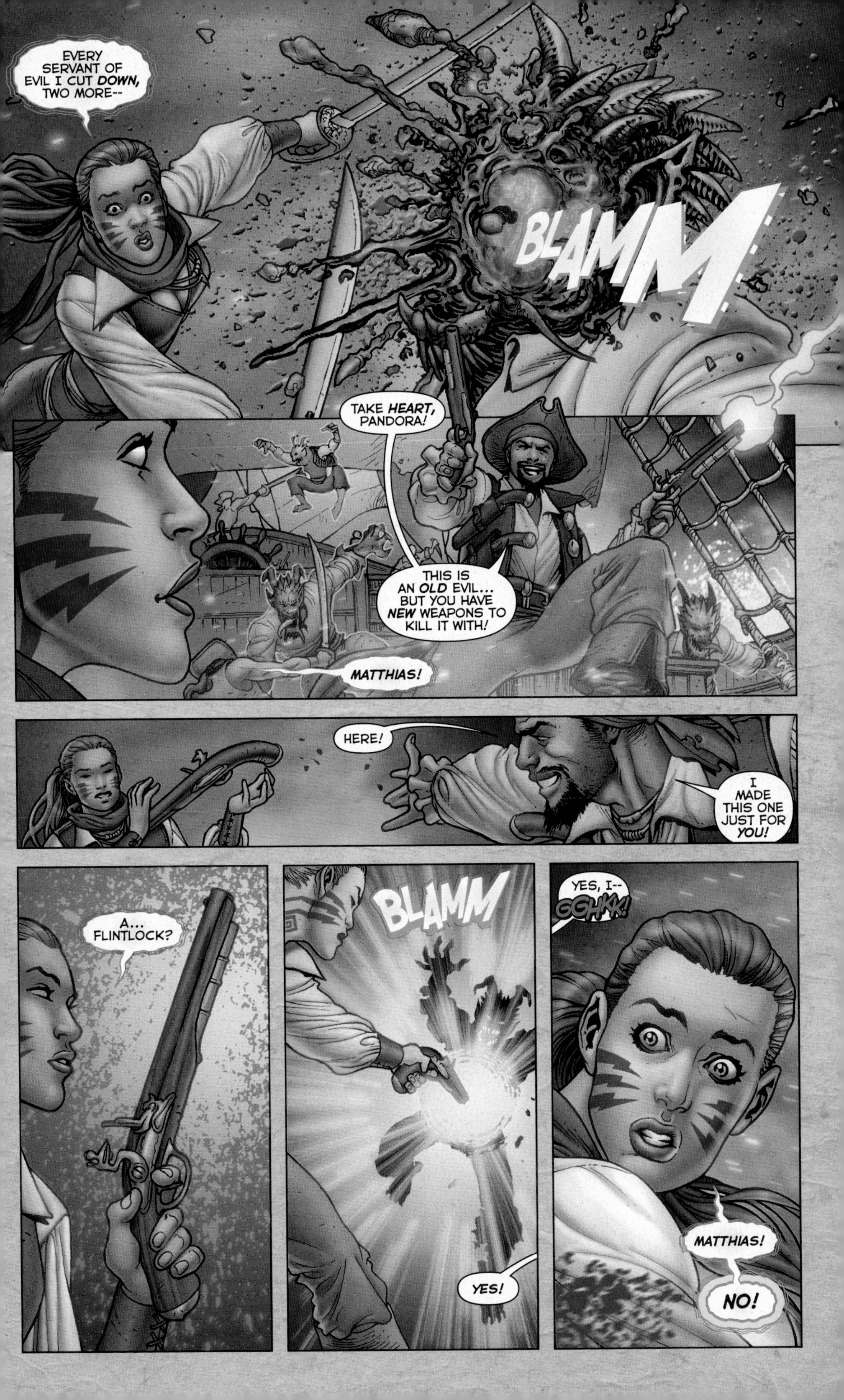
EVERY SERVANT OF EVIL I CUT DOWN, TWO MORE--
BLAMM
TAKE HEART, PANDORA!
THIS IS AN OLD EVIL... BUT YOU HAVE NEW WEAPONS TO KILL IT WITH!
MATTHIAS!
HERE!
I MADE THIS ONE JUST FOR YOU!
A... FLINTLOCK?
BLAMM
YES!
YES, I--
GGHKK!
MATTHIAS!
NO!

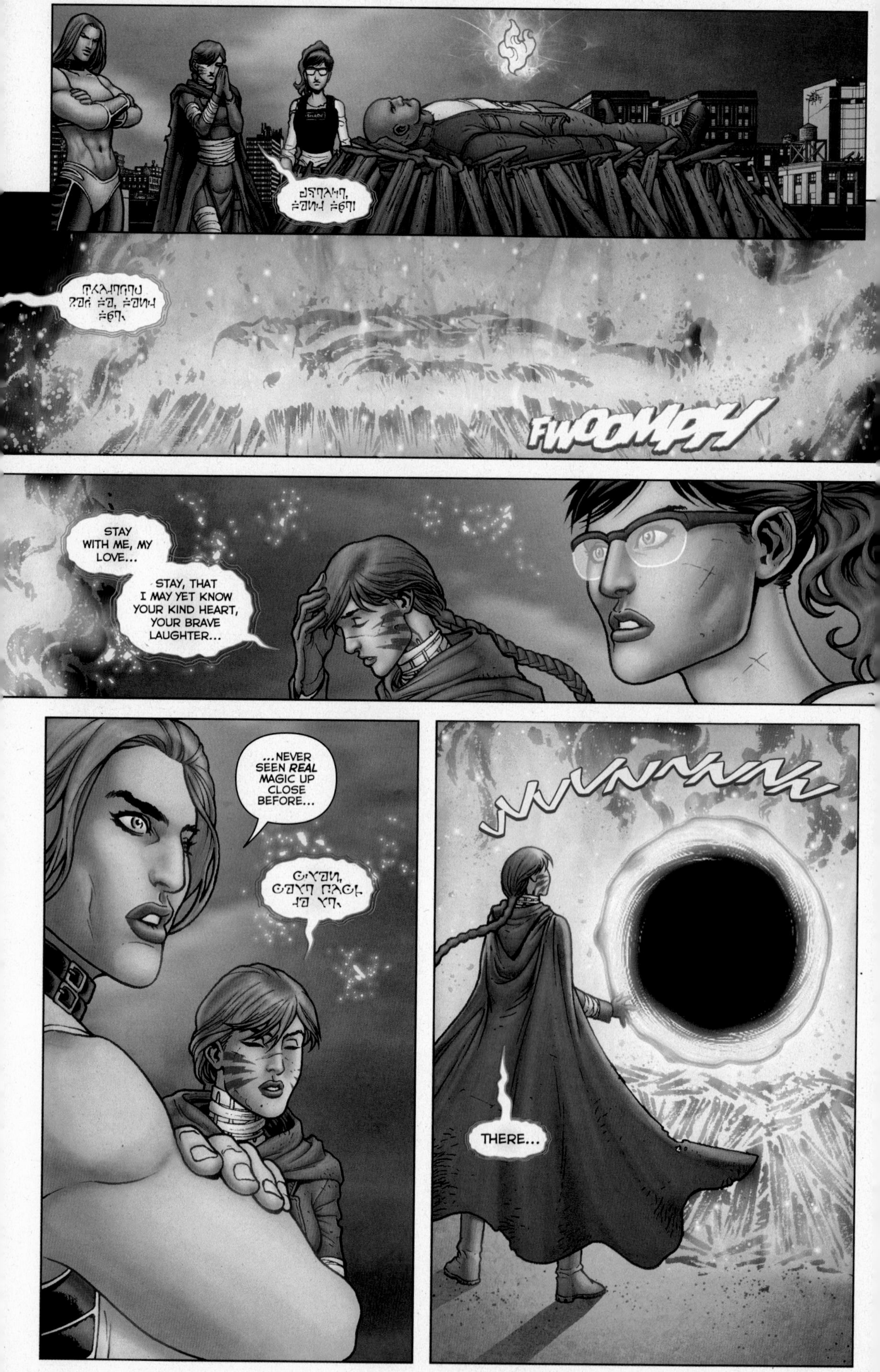
FWOOMPH
STAY WITH ME, MY LOVE...
STAY, THAT I MAY YET KNOW YOUR KIND HEART, YOUR BRAVE LAUGHTER...
...NEVER SEEN *REAL* MAGIC UP CLOSE BEFORE...
THERE...

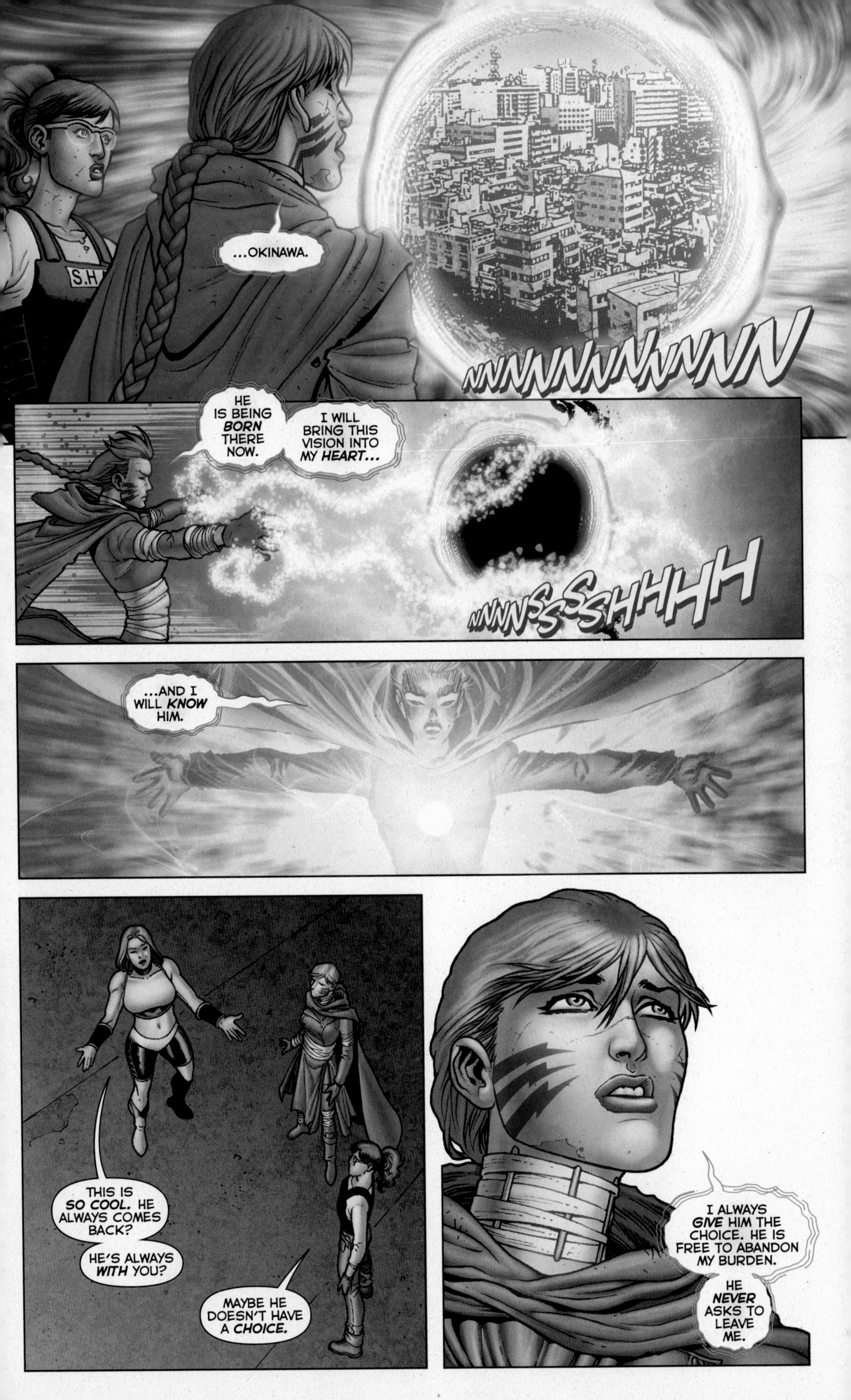

S.H
...OKINAWA.
NNNNNNNNNNNNN
HE IS BEING BORN THERE NOW.
I WILL BRING THIS VISION INTO MY HEART...
NNNNSSSHHHH
...AND I WILL KNOW HIM.
THIS IS SO COOL. HE ALWAYS COMES BACK?
HE'S ALWAYS WITH YOU?
MAYBE HE DOESN'T HAVE A CHOICE.
I ALWAYS GIVE HIM THE CHOICE. HE IS FREE TO ABANDON MY BURDEN.
HE NEVER ASKS TO LEAVE ME.

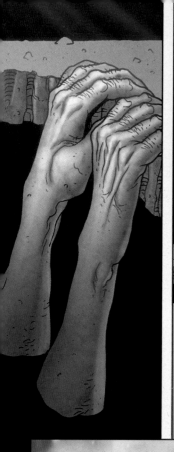

"DO YOU THINK I AM A MONSTER?"

DON'T *ANSWER* THAT, COP.

I'M *SO* READY TO SNAP YOUR SCRAWNY NECK.

I'M JUST *SAYING.* I HAVE MY DOUBTS.

YOU'RE AN IMMORTAL CREATURE, SO FAR REMOVED FROM *HUMAN* IT'S IMPOSSIBLE TO IMAGINE YOU CAN UNDERSTAND HOW WE *FEEL.*

I'M STILL TRYING TO FIGURE OUT IF I SHOULD *NEUTRALIZE* YOU.

I MEAN, I'M NOT *HUMAN* MYSELF. I'M A WERECROW.

WE *MONSTERS,* WE HAVE A REAL KNACK FOR *CAMOUFLAGE.*

YOU *LOOK* LIKE YOU CARE. YOU *SOUND* LIKE A GOOD PERSON...

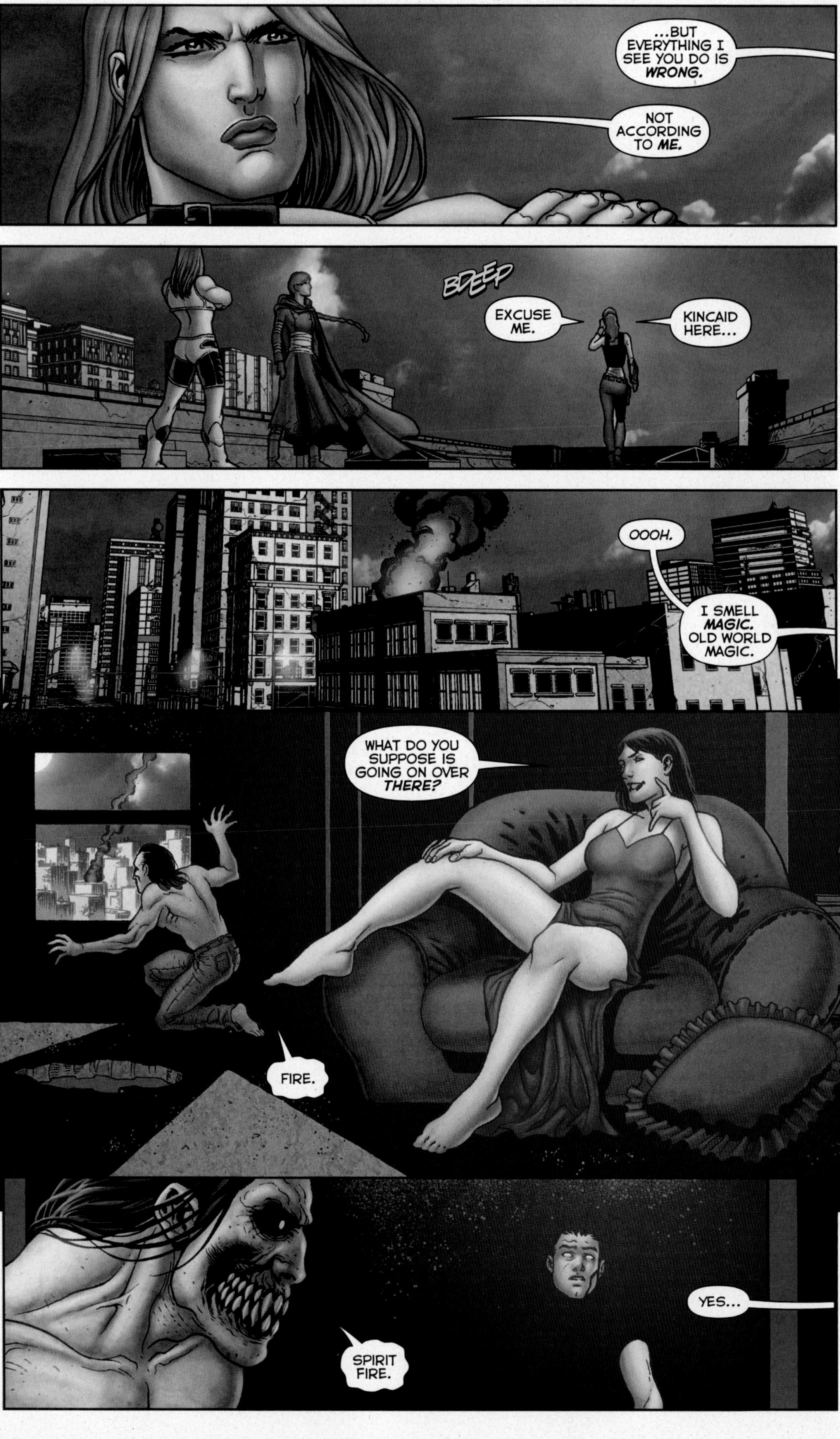
...BUT EVERYTHING I SEE YOU DO IS WRONG.
NOT ACCORDING TO ME.
BDEEP
EXCUSE ME.
KINCAID HERE...
OOOH.
I SMELL MAGIC. OLD WORLD MAGIC.
WHAT DO YOU SUPPOSE IS GOING ON OVER THERE?
FIRE.
SPIRIT FIRE.
YES...

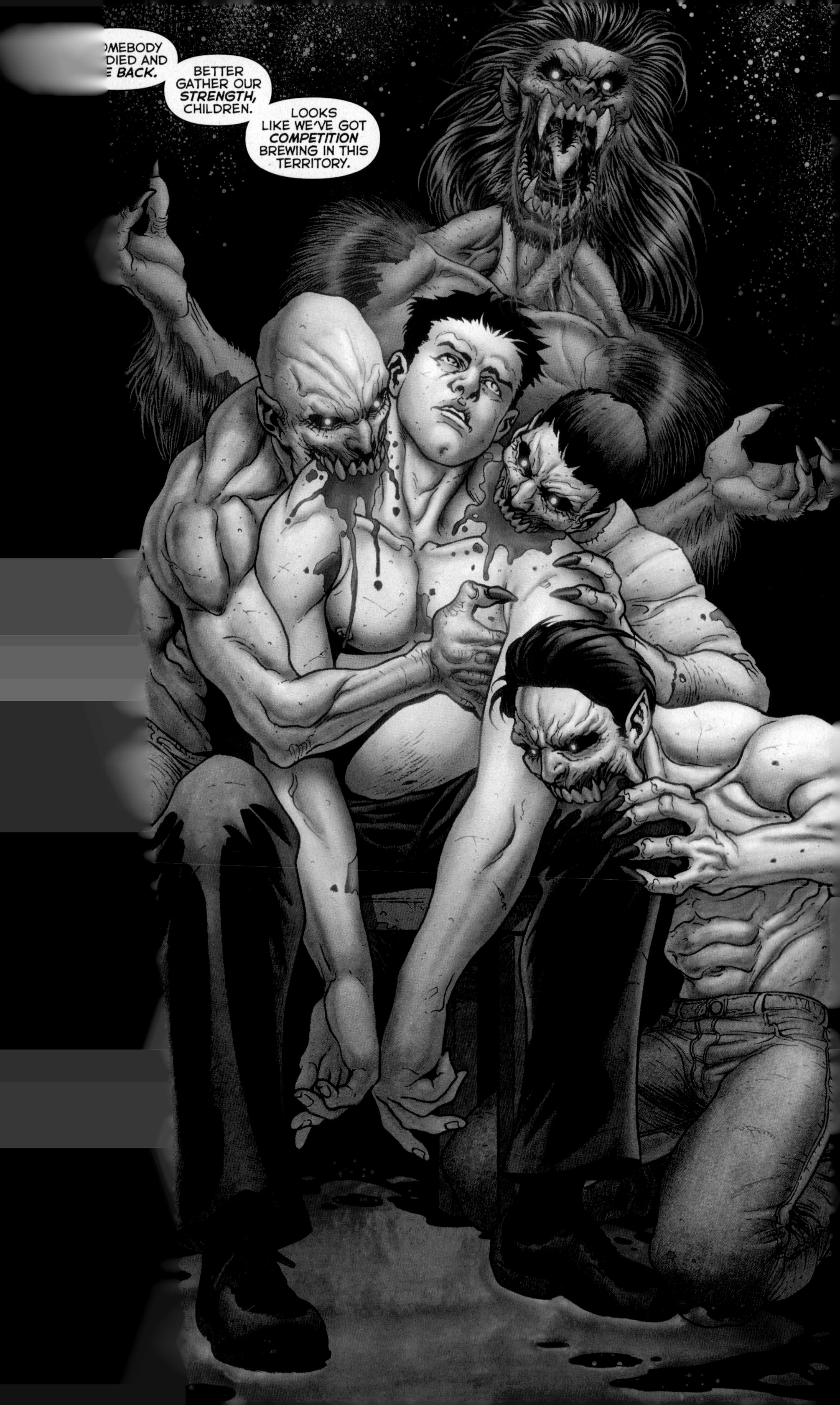

OMEBODY DIED AND E BACK.
BETTER GATHER OUR STRENGTH, CHILDREN.
LOOKS LIKE WE'VE GOT COMPETITION BREWING IN THIS TERRITORY.

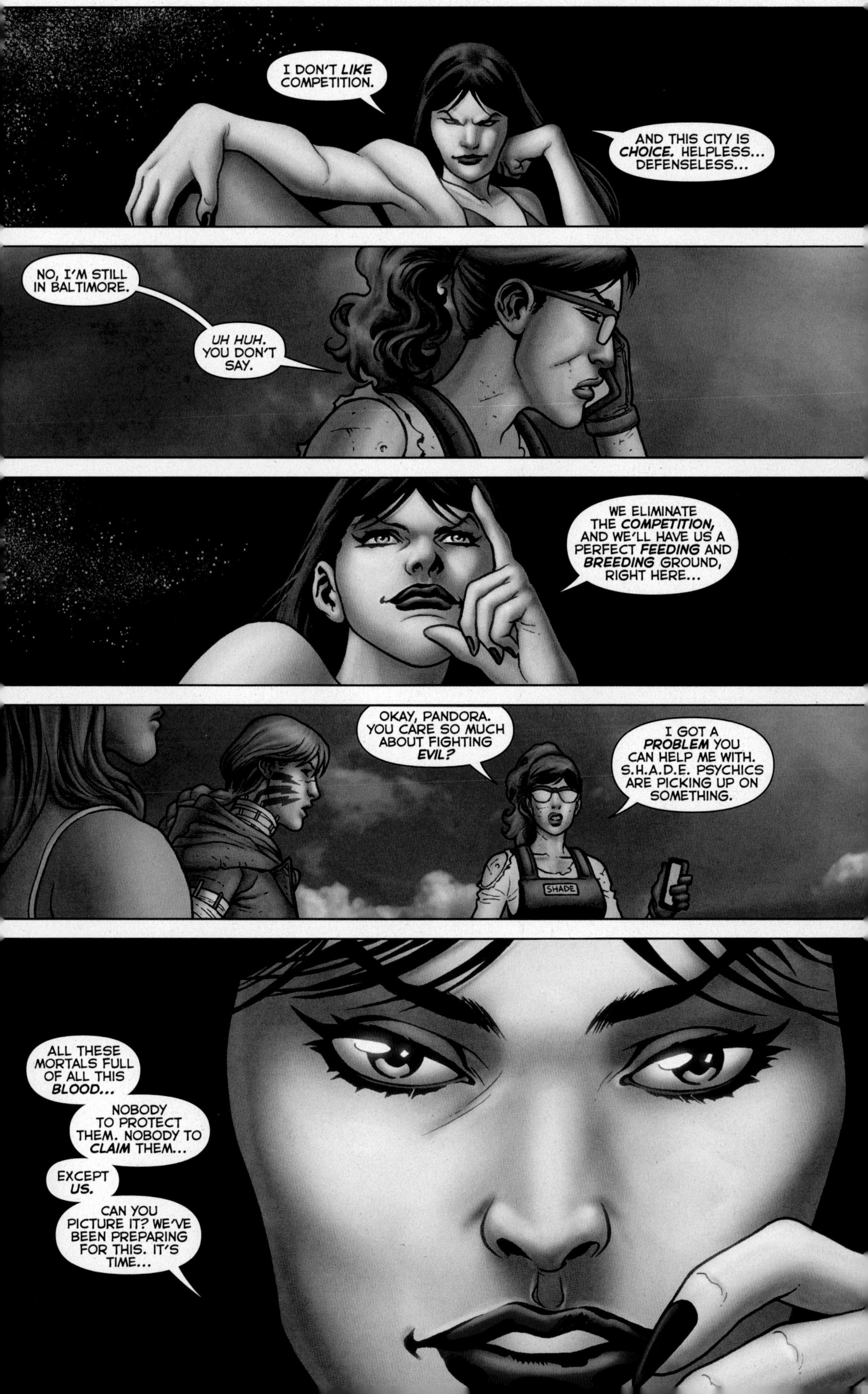
I DON'T *LIKE* COMPETITION.
AND THIS CITY IS *CHOICE.* HELPLESS... DEFENSELESS...
NO, I'M STILL IN BALTIMORE.
UH HUH. YOU DON'T SAY.
WE ELIMINATE THE *COMPETITION,* AND WE'LL HAVE US A PERFECT *FEEDING* AND *BREEDING* GROUND, RIGHT HERE...
OKAY, PANDORA. YOU CARE SO MUCH ABOUT FIGHTING *EVIL?*
I GOT A *PROBLEM* YOU CAN HELP ME WITH. S.H.A.D.E. PSYCHICS ARE PICKING UP ON SOMETHING.
SHADE
ALL THESE MORTALS FULL OF ALL THIS *BLOOD...*
NOBODY TO PROTECT THEM. NOBODY TO *CLAIM* THEM...
EXCEPT *US.*
CAN YOU PICTURE IT? WE'VE BEEN PREPARING FOR THIS. IT'S TIME...

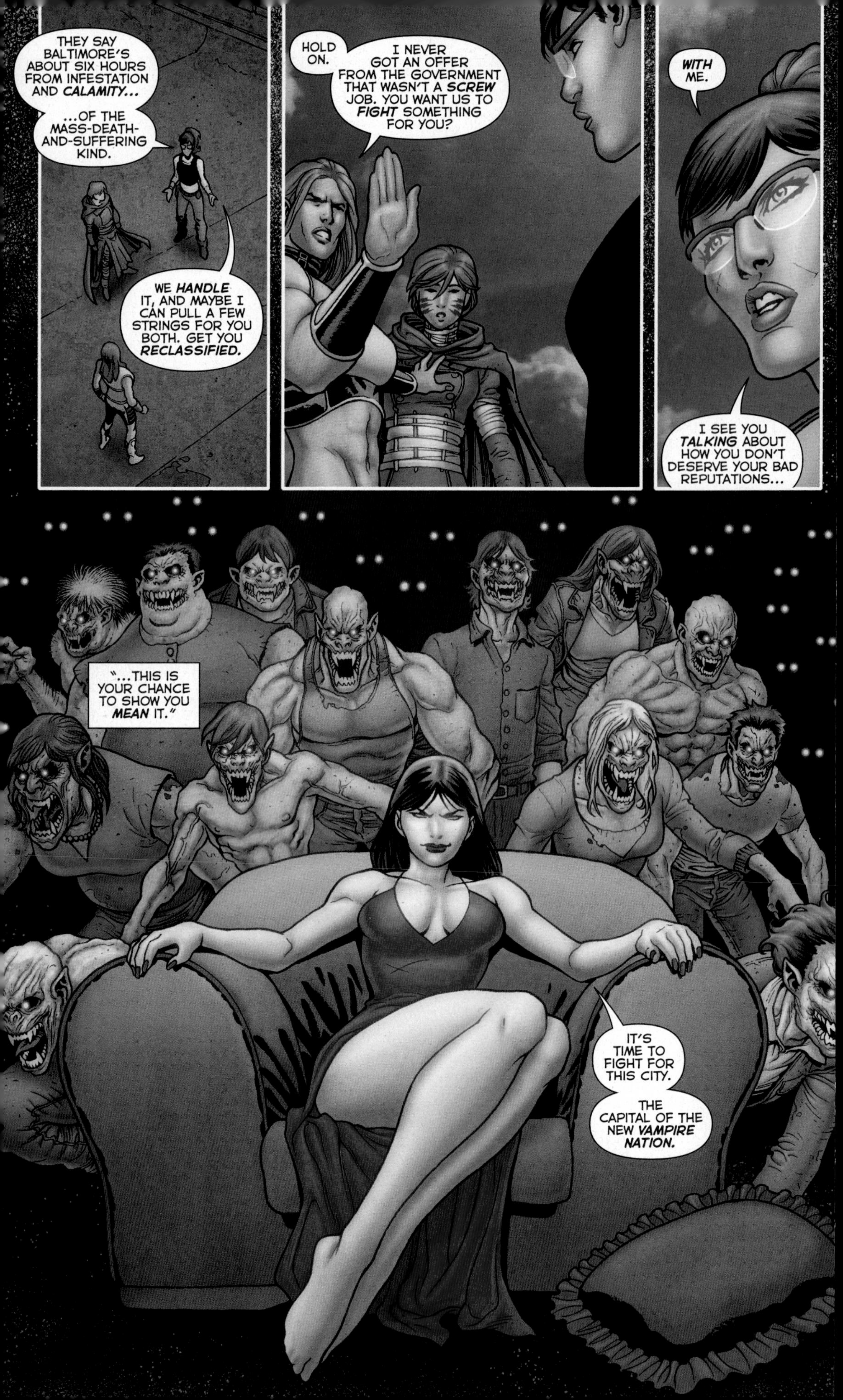
THEY SAY BALTIMORE'S ABOUT SIX HOURS FROM INFESTATION AND *CALAMITY...*
...OF THE MASS-DEATH-AND-SUFFERING KIND.
WE *HANDLE* IT, AND MAYBE I CAN PULL A FEW STRINGS FOR YOU BOTH. GET YOU *RECLASSIFIED.*
HOLD ON.
I NEVER GOT AN OFFER FROM THE GOVERNMENT THAT WASN'T A *SCREW* JOB. YOU WANT US TO *FIGHT* SOMETHING FOR YOU?
WITH ME.
I SEE YOU *TALKING* ABOUT HOW YOU DON'T DESERVE YOUR BAD REPUTATIONS...
"...THIS IS YOUR CHANCE TO SHOW YOU *MEAN* IT."
IT'S TIME TO FIGHT FOR THIS CITY.
THE CAPITAL OF THE NEW *VAMPIRE NATION.*

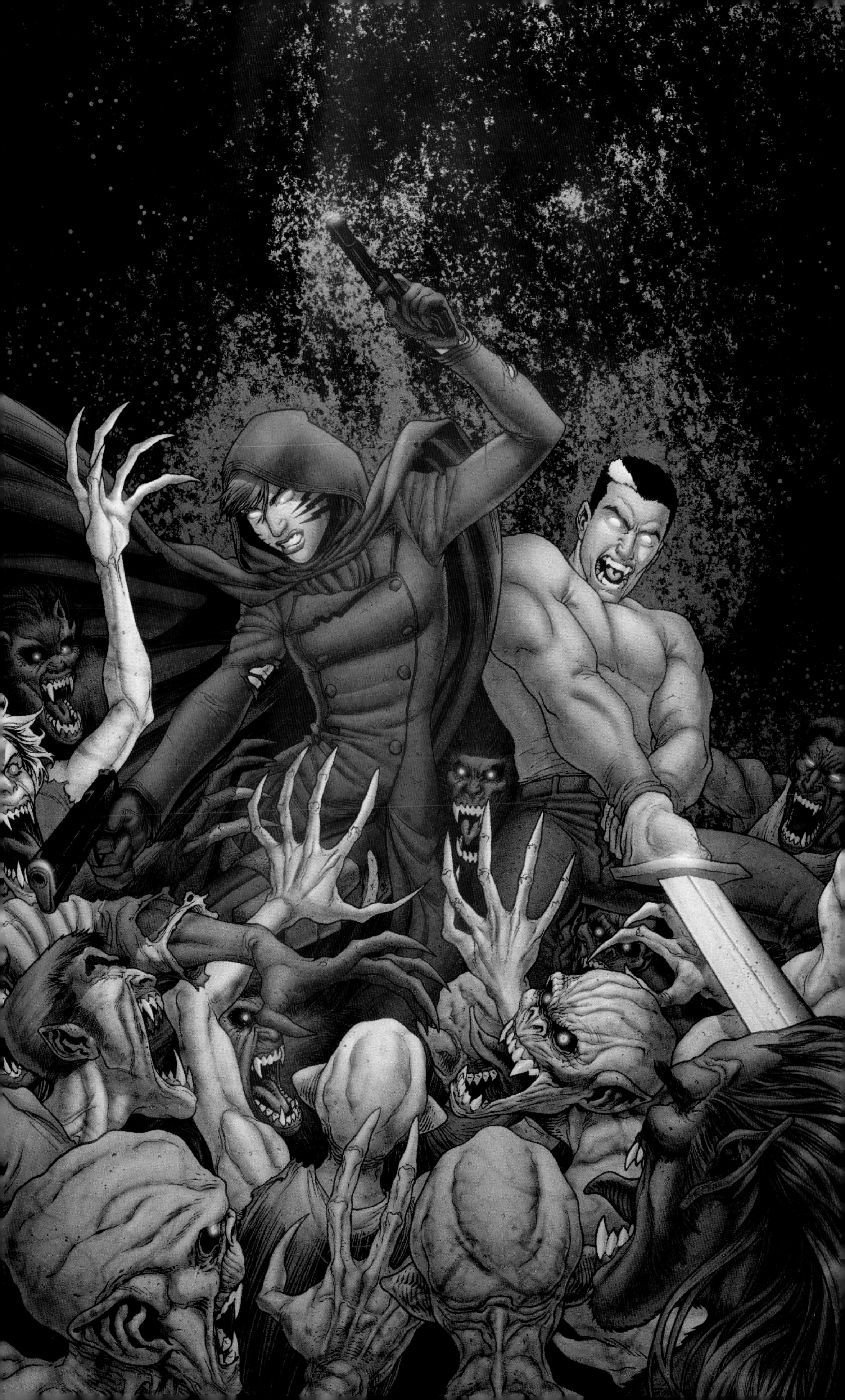

THE HALFWAY PLACE

RAY FAWKES
writer

TOM DERENICK
breakdowns

FRANCIS PORTELA
artist

ANDEW DALHOUSE
colorist

TRAVIS LANHAM
letterer

cover art by
FRANCIS PORTELA

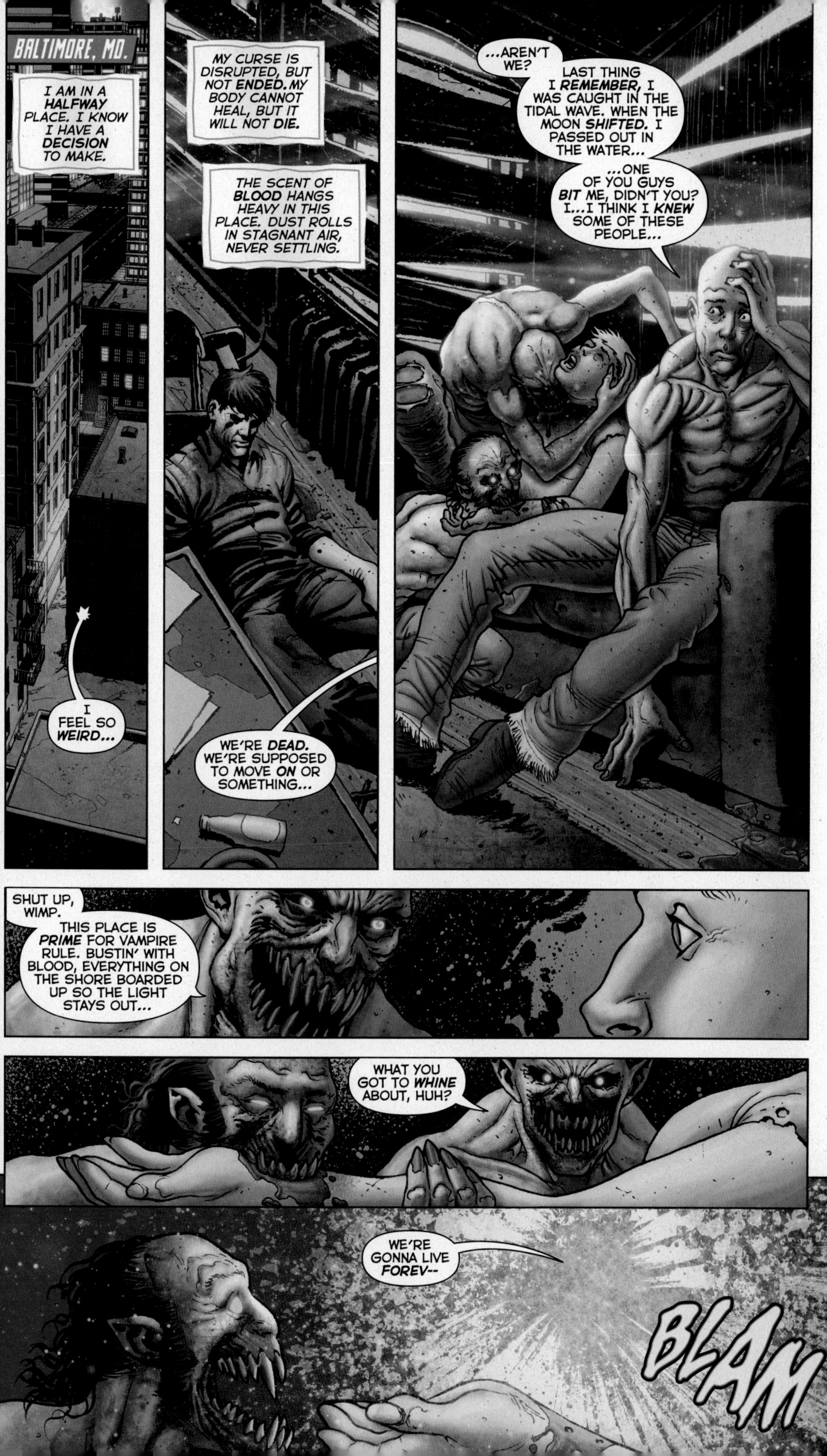
BALTIMORE, MD.
I AM IN A HALFWAY PLACE. I KNOW I HAVE A DECISION TO MAKE.
I FEEL SO WEIRD...
MY CURSE IS DISRUPTED, BUT NOT ENDED. MY BODY CANNOT HEAL, BUT IT WILL NOT DIE.
THE SCENT OF BLOOD HANGS HEAVY IN THIS PLACE. DUST ROLLS IN STAGNANT AIR, NEVER SETTLING.
WE'RE DEAD. WE'RE SUPPOSED TO MOVE ON OR SOMETHING...
...AREN'T WE?
LAST THING I REMEMBER, I WAS CAUGHT IN THE TIDAL WAVE. WHEN THE MOON SHIFTED, I PASSED OUT IN THE WATER...
...ONE OF YOU GUYS BIT ME, DIDN'T YOU? I...I THINK I KNEW SOME OF THESE PEOPLE...
SHUT UP, WIMP.
THIS PLACE IS PRIME FOR VAMPIRE RULE. BUSTIN' WITH BLOOD, EVERYTHING ON THE SHORE BOARDED UP SO THE LIGHT STAYS OUT...
WHAT YOU GOT TO WHINE ABOUT, HUH?
WE'RE GONNA LIVE FOREV--
BLAM

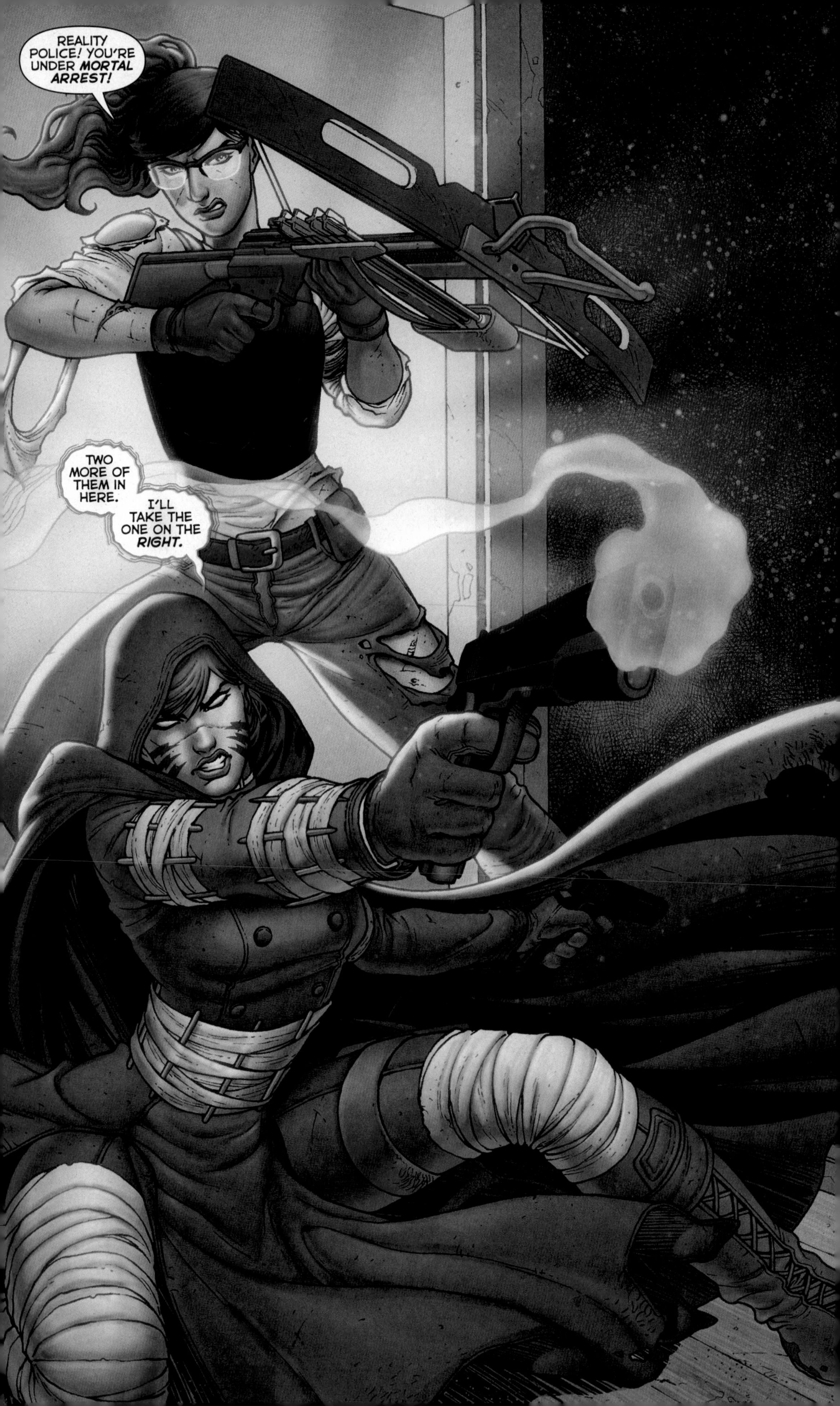
REALITY POLICE! YOU'RE UNDER MORTAL ARREST!
TWO MORE OF THEM IN HERE.
I'LL TAKE THE ONE ON THE RIGHT.

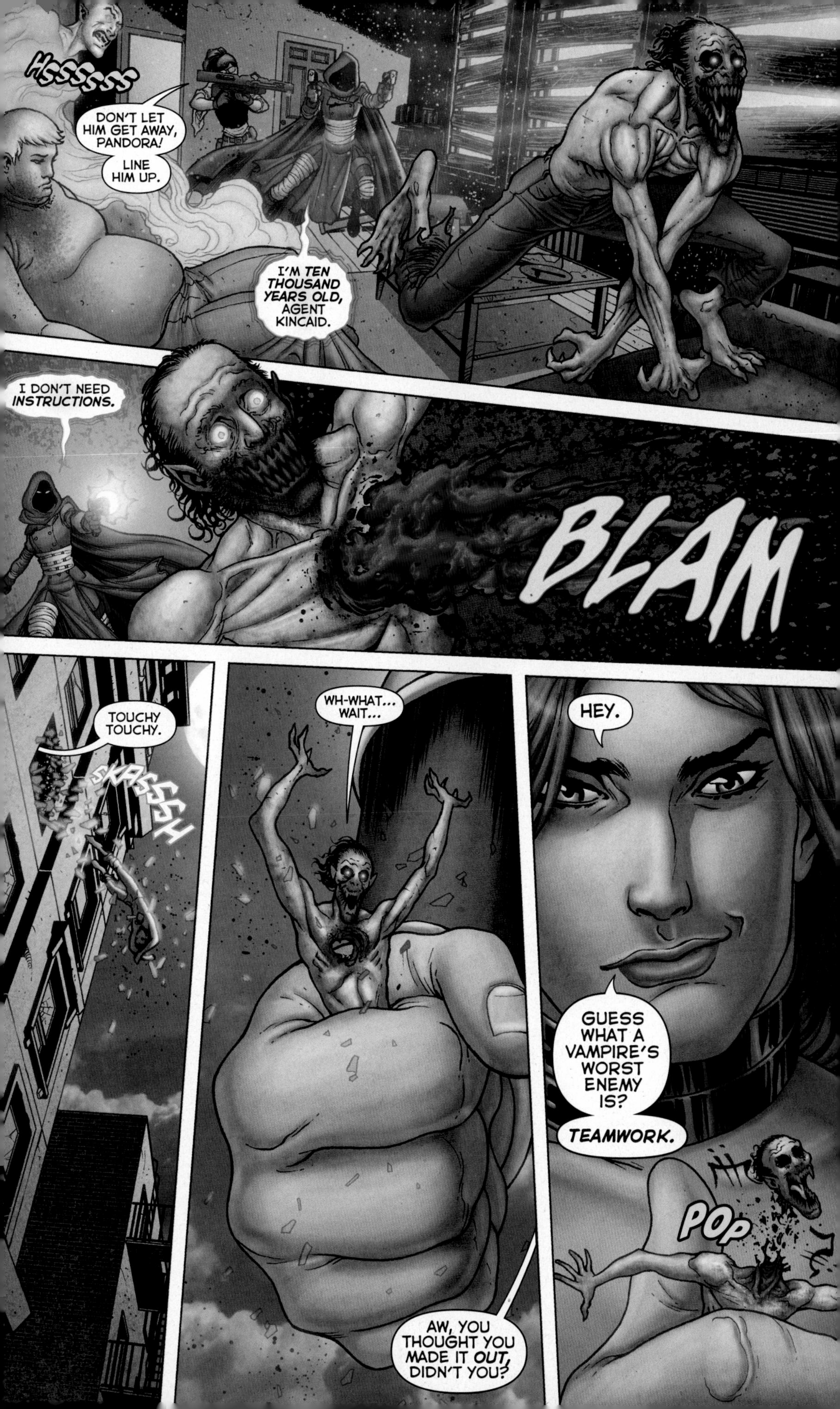
HSSSSSS
DON'T LET HIM GET AWAY, PANDORA!
LINE HIM UP.
I'M TEN THOUSAND YEARS OLD, AGENT KINCAID.
I DON'T NEED INSTRUCTIONS.
BLAM
TOUCHY TOUCHY.
SKASSSH
WH-WHAT... WAIT...
AW, YOU THOUGHT YOU MADE IT OUT, DIDN'T YOU?
HEY.
GUESS WHAT A VAMPIRE'S WORST ENEMY IS?
TEAMWORK.
POP

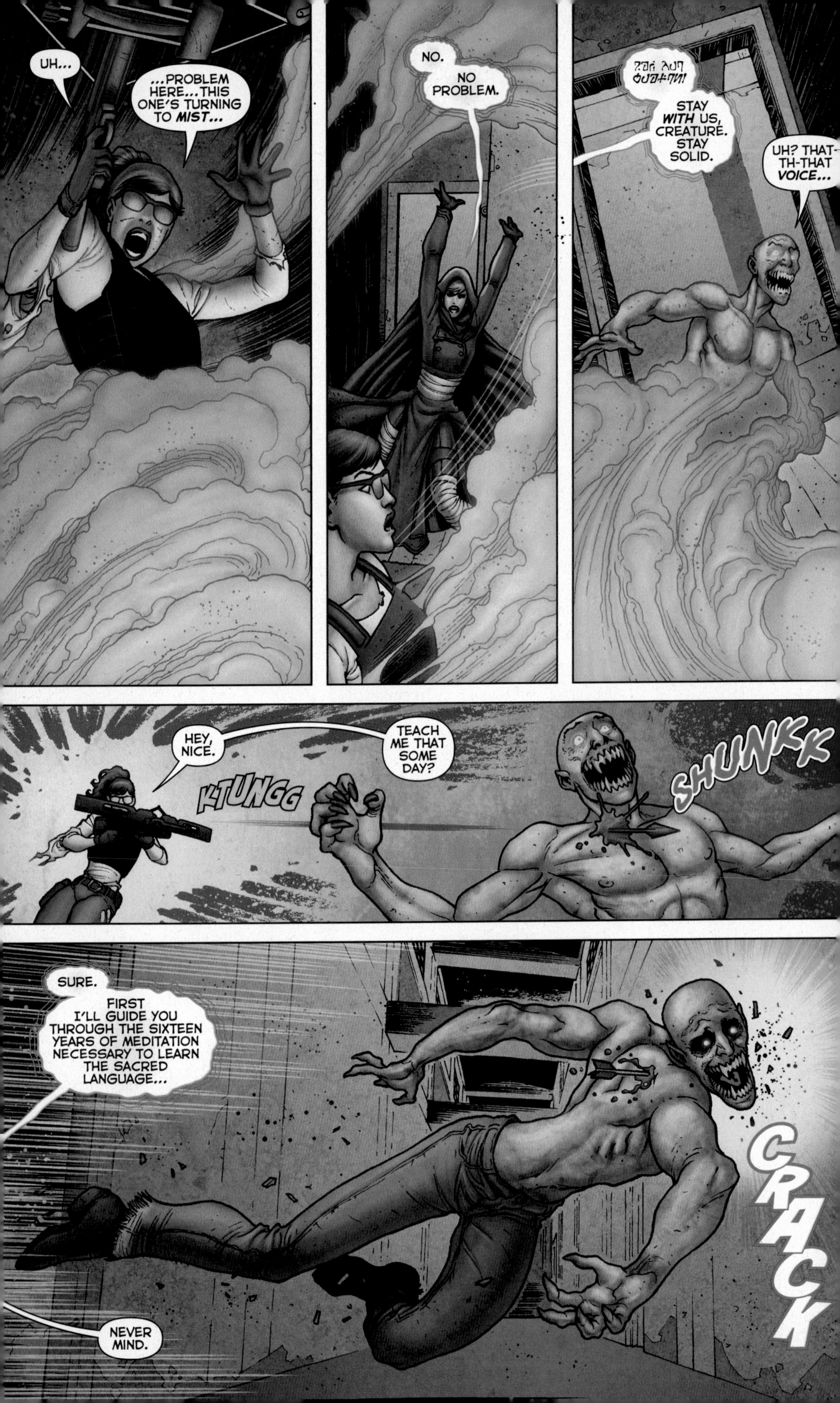
UH...
...PROBLEM HERE...THIS ONE'S TURNING TO MIST...
NO.
NO PROBLEM.
STAY WITH US, CREATURE. STAY SOLID.
UH? THAT-TH-THAT VOICE...
HEY, NICE.
TEACH ME THAT SOME DAY?
KTUNGG
SHUNKK
SURE.
FIRST I'LL GUIDE YOU THROUGH THE SIXTEEN YEARS OF MEDITATION NECESSARY TO LEARN THE SACRED LANGUAGE...
CRACK
NEVER MIND.

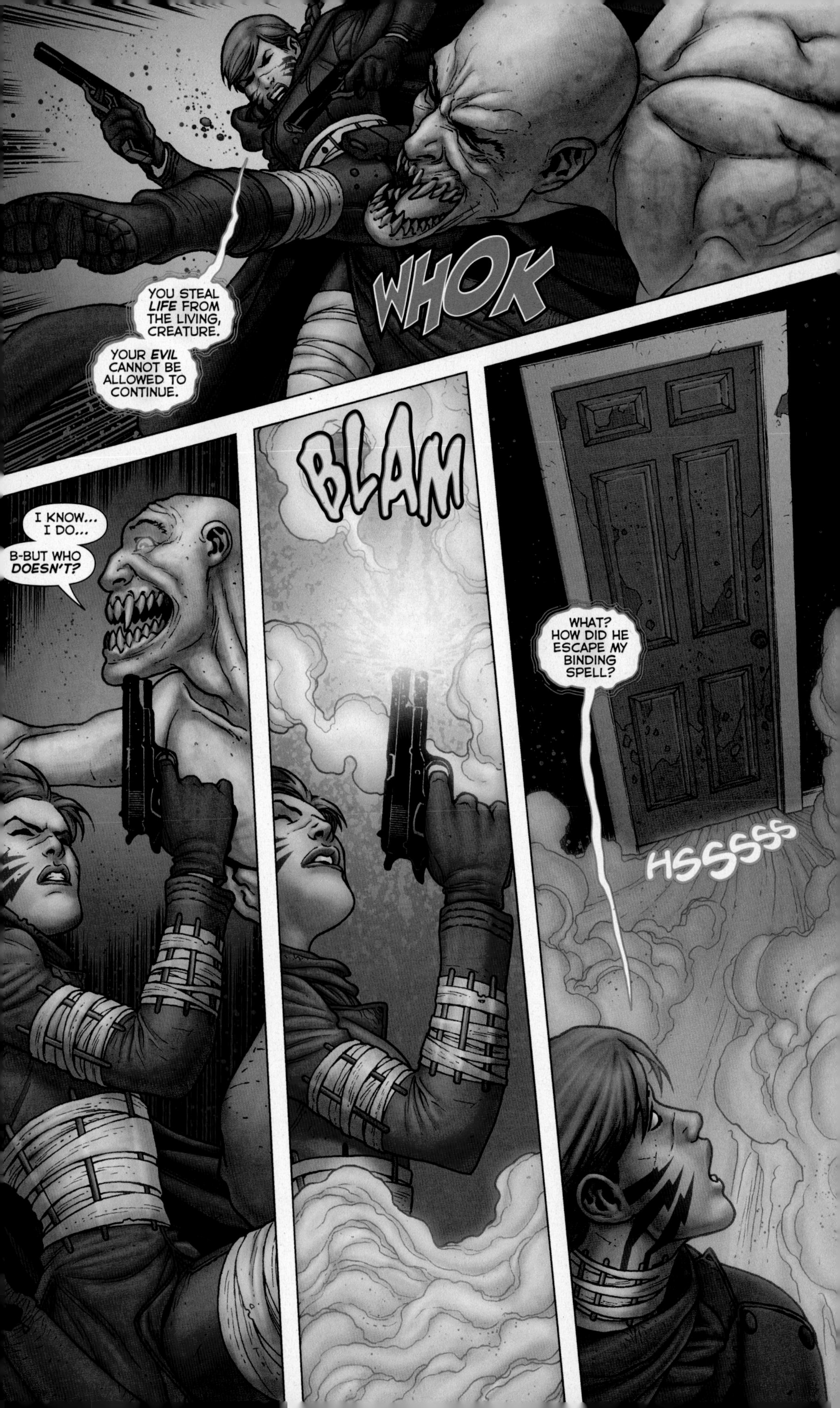
YOU STEAL *LIFE* FROM THE LIVING, CREATURE.
YOUR *EVIL* CANNOT BE ALLOWED TO CONTINUE.
WHOK
I KNOW... I DO...
B-BUT WHO *DOESN'T?*
BLAM
WHAT? HOW DID HE ESCAPE MY BINDING SPELL?
HSSSSS

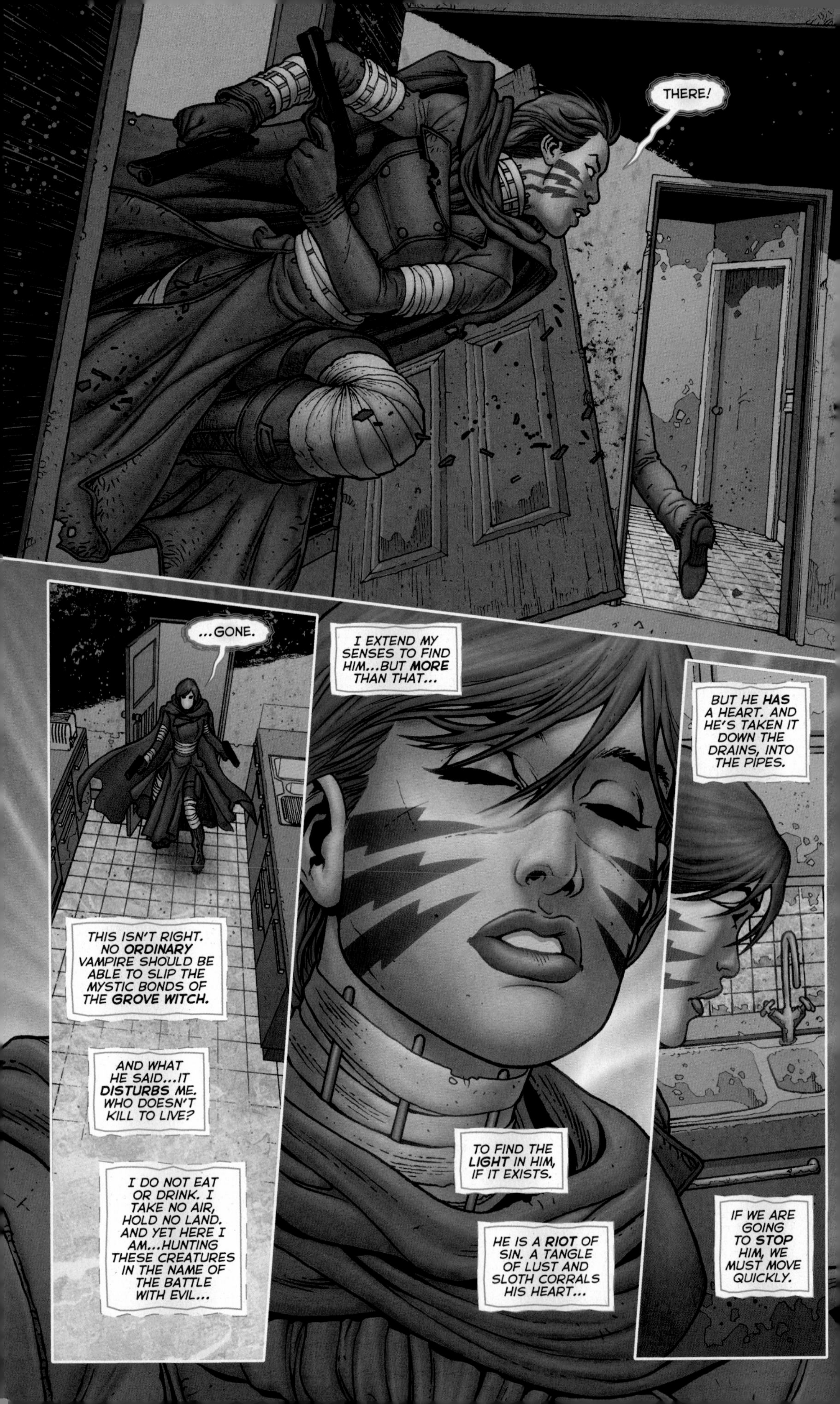
THERE!
...GONE.
THIS ISN'T RIGHT. NO ORDINARY VAMPIRE SHOULD BE ABLE TO SLIP THE MYSTIC BONDS OF THE GROVE WITCH.
AND WHAT HE SAID...IT DISTURBS ME. WHO DOESN'T KILL TO LIVE?
I DO NOT EAT OR DRINK. I TAKE NO AIR, HOLD NO LAND. AND YET HERE I AM...HUNTING THESE CREATURES IN THE NAME OF THE BATTLE WITH EVIL...
I EXTEND MY SENSES TO FIND HIM...BUT MORE THAN THAT...
TO FIND THE LIGHT IN HIM, IF IT EXISTS.
HE IS A RIOT OF SIN. A TANGLE OF LUST AND SLOTH CORRALS HIS HEART...
BUT HE HAS A HEART. AND HE'S TAKEN IT DOWN THE DRAINS, INTO THE PIPES.
IF WE ARE GOING TO STOP HIM, WE MUST MOVE QUICKLY.

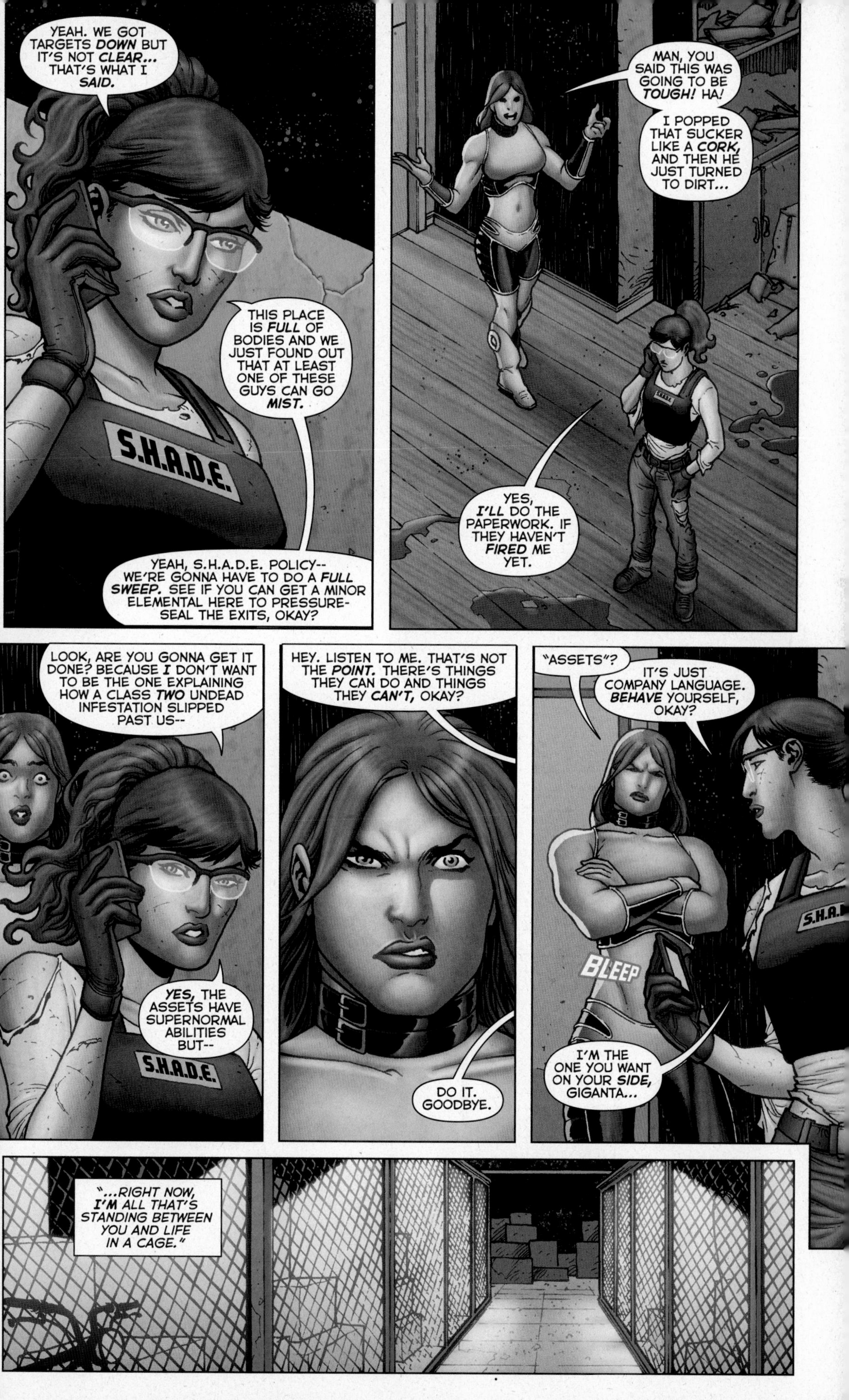
YEAH. WE GOT TARGETS DOWN BUT IT'S NOT CLEAR... THAT'S WHAT I SAID.
THIS PLACE IS FULL OF BODIES AND WE JUST FOUND OUT THAT AT LEAST ONE OF THESE GUYS CAN GO MIST.
S.H.A.D.E.
YEAH, S.H.A.D.E. POLICY-- WE'RE GONNA HAVE TO DO A FULL SWEEP. SEE IF YOU CAN GET A MINOR ELEMENTAL HERE TO PRESSURE-SEAL THE EXITS, OKAY?
MAN, YOU SAID THIS WAS GOING TO BE TOUGH! HA!
I POPPED THAT SUCKER LIKE A CORK, AND THEN HE JUST TURNED TO DIRT...
YES, I'LL DO THE PAPERWORK. IF THEY HAVEN'T FIRED ME YET.
LOOK, ARE YOU GONNA GET IT DONE? BECAUSE I DON'T WANT TO BE THE ONE EXPLAINING HOW A CLASS TWO UNDEAD INFESTATION SLIPPED PAST US--
YES, THE ASSETS HAVE SUPERNORMAL ABILITIES BUT--
S.H.A.D.E.
HEY. LISTEN TO ME. THAT'S NOT THE POINT. THERE'S THINGS THEY CAN DO AND THINGS THEY CAN'T, OKAY?
DO IT. GOODBYE.
"ASSETS"?
IT'S JUST COMPANY LANGUAGE. BEHAVE YOURSELF, OKAY?
BLEEP
I'M THE ONE YOU WANT ON YOUR SIDE, GIGANTA...
"...RIGHT NOW, I'M ALL THAT'S STANDING BETWEEN YOU AND LIFE IN A CAGE."

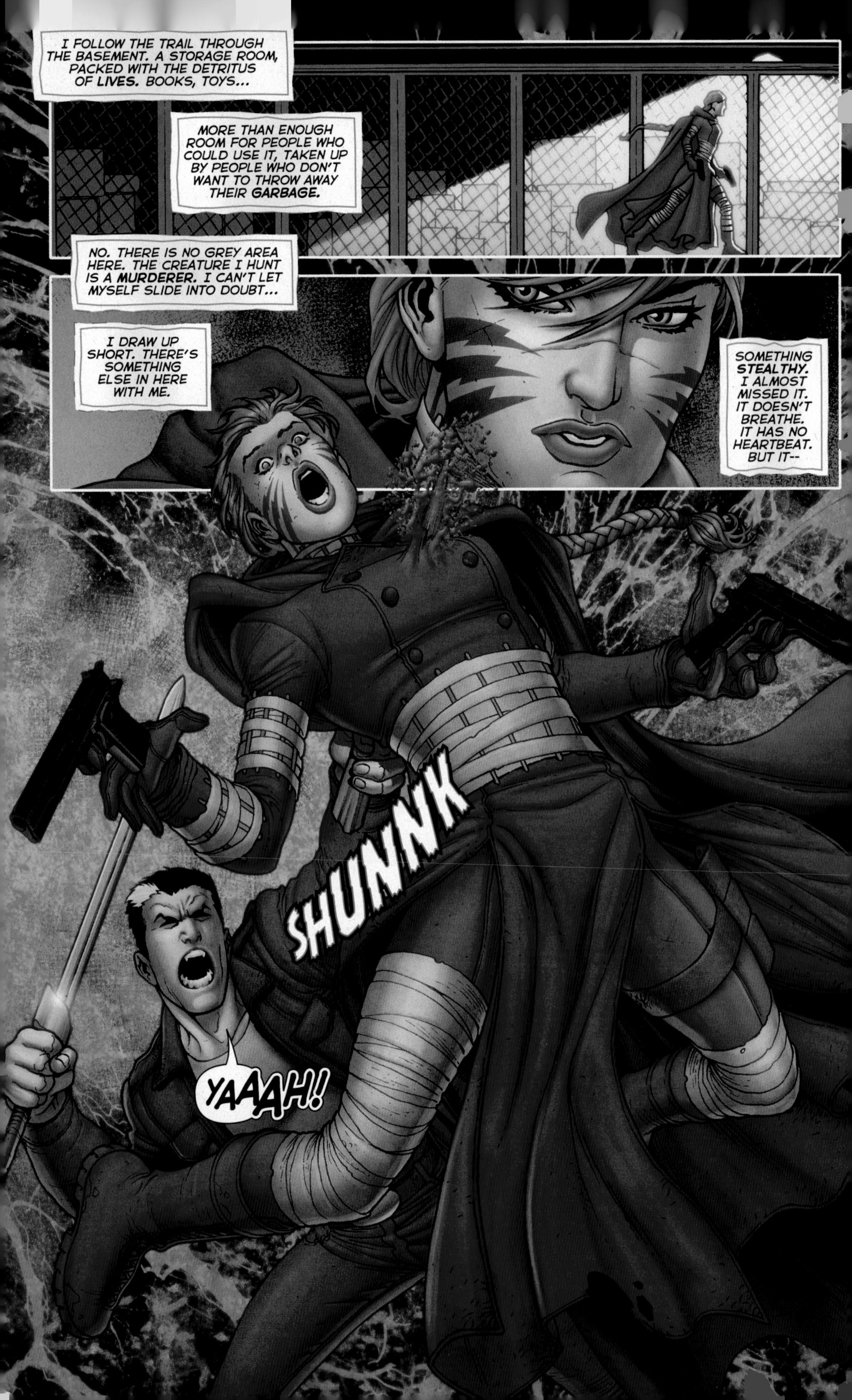
I FOLLOW THE TRAIL THROUGH THE BASEMENT. A STORAGE ROOM, PACKED WITH THE DETRITUS OF LIVES. BOOKS, TOYS...
MORE THAN ENOUGH ROOM FOR PEOPLE WHO COULD USE IT, TAKEN UP BY PEOPLE WHO DON'T WANT TO THROW AWAY THEIR GARBAGE.
NO. THERE IS NO GREY AREA HERE. THE CREATURE I HUNT IS A MURDERER. I CAN'T LET MYSELF SLIDE INTO DOUBT...
I DRAW UP SHORT. THERE'S SOMETHING ELSE IN HERE WITH ME.
SOMETHING STEALTHY. I ALMOST MISSED IT. IT DOESN'T BREATHE. IT HAS NO HEARTBEAT. BUT IT--
SHUNNK
YAAAH!

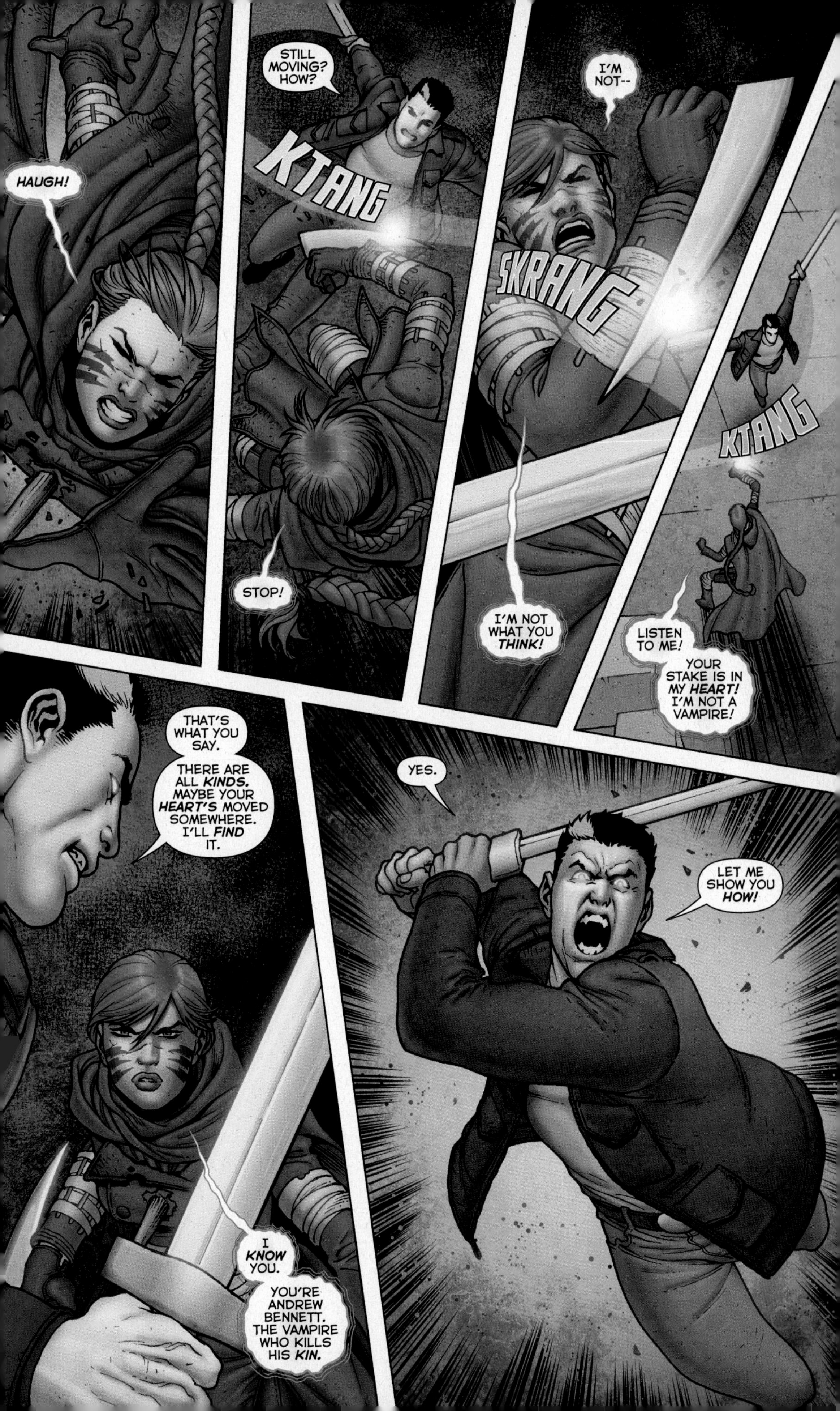
HAUGH!
STILL MOVING? HOW?
KTANG
STOP!
I'M NOT--
SKRANG
I'M NOT WHAT YOU *THINK!*
KTANG
LISTEN TO ME!
YOUR STAKE IS IN MY *HEART!* I'M NOT A VAMPIRE!
THAT'S WHAT YOU SAY.
THERE ARE ALL *KINDS.* MAYBE YOUR *HEART'S* MOVED SOMEWHERE. I'LL *FIND* IT.
I *KNOW* YOU.
YOU'RE ANDREW BENNETT. THE VAMPIRE WHO KILLS HIS *KIN.*
YES.
LET ME SHOW YOU *HOW!*

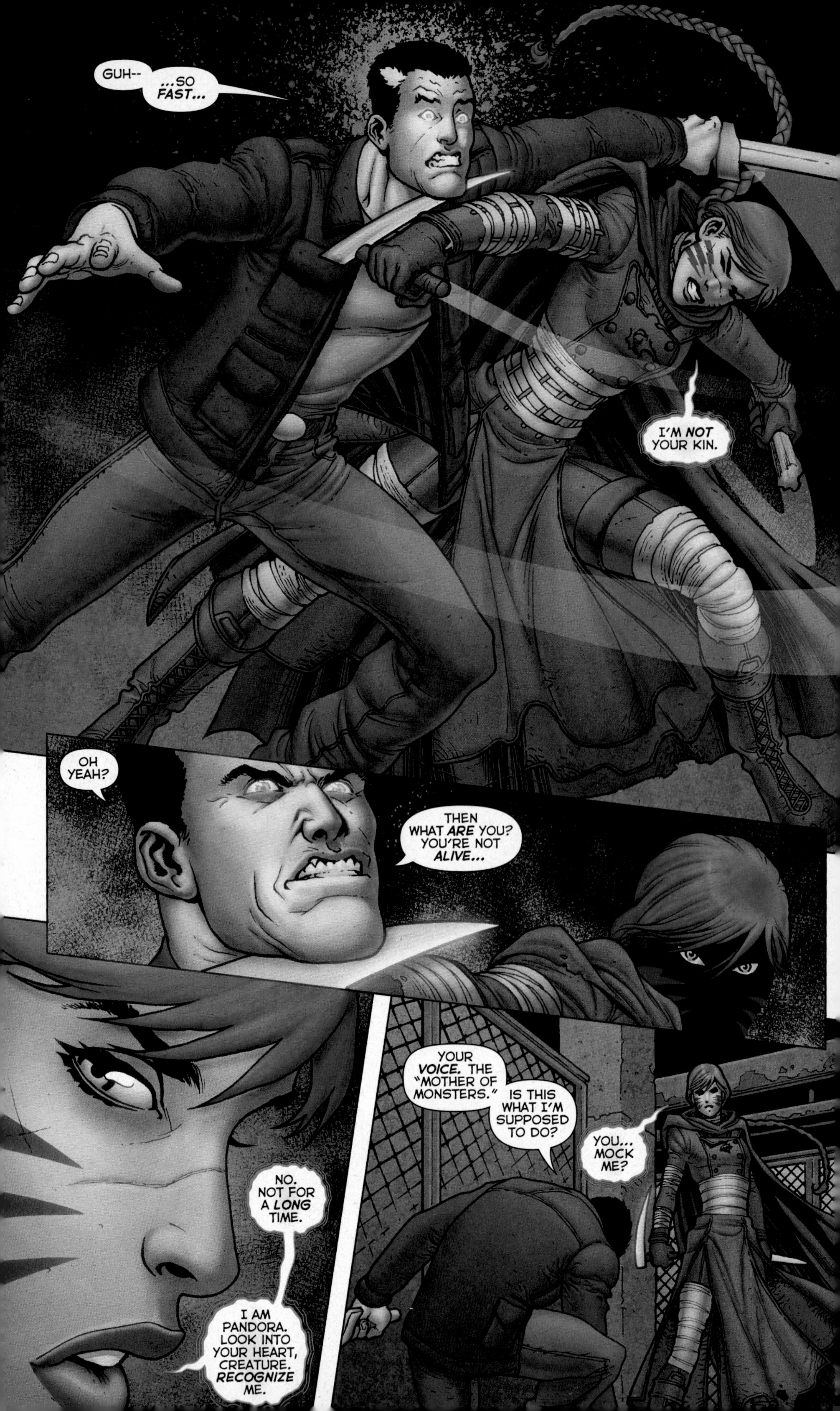
GUH--
...SO FAST...
I'M NOT YOUR KIN.
OH YEAH?
THEN WHAT ARE YOU? YOU'RE NOT ALIVE...
NO. NOT FOR A LONG TIME.
I AM PANDORA. LOOK INTO YOUR HEART, CREATURE. RECOGNIZE ME.
YOUR VOICE. THE "MOTHER OF MONSTERS." IS THIS WHAT I'M SUPPOSED TO DO?
YOU... MOCK ME?

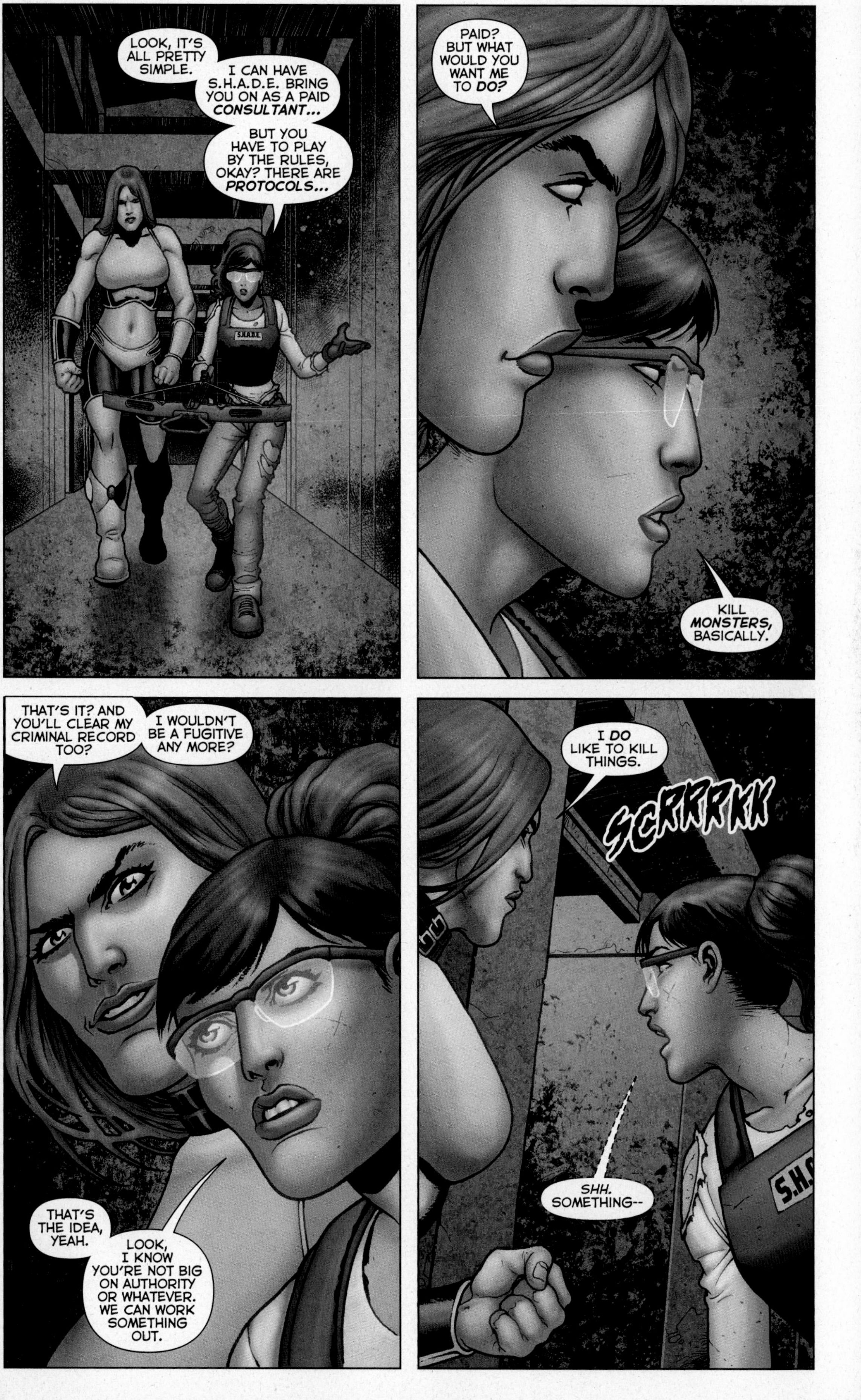
LOOK, IT'S ALL PRETTY SIMPLE.
I CAN HAVE S.H.A.D.E. BRING YOU ON AS A PAID CONSULTANT...
BUT YOU HAVE TO PLAY BY THE RULES, OKAY? THERE ARE PROTOCOLS...
S.H.A.D.E.
PAID? BUT WHAT WOULD YOU WANT ME TO DO?
KILL MONSTERS, BASICALLY.
THAT'S IT? AND YOU'LL CLEAR MY CRIMINAL RECORD TOO?
I WOULDN'T BE A FUGITIVE ANY MORE?
THAT'S THE IDEA, YEAH.
LOOK, I KNOW YOU'RE NOT BIG ON AUTHORITY OR WHATEVER. WE CAN WORK SOMETHING OUT.
I DO LIKE TO KILL THINGS.
SCRRRKK
SHH. SOMETHING--

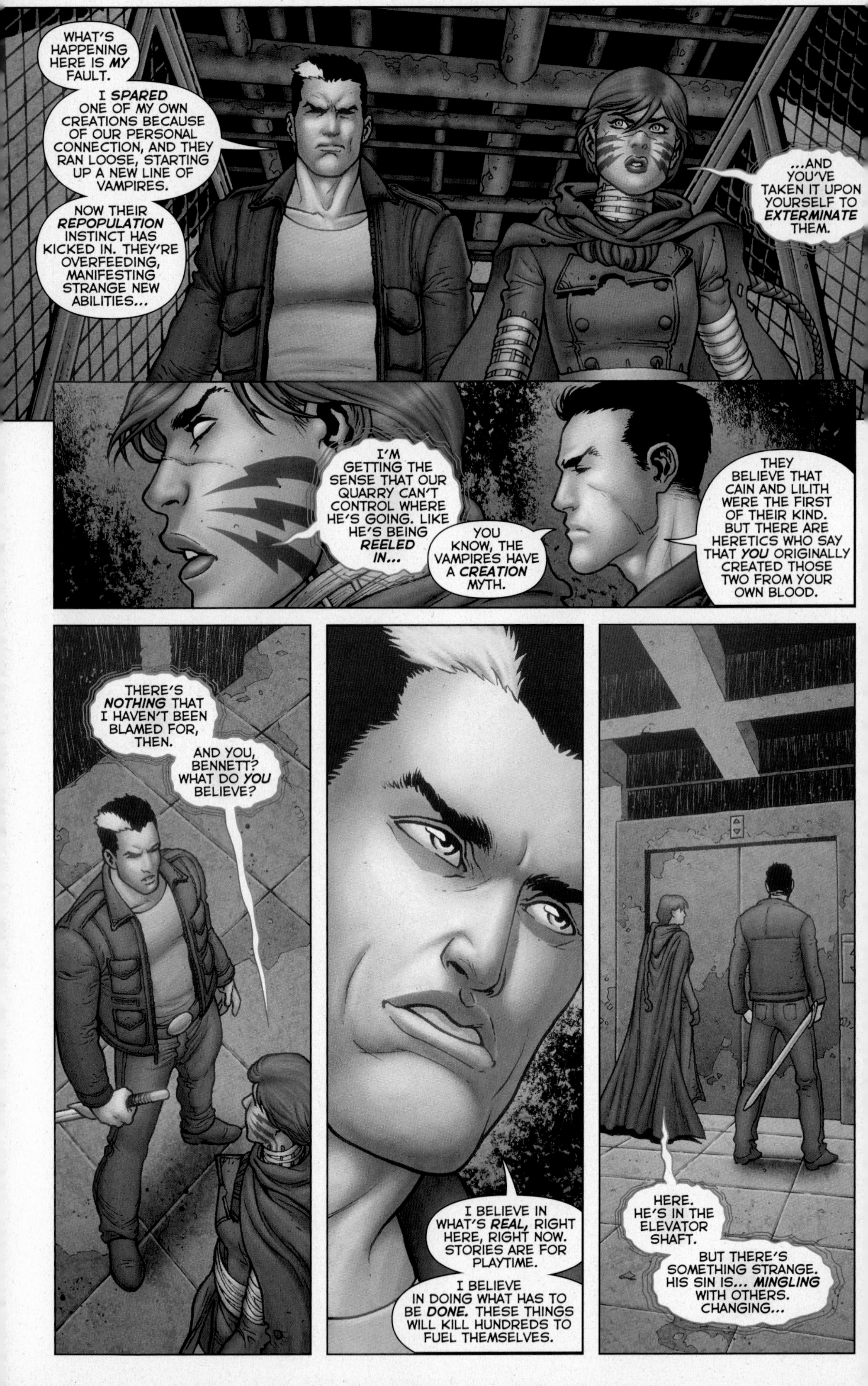
WHAT'S HAPPENING HERE IS MY FAULT.
I SPARED ONE OF MY OWN CREATIONS BECAUSE OF OUR PERSONAL CONNECTION, AND THEY RAN LOOSE, STARTING UP A NEW LINE OF VAMPIRES.
NOW THEIR REPOPULATION INSTINCT HAS KICKED IN. THEY'RE OVERFEEDING, MANIFESTING STRANGE NEW ABILITIES...
...AND YOU'VE TAKEN IT UPON YOURSELF TO EXTERMINATE THEM.
I'M GETTING THE SENSE THAT OUR QUARRY CAN'T CONTROL WHERE HE'S GOING. LIKE HE'S BEING REELED IN...
YOU KNOW, THE VAMPIRES HAVE A CREATION MYTH.
THEY BELIEVE THAT CAIN AND LILITH WERE THE FIRST OF THEIR KIND. BUT THERE ARE HERETICS WHO SAY THAT YOU ORIGINALLY CREATED THOSE TWO FROM YOUR OWN BLOOD.
THERE'S NOTHING THAT I HAVEN'T BEEN BLAMED FOR, THEN.
AND YOU, BENNETT? WHAT DO YOU BELIEVE?
I BELIEVE IN WHAT'S REAL, RIGHT HERE, RIGHT NOW. STORIES ARE FOR PLAYTIME.
I BELIEVE IN DOING WHAT HAS TO BE DONE. THESE THINGS WILL KILL HUNDREDS TO FUEL THEMSELVES.
HERE. HE'S IN THE ELEVATOR SHAFT.
BUT THERE'S SOMETHING STRANGE. HIS SIN IS... MINGLING WITH OTHERS. CHANGING...

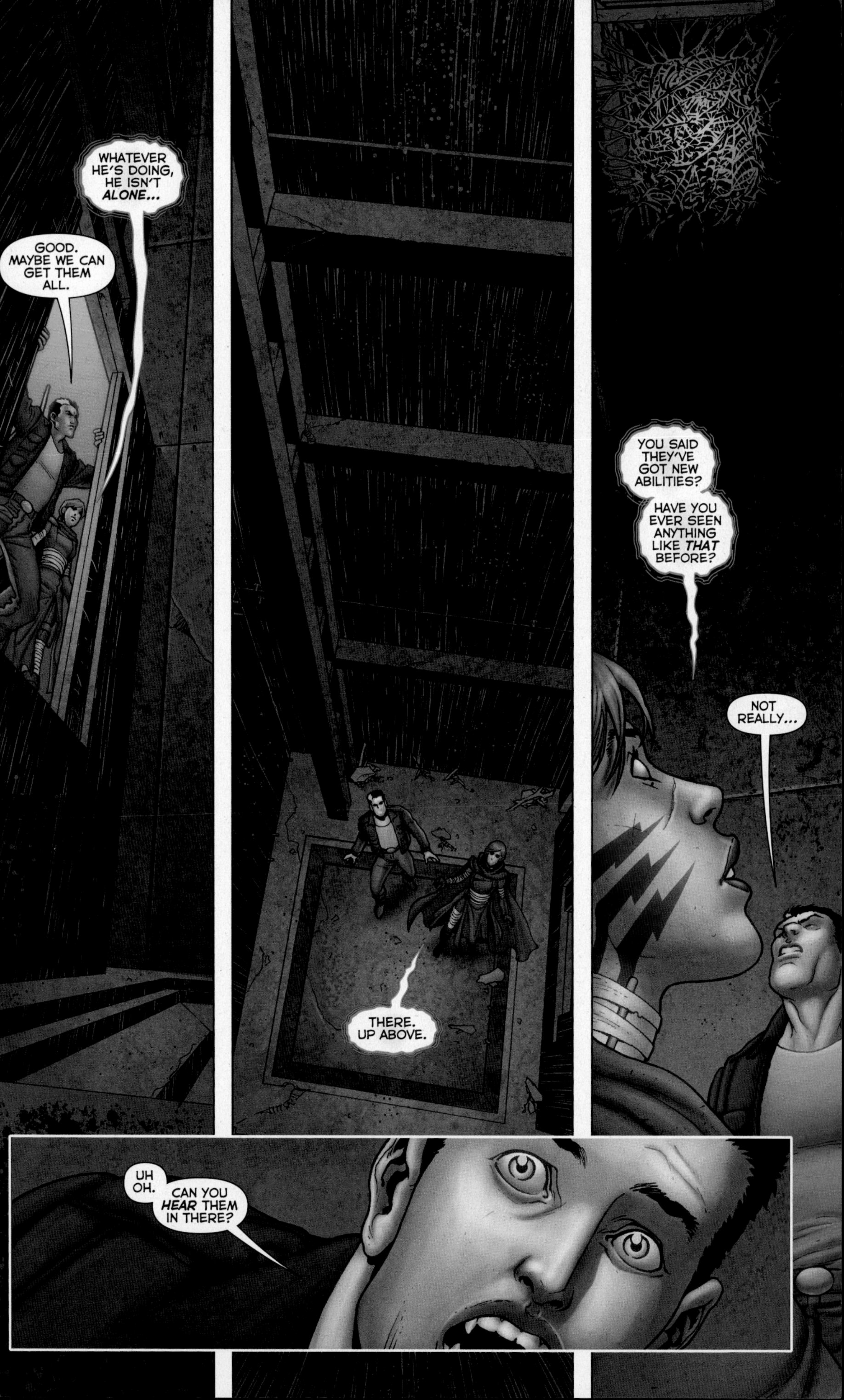
WHATEVER HE'S DOING, HE ISN'T *ALONE*...
GOOD. MAYBE WE CAN GET THEM ALL.
THERE. UP ABOVE.
YOU SAID THEY'VE GOT NEW ABILITIES?
HAVE YOU EVER SEEN ANYTHING LIKE *THAT* BEFORE?
NOT REALLY...
UH OH.
CAN YOU *HEAR* THEM IN THERE?

ELEVATOR SHAFT. HMM. I DON'T *LIKE* IT.

SCCRKKK

KRITCH SKKK

CAREFUL. WE'RE LOOKING AT SERIOUSLY RESTRICTED MOBILITY IN THERE.

YOU WON'T BE ABLE TO *GROW* MUCH.

HOW'S THIS?

IT'LL DO, I GUESS. ARE YOU MUCH *STRONGER* THAT WAY?

STRONGER THAN *YOU*.

STEADY...

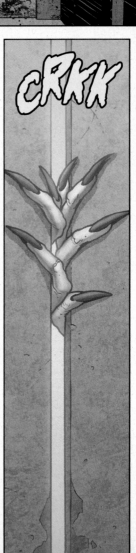

CRKK

HERE THEY COME!

KTUNGG

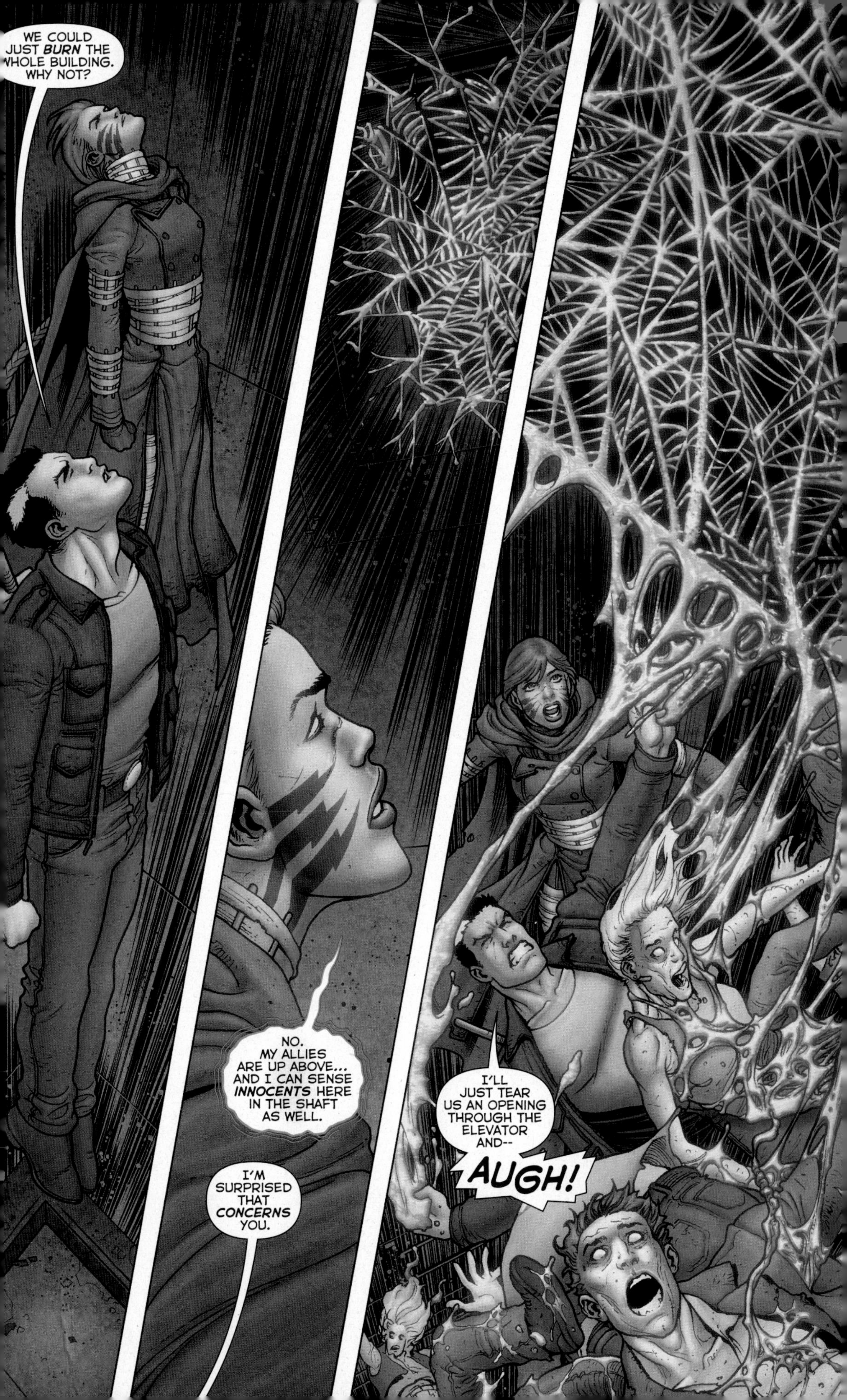
WE COULD JUST BURN THE WHOLE BUILDING. WHY NOT?
NO. MY ALLIES ARE UP ABOVE... AND I CAN SENSE INNOCENTS HERE IN THE SHAFT AS WELL.
I'M SURPRISED THAT CONCERNS YOU.
I'LL JUST TEAR US AN OPENING THROUGH THE ELEVATOR AND--
AUGH!

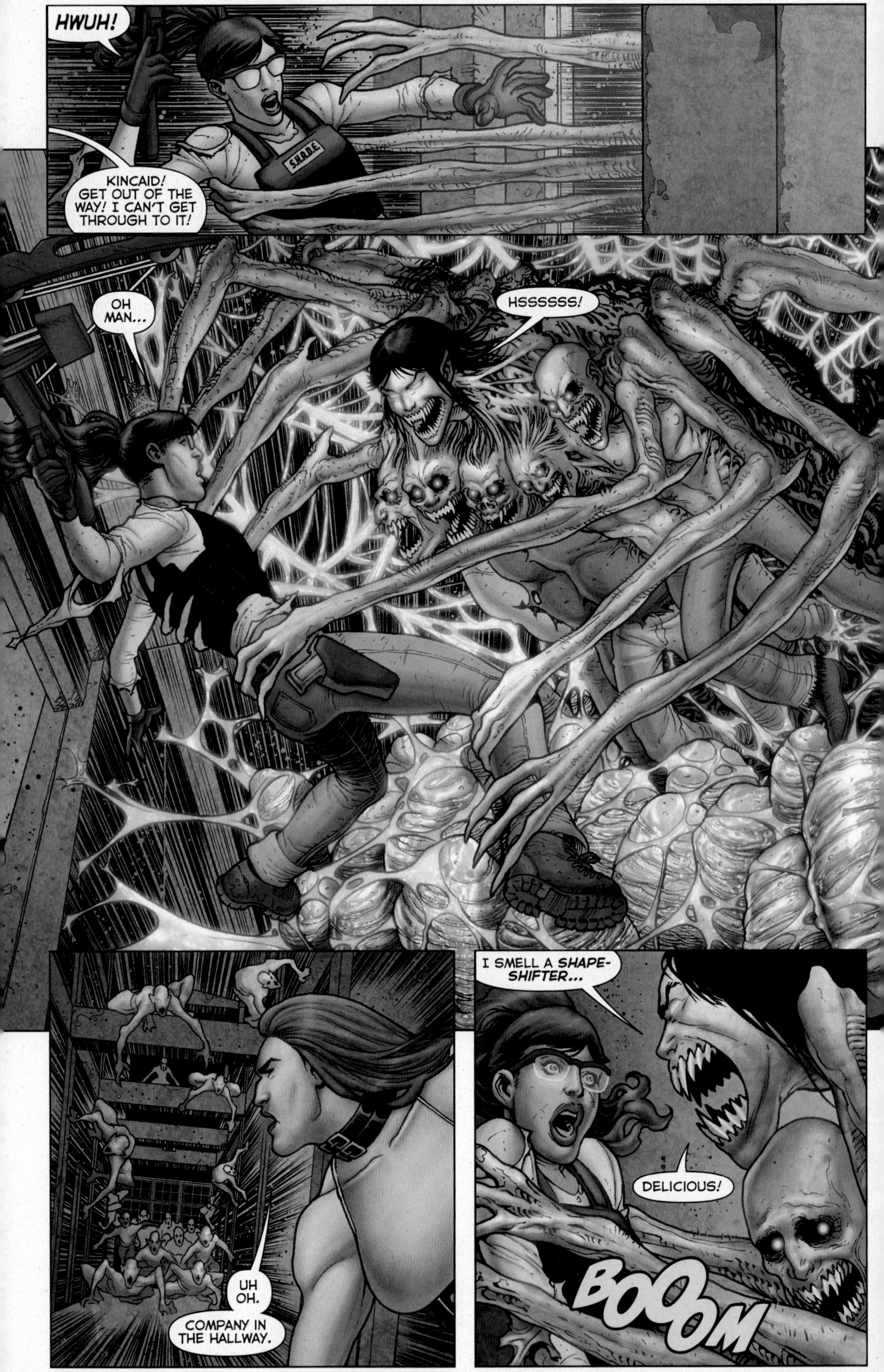
HWUH!
KINCAID! GET OUT OF THE WAY! I CAN'T GET THROUGH TO IT!
OH MAN...
HSSSSSS!
UH OH.
COMPANY IN THE HALLWAY.
I SMELL A SHAPE-SHIFTER...
DELICIOUS!
BOOOOM

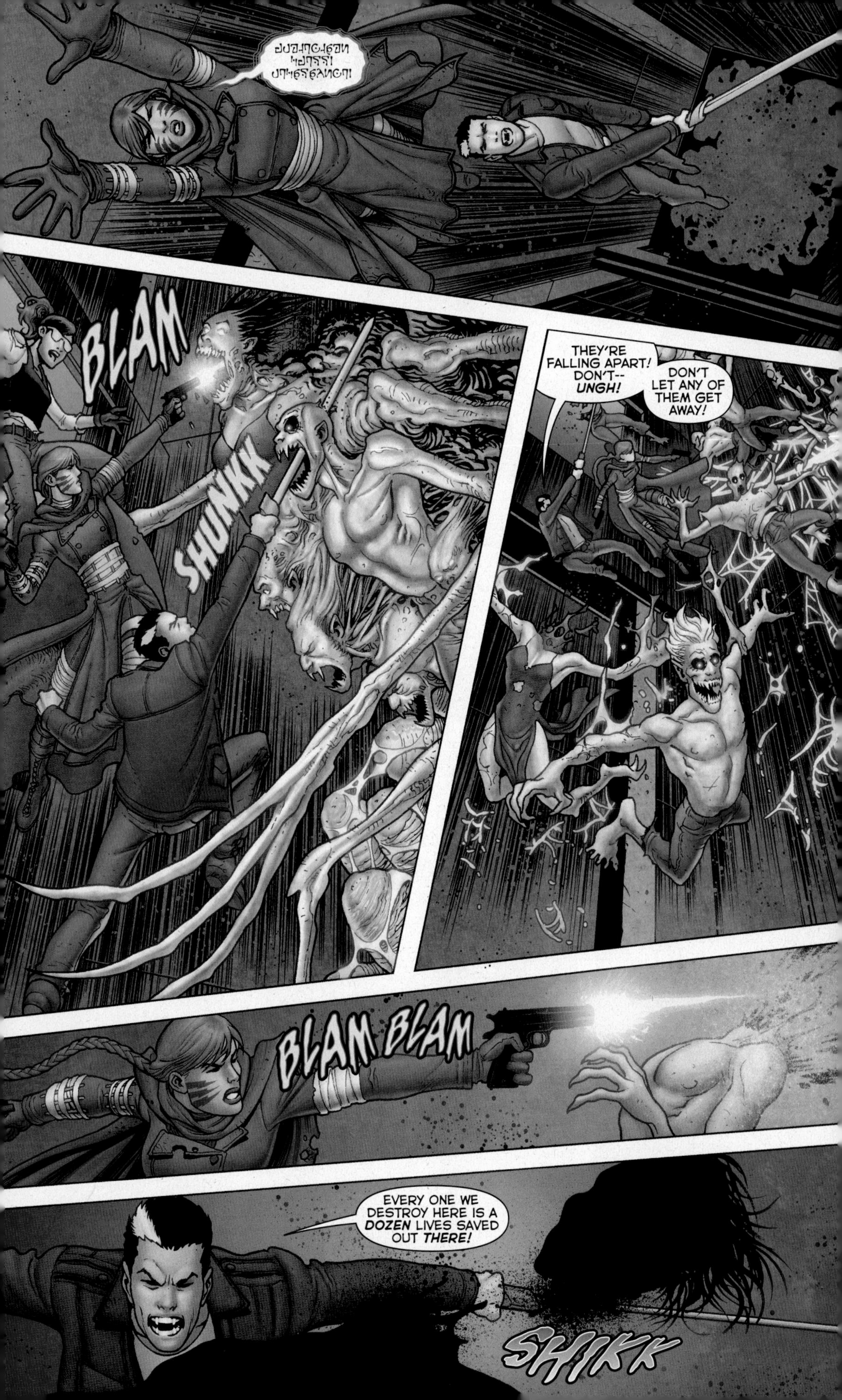
BLAM
SHUNKK
THEY'RE FALLING APART! DON'T-- *UNGH!*
DON'T LET ANY OF THEM GET AWAY!
BLAM BLAM
EVERY ONE WE DESTROY HERE IS A *DOZEN* LIVES SAVED OUT *THERE!*
SHIKK

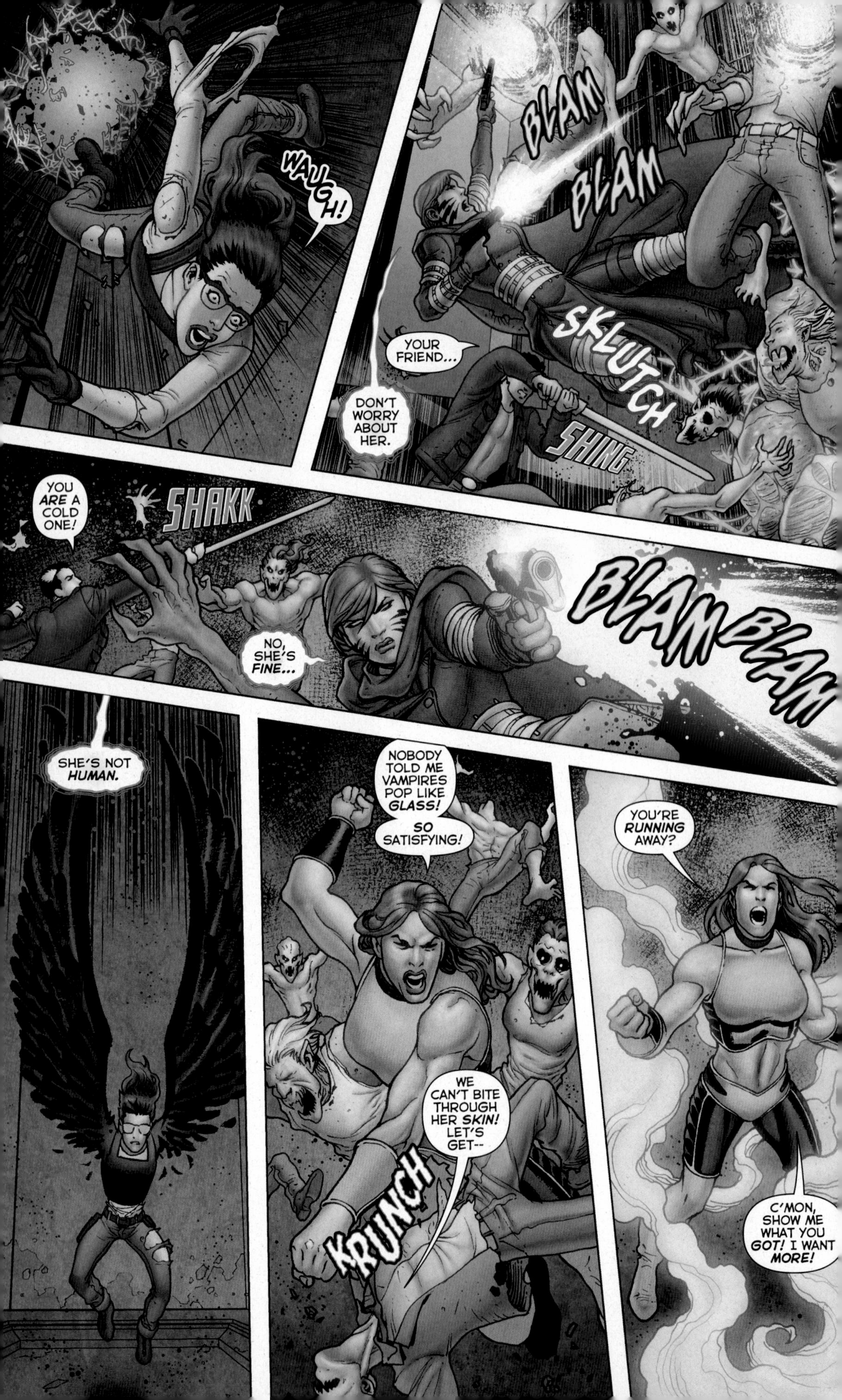
WAUGH!
BLAM
BLAM
YOUR FRIEND...
DON'T WORRY ABOUT HER.
SKLUTCH
SHING
YOU ARE A COLD ONE!
SHAKK
NO, SHE'S FINE...
BLAM BLAM
SHE'S NOT HUMAN.
NOBODY TOLD ME VAMPIRES POP LIKE GLASS!
SO SATISFYING!
WE CAN'T BITE THROUGH HER SKIN! LET'S GET--
KRUNCH
YOU'RE RUNNING AWAY?
C'MON, SHOW ME WHAT YOU GOT! I WANT MORE!

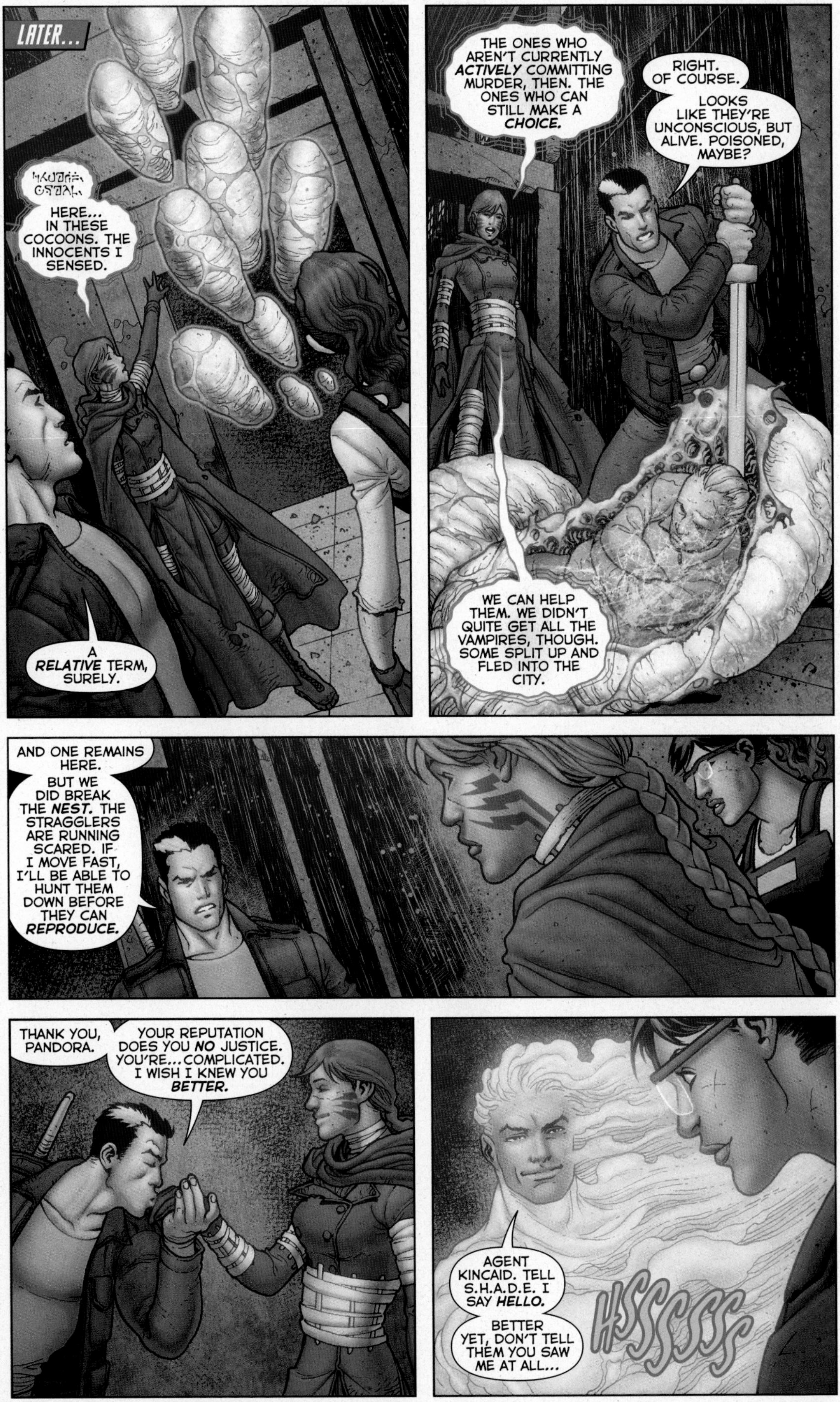
LATER...
HERE... IN THESE COCOONS. THE INNOCENTS I SENSED.
A RELATIVE TERM, SURELY.
THE ONES WHO AREN'T CURRENTLY ACTIVELY COMMITTING MURDER, THEN. THE ONES WHO CAN STILL MAKE A CHOICE.
RIGHT. OF COURSE.
LOOKS LIKE THEY'RE UNCONSCIOUS, BUT ALIVE. POISONED, MAYBE?
WE CAN HELP THEM. WE DIDN'T QUITE GET ALL THE VAMPIRES, THOUGH. SOME SPLIT UP AND FLED INTO THE CITY.
AND ONE REMAINS HERE.
BUT WE DID BREAK THE NEST. THE STRAGGLERS ARE RUNNING SCARED. IF I MOVE FAST, I'LL BE ABLE TO HUNT THEM DOWN BEFORE THEY CAN REPRODUCE.
THANK YOU, PANDORA.
YOUR REPUTATION DOES YOU NO JUSTICE. YOU'RE...COMPLICATED. I WISH I KNEW YOU BETTER.
AGENT KINCAID. TELL S.H.A.D.E. I SAY HELLO.
BETTER YET, DON'T TELL THEM YOU SAW ME AT ALL...
HSSSSSS

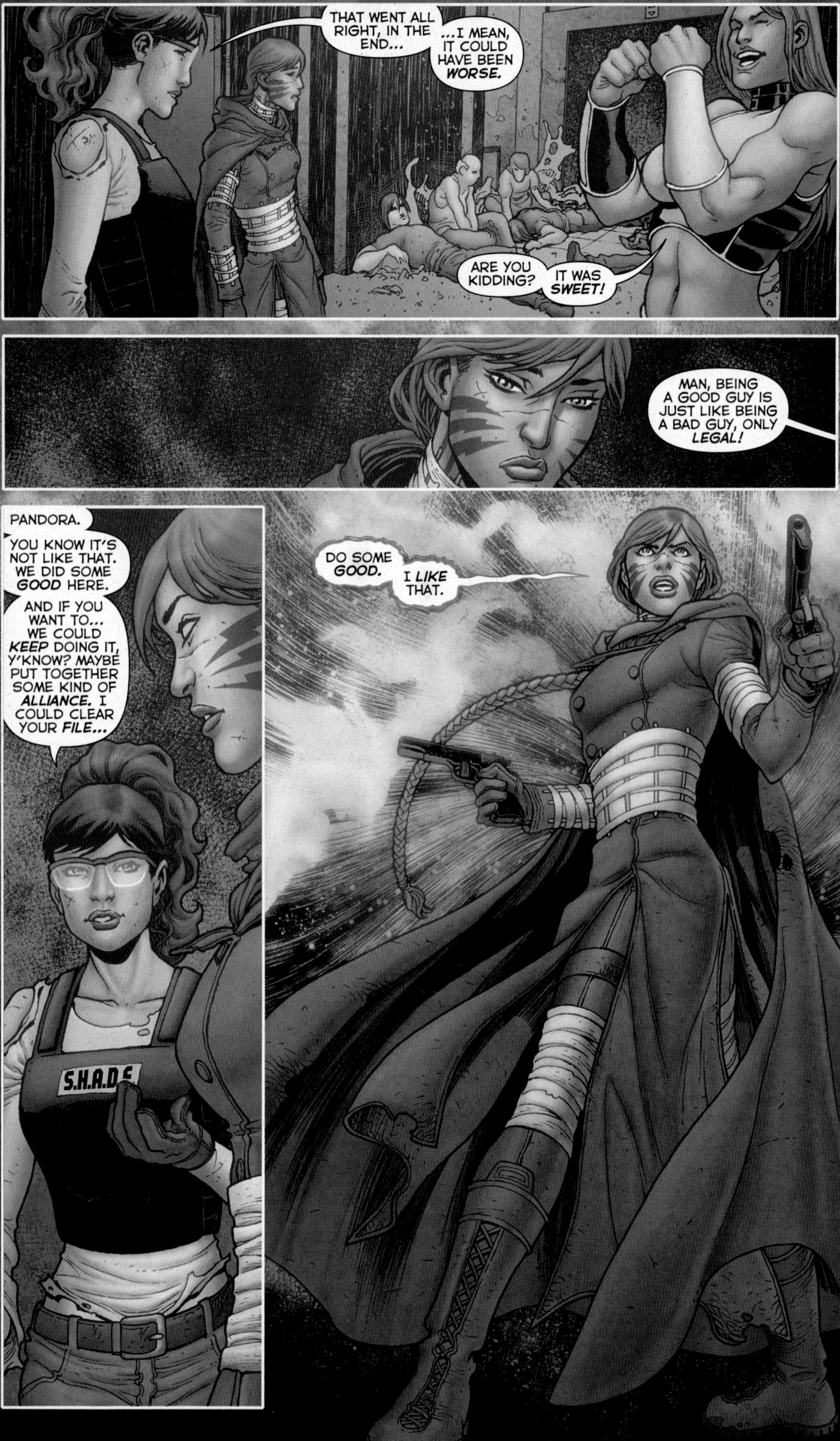
THAT WENT ALL RIGHT, IN THE END...
...I MEAN, IT COULD HAVE BEEN WORSE.
ARE YOU KIDDING?
IT WAS SWEET!
MAN, BEING A GOOD GUY IS JUST LIKE BEING A BAD GUY, ONLY LEGAL!
PANDORA.
YOU KNOW IT'S NOT LIKE THAT. WE DID SOME GOOD HERE.
AND IF YOU WANT TO... WE COULD KEEP DOING IT, Y'KNOW? MAYBE PUT TOGETHER SOME KIND OF ALLIANCE. I COULD CLEAR YOUR FILE...
DO SOME GOOD.
I LIKE THAT.
S.H.A.D.E.

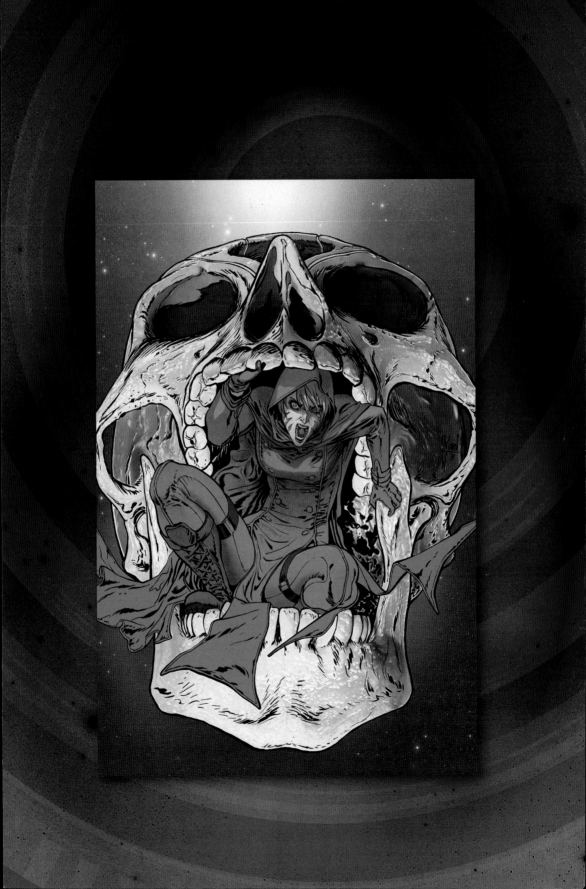

SACRIFICE

RAY FAWKES writer TOM DERENICK breakdowns FRANCIS PORTELA artist ANDEW DALHOUSE colorist TAYLOR ESPOSITO letterer
cover art by GUILLEM MARCH and TOMEU MOREY

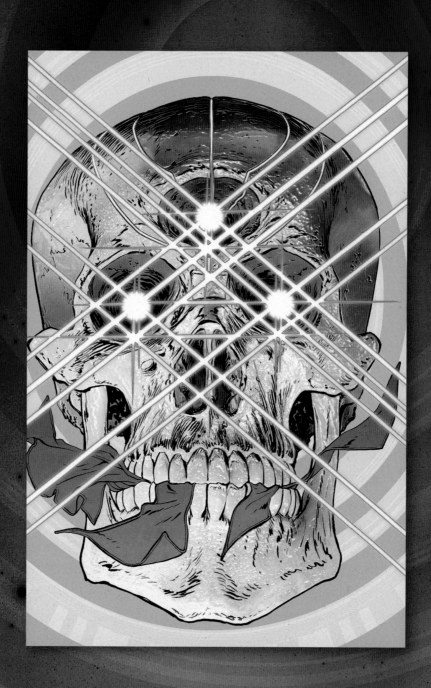

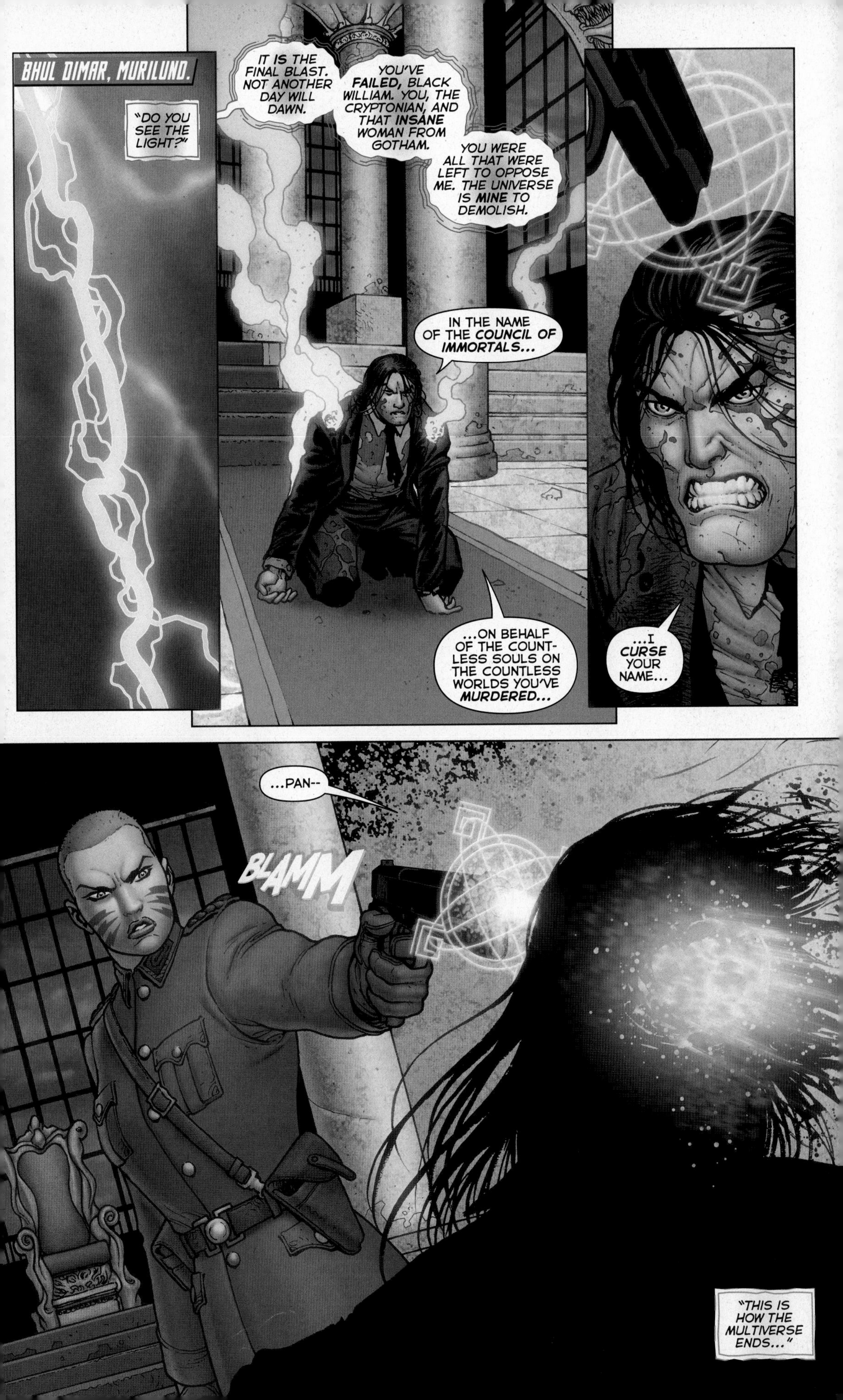
BHUL DIMAR, MURILUND.
"DO YOU SEE THE LIGHT?"
IT IS THE FINAL BLAST. NOT ANOTHER DAY WILL DAWN.
YOU'VE FAILED, BLACK WILLIAM. YOU, THE CRYPTONIAN, AND THAT INSANE WOMAN FROM GOTHAM.
YOU WERE ALL THAT WERE LEFT TO OPPOSE ME. THE UNIVERSE IS MINE TO DEMOLISH.
IN THE NAME OF THE COUNCIL OF IMMORTALS...
...ON BEHALF OF THE COUNTLESS SOULS ON THE COUNTLESS WORLDS YOU'VE MURDERED...
...I CURSE YOUR NAME...
...PAN--
BLAMM
"THIS IS HOW THE MULTIVERSE ENDS..."

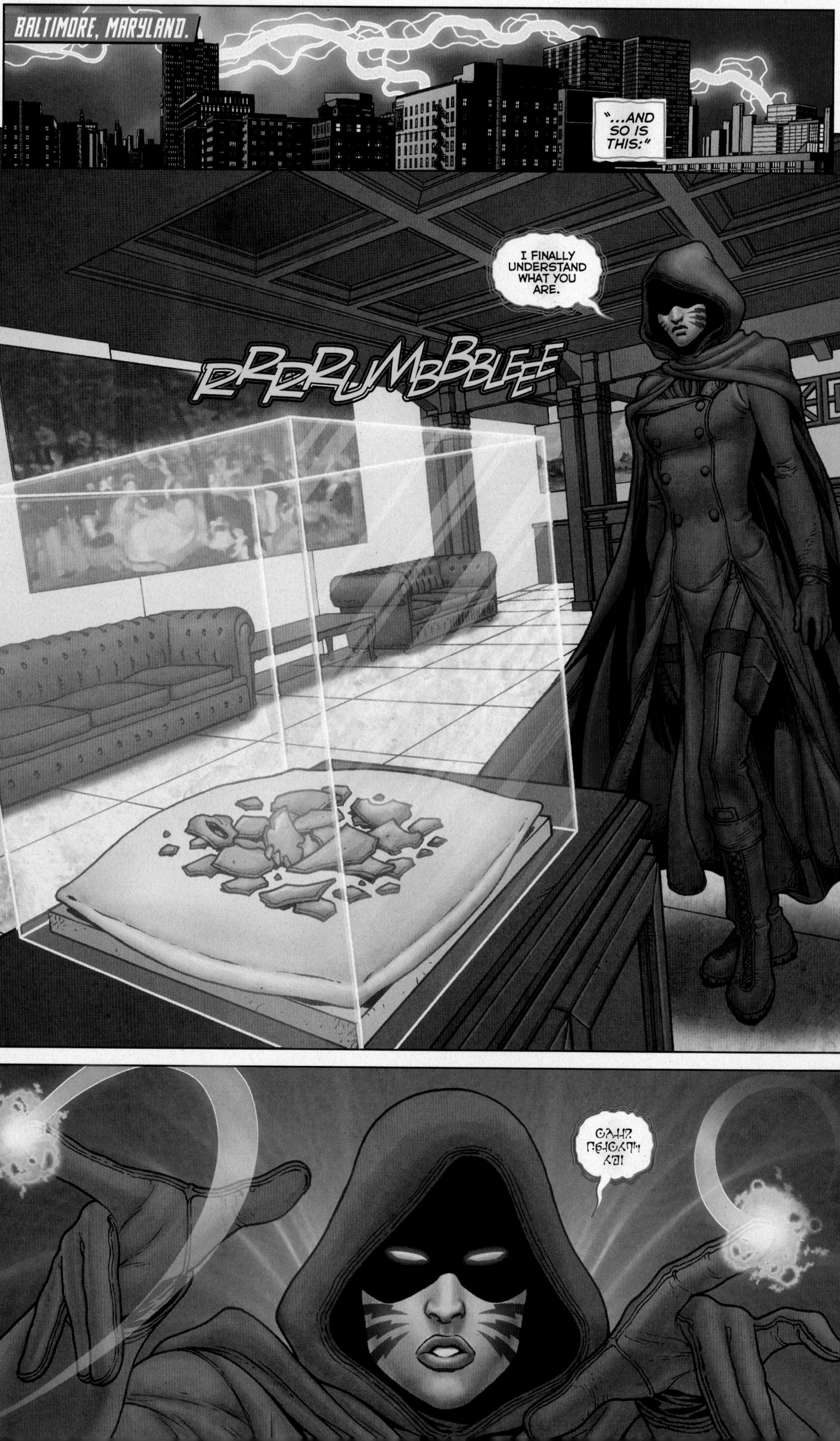
BALTIMORE, MARYLAND.
"...AND SO IS THIS:"
I FINALLY UNDERSTAND WHAT YOU ARE.
RRRRUMBBBLEEE

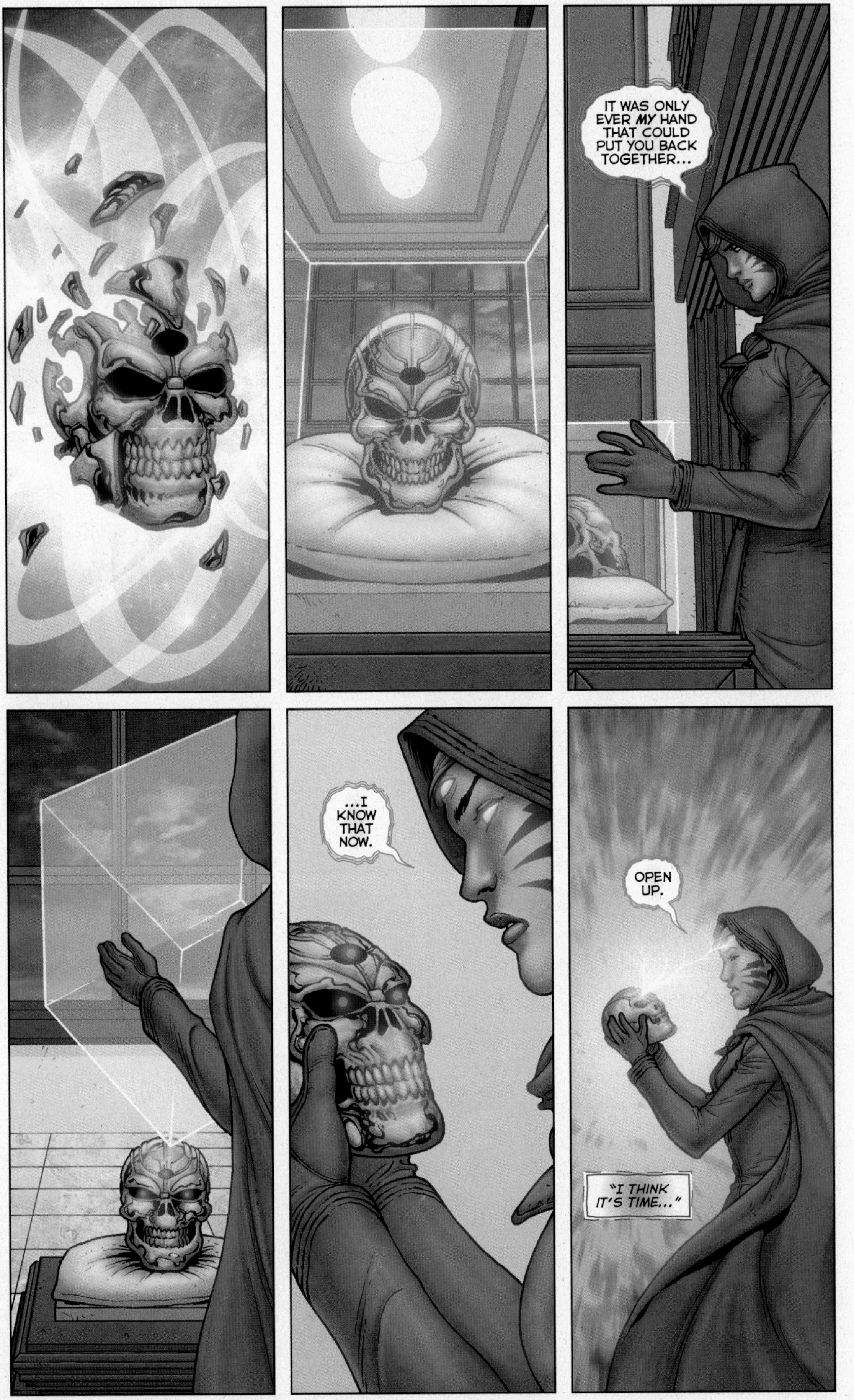
IT WAS ONLY EVER MY HAND THAT COULD PUT YOU BACK TOGETHER...
...I KNOW THAT NOW.
OPEN UP.
"I THINK IT'S TIME..."

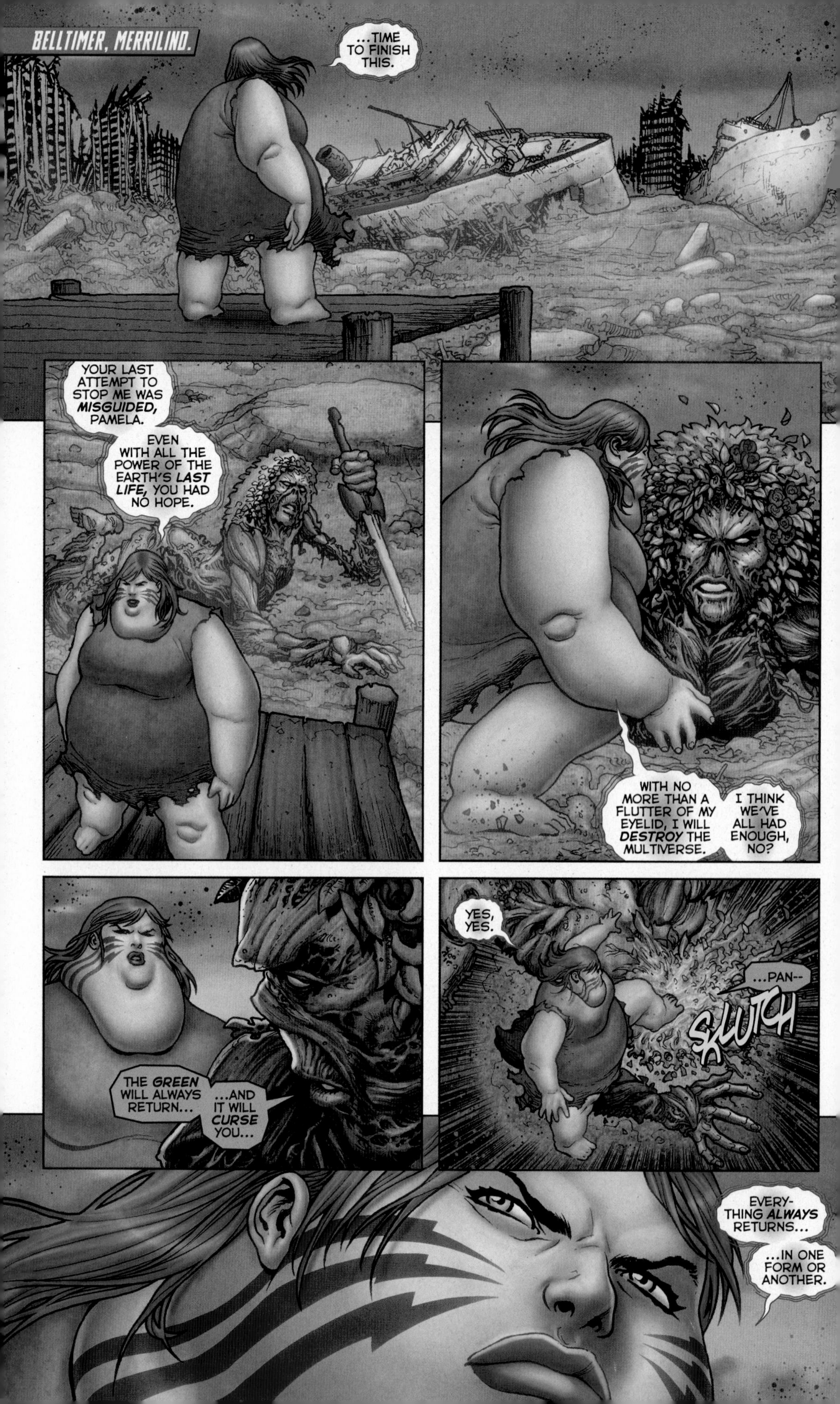
BELLTIMER, MERRILIND.
...TIME TO FINISH THIS.
YOUR LAST ATTEMPT TO STOP ME WAS MISGUIDED, PAMELA.
EVEN WITH ALL THE POWER OF THE EARTH'S LAST LIFE, YOU HAD NO HOPE.
WITH NO MORE THAN A FLUTTER OF MY EYELID, I WILL DESTROY THE MULTIVERSE.
I THINK WE'VE ALL HAD ENOUGH, NO?
THE GREEN WILL ALWAYS RETURN...
...AND IT WILL CURSE YOU...
YES, YES.
...PAN--
SKLUTCH
EVERY-THING ALWAYS RETURNS...
...IN ONE FORM OR ANOTHER.

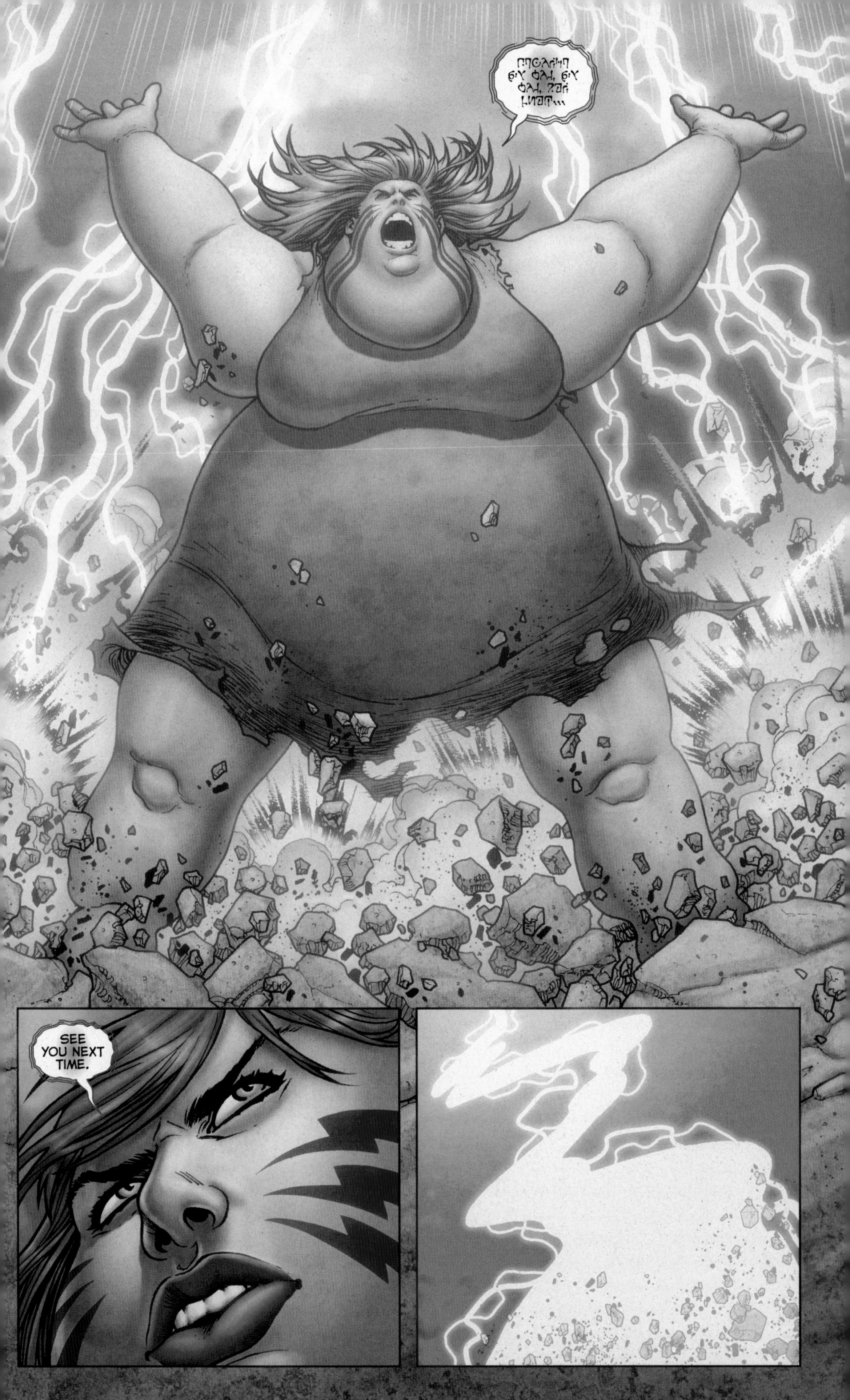
SEE YOU NEXT TIME.

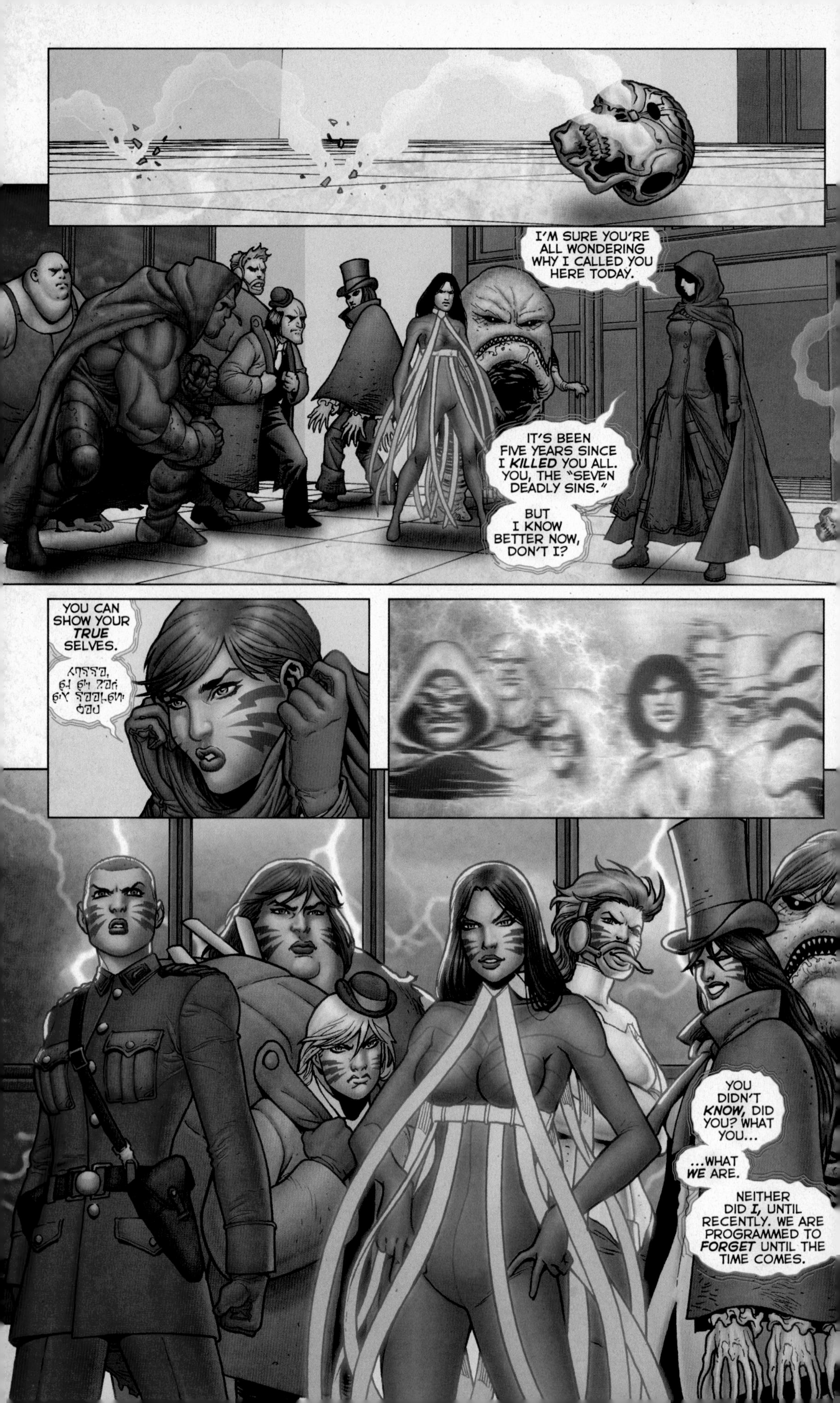
I'M SURE YOU'RE ALL WONDERING WHY I CALLED YOU HERE TODAY.
IT'S BEEN FIVE YEARS SINCE I KILLED YOU ALL. YOU, THE "SEVEN DEADLY SINS."
BUT I KNOW BETTER NOW, DON'T I?
YOU CAN SHOW YOUR TRUE SELVES.
YOU DIDN'T KNOW, DID YOU? WHAT YOU...
...WHAT WE ARE.
NEITHER DID I, UNTIL RECENTLY. WE ARE PROGRAMMED TO FORGET UNTIL THE TIME COMES.

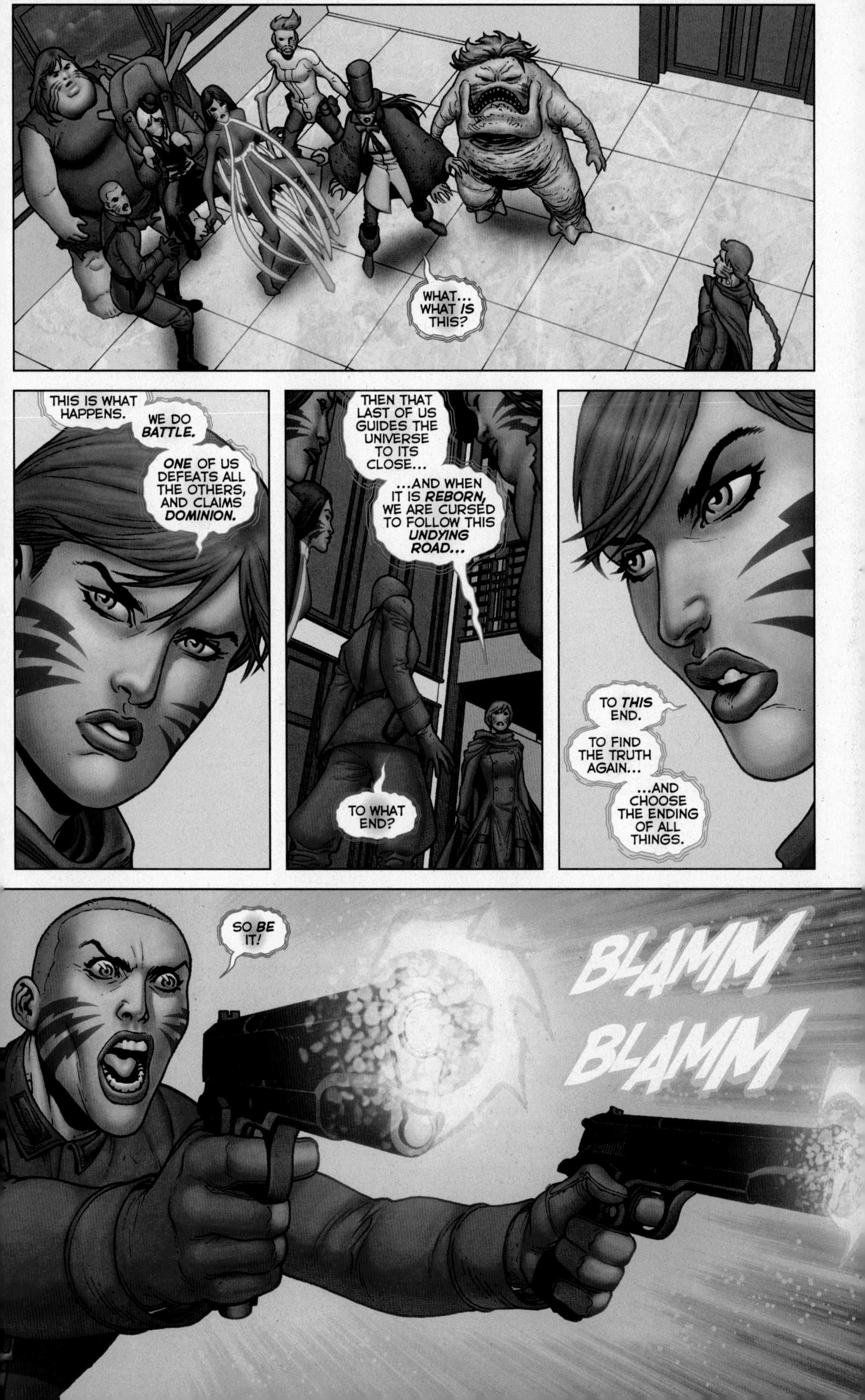
WHAT... WHAT IS THIS?
THIS IS WHAT HAPPENS.
WE DO BATTLE.
ONE OF US DEFEATS ALL THE OTHERS, AND CLAIMS DOMINION.
THEN THAT LAST OF US GUIDES THE UNIVERSE TO ITS CLOSE...
...AND WHEN IT IS REBORN, WE ARE CURSED TO FOLLOW THIS UNDYING ROAD...
TO WHAT END?
TO THIS END.
TO FIND THE TRUTH AGAIN...
...AND CHOOSE THE ENDING OF ALL THINGS.
SO BE IT!
BLAMM
BLAMM

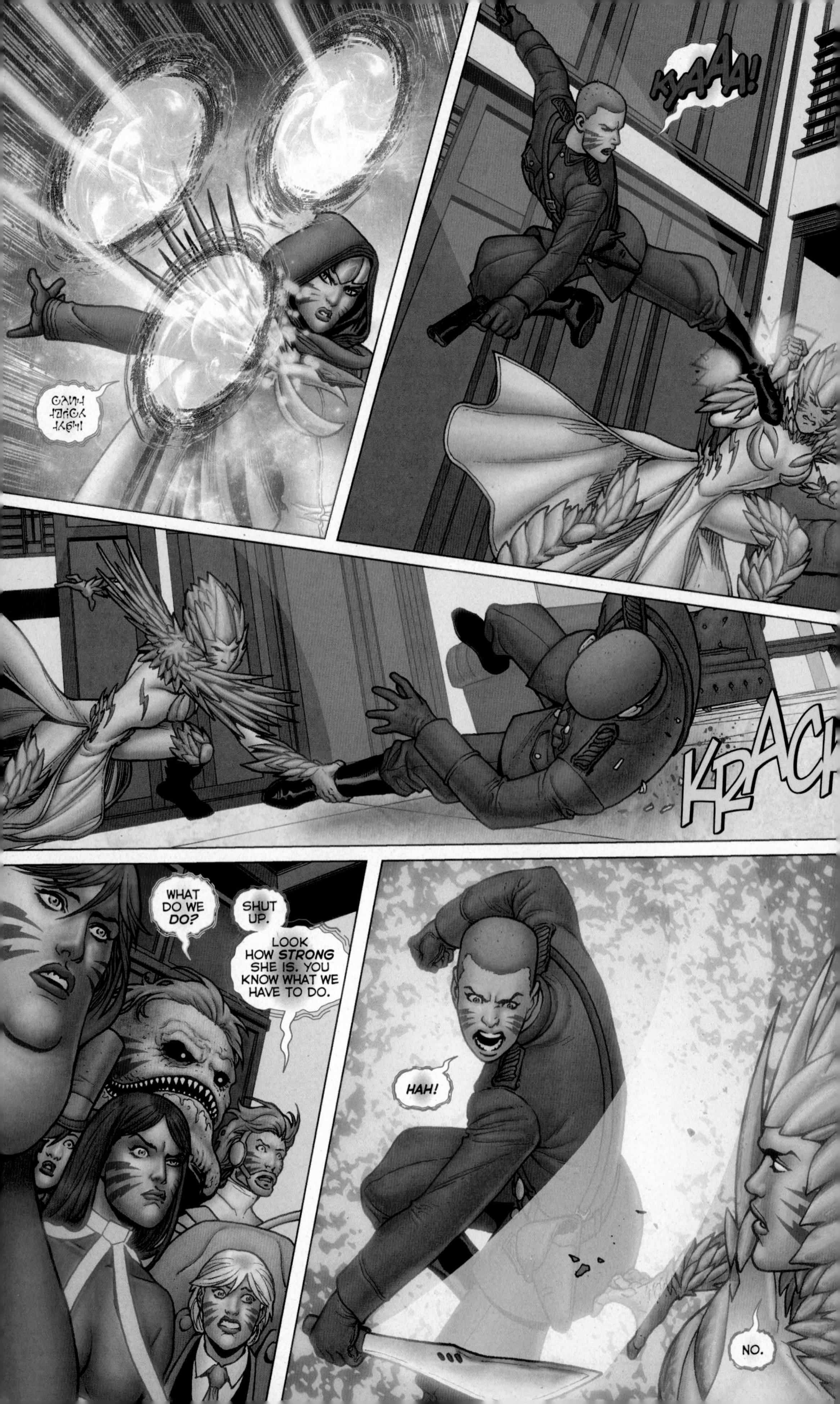
KYAAA!
KRACK
WHAT DO WE *DO?*
SHUT UP.
LOOK HOW **STRONG** SHE IS. YOU KNOW WHAT WE HAVE TO DO.
HAH!
NO.

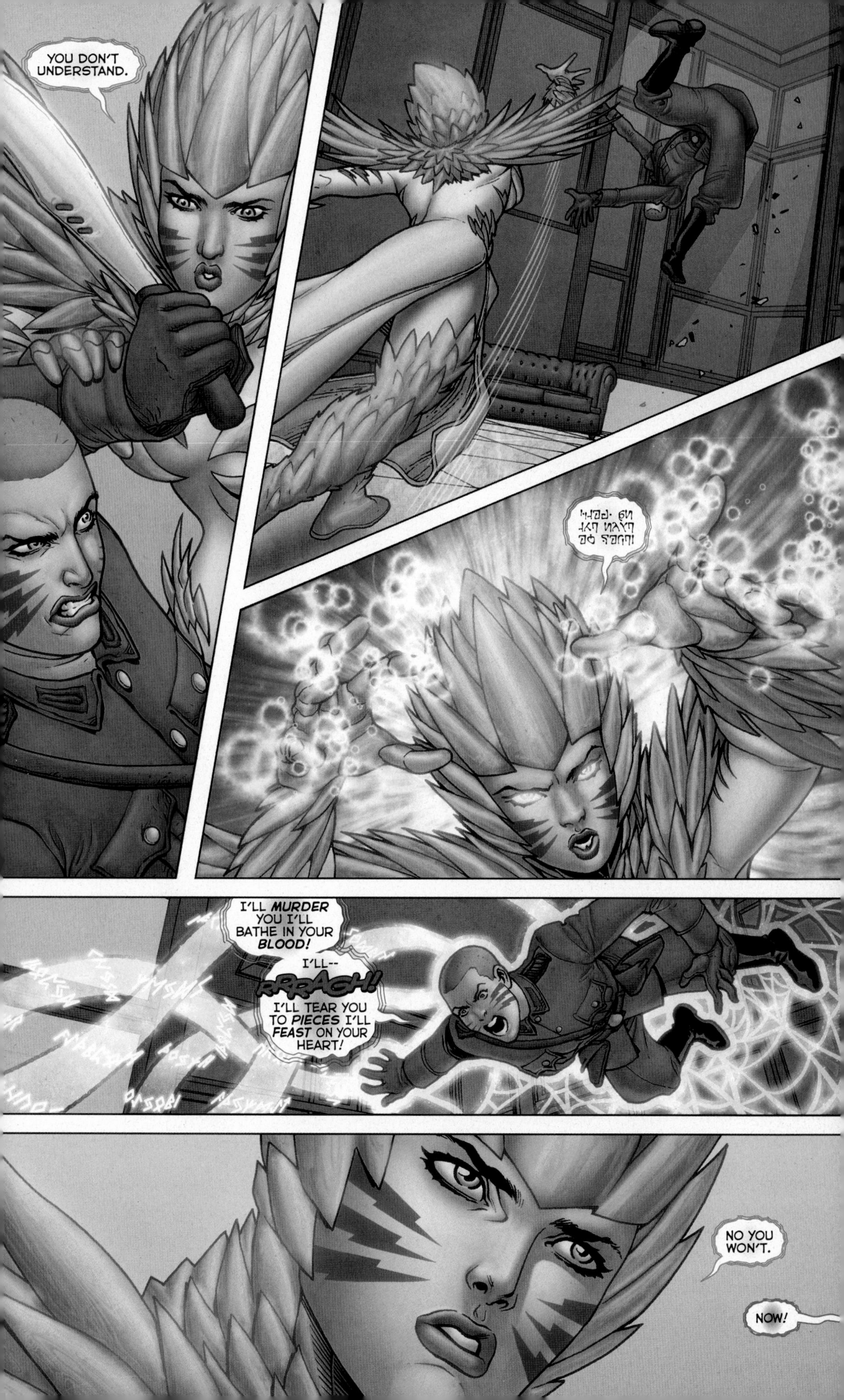
YOU DON'T UNDERSTAND.
I'LL *MURDER* YOU I'LL BATHE IN YOUR *BLOOD!*
I'LL--
RRRAGH!
I'LL TEAR YOU TO *PIECES* I'LL *FEAST* ON YOUR HEART!
NO YOU WON'T.
NOW!

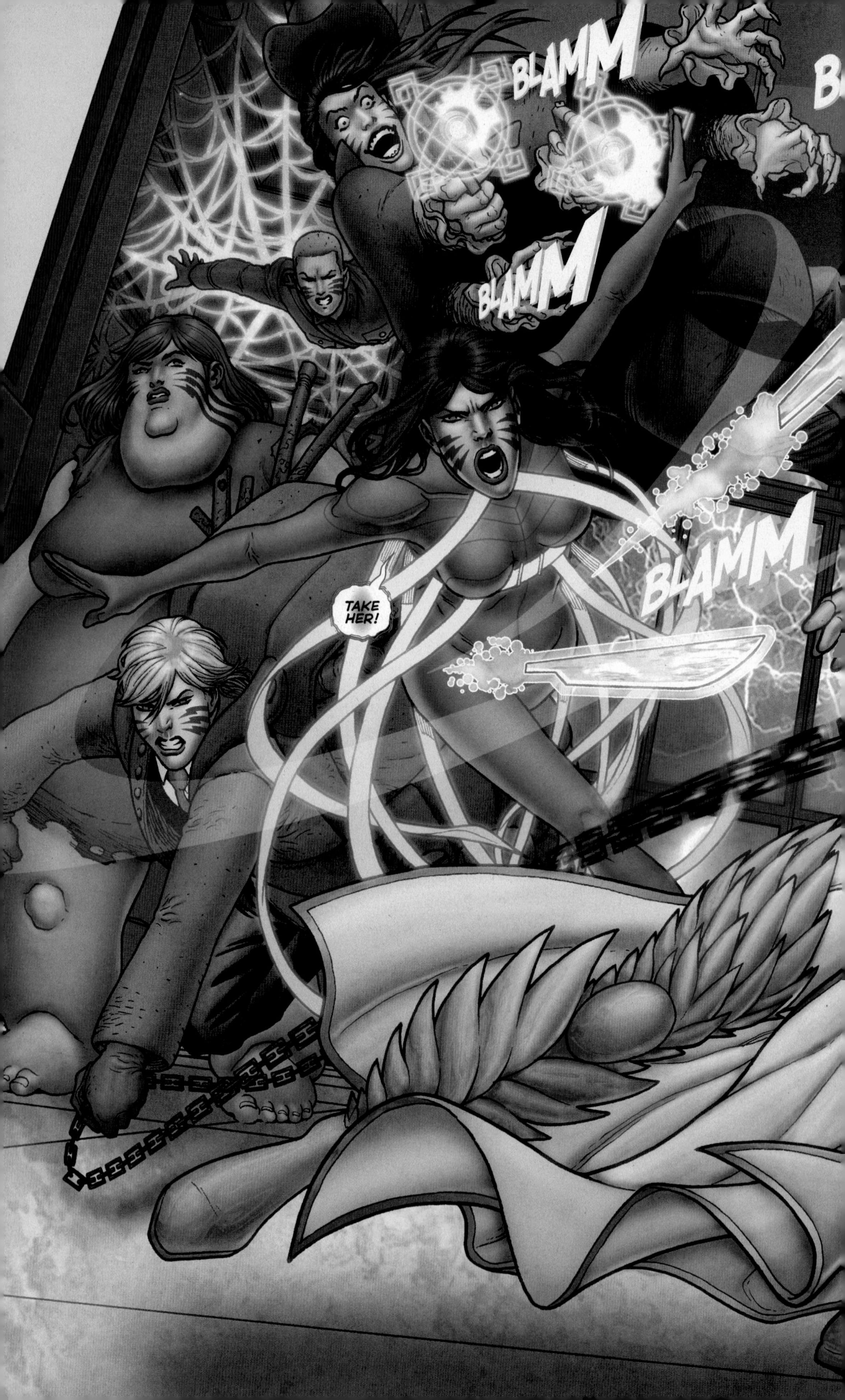
BLAMM
BLAMM
TAKE HER!
BLAMM

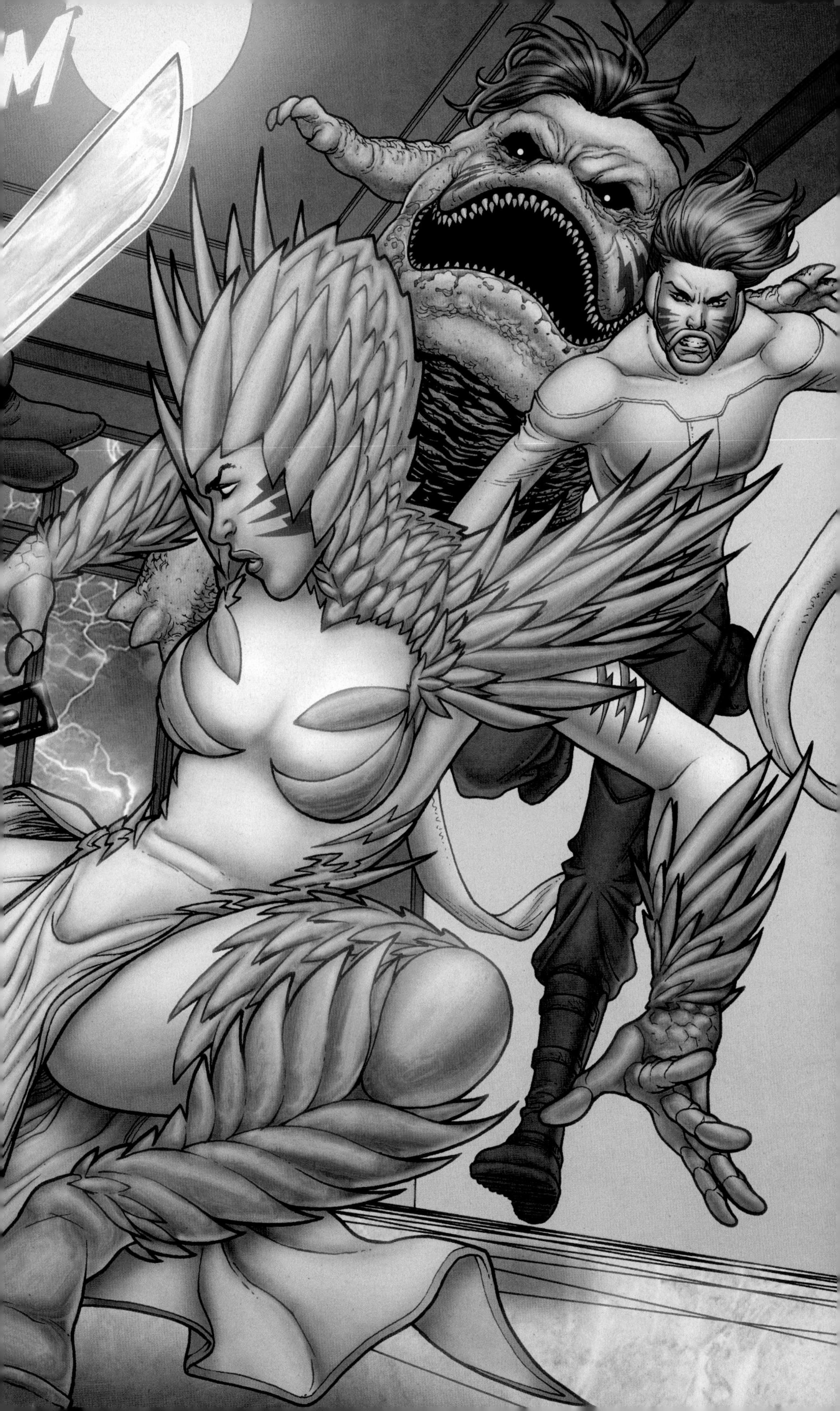

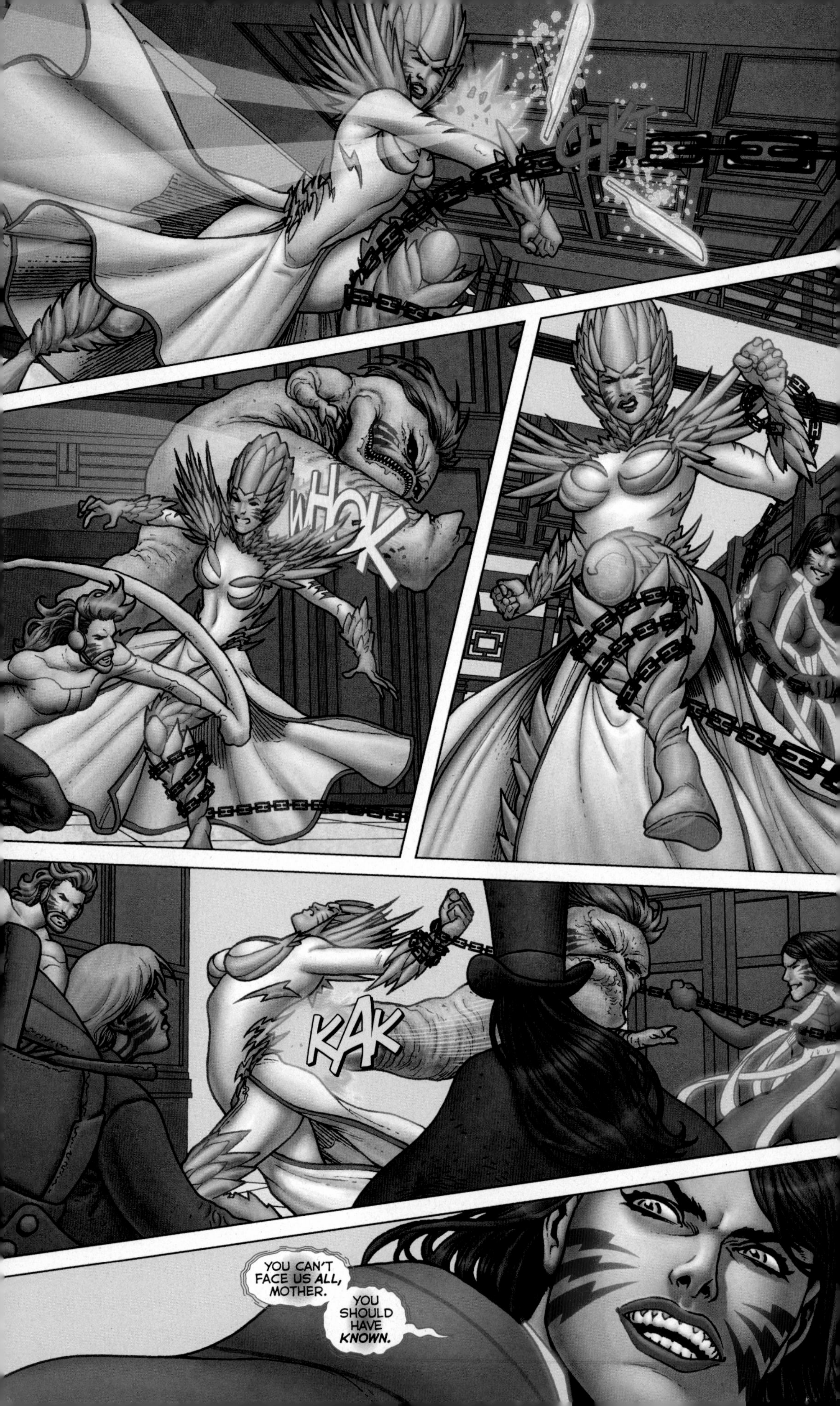
CHKT
WHOK
KAK
YOU CAN'T FACE US ALL, MOTHER.
YOU SHOULD HAVE KNOWN.

LISTEN TO ME.

LISTEN!

ᐁᑯᑫᑊ ᐅᑕ ᐸᐁᐧᐧ ᐅᐧ ᒣᐊᒣᐊ ᐅᐧ ᒃᐅᑕᐧᐧ ᐅᐧ

I **ALREADY** FACED YOU ALL.

I **DEFEATED** YOU FIVE YEARS AGO! **THIS** FIGHT IS LONG WON. FIRST, I SLEW ENVY IN THE TEMPLE OF HEPHAESTUS.

ALL THE WHILE IGNORING THE TEACHINGS OF **MANY** GREAT MASTERS.

THEN I BURNED THE **REST** OF YOU AWAY WHEN I REALIZED THAT **HOPE** DWELLED WITHIN ME...

...BUT IT TOOK ME **YEARS** AFTER TO FULLY UNDERSTAND MY **PURPOSE.**

NOW IT FALLS TO ME TO CHOOSE THE MEANS OF **THE END.**

SO WHY CALL US BACK? TO GLOAT?

NO...

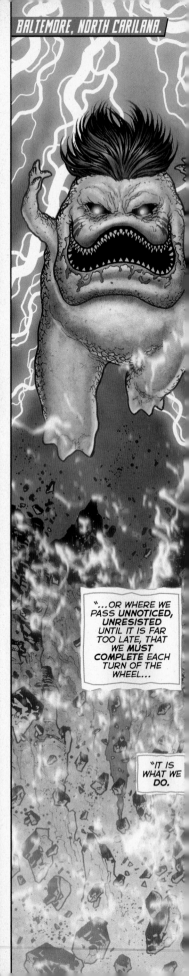

EROMITLAB, ONALYRAM.

"...THAT WOULD ONLY BRING US BACK TO THE BEGINNING AGAIN.

"EVERYTHING WOULD BE DIFFERENT, BUT IT WOULD RESTART.

"AND IN TIME, ONE WAY OR ANOTHER, WE WOULD RETURN TO THIS MOMENT OF ARMAGEDDON...

VUL-DE-NURR, MYRR-AH-LYDO.

"...WHERE THE LAST TITANS OF THE MULTIVERSE RISE UP AGAINST US, CURSING OUR NAME...

"...SHOWN IN THE END THAT OUR POWER FAR OUTSTRIPS THEIR VERY BEST. THAT WE CANNOT BE RESISTED...

BALTEMORE, NORTH CARILANA.

"...OR WHERE WE PASS UNNOTICED, UNRESISTED UNTIL IT IS FAR TOO LATE, THAT WE MUST COMPLETE EACH TURN OF THE WHEEL...

"IT IS WHAT WE DO.

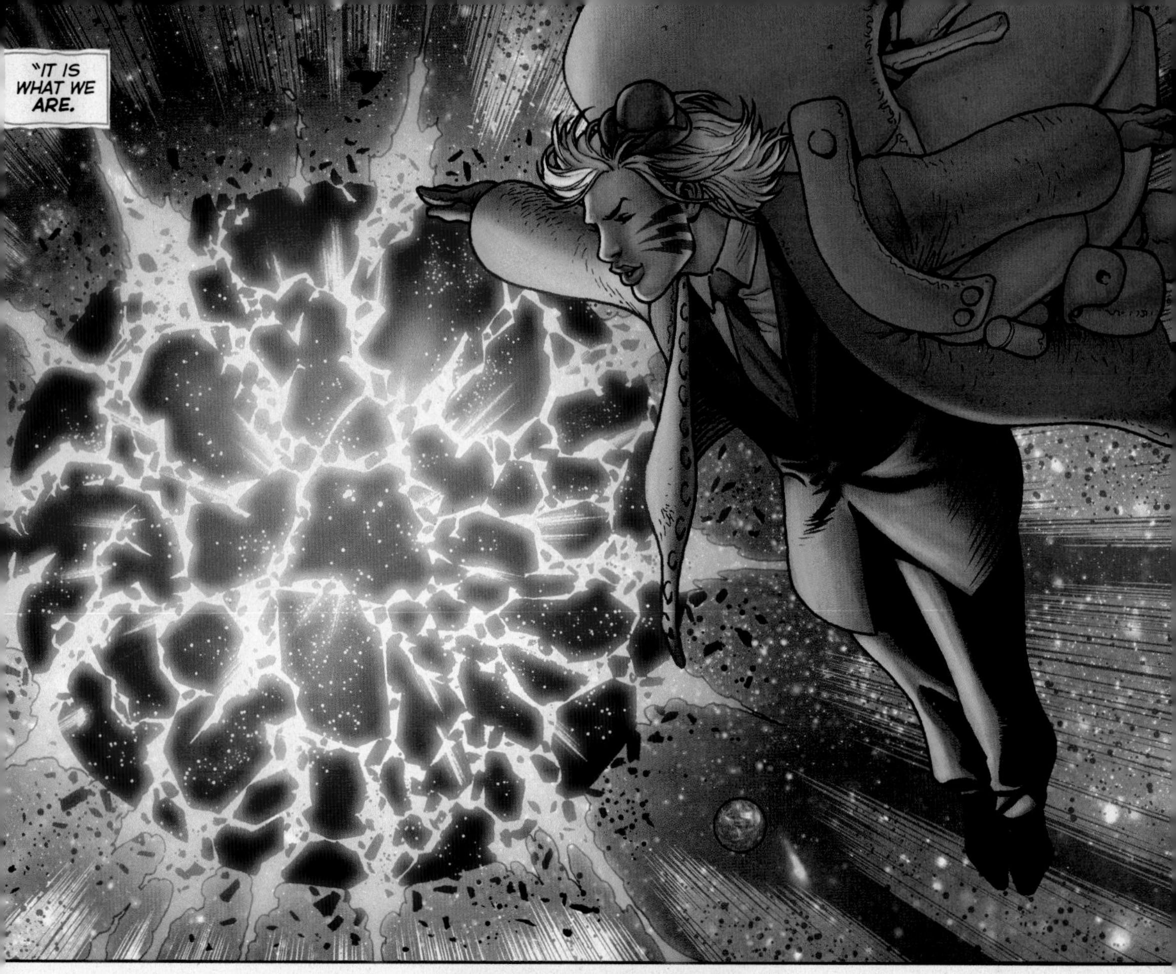
"IT IS WHAT WE ARE.

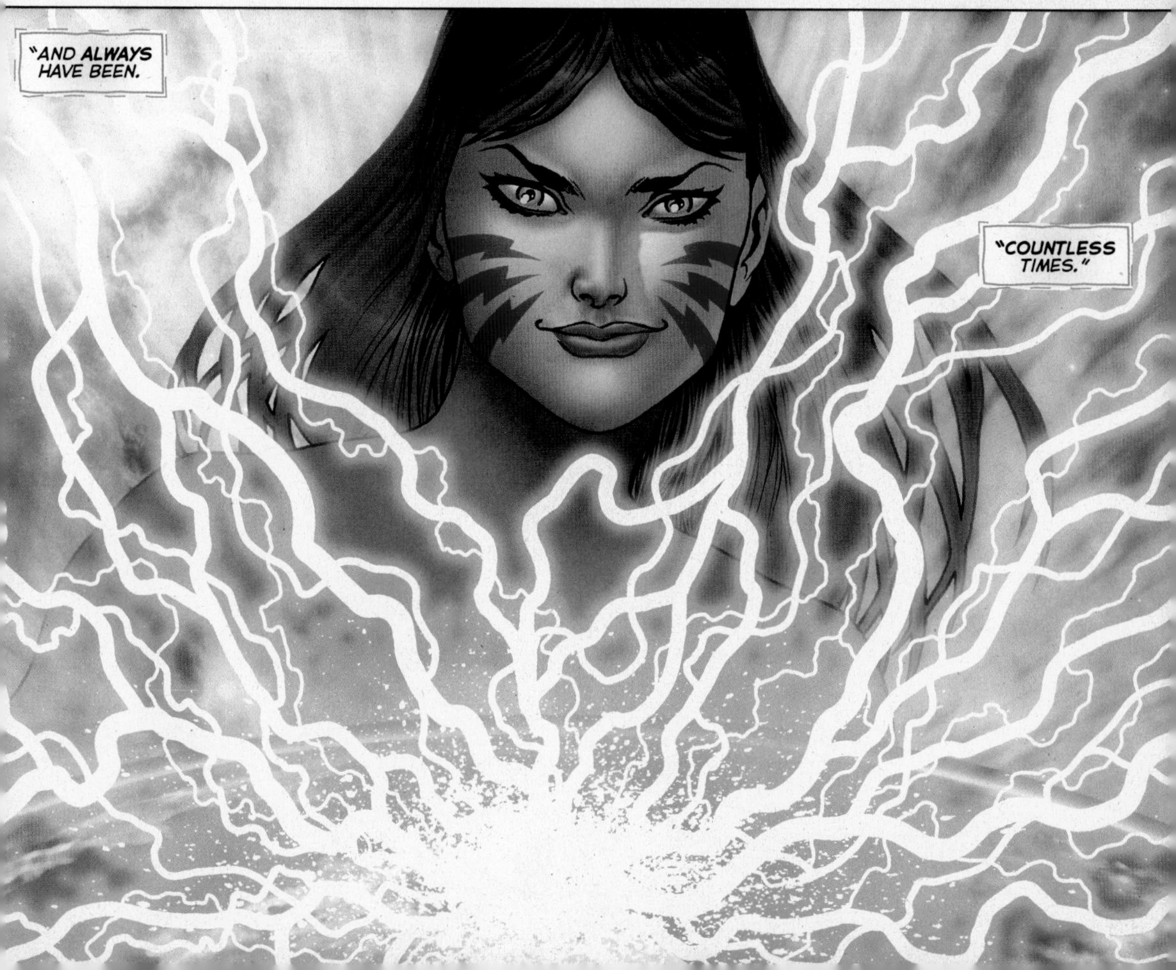
"AND ALWAYS HAVE BEEN.
"COUNTLESS TIMES."

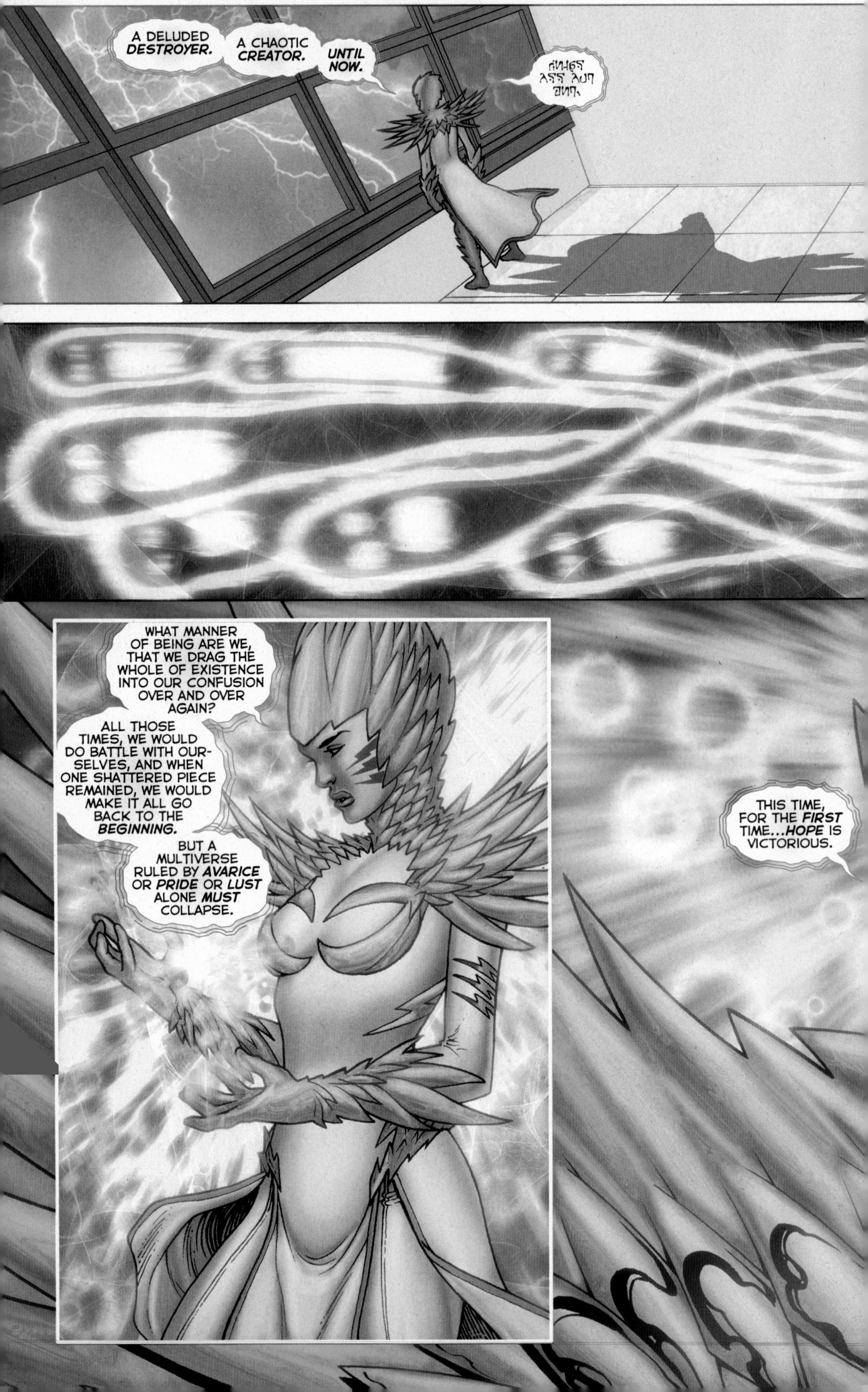
A DELUDED DESTROYER.
A CHAOTIC CREATOR.
UNTIL NOW.
WHAT MANNER OF BEING ARE WE, THAT WE DRAG THE WHOLE OF EXISTENCE INTO OUR CONFUSION OVER AND OVER AGAIN?
ALL THOSE TIMES, WE WOULD DO BATTLE WITH OURSELVES, AND WHEN ONE SHATTERED PIECE REMAINED, WE WOULD MAKE IT ALL GO BACK TO THE BEGINNING.
BUT A MULTIVERSE RULED BY AVARICE OR PRIDE OR LUST ALONE MUST COLLAPSE.
THIS TIME, FOR THE FIRST TIME...HOPE IS VICTORIOUS.

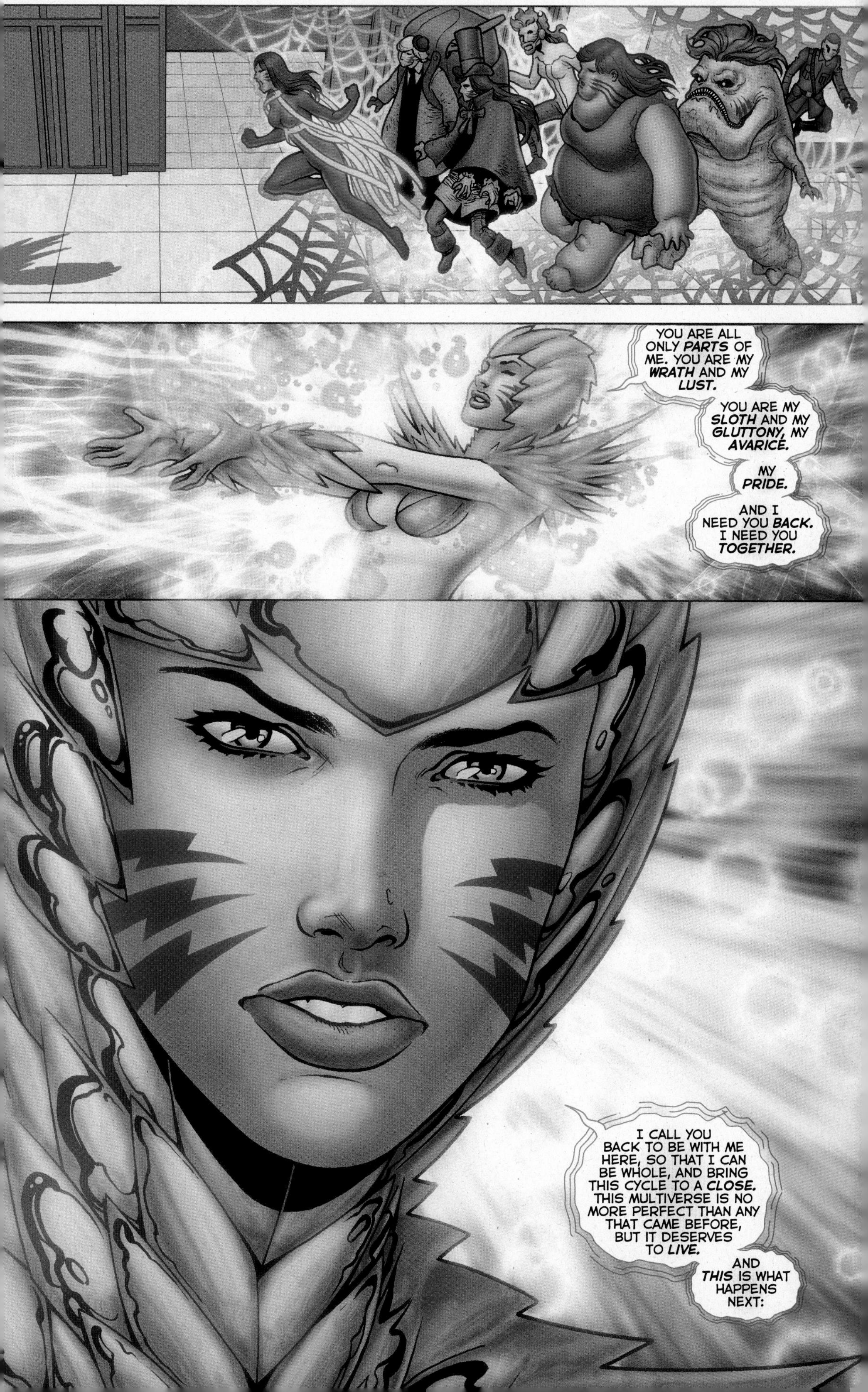
YOU ARE ALL ONLY PARTS OF ME. YOU ARE MY WRATH AND MY LUST.
YOU ARE MY SLOTH AND MY GLUTTONY, MY AVARICE.
MY PRIDE.
AND I NEED YOU BACK. I NEED YOU TOGETHER.
I CALL YOU BACK TO BE WITH ME HERE, SO THAT I CAN BE WHOLE, AND BRING THIS CYCLE TO A CLOSE. THIS MULTIVERSE IS NO MORE PERFECT THAN ANY THAT CAME BEFORE, BUT IT DESERVES TO LIVE.
AND THIS IS WHAT HAPPENS NEXT:

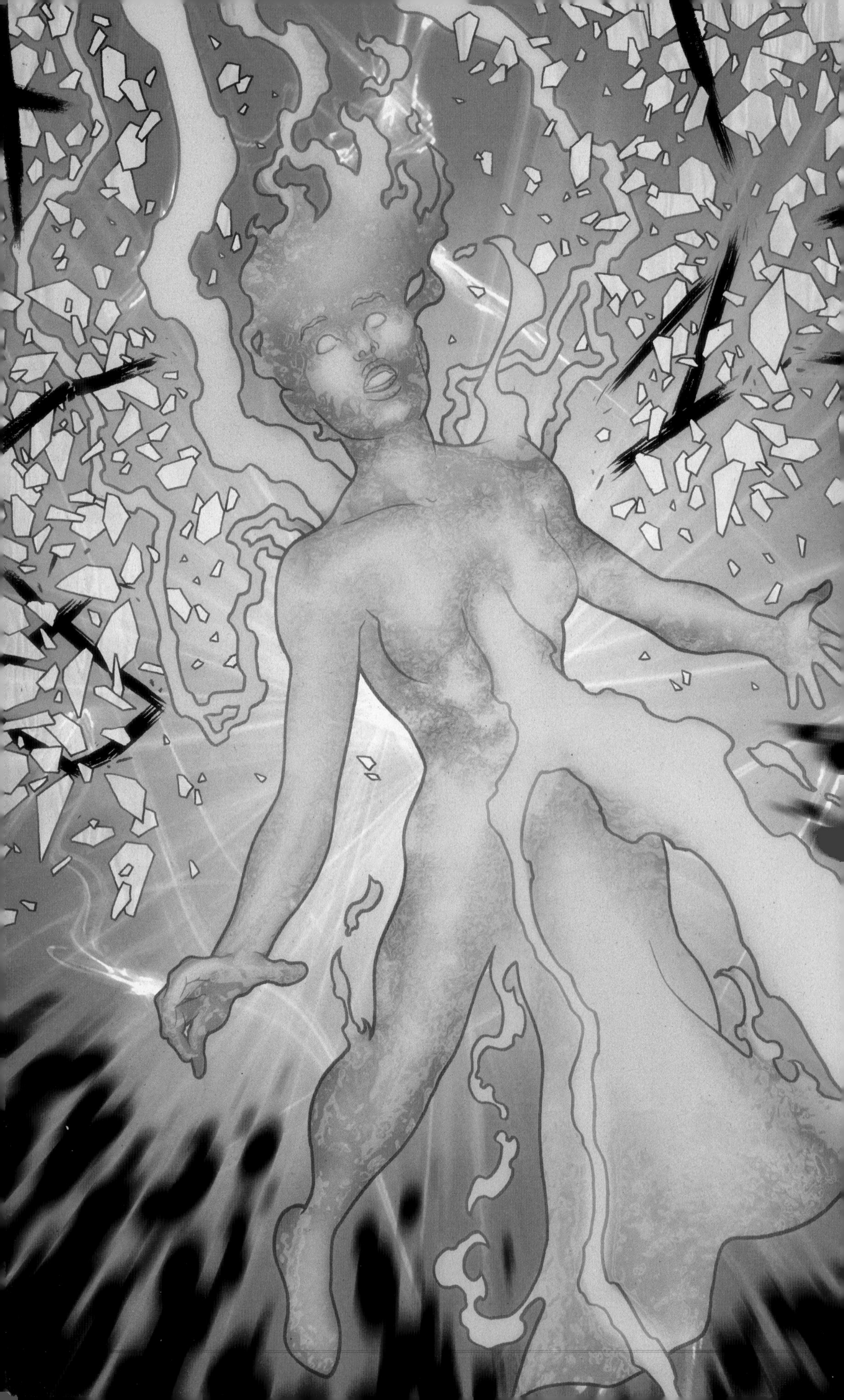

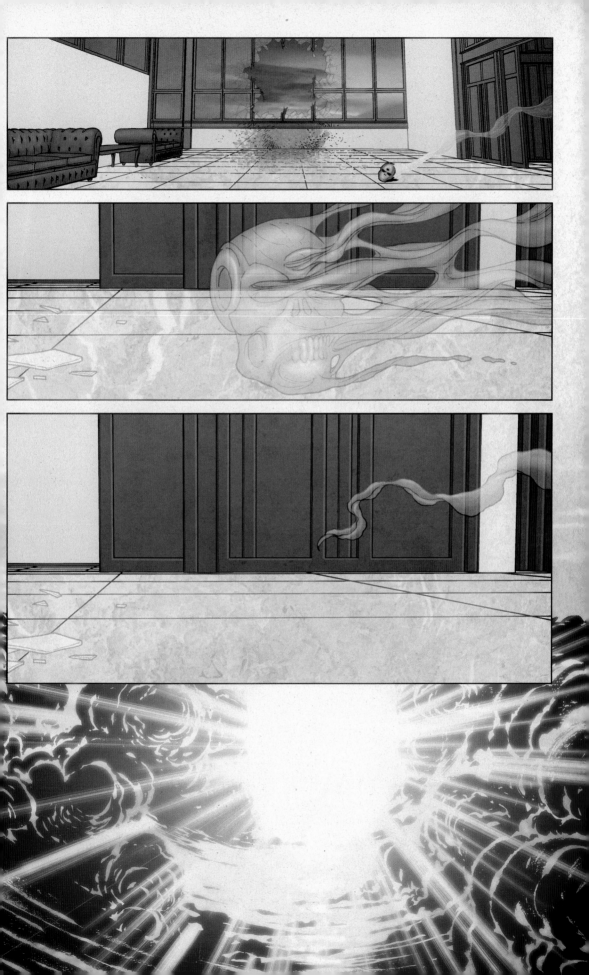

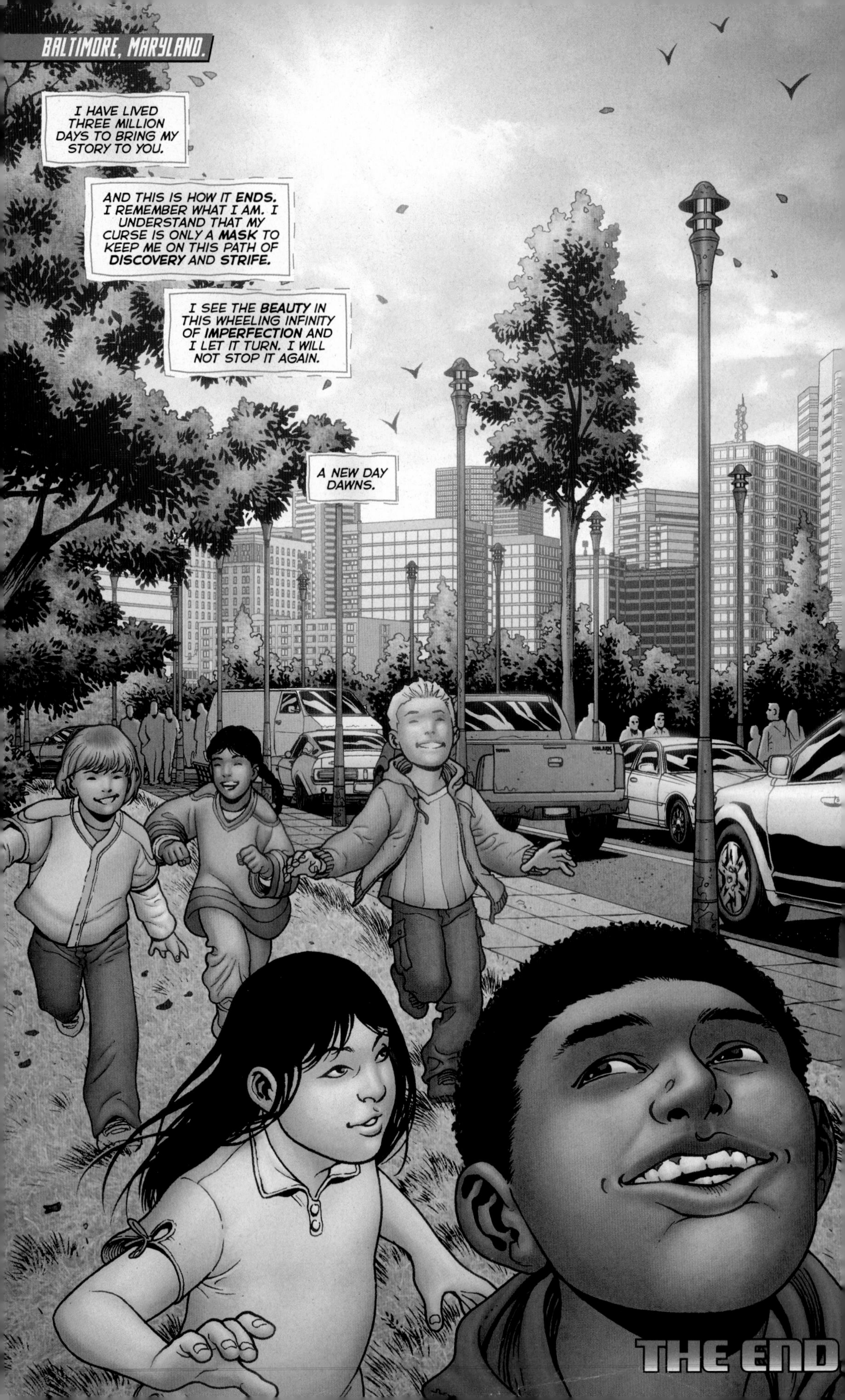
BALTIMORE, MARYLAND.
I HAVE LIVED THREE MILLION DAYS TO BRING MY STORY TO YOU.
AND THIS IS HOW IT ENDS. I REMEMBER WHAT I AM. I UNDERSTAND THAT MY CURSE IS ONLY A MASK TO KEEP ME ON THIS PATH OF DISCOVERY AND STRIFE.
I SEE THE BEAUTY IN THIS WHEELING INFINITY OF IMPERFECTION AND I LET IT TURN. I WILL NOT STOP IT AGAIN.
A NEW DAY DAWNS.
THE END